Model Railroad
Scenery and Detailing

Model Railroad Scenery and Detailing

Albert A. Sorensen

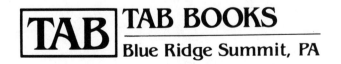

TAB BOOKS

Blue Ridge Summit, PA

FIRST EDITION
SECOND PRINTING

© 1990 by **TAB Books**.
TAB Books is a division of McGraw-Hill, Inc.

Library of Congress Cataloging-in-Publication Data

Sorensen, Albert A.
    Model railroad scenery and detailing / by Albert A. Sorensen.
      p. cm.
    Includes bibliographical references and index.
    ISBN 0-8306-3420-7
    1. Railroads—Models. I. Title.
TF197.S625 1990   90-37847
625.1′9—dc20   CIP

TAB Books offers software for sale. For information and a catalog, please contact TAB Software Department, Blue Ridge Summit, PA 17294-0850.

Acquisitions Editor: Jeff Worsinger
Book Editor: Kathleen Beiswenger
Production: Katherine G. Brown
Book Design: Jaclyn J. Boone   TAB1

Contents

Acknowledgments

In over 40 years of devotion to model railroading, I have learned the most from reading the writings of a relatively small number of persons. I never had the pleasure of personally meeting any of them, but I am very grateful for the time they took to write articles for magazines, and in some cases, books, on a hobby that they must have loved as much as I do.

These persons, some of them now deceased, who I consider the giants of the hobby are:

John Allen, who probably taught us all more about scenery than any other person. He showed us what attention to detail could do. He first developed many of the ideas and techniques that all of his successors have utilized. We can still learn more from studying his photographs than from almost any other source. Whatever the skill, probably no one has ever done it better than John.

John Armstrong, who wrote the "book" on layout design, treating the subject from a unified point of view. He integrated the requirements for operation, scenery, lighting, construction, and trackwork into a realistic approach to model railroad track layout.

Bill McClanahan, who devised many of the most popular scenery methods. Bill collected and published many of the other ideas from various sources, making them available to all modelers.

Linn Westcott, who, besides his long tenure as editor of *Model Railroader* magazine, wrote many magazine articles and books on a variety of subjects. His writings on benchwork remain particularly useful many years after their publication.

Frank Ellison, who first wrote about the similarities between a model railroad layout and a stage play. He developed many of the concepts of operation, so the trains could do something with realism and not just run around and around.

Malcolm Furlow, who is our closest modern approximation of a John Allen. His articles and books describe methods and show in their photos a rare skill for creating realistic effects with minimum effort.

John Olson, who is another contemporary modeler who can create layouts that are beautiful to see, and who can write about how it was done so anyone can understand what he did.

Bruce Chubb, who carried forth the ideas of realistic operations and wrote about them so they could be understood and applied. He showed how real railroads operate and how to duplicate these operations in miniature.

W. Allen McClelland, who, in his articles and book on how he designed and built his V&O railroad, showed everyone how an imaginary railroad could be made real in a basement. His planning made the history, the locale, and the execution all come out just right.

Art Curren, who has written many articles on the art of "kitbashing." He has inspired us to create new structures out of standard kits.

Jack Work, who wrote many of the definitive early articles on tree modeling, trackwork, and a variety of other subjects.

There have been a great many other authors who, through their writings in the model railroading magazines, have contributed to my enjoyment and knowledge of the hobby, and therefore to this book. I cannot acknowledge them individually, but I thank them collectively for their contributions. The credits to the magazines and books I have used as references are listed in the Bibliography.

I particularly thank my son-in-law, David E. Reed, who took all the photographs in this handbook. All of these photos are of my models, modules, and dioramas, with the exception of some that were taken on the layouts of Mary Barstow (Palos Verdes Pacific) and Hal Graebner (Sigma Lines), who I thank for their assistance. Special thanks also go to Brooks P. Bowman, who reviewed all of the text and made several helpful suggestions for improvements.

Finally, I thank my wife and children for accepting my many hobbies and for realizing how much pleasure they have brought to me over the years. I thank them for putting up with the loss of my time and company while I have been creating this handbook.

Introduction

This handbook covers materials, tools, methods, techniques, and procedures for creating scenic effects in miniature. Although the emphasis and examples are on scale model railroads, the material is almost equally applicable to all other miniatures, including military miniatures and dioramas, ships, airplanes, dollhouses, and architectural models.

This is a thorough, step-by-step guide to all scale modeling scenery methods and techniques, including basic construction, detailing, aging, weathering, etc. This handbook is meant to be a *continuing reference work* that can be consulted for information on how to handle any type of modeling problems pertaining to scenery and scenic detailing that might occur.

This book is much bigger and more complete than existing books that cover only parts of the same subjects. It is written to be equally useful to the beginner or to the most advanced modeler or professional model builder. All of the material is new and is not a reprint of magazine articles you have already seen. Rather than cover specific plans or projects, it gives the needed general information, from ideas and basics to details, to cover the scenery and detailing of anything you will ever want to build.

Features

☐ Handbook format for easy reference
☐ Latest developments and ideas
☐ Modular organization
☐ Systematic approach
☐ Comprehensive coverage
☐ Bigger and more complete than other books

- [ ] More illustrations and tables
- [ ] Easy to understand and apply
- [ ] Alternate approaches discussed
- [ ] Completely indexed and cross-referenced
- [ ] Includes hints, cautions, and safety advisories
- [ ] Provides cost/time/result tradeoffs
- [ ] Coverage by topics within each chapter
- [ ] Checklists to stimulate ideas
- [ ] Glossary of terms used

This handbook is organized into separate topics, each covering a specific subject, all highlighted by boldface headings. Chapters 1 and 2 contain general, background material. Chapters 4 through 11 cover the techniques or skills that will be useful for modeling. Chapters 12 through 20 deal with the specific methods used to create different models.

This handbook can be used in various ways. It can provide information on specific tools, materials, paints, adhesives, etc., or on construction methods involving casting, etching, painting, soldering, etc. Most of this information is found under the various topics in chapters 4 through 11.

It can also serve as a specific guide to the choice, planning, construction, and finishing of particular types of models or features, such as model cars, people, masonry, buildings, etc. This information is contained in chapters 12 through 20, which make up over half the handbook. That portion is organized in the logical sequence of model railroad layout construction, but the topics are self-contained, so you can consult them in any order.

The Appendix provides generally useful tables of data, including conversions, standards, and checklists. The Glossary defines all the terminology used throughout the book. A thorough Index makes finding a particular topic a simple task.

Handbook Use

Keep *Model Railroad Scenery and Detailing* by your workbench. You will repeatedly consult it for almost every modeling project you undertake. Here are some hints to help you use this handbook.

- [ ] Look up the type of model in the Index.
- [ ] Read about modeling methods applicable to that model in the referenced topics in chapters 12 through 20.
- [ ] Read about the needed techniques in topics in chapters 3 through 11.
- [ ] Use cross-references for additional information in other topics or in the Appendix.
- [ ] Use the Glossary to learn the definitions of words you find in the topics.

1

Overview

Model Railroad Scenery and Detailing uses the broadest possible definition of the word "scenery." *Scenery* is not just the duplication of nature as a setting for a model, but it is all aspects of the finishing of the model and its setting to create a feeling that you are seeing the real thing, only reproduced in miniature. It is the painting and finishing of the model, the creation of the background and foreground, the weeds and clutter . . . everything that is necessary to make some small items of metal, wood, and plastic seem to be lilliputian replicas of a larger world.

A model railroad could be built without scenery. The rails could be mounted directly to plywood, and the trains would run just as well. But, without scenery, there would be no illusion of reality. You would be just "playing with trains." No one else would be interested in your hobby, and your interest would soon lapse as well. A model railroad without scenery would be like an automobile without a body; it would run, but it wouldn't be pleasant to operate or to look at. See FIGS. 1-1A and 1-1B.

Scenery, in this broad definition, is also the thing that can distinguish one model railroad from another. All the basic locomotives and cars could be pretty much the same, but by the way they are finished, they become unique. Each modeler can create a different appearance to his railroad by the trackwork, the buildings, the backdrop, and how each are finished and detailed. Scenery is the place where creativity can be most utilized in model building.

REALITY AND SCALE

A "real" thing is something that can be seen or touched or otherwise sensed. By that definition, a model is just as real as the thing being modeled. To avoid the

Fig. 1-1A. Which layout would you prefer: One with bare benchwork and trackwork or the one shown in Fig. 1-1B?

Fig. 1-1B. A miniature of nature.

ambiguity of the word "real," we will refer to the full-sized object as the "modeled object" and the created representation of that object as the "model." The ultimate goal in modeling should be that the model be a (relatively) perfect miniature replica of the modeled object.

Model A smaller copy or imitation of a modeled full-sized object, made to scale.

Modeled object A material full-size thing, that occupies space and can be seen or touched.

Scale

Scale is the proportion that a model bears to the modeled object. The scale is stated in terms of the number of inches on the model that represents 1 foot on the modeled object. (In metric terms, this is stated in centimeters (cm) per meter.) For example, $1/4$-inch scale means that $1/4$ inch on the model is the equivalent of 1 foot on the modeled object. At that scale, if the modeled object measures 40 feet, the model should be $40 \times 1/4$ inch or 10 inches long.

Scale can also be represented as a decimal fraction of an inch per foot. In either case, the larger the scale, the larger the model.

Gauge

Do not confuse the words "scale" and "gauge." *Gauge* refers only to the width between the rails of the track. For American and Canadian railroads, standard gauge is 4 feet $8^{1/2}$ inches. *Narrow gauge* is any gauge less than standard. Various gauges, ranging from 2 feet, 2 feet 6 inches, 3 feet, 3 feet 6 inches, meter (39.37 inches), etc., were used. *Wide gauge* is any gauge larger than standard. Usually, when giving the scale, the absence of an added designation indicates standard gauge (for example, HO). Narrow gauge is usually indicated by a small *n*, followed by the gauge number in feet (example, On3).

Size Ratio

Size ratio is often a more useful representation of the relationship between the model and the modeled object. The *size ratio* is simply the proportion of the model size to the modeled object size. For $1/4$-inch scale, for example, the size ratio is 1:48, because there are 48 quarter-inches in 1 foot (4 per inch × 12 inches per foot).

In metric measurements, the scale and size ratio are more easily converted. For example, a scale of 1 cm per meter is a size ratio of 1:100. Because size ratio is really a fraction, the larger the number, the smaller the size of the model.

Scale	The "name" of the model size. Also the ratio of model dimensions (usually in inches) to modeled object dimensions (usually in feet). [Example: 0 scale: $1/4'' = 1'$]
Gauge	The width between the rails of the track.
Size ratio	The ratio of model size to modeled object size in the same units. [Example: 1:48]

Preferences

The preference for the selection of one scale and gauge over the others is up to the individual. The larger scales take more room, are more reliable in operation, cost more, and can be more easily and completely detailed. The smaller scales can give more operation in a given space and can cost less; the availability of equipment also might be better (N and HO). Standard gauge equipment is easier to acquire at a lower cost, but narrow gauge can give more operation in the same space for its higher cost and time taken. It is your hobby and your choice.

TABLE 1-1 shows the scale and size ratios for the more common modeling scales. TABLE 1-2 provides the formulas for converting between scale and size ratios, and between model and modeled object dimensions. TABLE 1-3 shows the percent enlargement or reduction necessary to convert model railroad drawings or plans between scales. TABLE 1-4 allows a quick conversion from prototype (modeled object) dimensions to model dimensions in the common model railroad scales.

FIDELITY AND PLAUSIBILITY

To capture the effect of the modeled object in the miniature that you create, you must have fidelity. You gain fidelity when you faithfully match the model to the modeled object in several considerations:

- ☐ Scale—proportional to size ratio
- ☐ Form—shape/configuration of the model
- ☐ Texture—basic to material and methods
- ☐ Color—independent of size ratio
- ☐ Gloss—dependent on the finishing
- ☐ Aging—the final touch of reality

Color includes hue, value, and intensity. Texture and gloss determine the reflectivity of light. Aging (and weathering) modify and give variation to the surfaces. Surfaces can be new or old, clean or dirty, shiny or dull. Whether natural or man-made, age, weather, and dirt modify surface appearance with time.

Table 1-1. *Scale Relationships*

Size Ratio	Scale (in/ft)	Model Railroad Designation	Commonly Used in Model:
1:220	0.055	Z	Railroads
1:160	0.075	N	Railroads
1:120	0.100	TT	Railroads
1:100	0.120	—	Architectural
1:87.1	0.138	HO%	Railroads
1:76	0.158	OO%	Railroads
1:72	$1/12$	—	Aircraft, military, ships
1:64	$3/16$	S	Railroads, architectural
1:48	$1/4$	O	Railroads, aircraft
1:45	$17/64$	O*	Railroads
1:35	0.343	—	Military
1:32	$3/8$	—	Aircraft, cars, ships
1:25	0.480	—	Cars
1:24	$1/2$	G	Railroads, cars, dollhouses
1:18	$3/4$	#	Railroads
1:12	1	#	Railroads, dollhouses
1:9	$1 1/2$	#	Railroads
1:1	12	—	Full scale

* – O Scale variation
\# – Live steam scales
% – HO is 3.5 mm = 1 foot; OO is 4 mm = 1 foot

Table 1-2. *Formulas for Conversion*

Between Scale and Size Ratios	Examples: HO
Scale (in/ft) = 12/Size Ratio	12/87 = 0.1379
Size Ratio = 12/Scale (in/ft)	12/0.1379 = 97

Between Model and Modeled Object Dimensions

$$\text{Model Dim.} = \frac{\text{Modeled Object Dim.}}{\text{Size Ratio}}$$

Example: 18′ in HO: 18/87 = 0.02069′
= 2.483″

Modeled Obj Dim. = Model Dim. × Size Ratio

Example: 1.75″ on HO model
1.75 × 87 = 152.25″ = 12.688′

Note: Model and modeled object dimensions will be in the same units

Table 1-3. *Drawing Conversion Ratios between Scales*
(Enlargement/Reduction Factor)

Original Scale	Z	N	TT	HO	OO	S	O	G	
				Desired Scale					
Z	—	138	183	253	289	344	458	917	
N	72	—	133	184	211	250	333	667	
TT	55	75	—	138	158	188	250	500	Percent
HO	40	54	73	—	114	136	181	363	Enlargement
OO	35	48	63	87	—	119	158	317	
S	29	40	53	74	84	—	133	267	
O	22	30	40	55	63	75	—	200	

Percent Reduction

Table 1-4. *Scale Size (inches) of Prototype Dimensions*

Scale	1″	2″	4″	6″	1′	10′
			Prototype Dimension			
Z	.005	.009	.018	.027	.055	.545
N	.006	.013	.025	.038	.075	.750
TT	.008	.017	.033	.050	.100	1.000
HO	.011	.023	.046	.069	.138	1.379
OO	.013	.026	.053	.079	.158	1.579
S	.016	.031	.063	.094	.188	1.875
O	.021	.042	.083	.125	.250	2.500
G	.042	.083	.167	.250	.500	5.000

Example: 14′3″ in HO:
$$1.379 + (4).138 + .023 + .011 = 1.965 \text{ inch}$$

When the model is well done, it might resemble the modeled object so closely that it is hard to tell them apart in photographs (FIG. 1-2 AND COLOR INSERT). Even if this cannot be done perfectly, it is a worthy goal.

Fidelity	Faithfulness and accuracy in details.
Plausibility	Being worthy of belief; not being untrue.

Plausibility

Plausibility (or believability) is an important ingredient in creating the illusion of reality in a model scene. Things should look and feel right. Every element of the

Fig. 1-2. Is this a photograph of a model or the prototype? If it is hard to tell, then the modeling has been done well.

model should fit together to become a plausible unit. Even if the model does not represent an actual (prototype) scene or thing, or even if the modeled scene or thing never really existed, it should be done realistically, without anachronisms (see "History and Era," chapter 2), and it should not be unbelievable.

Each modeler should do what brings him or her pleasure. Some model railroaders enjoy operating trains above everything else. Some do not care what their rolling stock looks like, or whether their benchwork is bare or covered. Some would not think of covering their carefully crafted models under a coat of grime to make them "realistic." Others want to learn everything they can about full-sized railroading, and they want their model to represent that full-size thing as closely as possible.

Some try to copy exactly the full-size subject; some try to capture its spirit (modifying details so suit their needs); and some totally invent their own railroad (or whatever) complete with its own history . . . something that could have been. Even in the latter case, plausibility is desirable.

To do effective scenery modeling, you don't have to be an artist, although you will use many artist's techniques. You don't have to be a craftsman, but you will use methods and techniques from a variety of crafts. The thing you need is desire . . . to do a good job, to learn, and to observe nature so that you can try to duplicate it in model form.

Examination

To learn, there is no substitute for looking at things with your own eyes. Look at the mountains if you wish to model mountains. Look at the trees, the buildings, the locomotives, the cars, everything that you want to reproduce in miniature. If you can't visit the real thing, then the next best thing is research.

Examine architectural and topographic models, museum dioramas, and other three-dimensional model scenes (including other modeler's work). Look at photographs in books and magazines. Take photographs. Make copies of material that you will need. Your memory alone will not be good enough, and it can play tricks on you.

Finishing

Finishing is the word given to the steps beyond building that makes the model look real and that gives the illusion that what is being viewed is the actual modeled object/scene. As an illusionist (another name for a magician), you should learn all the tricks (magic) that you can, to hide some things and accentuate others.

Realism in finishing can be obtained by simple techniques, but always at the expense of some product of time and money. There are usually several alternative techniques possible to achieve (nearly) the same effect, but the cost in dollars and/or the time it takes might vary considerably between the options. Even the least expensive model kit can benefit greatly from the time taken to provide the detailing and finishing that can convert it from the common to the extraordinary (FIG. 1-3).

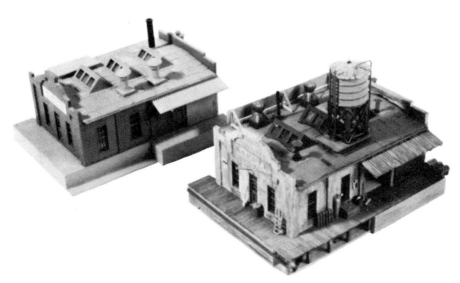

Fig. 1-3. Extra finishing and detailing of a standard kit can make a big difference.

Research and Reference Sources

Hobby shop:

Model railroading magazines (see Bibliography)
Walther's catalog (in your scale)
Model railroading books (see Bibliography)
Railfan magazines
Prototype railroad books
Other hobby books (boats, airplanes, dioramas, etc.)

National Model Railroad Association (NMRA):

Bulletins
Handbooks
NMRA conventions

Library—books, magazines, and newspapers on:

Railroad history
Period architecture
Geology
Locale history
Botany
Bridge engineering
Railroad engineering

Museums:

Railroad
Natural history
Science and industry
Maritime

Other:

Model railroad displays
Operating railroads
Layout tours
Photo slides
Pictorial calendars

In this handbook, there are usually several alternative methods presented for each aspect of the modeling. Comments are given about the effectiveness of the methods and techniques, and the relative cost in money and time. Recommendations are given, where appropriate, and cautions are given relative to safety hazards. Some techniques are not recommended because they create fumes or the probability of danger.

Natural vs. Man-Made

All modeled objects are either natural or man-made. Natural objects are those that would exist in the primeval state, without the modifications made by civilization. Man-made objects are all the roads, bridges, buildings, etc., that humankind has devised to modify nature to their will. When modeling, there are some important differences to keep in mind between natural and man-made objects.

There are no pure colors in nature (except for birds, flowers, insects, etc., all of which are very small in effect). There are no blacks, whites (except new snow), and few reds, oranges, yellows, or purples. Nature consists of variations, blends, and shades of:

- ☐ Blues—sky, reflections in water
- ☐ Greens—trees, grass, weeds, etc.
- ☐ Browns—trees, rocks, soil, dead foliage
- ☐ Greys—rocks, soil, tree trunks

Man can and does create much brighter colors, but except when they are very new, man-made surfaces also do not show pure colors. The colors of both natural and man-made surfaces fade with age, become coated with dirt and soil, and become stained by water-carried materials, dulling the initial purity of the colors.

Weather and age tend to make most colors lighter. Dirt can make light colors darker or dark colors lighter, generally coating them with the "earthy" colors of the soil and dirt in the region. Exceptions are rust marks, oil stains, and discoloration due to specific stains, wear, or deposits.

It should also be noted that straight lines, smooth surfaces, or areas of solid color do not occur in nature. Distance from the viewer makes all colors less intense (softer), lightens them, and shifts them toward the blue end of the spectrum. This is caused by atmospheric filtering and the effects of smoke, fog, and smog.

STAGECRAFT

A model railroad layout, module, or diorama can be compared to the theater. In the theater, something happens on the stage that the audience sees (and usually enjoys). Your layout, module, or diorama is also seen by an audience, whether it is just its creator, a few friends, or hundreds of people at a show.

Stagecraft is the art of creating a theatrical illusion. The illusion is that what the audience is seeing is real and is happening in real time; the audience is just eavesdropping on what is going on. While it is occurring in "full scale," time and distance and events might all be compressed. The stage is a window into the world that the author and director have created for them.

You do the same thing with your miniature scenes. You create an illusion of time and space and (in your case) size, to attempt to let your audience believe that what they are seeing is real. You can learn a lot from considering some of the things that happen on the stage and how those processes of creating illusions can be used in your model scenes.

Most of these ideas were first brought to print by the late Frank Ellison in his serial articles in *Model Railroader* in 1944, which were reprinted in 1964 and summarized in July 1976. His articles concentrated on the operations aspects of the theatre analogy, emphasizing the scenery aspects. You could build the greatest layout with the most complete detail and populate it with fantastic rolling stock and never operate it, but you would be missing the point of model railroading. It is as if you built a stage and hired the actors but never produced a play.

To quote Mr. Ellison, "For model railroading is definitely a play. It is the presentation of the drama of railroading in which the tracks are the stage, the buildings and scenery are the setting, the trains are the actors, and the operating schedule is the plot. We are not only model railroaders but potential members of the theater guild as well." He went on to say that the model railroader is "the playwright, producer, stage manager, and angel" of the production.

Mr. Ellison was particularly concerned with track design that would not limit the drama of the "play." Providing track that would only allow round-and-round running, would be more like watching "the smug and stilted wooden horses on a carrousel." He believed that the actors (trains) must be given individual personalities and conflicts and obstacles to overcome. All this must be done with precise timing (tempo) to build suspense, to sustain action, and to resolve crises.

He also believed, and showed on his own railroad, that the stage setting and costuming (scenery and finishing) were important to maintaining the dramatic illusion. There are many analogies between stagecraft and our model scenes.

Stage/Model Analogies

On the Stage	*On the Model*
☐ The stage	☐ Base and track
☐ Settings/scenery	☐ Scenery, buildings, foliage
☐ Historical era	☐ Historical era
☐ Characters/players	☐ Trains, vehicles
☐ Tempo	☐ Timing of trains
☐ Lighting/ambiance	☐ Lighting, color
☐ Sound/music	☐ Sound (if used)
☐ Acts/scenes	☐ Visually separate scenes
☐ Audience	☐ Operators, spectators
☐ Backdrop	☐ Backdrop

The theatrical backdrop and flats are directly analogous to the model. They serve the same purpose of hiding things that should not be seen and suggesting in two dimensions a three-dimensional scene of near-infinite depth. At the same time, they should not detract from the stars (trains). In the theater, they are often only a vague suggestion of reality, specifically designed to not draw attention to themselves.

In the theater, the audience stays seated and the scenes are separated by time and the falling and rising of the curtain. On the model layout, you separate scenes spatially and you must turn your head or walk between them to see each scene. But you do have different scenes, each of which should be as complete as possible and should tell a part of your story.

Whimsey and humor are often used on the stage and can also find effective application on the layout. Small scenes can have a humorous theme. Signs can make a pun or kid a fellow modeler. Everything of this sort should be kept subtle to be effective so that it does not become a burlesque.

The scenes might also be imaginatively done so that they display some tension, suspense, or mystery. This should not include the "which tunnel is the train going to pop out of next" variety, but perhaps might be rearing horses, cars stalled on the tracks, or other scenes of conflict and potential danger.

PERSPECTIVE

Things appear to be smaller when they are farther away. That fact is the main thing one needs to know about perspective. Artists use this effect to provide a three-dimensional illusion to their two-dimensional drawings or paintings.

Forced Perspective

Besides the obvious application of perspective to backdrops, which is really another form of a painting, a knowledge of perspective effects can be used to create a *forced perspective*. This is a three-dimensional falsifying of the size of objects beyond the foreground by making them smaller than scale to create the illusion that they are farther away than they really are.

In forced perspective, the structures and objects in the foreground are made to scale size, but structures and objects are gradually reduced to below scale size as they are farther away. If done properly, this makes it seem that the scene is much deeper than it really is. FIGURE 1-4 shows an example.

Only structures and objects that have an obvious size will work for this illusion. The best things to use are man-made things that people "know" the size of. Rocks and weeds will not work. Trees might, if they are the same type of tree that is used in the foreground, so the comparison is obvious. The best choices are buildings, cars, people, poles, fences, etc. Streets and roads can also be made narrower as they get farther away. Often, you can use structures, vehicles, and people that are made for the next smaller scale(s).

As the size decreases, so should the intensity of the colors because every-

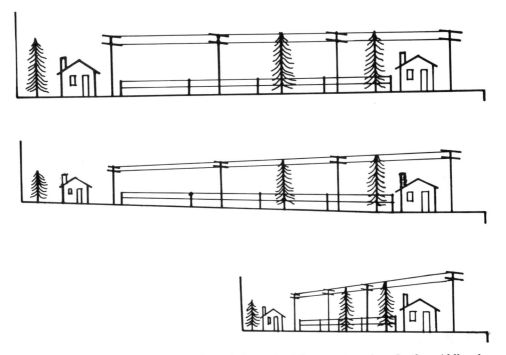

Fig. 1-4. At top, all objects are of equal size and with correct spacing. In the middle, the perspective is forced by making background trees, buildings, etc., smaller at increasing distance. At the bottom, the distances between objects that are farther away are compressed.

thing looks more hazy in the distance. This effect can be forced, just as the size is, to make things seem farther away. Note that the textures should also get finer and less distinct with distance.

Selective Compression

A trick that can be used to make the layout seem larger than it really is, is *selective compression*. The idea is to place man-made objects or structures, whose size you really know, closer together, or make them smaller so that it will appear the space between them is larger than it is. An example would be placing telephone poles or fence post closer together than scale distance.

Care must be taken that the exaggeration is not too great. Spacings down to about two-thirds of the actual should probably be the limit. Ground slopes can also be increased, but no more than 30 to 50 percent.

The term selective compression is also applied when it is used to make a large building smaller so that it will fit into the space available and not overwhelm the remainder of the layout. The approach is to consider the essential features of the building but to leave out length or height that is repetitious. For example, if a building is made up of 10 similar segments, it might still be convincingly modeled by reproducing only six of these. Smokestacks might be shortened. Window and door sizes might be slightly reduced. Such tricks can serve to make something appear bigger than it is (FIG. 1-5).

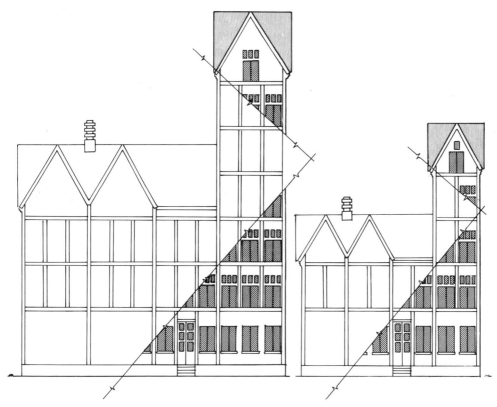

Fig. 1-5. The size of a building can be ''selectively compressed'' to create a smaller modeled building that still captures the feeling of the prototype.

2

Observation

To reproduce a modeled object in miniature, you must first understand what the object (scene, building, etc.) looks like and why it looks like it does. You must observe nature and the works of man to really see why one kind of a tree looks different than another kind, why mountains are shaped the way they are, why water flows where it does, and why a building will look right or wrong in a particular setting.

You can do this observation by visiting real scenes and places, or by looking at photographs of real things. Beware of looking at photographs of models for reference, because they might not have been done correctly. Memories are imperfect in retaining visual images, so photographs are always necessary for reference.

Perhaps even more important than observing is understanding why things are (or were) as they appear. Painful as it might be, you have to learn some more about the world around you to be able to represent it realistically. This chapter is about the "what and why" of geology, botony, architecture, history, and other such subjects that you might once have considered dull and useless.

GEOLOGY AND BOTANY

You know from your observations that the shape of the land varies from place to place. In general, the land is fairly flat in the middle portion or great plains, of the United States and Canada. In both the east and the west there are mountain ranges. Those mountains are different because they are of different age and the effects of erosion have been different on them.

The mountains in the eastern half of the continent have gentler slopes and more rounded tops because they are older. The mountains of the west are taller, sharper, and much more rugged. They often rise quite abruptly from flat land. Their canyons are steep and rocky.

If you are to create a realistic setting for your model railroad, you should know at least a little about the geology of the area that the railroad is located in. Besides the few basics presented in this chapter, you will need to examine photographs of the region and, if possible, visit the area and take your own photographs and form your own mental images. You will need to note not only the spectacular portions but those portions that are duller, and how the transitions between these separate portions occur and appear.

If there is nothing else that you remember, it should be that all the erosive effects of nature, be they from wind or water, tend to move things from higher elevations to lower ones. Always imagine what the forces of gravity will do to rocks and soil, grass and trees; and you can't go too far wrong.

Water Effects

Water falls from the skies as rain or snow. Except for that portion that evaporates along the way, it all eventually finds its way to the oceans. If it starts high in the mountains, that way is long and winding; starting from the little rivulets, forming into streams, dropping over waterfalls, roaring through gorges, becoming bigger and wider. Eventually it forms a river and then, more slowly, continues on to the sea.

The steeper the incline that the water flows down, the faster the water flows, and the more power it contains to move sand and rocks and trees, or anything else that gets in its way. The erosive forces are proportional to the quantity of water and the steepness of slope. Erosion occurs both vertically and laterally. The outer bank of turns and the foot of falls or rapids will be eaten away horizontally (FIG. 2-1).

Where the water flow is slower, the forces carrying sediment and driftwood are less. This debris will precipitate out or be deposited, leaving silt, for example, on the inside banks of river bends. The outer bank will tend to be steep and cut away, and the inner bank will be gentler because it has been built up by these deposits.

A lake is formed naturally by a glacial depression or by a natural damming caused by landslides or debris or silt buildup. Beavers can also form lakes by creating their dams. Often lakes will silt up and become swampy, and eventually they will become meadows.

Man has done much to create additional lakes, for both scenic and practical purposes. These lakes might be for livestock watering (stock ponds), for flood or erosion control, to provide a source of irrigation water, to provide water for hydroelectric power generation, or to provide water for fishing, boating, or other water recreation. Man-made dams can be simple, low, earthen mounds or rock and earth constructions, or they can range up to the giant concrete structures necessary to dam mighty rivers or create large lakes.

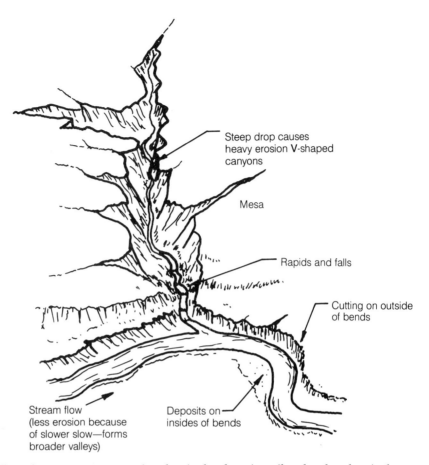

Steep drop causes
heavy erosion V-shaped
canyons

Mesa

Rapids and falls

Cutting on outside
of bends

Stream flow
(less erosion because
of slower slow—forms
broader valleys)

Deposits on
insides of bends

Fig. 2-1. Running water causes erosion, but it also deposits soil and rocks when it slows.

Flat Land

In flat land, the slopes are very gentle and the rivers and streams meander along. There is little erosion and the water level is often only a little below the level of the land. The soil might consist of sand, loam, clay, gravel, or peat. It might be of almost any color from black, through the browns, yellowish, even red. Any rocks that show would be unusual.

Lower areas might become swampy. The foliage will depend on the rainfall, ranging from lush to scant. In desert areas, a few tufts of grass and some sage-brush and mesquite might be all that will grow.

The railroad roadbed will usually be somewhat elevated on a fill above the level of the surrounding terrain. This is done for drainage reasons. Crossings of streams and dry washes will be over culverts and low trestles.

Hills

Hills can be the remnants of glacial fallout, or they can be very old worn-away mountains. They might contain no rock at all, or they might be almost wholly rock. Streams will tend to flow between the hills, and they might cut into them, exposing banks of soil or rock outcroppings. Erosive forces cause many ravines, dry washes, and arroyos to form on and between hills (FIG. 2-2).

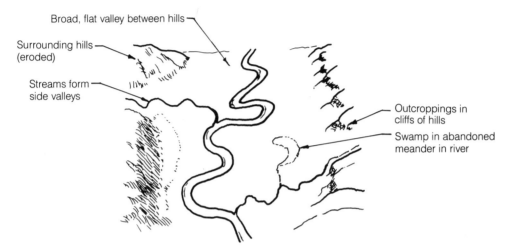

Fig. 2-2. In hilly or nearly flat land, there will be swamps, meandering streams, rock outcroppings, small cliffs and ravines.

Small ponds or swamps might form in pockets between the hills. If possible, the railroads go around the hills. When that cannot be avoided, they must use cuts, fills, trestles, etc., to go through them, trying to keep the total volume of dirt for cut and fill about equal. Tunnels are usually not used in hilly country because open cuts are less costly.

Rock strata might lie at angles even under gently sloping terrain. The soil will erode away, exposing the rock layers. Streams descending over such terrain will form small waterfalls at these transitions.

As the hills get larger, the water erosion washes more material down into the valleys, and the valleys tend to take on a U shape, with a relatively flat center. The larger streams and rivers are found in these valleys. The valleys themselves might have little slope and are much like flat land in their characteristics.

Soil erosion occurs more rapidly on steeper slopes. A small gully near the top of a hill might become quite large near the bottom due to the increasing volume of water flow during storms. The fallout from the gully will form a small delta at the base of the hill from the soil from the washed out area. Gullies are most likely to start where animal paths, unpaved roads, or bad farming practices have let too much runoff concentrate in one place.

Foliage is determined by total rainfall and by the underground water courses. If the countryside is arid, then almost all the trees will grow in the ravines and along stream beds, even though they might be dry most of the time.

Mountains

Mountains occur because of an uplift of the earth's crust. This process takes millions of years, but the uplift still occurs faster than the erosion can wear the mountain down. Most mountains are not formed by volcanic action, either by lava flow or by cinders. Mountains typically are composed of a mixture of gravel, soil, and rock, although the rock percentage might be quite high. It is rare that a mountain will be monolithic (solid rock).

As the mountains rise, the streams do their thing, cutting paths as they provide the drainage for the rain and melting snow. The water flows faster because of the steep slopes, and the cutting occurs even through the rock. This results in V-shaped canyons with relatively steep slopes. These slopes appear to be steeper than they are because they rarely exceed 45 degrees. There are few nonerosive cliffs.

To cross the mountains, railroads usually follow the valleys, gaining altitude as they are able, to eventually cross over a divide and proceed, in the same manner, down the other side. The roadbed might have to be blasted from the mountainside to form a shelf part way up the canyon wall. Fills, trestles, bridges, and culverts are used extensively to cross the side ravines and water courses. Tunnels, steep cuts, and retaining walls might be necessary to find a way through the promontories and rock escarpments.

Often a railroad must cross the valley to gain a better route or double back for more altitude. This will require a large trestle or bridge, some of which might be quite spectacular. Sometimes long tunnels must cut through a ridge or through the summit. These tunnels might be curved and will usually have a grade. Occasionally, the track might cross over itself as the elevation is gained.

Mountain foliage grows wherever the scant soil will permit it—on the flatter slopes and sometimes between the rocks. Towns in the mountains are usually located in valleys that were once meadows, where a natural dam might have once formed a lake. They tend to be long and narrow, like the valley they are in.

Even in the same range of mountains, the rock strata might vary greatly in color, size, and tilt. Usually, on the model, it is better to keep the various rocks fairly similar within a given area. Water usually flows year-round in the mountains. This can provide some marvelous effects, including rapids and waterfalls.

Rocks

Rocks are generally of two types, igneous and sedimentary. *Igneous rocks* were originally formed from volcanic action. Included in this category are basalt, granite, lava, and pumice. Igneous rocks usually are not layered. *Sedimentary rocks* were formed originally from the pressure of overlaying earth or water on layers of sand, silt, clay, vegetable matter, or animal skeletons. Over the centuries, clay becomes shale, sand becomes sandstone, gravel becomes conglomerate, plant life becomes peat or coal, and sea life remains become limestone or chalk.

Sedimentary rock forms in layers, often separated (stratified) by layers of other sedimentary rock varieties, or by clay or sand. While these layers are level when formed, they are often tilted by subterranean forces into domes or sloping sheets. Erosion then acts, exposing some of these layers and the strata of the rocks.

A third type of rock, formed from sedimentary rock by additional heat and pressure, is called *metamorphic rock*. Examples are marble, formed from limestone; and slate, formed from shale. These rocks also occur in layers.

"Solid" rock isn't really that solid because it is usually split by expansion cracks and joints, caused by temperature changes or earth movement. Rocks are also split by earthquake faults, which usually result in a differential shifting of elevation on opposite sides of the fault. This can displace the layers in sedimentary rock formations. The cracks are gradually enlarged by frost and tree roots. Eventually, portions of the rock might separate from the face and fall down the mountain, either as large boulders or as exfoliated rock. This fallout is called *talus*.

Soil and Rock Colors

To duplicate the colors, there is no substitute for using samples picked up on the site. Note that, because of the effects of scaling, the average color is generally lighter than that of the samples.

Soil can be just about any color, from near black to almost any shade of brown (umber or sienna) or dark gray. Clay will be lighter brown, ochre, and various shades of red-brown. Some clay is even a bluish color. Loam or peat is quite dark, almost black. Sand will tend to be lighter than soil, sometimes white on beaches, but usually a light tan.

Igneous rocks vary a great deal in color. Granite is usually shades of gray, ranging from fairly dark to quite light. Lava and pumice can range from black, through the grays, to a rust color. Basalt tends to be darker than granite. Streaks of other colors, including reds, blues, and browns, can occur in igneous rocks.

Sandstone is usually light tan but can vary darker from that. It might also be tinged with other colors, particularly rust. Limestone varies from a normal light gray up to almost black. Much of this variation is due to weathering. Marbles can be almost any color. Slate is very dark gray to black. Chalk can vary from white to light gray.

Vegetation

The natural foliage of each region varies as much as the geology. The primary influence is climate. Climate is determined by the latitude (how far north), by the elevation, by the annual rainfall, and by microclimate effects (wind, shade, etc.).

Each variety of tree or plant has limits to where it can grow in terms of temperature range, water requirements, amount of light, and wind conditions. In addition, even with the proper environment, it might not grow in a particular area simply because it is not native to that area. The forces of nature might never have scattered seeds in that specific place because it was too far removed from regions where it was native.

Besides the instruction to observe what grows in the area you wish to model, there are a few general guidelines that can be provided. Arid regions support less plant growth than wetter regions. What plants there are must conserve the little moisture that does fall. This includes sagebrush, a few grasses, a variety of cacti, ocotillo, and mesquite and similar trees. The foliage tends to grow along washes because this concentrates the sparse rainfall. Palm trees grow only where there is a fairly constant supply of water. In areas with even more water, cottonwoods might be found.

Very high altitudes also have little vegetation. A few grasses, some lichen and algae, mosses, and dwarf conifer trees are all that can survive. As one goes down the mountain (FIG. 2-3), the trees get bigger, but they remain all conifers. Still farther down, some hardly deciduous trees, such as aspens, start to appear. The conifers can become very large, with pines, cedars, firs, etc., predominating.

In the far north, the situation is somewhat similar to that at high altitudes. The trees are few and stunted. Willows and tamaracks are found. Conifers are usually rare. Much of the land is permafrost or is covered by summer bogs full of water plants.

Near sea level, in warm climates, virtually everything can grow. In the better soils or in wetter areas, the trees are mostly deciduous, although many of these are of the evergreen type. Cypress trees might grow in the water. The undergrowth usually forms a jungle of plants, shrubs, and vines.

In between these extremes, almost anything in the plant world can and does occur. Poorer soils usually will support conifers, such as pines, better than deciduous trees. The richer soils will have a wide mixture of trees and plants because the fertility will allow few restrictions on growth. Usually, the latitude and the degree to which the land has been cleared will determine the foliage that is most common.

HISTORY AND ERA

Every model should be created with an idea of the approximate time that is being modeled. For model railroads, this is usually determined by the type of railroad equipment you prefer. For mainline railroads, this means that if you prefer all steam, the era should be prior to about 1940. If you wish to have both steam and diesels, then the time should be sometime between 1940 and 1955. If you prefer all diesels, then it should be sometime after about 1955.

If you are modeling narrow gauge, then you must choose an era when narrow gauge existed. This is generally consistent with the all-steam time frame of pre-1940. Modeling a time era prior to about 1910 gets more difficult due to a lack

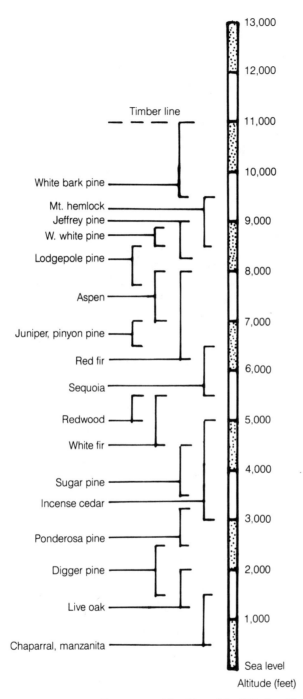

Fig. 2-3. *The main tree species will vary considerably with altitude. (California Sierras)*

of available equipment. Modeling a railroad of the nineteenth century, while an interesting project, can give real difficulties in recreating the equipment.

History

If you are modeling a prototype railroad, then the history of your portion of that railroad must be consistent with the actual history of the real railroad. Your portion might be an imaginary division or branch of the prototype, allowing you to create a unique history for just that portion. If your railroad is wholly imaginary, the railroad's history will also be imaginary, but it should fit in with the "real" history of the place and time depicted.

Create a history, complete with the names of the towns, the dates when things happened, the names of principal citizens, etc. It will add to the fun of the model, while creating an overall scenario into which everything will fit. It will explain why the railroad was built, what was built, when things happened, where it is, how it was done, and who did it.

Anachronisms

An *anachronism* is something that appears in a scene that should not be there because it did not exist at the time depicted. Avoid such out-of-place items because they display a lack of temporal fidelity in the model, and they serve as a lightning rod to draw the jibes of observers (FIG. 2-4).

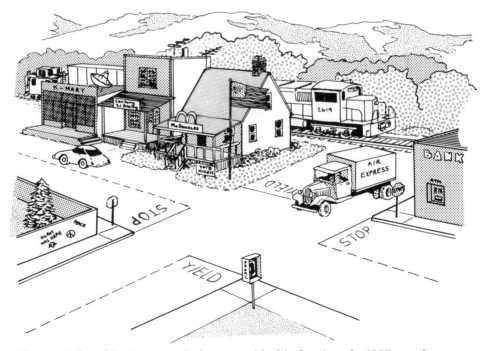

Fig. 2-4. *What things can you find wrong with this drawing of a 1937 scene?*

Anachronisms can only be avoided by thorough historical research and rigid adherence to observing which things could have been present in the era being modeled. The most obvious errors occur with automobiles, trucks, and railroad locomotives and cars. Before using them, determine when they were first built and how they were painted and lettered at the time being modeled.

Never buy a model locomotive or car without knowing the date the prototype was made. Look at the fine print on the freight car lettering to see the "built" date. Other, less obvious, things to watch for are building signs, advertisements, road signs, clothing, and building architecture.

Anything that existed before the era being modeled is possible (however unlikely) to still exist at any later time. Things that only were developed later could not exist before their first appearance in the world. Natural things are not a problem because they have always existed. Man-made things cause the trouble because their styles are fleeting and usually very identifiable to a specific time.

The only sure way to avoid anachronisms is to do plenty of research and only model things that you know from photographs or written accounts that existed at the time being modeled, or at any earlier time.

Checklist of Possible Anachronisms

Model Year:	Styles:	Highway Signs/Lines
Autos	Lettering	Signs
Trucks, Buses	Architecture	Graffiti
First Built:	Clothing	Flags
Locomotives	Signs	Signals
Freight Cars	Antennas	Advertisements
Passenger Cars	Street Lights	Business Names

ARCHITECTURE

Just as with clothing, architecture has styles that change with time and the tastes of people. A building can be dated quite closely by its appearance in terms of its design, its ornamentation, its construction, its choice of materials, its finish—all the details that constitute its architecture.

Architectural styles also vary with the region. Certain styles are typical of certain parts of the country. Some building types are typical of New England, or the seacoast, or the West. The choice of the architecture can thus help to set the locale for the railroad being modeled. FIGURE 2-5 shows how recognizable differences in home locations can be.

The buildings built by a railroad will usually have some architectural commonality. This can serve as a unifying feature for your model railroad. This includes not only the depots and freight houses but miscellaneous sheds and outbuildings, water tanks, etc. They might include rooflines, roofing choice, amount of gingerbread, type of siding, etc., besides the obvious "company" color scheme.

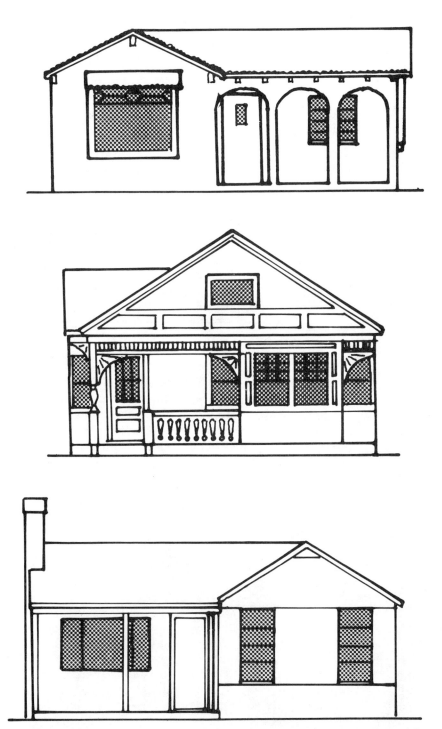

***Fig.* 2-5.** *Four examples of regional architectural differences: California mission, Queen Anne cottage, Western tract, and Cape Cod colonial houses.*

Fig. 2-5. Continued.

The architecture style of most European and other foreign buildings is quite different from those of North America. This is important to note because there are many excellent plastic building kit models available from European sources that cannot be used without modifications. Often, removal of some of the gingerbread will make the models acceptable. In other cases, the rooflines are so different that the conversions will still be obvious (FIG. 2-6).

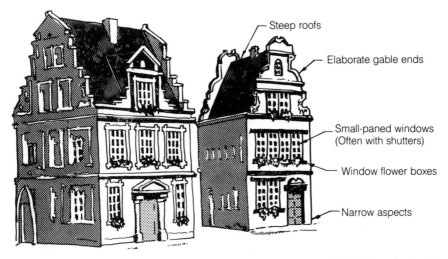

Fig. 2-6. European buildings can look a lot different than those of the US and Canada.

3

Environment

The environment you create for your model, for its display and operation, and for yourself and those who view it is extremely important. This environment consists of the proper temperatures, humidity, lighting, and safety; and of the added enhancements that lighting, sound, and even smell can provide. Environment also means preventing the buildup of dust and dirt and cleaning the model when typical preventive techniques prove inadequate, as they usually do.

LOCATION

If at all possible, locate your model railroad layout in its own room, preferably a room with a finished ceiling and tiled or carpeted floors. Cover the walls from the layout top to the ceiling with the backdrop. Complete the ceiling, the backdrops, and the lighting before you put the layout in because access will be difficult later. Wait to finish or surface the floor until the layout is complete because many things will be spilled on it along the way.

Close off the room from the rest of the house, or other building, with doors and windows that close tightly. Provide for heating in winter and cooling in summer so that you can enjoy your time there on a year-round basis. The room needs its own lighting system and, if necessary, a way to control excessively low or high humidity. Try to keep the room off limits to children, pets, and insects. Separate the room from a workshop, laundry, or other area where dust is produced.

A module should have either the same provisions as a full layout, or at least its storage area should be dry, secure, and dust free. A diorama or an individual model is best kept in a custom-built plastic display case or in cabinets behind glass or plastic doors. Thus protected, delicate models can survive indefinite exposure to room dust, exuberant children, and unrestrained pets.

LIGHTING

Lighting provides illumination for the entire layout. Lights can be designed to simulate outdoor sunlight and light from the sky. Good layout illumination might be the single most neglected aspect of creating a superior model scene. This is unnecessary because providing adequate lighting is relatively easy and inexpensive.

Plan the lighting from the beginning as an integral part of the track planning and scenery and layout design. Even if this is not done at first, you can still make many postcompletion improvements in layout illumination systems.

Illumination Functions

The lighting system should fulfill a number of different functions. Lighting should:

- ☐ Be safe
- ☐ Simulate natural sunlight
- ☐ Generate only natural effects
- ☐ Be inexpensive to install
- ☐ Be inexpensive to operate
- ☐ Be accessible for maintenance
- ☐ Provide the proper light color balance
- ☐ Provide relatively uniform lighting intensity
- ☐ Be controllable (on/off as a minimum)

Lighting should not:

- ☐ Shine into the eyes of the viewers
- ☐ Generate too much heat
- ☐ Cast multiple shadows in any single scene
- ☐ Cast shadows on the backdrop
- ☐ Cast shadows of viewers on the layout
- ☐ Interfere physically with the viewers/operators

Safety is listed first because it is most important. This includes not overloading the circuits, avoiding inflammable materials near the lights, providing proper ventilation for light cooling, preventing contact with hot bulbs or electrical wiring, and providing proper grounding of the isolated high-voltage circuits.

Bulb Choice

Ordinary household-type, inside-frosted incandescent bulbs are the best choice for illumination, in most cases. They come in a wide variety of sizes—25, 40, 60, 75, 100, etc., watts. They can be mounted in inexpensive sockets; use the ceramic or porcelain sockets, not plastic. And they give a good simulation of the color of sunlight. Many, smaller wattage bulbs are better than a few larger bulbs because they give a more even overall effect and eliminate "hot spots."

There are also many advantages to using fluorescent tubes. They are more efficient and thus produce more light per watt of electricity used. They run cooler and they last longer. They cost more originally, but the savings are made up in long-term energy costs. They come in tubes of length proportional to the wattage (a 40-watt bulb is 48 inches long).

A major disadvantage is that fluorescent tubes do not produce a color balance that is even close to sunlight. This includes both the common types, "daylight" and "cool white." Special, more-expensive bulbs (such as GE Chroma 50 or Sylvania Natural) might be obtained, on special order, that approximate the color spectrum of incandescent lights. Fluorescent lighting is also not as flexible in tailoring the illumination to the space available. Another disadvantage is that, because of their length, fluorescent tubes produce an unnatural "shadowless" lighting.

The color balance of incandescent bulbs gets more "yellow" as the wattage size of the bulb, or the voltage, is reduced. The efficiency also goes down rapidly with voltage, although the bulb life goes up tremendously. Unless access is very difficult, it is more economical to operate these bulbs at full voltage, rather than use more bulbs operating at slightly lower voltage for the same illumination. This is because the long-term costs of the electricity are several times greater than the bulb cost. The larger bulbs are also more efficient than the smaller ones, a difference of nearly a factor of two between a 25-watt and a 100-watt bulb.

Intensity

The intensity of illumination is measured in *foot-candles* (fc). If you have a suitable light meter, use it to directly measure the light on the surface of the layout. The desired intensity is determined by what looks right to you. Note that the appearance will be affected, in part, by the illumination of other parts of the layout room, such as the front boards, aisles, operators/viewers, etc. If these other portions are kept darker (like the audience in a theater), then lower intensity lighting on the layout will look like the sunlight it is supposed to represent. The actual average layout illumination should probably be no less than 30 fc, and preferably up to about 100 fc.

Light Placement

Place the lights above the layout, as high as possible and as close to the front as possible. If it can be done with adequate head clearance and without causing spectator shadows, place the lights in front of the layout edge, above the aisleways (FIG. 3-1). If possible, trace the layout perimeter (next to the aisleways) on the ceiling overhead with a valance to hide the lights.

Place the lights no farther apart than their height above the layout surface. The closer they are placed together, the less trouble there will be with multiple

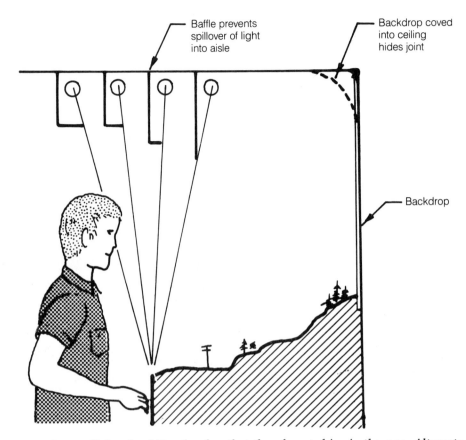

Fig. 3-1. *Layout lights should be placed so that they do not shine in the eyes. Alternate light placement requires baffles of different shapes.*

shadows; the lighting then becomes more diffuse and shadowless, particularly in the foreground.

Light intensity diminishes inversely as the square of the distance. This means that as the lights are put farther away, more lights are needed. The number, wattage, and location of the lights is a compromise between all these factors.

The bulbs might need individual reflective baffles, or shades, to direct and control the light. Snip these out of metal; large tin cans are a good source. A wooden baffle, placed on the aisle side of the lights, might be useful to prevent the lights from shining where they are not wanted, particularly into the eyes of the viewers. All baffles must give adequate head clearance for your tallest viewers. They must also be designed to safely take the heat from the lamps without any danger of combustion.

If the layout consists of a number of detailed scenes, with less-detailed areas between them, consider a higher level of illumination for the detailed portions (FIG. 3-2). This can also help reduce problems with shadows because the multiple shadows will tend to fall into the less interesting areas. Note that the entire lay-

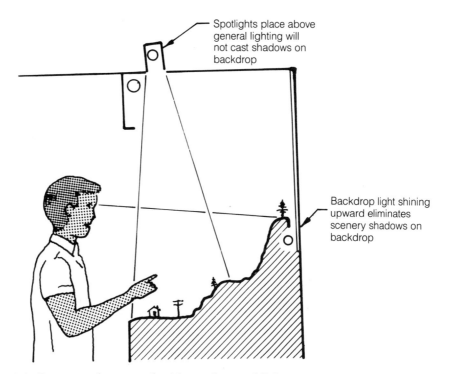

Spotlights place above general lighting will not cast shadows on backdrop

Backdrop light shining upward eliminates scenery shadows on backdrop

Fig. 3-2. *Scenes can be accented with supplemental lights.*

out does not need completely uniform illumination. Differences can be accounted for by the "clouds" in the "sky." Again, what is important is what looks right!

It might also be desirable to incorporate dimmers in the lighting circuits so that the light level can be varied, either to save energy or to provide dawn and dusk lighting effects. Needless to say, the lights should have convenient on/off switches to turn them completely off and to simulate "night." Blue night lighting, which simulates moon and starlight, might also be used. If these lights are left on during the "day," they can help balance the color spectra.

Photographic Lighting

The best lighting for photography is provided free by natural sunlight. No artificial light can even begin to compare with sunlight for color intensity or brilliance. If you can take the model, diorama, or module outside for photography, that is your best option. Choose the time of day to provide the proper angle for the light, and use white or shiny reflectors to bounce the light into shadow areas to reduce the contrast. Be careful of the background so that it is out of focus or compatible with the subject being photographed.

Often it is inconvenient or impossible to move the model outside. The photography must then be done where the model is located. Take black-and-white photos indoors by using normal layout lighting, possibly augmented with bounce reflectors, or by using normal lighting plus supplemental lighting. Use the same outdoor film, with an appropriate exposure time adjustment, of course.

With color shots there are more problems. Artificial light is much more yellow than sunlight, and this must be compensated for either in the film choice or the lighting or both. Unfortunately, there is no really compatible combination for fluorescent lighting, so if your normal lights are fluorescent, turn them off while taking photographs. Accommodate incandescent lights either by using special film balanced for this light, such as Kodak Ektachrome Tungsten 160, or by using daylight film combined with an 80A conversion filter. The latter is probably preferable for most cases.

Supplemental lights should use tungsten filament incandescent bulbs. They need not be the photoflood variety; common household bulbs mounted in inexpensive clamp-on sockets with reflectors are fine. Because the camera will be tripod-mounted and actuated by timer or cable release, the exposure times can be long and a high intensity of light not needed, even with slow color films. Always use the lowest wattage bulbs that will work (the limitation might be the light meter used), combined with the slowest film speed (less grain and better resolution), and the smallest aperture opening (f22 or higher). This trades time for cost.

Model Lights

You can provide considerable drama to your scenes by including miniature lighting into the models. This includes the lights inside the rooms of the buildings, the outside yard lights, motor vehicle lights, signal lighting, and the lights in the locomotives and cars. When the layout lights are dimmed or extinguished, the lights shining from the models give a whole new magic to the scenes. Operate all model lights at reduced voltage to increase the bulb life. This gives the added advantage of keeping the effect subtle, which adds to the realism.

Some modelers have also added sunrise, sunset, and moonlight effects, which allows them to simulate operations over 24 hours. Elaborate systems have been built with all lights operating from timers and dimmers to give preprogrammed sequences. More information on model lights is given in "Miscellaneous," chapter 20.

TEMPERATURE AND HUMIDITY

Large changes of temperature or humidity can destroy your model or make it inoperable. Very high or low temperatures or very high humidity will make your layout very uncomfortable as either a place to work or to operate or view the trains and scenery. Materials expand and contract with changes in temperature or moisture content. This can distort the rails, cause cracks to form, delaminate materials, and cause other woes that are best not experienced.

Build, display, and operate your layout/diorama/model in an area that is continuously controlled in temperature and humidity, at least to the same extent as the rooms you live in. Avoid unheated garages and attics. If you live in an area with high summer temperatures, consider air conditioning. If high humidity (over 70 percent) is a problem, consider a separate dehumidifier for your layout room. If the humidity gets extremely low (under 15 percent), consider a humidifier.

SOUND

The use of sound can enhance the realism of the model. Systems are available that emit the sounds of the locomotive from speakers in the locomotive or tender. These sounds can include whistles, bells, air pumps, brakes, horns, and motor roar. Steam exhaust sounds can be synchronized to the driver rotation. Some of the sounds are prerecorded on tapes, and some are electronically synthesized and initiated by operator control. The sound travels to the locomotive over carrier signals superimposed on the normal voltages on the track.

The sound can also be fixed to come from speakers hidden under the scenery. The sounds might simulate a sawmill, a playground, rapids, a frog pond, an industrial plant, traffic noises, etc. Keep the effect subtle and localized. Loop-to-loop tape cassettes can be used as the sound sources, playing through low-cost players.

SMELL

The sense of smell is an extremely powerful one, bringing to memory images that have been long buried. Now various artificial odors are available to create the pleasant and unpleasant smells that can add to the perceived reality of a scene. Coal smoke, diesel fumes, a pine forest, a stockyard, a flower garden, burning leaves, and fresh cut grass are just a few examples of smells that could be used. It is important that these odors be kept subtle and close to their source for them to be effective.

Also consider the general smell of the layout or model. It should not smell like what it really is . . . a collection of wood and plaster. It particularly should not smell of stale cigarette or cigar smoke. It should have no smell at all, or at least a clean, masking smell that freshens the air. Spray or solid air fresheners can provide just the right effect.

CLEANING

To preserve the reality you have labored to achieve, it is necessary to keep the scenery and models clean. The best way is by preventing dirt and dust from accumulating. Make every attempt to reduce the dust in the room your layout or model is in. A finished ceiling and a sealed or tiled floor will help a great deal. Try to do any construction work that creates dust in another area. If your workbench is close to the layout, consider buying a separate exhaust fan for the workbench area.

Make sure you change or clean your furnace filter regularly. You might consider installing one of the new electronic filters. If it is possible, try to have a positive pressure in the layout room, relative to adjacent areas, that will keep dirt out.

Unless smoking is a necessity based on your own strong urges, attempt to enforce a no-smoking rule in the room.

In spite of all these things, dust will fall and collect on the railroad. That dust will not be to scale and it will not add anything to the layout. Remove it periodically. The best way is by vacuuming.

Use a tank-type vacuum cleaner with a hose and wand with a piece of nylon hosiery over the end of the wand, held on with a rubber band. Use a very soft 1-inch brush in one hand and the wand in the other. Gently brush the scenery, structures, etc., with the brush, while sucking up the dust. The nylon hosiery material keeps any loose scenery material or details from being lost. It would probably be helpful to have a second person help you by guiding the vacuum hose away from anything delicate.

Another choice is the new small cordless vacuum cleaners. Some of these are made specifically for dusting small models. Others might need some modification of the nozzle (with cardboard tubes, etc.) to provide a suitable end configuration. The main advantage is the light weight and ease of handling, compared to a tank-type vacuum cleaner.

Remove dust from still water (lakes, ponds, etc.) to keep these areas looking "wet." You can clean resin, glass, and plastic "water" with a good furniture polish.

If you have modeled a small diorama or individual model, consider buying or making an acrylic plastic case for display and protection. This can virtually eliminate the need for cleaning, as well as serve as a protection to the model from pets, vermin, and small children. You also can use display cases with sliding doors to contain and show off the models.

SAFETY

Throughout this handbook, safety cautions and advisories will be given in almost every topic. *Do not ignore these.* It would be tragic if the hobby that you have chosen to bring relaxation and enjoyment should, through carelessness, bring you an injury, a loss of sight, a loss of a finger or limb, a reduction of your life span through breathing or absorbing poisons, or even in the worst case, your death. These things have happened to others. They can happen to you!

The most dangerous hazards are those caused by inhaling fumes from some of the paints and chemicals that are used. These dangers are particularly insidious because you might not realize the damage to your system until hours, days, or even years after the exposure. Do not spray paint in confined areas. *Always* wear a respirator-type protective mask. Never use carbon tetrachloride for any purpose.

All hobby accidents and hazards are preventable by using tools properly, wearing protective gear, and rigid adhering to simple rules. Do not take short cuts and try to get by with something that you know is unsafe . . . even one time. That might be the time that gets you!

These Things Could Happen to You . . . If You Don't Follow Safety Precautions!

- ☐ Loss of fingers
- ☐ Severe cuts
- ☐ Loss of an eye
- ☐ Electric shock
- ☐ Explosion
- ☐ Burns (thermal or chemical)
- ☐ Allergic reactions
- ☐ Respiratory distress
- ☐ Emphysema
- ☐ Sickness
- ☐ Poisoning
- ☐ Lung cancer
- ☐ Death

4

Techniques

Technique allows you to create a model that closely imitates the modeled object. Technique uses materials and tools, adhesives and fasteners, through construction, finishing, aging/weathering, lettering, etc., together with methods specific to what you are modeling; to create the models in whatever detail you desire. It is the collection of skills that you need. The various techniques are covered in chapters 4 through 11. Specific methods and procedures are detailed in chapters 12 through 20.

APPROACH

The approach to creating a model layout, module, scene, or diorama is to first plan what you want to do; then consider the options available, choosing the option to use based on the trade between the effect desired and the cost/labor involved; and then execute and create the model. These steps are illustrated in FIG. 4-1.

PLANNING

Planning consists, more than anything else, of determining what it is *you* want. What do you want to model, and how do you want to do it? How much time do you want to spend? What is the effect that you want to create? What compromises are you willing to make with yourself in what you do? In the final analysis, it is only you that you have to please. It is your model and you make the rules.

You should have a general plan for your model. Whether it is a layout, large or small; a module, one or several; a diorama; or a single locomotive or car; what do you want it to look like when it is done? Good planning will yield good models (FIG. 4-2).

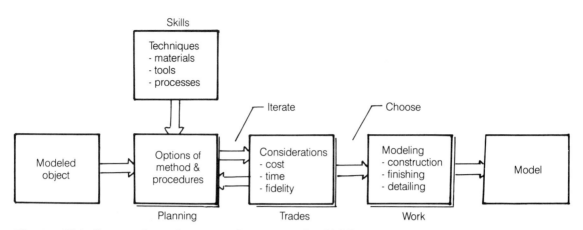

Fig. 4-1. This diagram shows the systematic steps one should follow in creating a model.

Fig. 4-2. From constructing the smallest building or railroad car, to the most elaborate layout, to create fine models it is necessary to have and follow a plan.

To plan, you must have knowledge. Knowledge is either gained slowly, and often painfully, by experience, or more quickly by reading what others have learned and written down. Experience can come from the past or can be gained by observation. If what you want to model can still actually be seen, there is no substitute for seeing, and photographing, it.

In most cases, however, you must read the books or magazines devoted to the prototypes, or the books (such as this one) or magazines devoted to the models. It is almost mandatory to regularly read at least one of the several fine model railroading magazines to learn what others are doing, to learn techniques, to get ideas, to learn about new products, etc. (See the Bibliography for a list of periodicals.)

Ideas

Ideas are the key. The human mind must collect and assimilate a lot of information before it can somehow collate and formulate that data into the ideas that lead to the plans for the models. The ideas do not have to be original, and seldom are. People almost always do things that are a combination of all that they have learned from others. You probably would not (or could not) copy a model that someone else made and do it exactly. Even when you build from the same kit, the resulting models are usually different in varying respects, either because of differences in skill or in intent.

Skills

What about skills? You probably are not equally skilled in all areas. You should attempt projects that are commensurate with your skills, perhaps pushing them a little, so that you can learn and become better. You probably are not equally handy with all tools. You might not have artistic ability. You might know nothing about electricity. But you don't have to be perfect . . . your skills do not have to match the abilities of anyone else. Your hobby is for you to have fun and to relax, not to put you back into the same rat race you are trying to escape from.

Your Goals

- ☐ Judge yourself against your own goals and capabilities.
- ☐ Use the work of others to educate and inspire you.
- ☐ Don't let what others have done intimidate you.
- ☐ Set realistic goals for yourself.
- ☐ Understand your resources and limitations.
- ☐ Expect to improve and reset your goals.

Rules

There are *no* rules you have to follow. If something pleases you, then that is all that matters. It is your hobby. It is supposed to relax you from the cares of the world, not create new tensions because you are not doing something "right" by someone else's rules. You can spend as little or as much time as you wish. You can create your own empire . . . even your own imaginary world. Whatever you do is right for you!

The subject of planning is covered in more specific detail in the topic, "Ideawork," chapter 13.

5

Materials

The choice of materials to use in making the model is very important because it will determine:

- ☐ How faithfully you can reproduce the modeled object in its texture;
- ☐ The tools, adhesives, and fasteners you can use;
- ☐ The specific methods you can use;
- ☐ The cost and time required.

The selection of the materials used is closely tied to the methods employed. This section will discuss material selection in general. Specific material selection options for methods are discussed in chapters 12 through 20.

The first choice for consideration should always be the same material as the full-sized object is made of; that is, use wood to model wood, etc. The choice must consider matching the texture as determined by the size ratio.

See TABLE 5-1 for a listing of full-sized materials and modeling materials. Often there is no identical model material that can be used. Usually this is because the texture of the full-sized material is just too coarse for the model.

A portion of a modeled object usually does not make a good model of itself. A small rock does not make a good model of a big rock or a rock face. A twig might not make a good model of a tree. Neither the detailing, the texture, nor the color will look right. The sizing is usually too massive and the texture is usually too coarse. The color, which you might think perfect, is usually not right, either.

A rock face, a tree, or anything else in nature is made up of many patches of color that the eye integrates together to tell the brain that "that looks like a real _____." Taking one of those color patches by itself will not give the right effect.

Table 5-1. Material Options for Modeling

Full-Sized Materials	Modeling Materials
Brick/block/stonework	Plaster (cast)
	Plastic (cast, sheet)
Concrete/asphalt	Plaster (cast, poured)
	Paper/paperboard
	Plastic (cast, sheet)
Earth	Earth
	Plaster (cast, poured)
	Foam plastic (stock, poured)
Fabrics	Fabrics
	Paper
Flesh/fur	Plastic (cast)
	Metal (cast)
Glass	Glass
	Plastic, clear (sheet)
Grass	Foam rubber (shredded)
	Sawdust
	Flock
Ice	Plastic, clear (poured)
Metal	Metal (stock, formed, cast)
	Paper/paperboard
	Plastic (stock, cast)
Rock	Rock
	Plaster (cast)
	Foam plastic (poured)
Rubber	Rubber
	Plastic (cast)
	Metal (cast)
Snow	Powder (plaster, etc.)
	Plaster (poured)
Stones	Stones
	Plaster (cast)
Trees	Twigs
	Weeds
	Lichen
	Grass Materials

Full-Sized Materials	Modeling Materials
Water	Water Plastic, clear (poured, sheet) Glass
Weeds/brush	Weeds Seeds Lichen
Wire	Wire Thread
Wood	Wood (stock, milled) Paper/paperboard Plastic (stock, cast)

Look at a big rock—it is not all one color. Look at a stone or small rock near it, even one broken off from it—it will probably be a single color.

COST

Usually the cost of the materials is a small consideration. It is often better to pay a little more to save much time and tedium. You will get a better result, will feel better about the model, and might not be tempted to redo it. It might also last longer and be less subject to warping and deterioration. An example might be the temptation to use balsa wood instead of basswood. The former will cost less, but it will take more time to reduce the fuzz, it will be harder to finish, it will not be as durable, and the wood grain will be out of scale.

Some of the main types of materials used for models are listed in TABLE 5-2. Some examples for wood, paper, and plastics are shown in FIG. 5-1.

Table 5-2. Materials Used for Models

Material	Type	Configuration
Wood	Bass	Sheet, strips, milled
Paper	Various	Sheet
Plastics	Styrene, ABS, epoxy, casting	Sheet, milled, cast
Plaster	Hydrocal, dental	Cast, precast
Foam	Rubber	Sheet, ground
Metal	Brass, white	Sheet, cast

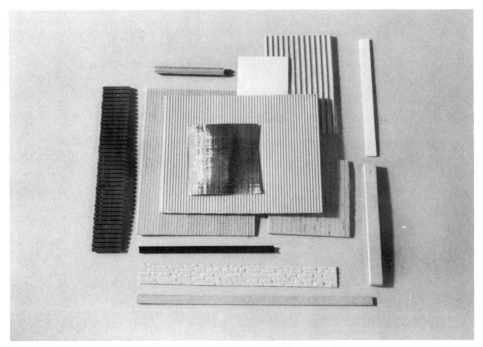

Fig. 5-1. *Some examples of common modeling materials, including wood, paper, and plastic.*

MATERIALS

Wood. The best general-purpose wood for models is basswood (American Linden). It has fine grain and is relatively hard. Substitutes might be walnut, clear white pine, or jelutong. The wood used should be free of knots and of uniform color and texture.

Paper. This also includes cardstock, cardboard, illustration board, Strathmore board, and foam core board. All of these materials have a smooth finish and are grainless. With proper texturing and finishing, they can be used to simulate many other materials.

Plastics. The best general-purpose plastic to use is virgin white styrene. It is easy to cut and shape, and it is pliable and easy to join. Do not use clear styrene, which is very brittle and shatters easily. Dark-colored styrenes contain pigments that have no advantages and make the material softer. Acrylonitrile-butadiene styrene (ABS) plastic is a useful variety of styrene that usually has a gray color. Acrylic plastics, such as Plexiglas®, Lucite®, and Acrylite®, are also useful.

Metals. Brass is the best all-around metal to use for models, if fabrication is involved. It is readily available and can be easily cut, formed, shaped, turned, soldered, or otherwise joined together. Aluminum is easy to work with but hard to join together because it cannot be soldered or welded by conventional techniques. Steel has limited application. White metal is commonly used for castings; this is an alloy of zinc, antimony, and lead. White metal cannot be easily soldered, and so it requires adhesives or fasteners for joining.

6

Tools

Tools are said to distinguish man from the animals. They are also what you use to build and finish your models. A craftsman is no better than his tools. Quality tools last longer, do a better job, and are much less expensive in the long run. Acquire tools as you need them. Keeping all of your modeling tools organized, handy, and protected in their own locked toolbox is a very good idea.

Learn how to correctly use each tool. Improperly used, tools can be dangerous, resulting in injuries, lost fingers or eyes, or permanent damage to your health. Never use a tool for any purpose other than the one for which it was intended. It is a good practice to wear plastic safety glasses when working with any tool. It should be mandatory when working with power tools. (Also see safety cautions under the topic, "Airbrushing," in chapter 9.)

Tools can be broadly categorized into those used for measuring, cutting, holding, smoothing, joining, and painting. Some tools can be obtained in motorized form (power tools). TABLE 6-1 lists suggested tools for the modeler, with the tools listed in columns according to priority of need.

MEASURING TOOLS

Measuring tools (FIG. 6-1) include rules, gauges, dividers, scribes, squares, and markers.

Rules

As a minimum, you should have two metal rules, one graduated in feet and inches (or meters and centimeters) in the scale you are modeling, and one graduated in inches (and/or centimeters) and fractions thereof. They should each be

Table 6-1. *Modeler's Suggested Tool List*

Type	Need	Nice	Luxury
Knives	X-Acto handle, #1 X-Acto blades, #11, #16* Razor blades, single edge*	X-Acto handles, #2, #5 X-Acto blades, #19* Utility knife, with blades*	Dupli-Cutter Paper Shear Chopper
Saws	Razor saw handle Razor saw blade, extra fine Mitre box (wood or metal)	Razor saw blade, fine Razor saw blade, medium Crosscut saw, small Mini hacksaw, with blades	Jewelers saw with blades
Pliers	Needle-nose, medium Household, small	Needle-nose, small Chain-nose, small	Clamping, small
Cutters	Scissors, common Pliers, diagonal cutting Pliers, end-cutting	Sheet-metal snips	
Files	Medium, 6-inch Fine, 6-inch Jewelers set, with handle	Wood rasp, 10-inch	Riffler files
Abrasives	Fingernail sanding slats Sanding stick	Sandpaper* Emery paper* Surform tool	
Clamps	Cross-action clamps, X-Acto C clamps, plastic Clothespins, spring type Rubber bands* Weights, miscellaneous	C clamps, metal	Forceps Magnetic jig
Rules	Scale gauge/rule, 6-12-inch metal Inch/cm rule, 12-inch metal Pocket rule, retracting	Square, combination	Square, machinist's

Type	Need	Nice	Luxury
Brushes	Round tip, assorted sizes Flat tip, assorted sizes	Regular, 1, 2 inch	
Drill Bits	Fractional (or metric) to $1/4$ inch Numbered, 61-80	Numbered, 1-60 Fractional (or metric) to $1/2$ inch	
Tweezers	Offset needle tip Broad bill tip	Needle tip	
Screwdrivers	Jeweler's set Small, regular	Small, Phillips	Hex drivers, small
Markers	Pencils* Marking pens* Scribe Dividers	Center punch	
Gauges	Vernier caliper	Drill gauge Micrometer	
Air Brush		Single-action Air supply Respirator, with filters* Siphon bottles	Dual action
Bench Aids	Cutting board Toolbox Lamp, adjustable	Machinist's vise, small Vise, multi-angle Magnifier, clamp-on	Jeweler's hand vise Surface plate
Joining		Soldering iron, solder* Glue gun, glue sticks* Staple gun, staples*	Butane torch, small Micronox torch
Miscellaneous	Eye goggles, protective Pin vise	File card Wire brush, small Burnishing stick Tap set Hammer, small	Die set
Power Tools	Motor tool, with accessories	Motor tool speed control Motor tool flexible shaft Drill motor, $1/4$ inch Saber saw	Spray booth Accurate drill press Mini table saw Belt/disk sander

*–Optional

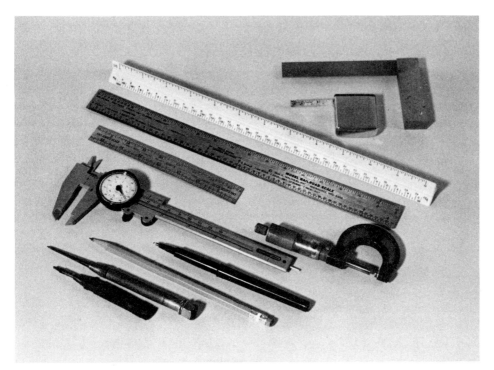

Fig. 6-1. *Examples of useful modeler's measuring tools.*

from 6 to 12 inches long. Rules graduated in other than your scale might also be useful if you are using plans drawn in that scale. Rules are also available that have multiple scale graduations on the same rule, but these require you to look each time to get the right part of the rule. Besides measuring, these rules will also be useful as a straightedge to guide your knife when cutting. A small pocket retracting rule capable of measuring up to 6 feet can also be useful, particularly for benchwork and trackwork purposes.

Gauges

A useful addition is a caliper or a micrometer. The former comes in the more-popular scales or in inches or centimeters. Calipers can have a dial for reading or a vernier readout. Micrometers are available in inch or centimeter vernier or dial readouts. Micrometers are for very accurate measurements of an inch or under. Calipers can measure lengths up to several inches.

Dividers

Dividers, like the ones used by draftsmen, can be useful for transferring dimensions between drawings and from drawings to materials. You also can use their sharp points for putting simulated nailheads into wood. Proportional dividers can be used for direct scaling up or down between plans in different scales.

Markers

Markers include pencils, pens, scribes, etc., that are used to mark the material for cutting. Pencils should be 4H or harder. You can buy scribes or make them by forcing a sharpened pin or nail into a wooden dowel. Machinist's marking dye might be useful so that lines scribed onto metal can be seen. You can use a small center punch to mark holes to be drilled in metal or plastic.

Squares

A 6-inch combination square or a small 3-inch machinist's square can be useful when squaring and marking materials.

CUTTING TOOLS

Cutting tools (FIG. 6-2) include knives, saws, cutters, drills, and taps and dies.

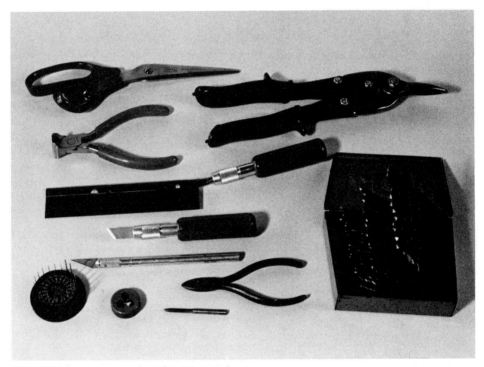

Fig. 6-2. Several examples of cutting tools.

Knives

The most basic modeler's tool is the knife. The most useful form of the knife is the type made by X-Acto, in three different handle sizes and with a large variety of blade sizes and shapes. To begin with, get the small handle (#1) and a package each of #11 and #16 blades. Later, you can add the medium-sized (#2) or large (#5) handles and other blades. (The two larger handles take larger size blades).

The most useful blade is the #11. It is long and pointed but with a fragile tip. It might be overlong for some cuts. The #16 blade is shorter and more durable. The most important thing in using these blades is that they must be sharp because if they are not, they will crush the material rather than cut it. They can be sharpened using a small sharpening stone, followed by stropping on jeweler's rouge on a strip of leather. At their cost, however, it is easier to buy new blades than to go to this trouble.

It is often desirable to have a duller blade as well as the sharp one. Mark or color the handles to tell them apart. A #11 blade with just the tip broken off makes an ideal tool for scribing lines in plastic or for scribing plastic prior to breaking it apart. When used backwards, it can chisel out a clean groove, stripping out a curl of the plastic. A sharp knife, used for scribing, will raise ridges alongside the cut, which must be filed down.

Blades with concave or convex curves are generally less useful, although the #9 (convex) is sometimes handy. Medical scalpels are not very useful, and they are expensive.

The safest knife is a sharp knife. The blades are inexpensive, and it is false economy to use them too long. For cutting safety, always cut so that the knife is moving away from the hand holding the material. If a slip occurs, it will not cut you. If possible, use a metal guide when doing any cutting. Have a safe place to put your knife when you are not using it. Add a "bulge" to the handle so it will not roll. If it does, get out of the way and do not try to catch it.

Razor Blades. Single-edge razor blades are inexpensive when bought as industrial grade in hardware stores in quantities of 100. They are very useful for a variety of cutting applications. They should be disposed of when no longer sharp.

Utility Knife. Larger knives, called utility knives, with replaceable blades are also useful for a variety of cutting chores, particularly when cutting paperboard or wallboard.

Saws

An essential modeler's tool is a Zona or razor saw, a backsaw type made especially for models. They can be used to cut either wood or plastic. They come with various numbers of teeth per inch (30 to 40). These saws have a thin (0.010-inch) blade, reinforced at the top, and cut on the push stroke. Use saws with the finest teeth for sawing wood. You also can hold saws in a small purchased or home-made mitre box. Some are available with removable handles and different depths of cut, ranging from one to two inches. They are not recommended for cutting metal.

Metal can be cut with a small hacksaw or with a jeweler's saw, depending on the thickness of the metal. Either has replaceable blades, but the jeweler's saw blades are quite delicate. They have from 30 to 80 teeth per inch and are designed to cut on the pull stroke. This saw can cut very thin metal very accurately. The thinner the metal being cut, the more and finer the teeth need to be. The blade must be kept straight and quite taut.

A small crosscut saw can be used to cut wood too large for the razor saws. In any case, the smaller tooth sizes will be most useful for model work. A keyhole saw can also be handy for cutting plywood if you do not have a power saber saw.

Cutters

Cutters include a variety of purchased and homemade devices that allow a single-edge razor blade to accurately cut material in duplicate lengths. The blade might move in a pivoted-lever or parallel-shearing motion. Various types of jigs and stops can hold the material and control the cut length. Examples of these devices are the Dupli-Cutter, the Chopper, and the Shay wood miter. These devices are extremely useful for repetitive cutting of stripwood. Be sure to replace the blade often to keep it sharp.

Scissors. Common household scissors are essential for your tool kit. Use them to cut paper as well as thin plastic and paperboard. Metal shears might also be useful, in the smaller sizes.

Drills

The drill bits you buy should all be of the "high-speed" type. Buy drills as sets, in a container that holds each drill bit in its proper place. Modelers should have a set that ranges from numbers 61 to 80 (which are the very small sizes), and a set that ranges in fractional sizes from $1/16$ inch to $1/2$ inch. Fractional drill sizes larger than $1/2$ inch or numbered or lettered drill sizes larger than number 61 are optional.

Drills can be used in a motor tool, a miniature drill press, or held in a pin vise. The latter has several chuck sizes and allows you to use your hand to hold the drill for the drilling operation. Resharpening drill bits of smaller than $1/16$ inch is difficult and unlikely to be successful. Above that size, it is worth it, if you can learn how to do it.

Start drills in a center-punched dimple or a scribed mark. Lubricate drills used in metal with cutting oil. Lubricate those used in plastics with soap, bees wax, or paraffin. The smaller size drills are very fragile and are subject to breakage, even with careful use.

Taps and Dies

Taps can be useful for model work. Dies have much less applicability. Taps are used to create threads inside drilled holes so that machine screws can be retained. Dies are used for forming threads on the outside of rod stock. A useful range of sizes is 00-90, 0-80, 1-72, 2-56, and 4-40. The first number is a reference designation proportional to size, and the second number is the threads per inch. Useful metric sizes are 1 mm, 1.4 mm, and 2 mm. Taps can be held in a tap handle or (for these sizes) in a pin vise. Dies require a special die holder.

HOLDING TOOLS

The most useful holding tool is the human hand. Unfortunately, it is too large, or too weak, or too few in number to fulfill all the holding jobs required. Holding tools (FIG. 6-3) include pliers, clamps, tweezers, vises, weights, and jigs and fixtures.

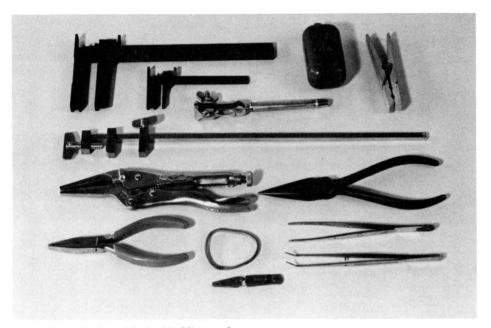

Fig. 6-3. Typical model-sized holding tools.

Pliers

The available variety of pliers is almost endless. For modeling purposes, the largest useful pliers is the common household slip-joint or "gas" pliers. Among its thousands of uses, it is very handy for opening stuck paint jar tops.

The most useful miniature pliers is the shorter version of the needle-nose type. These small pliers are available in different lengths in round nose, flat nose, long needle nose, etc. A selection of several types can often be obtained at a hardware store for relatively low cost. If you are going to spike rail, however, one really good pair that feels just right to you, will be worth its weight in gold.

Also in the general category of pliers are a variety of plier-type cutters or nippers, including diagonal cutters, flush end cutters, etc. Some are made especially for cutting model railroad rail to length without leaving a rough end.

Clamps

The least expensive clamp is the common wooden spring-action clothespin. It can be used as is or as modified in a variety of ways. There is probably no better clamp for holding two surfaces together while the glue dries. These are now made in a miniature version (for craft use) that is about 1³/₄ inch long.

A small metal version of a clothespin is made by X-Acto. These are called cross-action clamps. They are used in a similar manner but for smaller jobs and in tighter places.

A variety of different size and shape plastic C clamps are available for modelers. These are useful for clamping or holding larger models or pieces of material. Metal bar clamps are also available for model applications. Either type is adjustable over a range of several inches. Regular metal C clamps are useful when doing benchwork or trackwork.

Although it is not a clamp, the common rubber band is a helpful tool for clamping and holding models and materials together while the glue is setting. The cost is minimal (or free) and the size range is very large. Caution must be used that the rubber bands do not distort the model or the material, however, because the force they exert can be made quite high.

Tweezers

Tweezers come in a great variety of sizes and tip configurations. Several different types are necessary to suit the shapes and sizes of materials to be handled. Choose ones that are not too heavy or too stiff. If they are too stiff, your hand will tire while holding them closed.

The most useful tweezers are probably the offset fine-tip type. A second choice would be a broader (¹/₈ inch) straight-tip type. From there, the choices are open and up to the individual. Tweezers can be normally open or normally closed (reverse action), and can have provisions for locking them closed. Hemostats are a special type of tweezers made for the medical clamping of blood vessels; they can be useful, but they are expensive.

Vises

The most useful modeler's vise is called a machinist's vise. It is about $3 \times 3 \times 6$ inches in size and can hold material up to 3 inches thick. Another useful vise is a small adjustable one, such as a PanaVise, that can clamp onto your workbench, or attach with suction. It has a universal joint that swivels and locks in any position. The jaws will hold material up to 1 inch thick, but it will not hold material as firmly as the machinist's vise.

In the category of very small vises are pin vises, used for holding small drills and taps (or pins); and the jeweler's hand vise, used for holding small pieces of material or castings while they are being worked on.

Weights

Often there is no other way to hold materials together while the glue is drying that is as good as weights. While you can use books, or rocks, or most anything heavy, some special-purpose model weights can easily be bought or fabricated at low cost. They will do a better job, will have greater mass for size, and will let you see what you are doing better.

One choice is lead fishing weights. If you live near the ocean, deep sea lead weights are available in sizes of 1 pound and more. Even smaller weights of 1 or 2 ounces can be useful. The cost is quite reasonable.

A second choice is lead or metal bar stock. This can be cut to various lengths to suit the jobs. The lead is available at plumbing supply stores and is melted to make seals in drain pipes.

Steel or iron bar stock can be obtained from welding shops. Old railroad spikes make good weights, and large steel bolts or nuts can be useful. Often these items are scraps that no one but you wants, so the price will be little or nothing.

Jigs and Fixtures

One of the handiest tools for making model buildings is a magnetic jig made for dollhouse modelers. It consists of a steel plate, some aluminum angles forming a corner, and several magnets used to hold items while they are being glued. The tool is about 12 × 12 inches. A surface plate can also be useful, and besides its intended use as an accurate base for measurements, it can also be used with magnets as a gluing jig.

The variety of jigs and fixtures that can be useful for cutting or assembling or gluing is essentially endless. Any time that a number of things need to be fabricated that are the same size and shape, use a jig/fixture to ensure uniformity and save time and work.

SMOOTHING TOOLS

Smoothing tools (FIG. 6-4) include the various files and abrasives.

Files

Several types of small files, such as a small set of needle or pattern files, will be useful to the modeler. A good addition is a pair of small (6- to 9-inch) mill files in medium- and fine-tooth sizes. The mill file is used for filing larger expanses of wood, metal, plaster, or plastic. You might wish to use handles with these files to hold them better and protect your hand. A larger wood rasp is useful when working with scenery shaping, particularly with foam.

Files are designed to cut on the push (away from the tang end) stroke. Start work with the larger files and finish with smaller ones. Keep files clean so they work effectively. Some metals and plastics tend to gum up the grooves, which must then be cleaned out individually or with a small file card or a suede brush with brass bristles. Gumming can be reduced by using appropriate lubrication while filing (oil for metals, water for plastic). Riffler files are curved needle files and are of limited use.

Fig. 6-4. Some typical model smoothing tools (files and abrasives).

Abrasives

The most common abrasive is sandpaper. It can be obtained in a large variety of roughnesses and with different backings and abrasive materials. Commercial wet-or-dry 10-×-12-inch sheets in grits of various sizes are a good first purchase. These sheets can be cut to smaller sizes.

The emery boards used for manicuring are very useful. They have a different roughness on each side. They are inexpensive and can be trimmed to size for special applications. It is also handy to make several sanding sticks. These are wooden sticks 1/2 inch to 1 inch wide, 1/4 inch thick, and about 6 to 9 inches long. Ordinary sandpaper is trimmed and contact-cemented to each side. These are for the heavier jobs that emery boards are too small to do.

JOINING TOOLS

Joining tools (FIG. 6-5) include those used for manipulating fasteners (screwdrivers, etc.) and for soldering, gluing, stapling, and fastening.

Screwdrivers

It is essential to have a small set of jeweler's screwdrivers. You should have three or more sizes with flat blades and one or more cross-point (Phillips) blades.

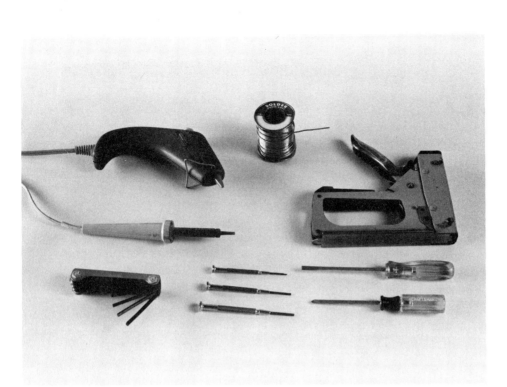

Fig. 6-5. Joining tools useful in modeling include screwdrivers, soldering, gluing, stapling, and fastening tools.

Other blades for Allen-head screws, or with miniature wrenches are not really necessary. You should also own one or more regular screwdrivers with flat end blades and with Phillips end blades for use with larger-than-model tasks. A set of small hex nut drivers can be an eventual addition to your inventory.

Soldering

Soldering can be done with large or small soldering irons, a soldering gun, or a torch using butane or Micronox/butane. All of these are not needed by the average modeler. Which is used is determined by the job to be done because each is best for a particular function. A soldering gun is primarily useful for electrical wiring.

A microtorch (small size for models) or a large soldering iron is used mainly for soldering of brass sheet or castings, where a lot of heat is necessary. Use a torch if high-temperature solders are to be used. Carbon electrode soldering tweezers, which make use of resistance soldering, can also be useful. You can use a small soldering iron for electrical wiring and for small metal joining jobs. More information on choices of soldering tools and materials is in "Metal Construction" in chapter 8.

PAINTING TOOLS

Painting tools include those used for brushing and airbrushing. These tools, their selection, and use are discussed in detail in "Brushing and Airbrushing" in chapter 9.

Also particularly note the safety cautions and the need for a respirator (face mask) while doing spray painting. Indoor spray painting should be done only in a spray booth that exhausts to the outside.

TOOL AIDS

Aids include a great variety of miscellaneous devices, including toolboxes, lights, magnifiers, cutting boards, and surface plates. Examples of some of the many types of tool aids are shown in FIG. 6-6.

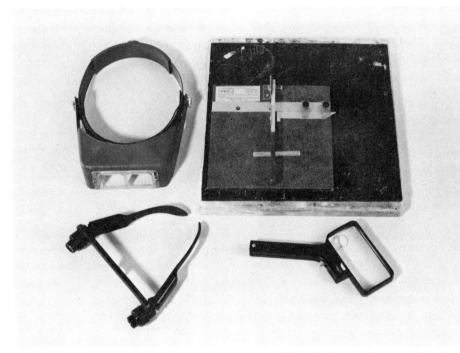

Fig. 6-6. Various kinds of tool aids, such as magnifiers, lights, and cutting boards, can help the modeling and save time.

Toolboxes

Using a toolbox to keep all of your smaller modeling tools together in one organized place will prove to be very important for a number of reasons. A toolbox tends to keep the tools from being lost, misplaced, or used for other household jobs. The toolbox can be locked up to keep "little hands" out. The tools will stay sharper and more rust free if they are stored this way. Wood or metal toolboxes can be built or bought.

Lights

Adequate lighting for the workbench is very important, both to preserve your eyesight and to allow you to see well enough to produce the best possible models. Either fluorescent or incandescent lighting can be used. Flexible arm, drafting type lamps are recommended to position light where needed. Lights are also available with built-in magnifiers. For some operations, it is important to duplicate the light type and intensity of the layout so that the colors appear the same.

Magnifiers

Most persons can benefit from magnification when working on small details on models. The most convenient magnifier is the type that clamps onto the head, over glasses (if any), and that can be raised out of the way when not needed. Small magnifying glasses or loupes also work.

Cutting Boards

Use a piece of Masonite, pressed board, plastic, or hard rubber as a cutting board. Do not use a material with a grain (such as wood) as it might divert the knife.

POWER TOOLS

Power tools are not essential, but they can save a lot of time and often result in a better job. Most power tools are powered from a wall outlet, but some are available in cordless, rechargeable battery types. This choice is up to you. Power tools (FIG. 6-7) include motor tools, drill motors, spray booth, power saws, drill presses, saber saws, and sanders.

Power tools require constant attention to safety. This includes using electricity safely to avoid shock or electrocution, as well as using sharp tools safely to avoid loss of skin, fingers, and other body parts. All power tools can be dangerous! Constant use can bring complacency that results in carelessness that results in injuries.

The most dangerous tools are rotary saws, or motor tools or drill motors that turn larger cutting tools at high peripheral speeds. In case of accident, the least that could happen is the destruction of what you are working on. Keep the speeds no higher than necessary. Make sure the tools are adequately grounded. Keep your fingers well out of the way. Wear safety goggles.

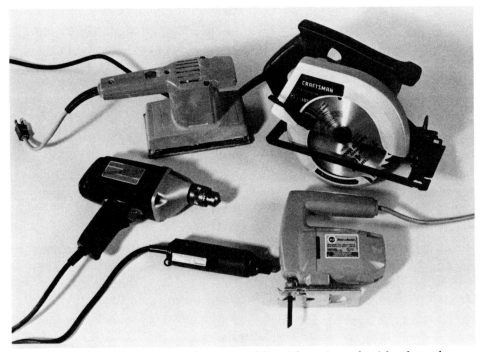

Fig. 6-7. *Small power tools can make most modeling jobs easier and quicker, but safety can be a concern.*

Motor Tools

The small, universal motor tool, with its variety of attachments, is the single most useful power tool. Those made by Dremel, and others, come with various chuck sizes and a large assortment of compatible cutting bits, rasps, saws, etc., that can handle a variety of jobs.

Not all the accessory tools that come in an assortment are useful. The handiest are the variously shaped steel-cutting bits, the sanding drums, the rubber-bonded abrasive wheels (for polishing), wire brushes, and the abrasive cutting discs.

Abrasive cutting discs are quite delicate, but they provide an ideal tool to cut rail to length. Be sure to wear goggles when using them. A new type of abrasive cutting disc has nylon filaments that prevent shattering. Steel saw blades are no longer available. Even if you have them, do not use them because they present severe safety hazards.

These motor tools come with either built-in or separate speed controllers (which are a useful addition). Other features might include foot controllers, flexible extension shafts, mounting bases, fixtures that allow you to use the tool as a drill press, and other accessories.

Drill Motor

This tool is the single most useful household power tool, and as such, it has many hobby applications, particularly for benchwork and trackwork. Choose a drill motor with a 1/4-inch or 3/8-inch capacity chuck and with reversing and speed control capability. This tool can be used for driving screws as well as drilling holes.

Spray Booth

This subject is covered in more detail under the topic, "Airbrushing," in chapter 9. Suffice it to say that it can save your health if you insist on doing spray painting indoors.

Accurate Drill Press

This tool can provide extremely accurate drilling of holes in model-sized materials using the smallest drill bits. The motor should have a speed control. Either the motor/chuck portion (preferable) or the worktable should move up and down. The worktable also might have a lateral motion adjustment.

Saber Saw

This tool is worth its weight in gold when large amounts of roadbed material must be cut out. These saws come with replaceable blades in a variety of tooth sizes and types.

Table Saw

Miniature versions of the woodworker's table saw are available for modelers. These are useful if you cut a lot of wood or plastic. Often you can use a full-sized table saw with a fine-toothed "plywood" blade for these jobs, if one is available.

Sanders

Power sanders are available as hand-held orbital sanders, belt sanders, or disk sanders; and as bench-mounted belt and/or disk sanders. The most useful, for these modeling applications, is probably a small, bench-mounted combination belt and disk sander. Like the table saw, this is a luxury item not needed by most modelers.

SCENERY TOOLS

There are a number of additional tools, many of which you might already have around the house, that will be needed for the various scenery construction methods discussed in chapters 15, 16, and 17. These tools, and their use, will be discussed in detail as they are needed.

Scenery Tools

Pump-type plastic spray bottles, adjustable nozzle
Plastic squeeze bottles, large size
Paintbrushes, 1", 1$^1/_2$", and 2" wide
Measuring cup
Measuring spoon set
Teaspoon
Eyedroppers
Rubber kitchen spatula
Butter knife
Small trowel
Containers with lids (jars, coffee cans, etc.)

7

Adhesives
and Fasteners

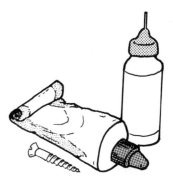

Adhesives and fasteners are alternative means of joining parts together. Soldering, brazing, and welding are other techniques. Soldering tools are covered briefly in the topic, "Joining Tools," in chapter 6. Soldering is covered at length in the topic, "Metal Construction," in chapter 8.

ADHESIVES

There are a great many adhesives available that you can use, each with its particular applications. No single adhesive is universal. The variety is necessary to ideally bond materials of different types and porosities together (FIG. 7-1).

Acetate Cement

Acetate cement includes the model airplane and household cements available in tubes. They are made of celluloid dissolved in acetone, with added ingredients to facilitate strength and fast drying. They are very fast drying, almost too fast, and are useful primarily for wood or paper. They have a strong odor, are relatively weak, are relatively expensive, and give off harmful fumes. They are not suitable for joining metal or styrene plastics. Other types of cements have made acetate cements a poorer choice for almost any joining job.

Plastic Cement

There are several types of cements made for use with plastics. The best type to use for joining styrene is the liquid type. Apply it sparingly with a small brush, using capillary action to draw the cement into the joint. It will dry in minutes to partial strength, but it will take several hours for the joint to reach full strength.

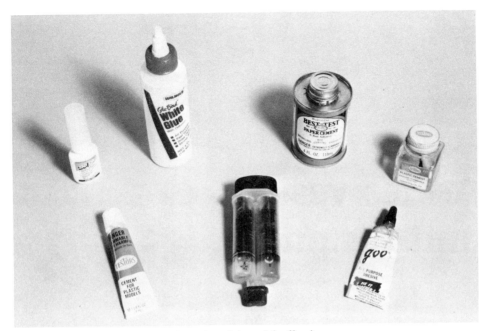

Fig. 7-1. There are a large variety of useful model adhesives.

This cement has a bad odor. Do not breathe the fumes and avoid skin contact. The cement is also flammable. The cost is low because the amount used is so little. This liquid plastic cement contains methyl isobutyl ketone and methyl cellosolve acetate. Examples of liquid plastic cements are Testors' Plastic Cement, Pactra's C-ment, Plastruct's Plastic Weld, and Micro Scale's Micro Weld. These vary somewhat in thickness. Experiment to determine which works best for you.

A similar, but thicker, formulation is available in tubes. This is sometimes called "plastic model cement." It dries a little slower, is somewhat messier, is slightly more expensive, and is less strong. It must be applied thinly to one or both pieces before they are joined. It is not as useful as the liquid type, and it tends to make a less neat joint. It can be useful for attaching gussets and strengthening layers to the back of plastic surfaces, where its gap filling properties are an advantage.

Use ethylene dichloride (EDC) for joining Lucite, Plexiglas, or other acrylic plastics. This is applied using capillary action. It will not etch the acrylics. Plastruct makes a liquid bonding agent called Weld-On, which can be used for bonding ABS plastics.

White Glue

White resin-emulsion adhesives are sold under a variety of trade names, such as Elmer's and Glu-Bird. All are known generically as white glue. They usually come in a polyethylene squeeze bottle. White glue is used as the primary adhesive for joining porous materials such as wood, paper, styrene foam, and fabric.

It is very inexpensive, forms a strong bond, is slow drying, and dries transparent. You can use it full strength or thin it with water when it is used as a bonding agent for loose scenic materials.

White glues consist of polyvinyl acetate suspended in water. For the glue to work, the water must evaporate, be absorbed into the materials, or flow away. Apply the glue to one or both materials and clamp them together until the glue dries (several hours). While it is still wet, excess glue can be wiped off with a wet cloth. White glues are very safe to use because they are nontoxic, nonflammable, and almost odorless.

Yellow Glue

A similar glue, called aliphatic resin, comes in similar packaging to white glue and can be used in the same manner. Its advantage is that it is stronger on wood-to-wood joints and dries a little faster. It is more expensive, has a more yellow color, and does not dry as transparent.

Contact Cement

These cements are normally used by applying them thinly to both surfaces to be joined, letting the cement dry until tacky (5 to 10 minutes), and then pressing the surfaces together. These cements are made of resin ingredients and take a very long time to dry thoroughly. Examples are Walther's Goo and Goodyear's Pliobond. They can be used to bond nonporous or porous materials to each other. The most useful modeling application is in joining corrugated aluminum to paperboard or wood. They are very messy to use and are relatively expensive.

When the two dry, cement-coated surfaces are brought together they will bond instantly. It will be almost impossible to get them apart again, so they must be properly aligned in advance. This can be done by using a paper slip sheet (any kind of paper). This is placed between the two surfaces (but will not stick to either). Matching edges of the surfaces are then aligned, and the slip sheet is pulled out as the surfaces are pressed together. Contact cements are extremely flammable, and they are also toxic (when wet) to the skin. Do not breathe the vapors.

Rubber Cement

Rubber cement can also be used as a contact cement, though it is not as good as genuine contact cements at joining nonporous materials. It is best used for joining paper materials. Excess rubber cement can usually be rubbed off. It can also be used to make temporary bonds, if only a little is used. Rubber cements are also available in spray cans.

Epoxy Cement

Epoxy cements come as two solutions, which must be mixed in an equal ratio prior to use. Depending on the formulation, the setting time can vary from a few minutes to an hour or more. It cures chemically, rather than drying like glue. It can bind nonporous materials together with surprising strength. It is a good gap filler and can bond materials that don't fit too well. It can retain its strength to 200°F, which can be of advantage in some applications. The fumes are unpleasant; keep the cement away from your skin as it is toxic upon contact. The most convenient form to buy epoxy in is a twin-tube dispenser. It must be mixed only just prior to use. It is expensive.

ACC

These alpha cyanoacrylate cements are sold under a variety of brand names, such as Hot Stuff, Krazy Glue, Zap, etc. They come in small polyethylene containers with a fine Teflon spout or nozzle applicator. A very small amount will join almost any two materials together, if the fit is good. It is used by letting capillary action carry the thin liquid into the joint. The bonding is quite rapid. Use caution so that your fingers or clamps do not become a part of the bond. Acetone or nail polish remover can serve as a solvent to "unstick" things.

Different types of ACC have different drying time and different gap-filling capabilities. An accelerator is available that will cause almost instant bonding. Baking soda can be added as a gap filler. In any case, the bonds have good strength but will yield to shock. Curing occurs due to the microscopic moisture that clings to the surfaces, although they should not actually be wet. The thinnest possible film will give the most strength and the fastest bonding time. The bond will weaken at 150°F.

A small container of ACC seems expensive, but only tiny quantities are used. The adhesive has a limited life, which can be extended by storing it in the refrigerator. It gives off toxic fumes, and keep it off your skin. Wear safety goggles when using it to prevent an accidental drop from flying into your eye, which could cause permanent blindness.

Silicone Sealant

This material, sold for bathtub caulking and other uses, can be a handy adhesive for some purposes. Its advantage is that it remains flexible, is waterproof, and will not shrink or crack. It can be used for mounting window material in structures, and it makes a good adhesive to use to mount motor vehicles and creatures to the layout surface. Use the type that dries colorless.

Liquid Metals

Liquid metals are powdered metal added to a vinyl resin dissolved in a solvent. After a day's drying, they are very hard and can be cut, filed, and drilled like metal. They are probably more useful as fillings or to make castings than as adhesives.

Urethane Bond

This adhesive, made by Dow Corning, is an epoxy-like glue that will bond just about anything. It is one of the few adhesives that will bond Delrin or nylon. At the same time, it is difficult to use because it is almost impossible to remove from anything (including the skin) that it gets on inadvertently.

Adhesive Usage

TABLE 7-1 is a guide to the various adhesives and shows which to use with different materials. When bonding dissimilar materials to each other, choose the adhesive most compatible with both materials. The time for setting and complete curing also varies with the adhesive used. A rough guide of these times is shown in TABLE 7-2.

FASTENERS

Fasteners for model work include nails (of various sorts), wood screws, machine screws, and rivets. Fastening also includes use of soldering and brazing.

Machine screws are available in brass, nylon, and steel, and with head configurations that are round, flat, hex, and filister. The useful sizes for models are 00–90, 0–80, 1–72, 2–56, 4–40, and the smaller metric sizes. They are available in a variety of lengths. See the Appendix for clearance and tap drill sizes.

Wood screws for small models come in brass or steel, with round or flat heads in a range of sizes indicated by head size and length. Self-tapping screws can be used for metals or plastics. They are usually steel and have round or pan heads.

Table 7-1. Adhesive Use Guide

Adhesive	Wood	Paper	Plastic	Foam	Metal	Plaster
White glue	+ +	+		+ +		+ +
Epoxy	+	+		+	+ +	+
ACC	+		+		+ +	
Contact cement	+ +	+ +	+ +		+ +	
Rubber cement	+	+ +	+		+	
Plastic cement		+	+			+
Plastic weld			+ +			
Acetate cement	+	+ +				

+ good; + + best

Table 7-2. Adhesive Setting and Curing Times

Adhesive	Setting Time (Min.)	Curing Time (Hours)
White glue	30–60	24
Yellow glue	20–40	24
Epoxy (quick set)	5–10	12
Epoxy (slow set)	120–240	24
ACC	$1/10 – 1/2$	2
Contact cement	0	24
Plastic cement	$1/2 – 1$	8

8

Construction

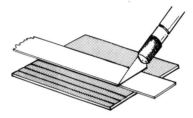

Good construction results require knowledge of the tools to be used, the materials you are working with, and how to best use the tools with the materials. In the topics on construction that follow, the techniques are described as a function of the materials, including wood, paperboard, plastic, metal, casting, and etching.

DEFINITIONS

Some terms are used that require definitions. *Ready-to-run* or *ready-to-use* models are those sold as complete and ready to use as-is, without further assembly or painting.

With the possible exception of custom-finished brass locomotives and cars, all models can benefit from additional work, including lubrication, flash cleanup, repainting or flat overspraying, aging and weathering. *Upgrading* is the term used to describe operations performed on ready-to-run/use models that add more detail and/or make them more representative of the prototype.

Kit-built refers to any model built from a kit. If it is *stock*, then it has been built according to the kit plans/instructions. *Modified* means that the model has been changed in some ways from what was described in the kit.

Kitbashing is the term used to describe combining parts from one or more kits to create a unique model, to add detail, or to represent a particular prototype that is different than the one in the kit. *Cross-kitted* means the same as kitbashed. Kit models can also be upgraded, of course.

Scratchbuilt means that the model has been built largely from stock materials. The terminology *mostly scratchbuilt* allows addition of purchased parts for details (particularly for castings). The difference is a matter of degree of purity and is not really important in the end result.

WOOD CONSTRUCTION

Construction with wood includes use of stock materials that are available in plain sheets of varying thickness, in scribed or milled sheets (simulating building siding), in strips of dimensional and scale sizes, and in structural shapes (such as I, H, and T beams).

Any of these materials might be a part of ready-made models, of kits, or may be purchased as stock. Kits will often have the materials cut to length and the openings cut out. The techniques used for cutting, fitting, and bonding the materials are the same in any case.

Cutting

Cut wood sheet material of 1/16 inch thickness or less with a sharp knife, using a metal straightedge and repeated, light strokes. Make cuts deeper than this with a razor saw. When cutting with the grain, care must be taken that the grain does not divert the knife or saw from the desired line.

Do stripwood cutting with a sharp knife or (preferably) with a single-edge razor blade. Cut multiple boards of the same length by using jigs or commercial cutting devices (such as Chopper, etc.).

Scribing

Scribe lines, such as to simulate individual boards, with a sharp knife, drawing it along a metal straightedge in several light strokes. Carefully scribe all lines about the same depth. Also be careful that the grain of the wood does not draw the knife away from the straightedge.

Openings

When cutting openings in sheet stock, such as for doors and windows, mark the rectangle for the hole accurately on the front surface of the material using a metal straightedge and a sharp pencil. Mark the part to be removed with an X. Cut away the material using a sharp knife, allowing a slight margin inside the lines. Carefully sand away the remaining material to the scribe lines. If another item, such as a door or window casting, is to fit into the hole, continue to trial fit the item as the sanding is done to ensure an exact fit.

Texturing

You can provide additional texture to wood by distressing the surface with a razor saw, a file, a file brush, sandpaper, knife, etc. Whatever the method, the intent is to cause the wood to look worn or rougher than the new stock is. You can cut stripwood so that it appears split at the ends, or break parts instead of cutting them to simulate full-sized breaks. You also can cut or scribe knotholes and grain patterns into the wood. Remove the fuzz that is raised with a final sanding.

Drilling

The main precaution for drilling holes in wood is to be aware of the grain and the effect this has on the nonuniformity of material density. Holes drilled in wood will be less precise than those drilled in more homogeneous materials, and they might not end up round or located where you wanted them. Mark the start of the hole with a small prick from a sharp point. Take care that the drilling does not cause forces that will split the wood.

Use low speed when drilling in wood and keep downward pressure moderate. Large-sized holes in thin materials are better made by cutting with a knife, rather than by drilling.

Hole Filling

You can fill holes (or cracks) with plastic wood or any of the hole fillers made for plastics. These fillers will shrink when dry, so repeated applications might be necessary. Sand the surface smooth and to the proper profile. Duplicate wood grain or other texture, if required. If the wood requires sealing, then use sanding sealer (made for model airplanes) or a clear flat finish.

Bonding

Wood is best bonded to wood or other porous materials using white or yellow glues. For bonding to other materials, see the topic, "Adhesive and Fasteners," in chapter 7.

PAPER CONSTRUCTION

This category of materials includes paper, cardstock, Strathmore board (5 to 25 thousands inch thick in 5 thousands increments), illustration board ($1/16$ inch), foam core board, and bristol board. Foam core board has a styrene foam core faced on both sides with smooth paper. It is light and warp free and comes in thicknesses of $1/8$, $3/16$, $1/4$, and $1/2$ inch.

Cutting

Make cuts for paper just as you did for wood, except make all cuts using repeated strokes with a sharp knife. There is no grain to divert the blade. Do not use sawing. For heavy cutting, a utility knife made for cutting mat board and similar materials, might be more convenient. Mark foam core board and cut on both sides.

Scribing

Scribing can be done just as it is for wood. Be careful that all scribed lines look similar.

Openings

Openings are cut using exactly the same technique as was previously described for wood.

Drilling

Avoid drilling paper. If it is necessary, use the same techniques as you used for wood. Better results are almost always obtained by cutting the holes using a knife.

Bonding

Paper is best bonded to paper, wood, or other porous materials using white or yellow glues. For bonding to other materials, see "Adhesives and Fasteners" in chapter 7.

Finishing

Strathmore or illustration board furnishes a good base finish for painting. Because paper products are porous, they might require sealing with more than one coat before they will give the smooth look to represent metal surfaces.

PLASTIC CONSTRUCTION

Construction with plastic includes use of both precast and preformed sheet and three-dimensional materials, and use of stock materials. Stock materials are available in plain sheets of varying thicknesses; in scribed or milled sheets (simulating building siding); in strips, tubes, and rods of dimensional and scale sizes; and in structural shapes, such as I, H, and T beams.

Flat castings include scale walls, brick, stone, roofs, etc. *Detail castings* include scale doors, windows, railings, steps, etc. Any of these materials or parts might be a part of ready-made models, or kits, or can be purchased as stock or parts. The techniques used for cutting, fitting, and bonding the materials are the same in any case.

Kit Parts

Cast parts are made by injection molding, which involves forcing molten plastic under pressure into multipart metal molds. No plastic kit or ready-to-run plastic model is really ready to use. The parts need cleanup, with flash removal and repainting, as a minimum. Kit parts must be trimmed and filed to fit properly before each joint is bonded/cemented together.

Do not remove kit parts from molding sprues until the parts are needed. The sprues make good holding handles for painting the parts. It is also easy to confuse the parts if they are removed from their identifying numbers on the spruce trees. Remove all parting lines and flash from the casting/molding process by scraping with a sharp knife and/or files.

When removing parts from the sprue, do not break them off. Cut them using a diagonal cutters/nippers, then use a knife and files to cut and file the sprue remnant away.

Cutting

You can cut sheet material up to $1/32$ inch thick with a knife. Use a metal straight-edge, holding it firmly in place, and several light cuts to separate the material. The cutting will raise a small lip on either side of the cut. Remove this by lightly scraping, filing, and/or sanding.

Cut sheet material between $1/32$ and $3/16$ inch by scoring and breaking along the line. Use a metal straightedge held firmly in place. Make the first light cut as you would for thin material, then make further cuts using the back side of a #11 blade that has had its tip broken off (about $1/32$ inch). This acts as a chisel to remove a plastic curl of material without raising ridges on either side of the cut. Make enough cuts to score about one-third of the way through the material. Hold the back of the cut line against the edge of your workbench, and snap the cut piece off. Trim up the cut edge with files and light sanding.

Cut sheet material greater than $3/16$ inch and items that are not flat with a razor saw. Use a blade with fine teeth that is reserved for only cutting plastics. Lubricate the blade with a little petroleum jelly. If possible, clamp the material being cut. Plastic or wood filler pieces might be necessary to properly clamp the shape that will be cut. Guard against the saw slipping and marring another area. Trim up the cut edges with files and light sanding.

Opening

When cutting openings in sheet stock, such as for doors and windows, scribe the rectangle for the hole accurately on the front surface of the material using a metal straightedge and a sharp knife blade. Mark the part to be removed with an **X**. Drill small holes at least $1/16$ inch inside the scribe lines. Cut away the material between the holes with a knife (many light cuts) or with a power motor tool. Then, starting with larger files and graduating to smaller ones, carefully file away the remaining material to the scribe lines. If another item, such as a door or window casting, is to fit into the hole, continue to trial fit the item as the filing is done to ensure an exact fit.

Scribing

You can scribe plastic sheet using the same technique you used for scoring. Use the back side of a broken blade, making several light cuts. Try to achieve the same depth and width for all scribed lines.

Texturing

Plastic can be textured to look more like wood. Techniques include use of sand-paper, small files, and knife blades. Try to simulate the grain of the wood, including cracks, splits, knots, etc. A light finishing sanding will remove any "fuzz" that is raised.

Drilling

Drilling holes in plastic is similar to drilling them in hardwood or metal. Mark the hole center with a small dimple made with a center punch or scribe. Keep the drill bit square with the work. Apply light pressure and turn the drill at low speeds (in motorized tools). High speeds will melt the plastic, rather than cut it. Use bee's wax for a lubricant. Frequently remove the drill from the hole and clear the chips away. Tapping holes in plastic is usually not very satisfactory.

Protection

When cutting or filing plastic material, some masking tape can provide valuable protection against tool slippage. On flat material, the tape can also be used as a cutting guide, in addition to the metal straightedge.

Removing Detail

Sometimes it is necessary to remove cast-on detail, such as rivets, handrails, etc., from plastic castings. This must be done very carefully to protect other detail from being removed inadvertently. Protect adjacent detail with tape. Carefully shave, scrape, and file the detail away, being careful not to remove too much material. X-Acto #17 or #18 chisel blades are ideal for this task. Use fine files and then No. 600 wet-or-dry sandpaper for the final portion so that the contours of the casting appear as though there had never been any detail there.

Hole Filling

Sometimes unwanted holes need to be filled or plugged. If they are small ($1/8$ inch or so), file them round and plug them with some scrap sprue material, filed to fit. Leave it a little long and file it flush after the cement is dry. If the hole is larger, such as an unwanted window opening, file the hole to a rectangular shape (if it isn't already). Carefully cut and file sheet material to just fit. Cement the filler piece so that it is flush with the side that shows. After the cement dries, fill in any gaps with plastic putty and sand to hide the joints.

Putty used for filling holes in plastic is available in several brands, including Squadron Green putty, Duralite Surfacing putty, Duco Spot-In Glaze, and Micro Scale Quick Silver. These putties can also be used for wood filling, but other products especially made for wood are better. The putty is spread into the hole and allowed to dry for at least 8 hours. It can then be scraped, filed, and sanded to the desired shape. It is slightly softer than the plastic. It shrinks somewhat if used in large holes or in thick layers. If this occurs, apply another coat after the first one has been completed.

Scraps of styrene can be saved in a small bottle (with a tight cover) filled with acetone. After a few days, the plastic will soften to the consistency of putty. It can then be used to make an excellent (and inexpensive) filler for plastics.

Other Operations

You can bend ABS plastic sheet to provide curved surfaces. You also can make small rods for piping, etc., by stretching plastic sprue material. Carefully heat the sprue over a candle flame. At just the right temperature, gently pull on the ends to create a filament of appropriate size. The temperature/timing is crucial because if the plastic gets too hot, it will melt or catch on fire; and if it is not warm enough, the filament will not be of uniform size. Fortunately, the raw material costs nothing. The resultant filaments are quite brittle and should only be used where they will not be exposed to handling. You can form rivets by the same techniques discussed in "Metal Construction."

Painting

If possible, paint most parts prior to assembly. Cast parts are most easily painted while still on the molding sprues. Try to form prefabricated subassemblies of parts that will be painted a common color. See "Finishes," chapter 9, for advice on the types of paints to use and other precautions when painting plastics. You might have to scrape off some paint where there will be a joint because plastic cements will not "weld" if paint is present in the joint.

Bonding

Cut and file plastic parts to fit closely together. If the fit is good, the resulting bonded joint will be strong. For tight-fitting joints, use a minimum amount of liquid plastic cement, applied from the back side using a small brush. Capillary action will pull the cement into the joint between the two pieces being joined. The cement will temporarily partially dissolve the plastic, forming a weld when the plastic rehardens.

If the joint is not a good fit, or in special cases, such as cementing long 45-degree corner joints on buildings, use tube-type plastic cement. Be careful that too much is not used and that it does not ooze out and smear on the "good" side of the plastic. Gussets or doublers are often desirable for reinforcing joints. These can be made of scrap or stock flat material.

Do not use either type of plastic cement for clear plastic window material. It will craze or cloud the surface. Use white glue or a clear silastic cement for this purpose.

Acrylic Plastic

This group of plastics is harder than polystyrene. It is very optically clear, but it scratches easily. It softens at 275°F for heat forming. Acrylic plastic is available in clear, tints, opaque colors, and textures. It can be bonded like styrene; or use EDC (ethylene dichloride), which is slow, or MC (methylene chlorate and chloroform), which is fast. Both of these chemicals are quite toxic.

METAL CONSTRUCTION

Metal is available as stock material in brass, copper, steel, aluminum, etc. Brass is by far the most useful metal for the miniature modeler. Stock comes in sheet, bar, rod, and wire configurations. Cast metal parts are available in brass and in white metal, an alloy well suited to centrifugal casting.

Cutting

Metal sheet up to 0.025 inch can be cut with metal shears. Precise cutting can be done with a jeweler's saw. Rough cutting to size can be done with an ordinary hacksaw. In almost every case, cut the metal oversize and file to exact dimensions. Choose files that are appropriate to the thickness of the material. Use the coarsest files first and reserve finer files for the final cuts.

Precise working in metal requires expensive tools such as milling machines, which are beyond the budget of ordinary modelers. Many simple milling operations also can be done using a drill press and a milling table, at greatly reduced cost and some loss in accuracy. Milling cutters look like drill bits, but they are designed differently to either cut on their sides or on their squared ends.

Turning

Round metal parts are made by turning the stock while scraping, shaving, filing, or grinding the metal away. The classic, and expensive, approach is a metal-cutting lathe. Surprisingly good results also can be obtained with less expensive tools, such as a drill press or a common motor tool. In either case, a table to stably rest the tool (usually a file) against is necessary. The tables can be purchased or fabricated.

Chuck a rod of suitable diameter into the collet/chuck. Guide a file against the rod, reducing the diameter where desired. By using small jeweler's files, and frequent measuring, almost any dimension can be held accurately.

Drilling

Metal drilling is similar to drilling in other materials if you compensate for the greater hardness of the metal. It is most difficult either to drill small holes in thick material or to drill large holes in thin material.

The most crucial element is the tool used to hold the drill bit. The simplest choice, usable for drills from no. 80 up to about 0.125 inch, in the *pin vise*. This is hand-held and twisted with finger motion. Most pin vises have separate chucks for the different size drill bit ranges.

Very little of the drill should be exposed so that breakage is minimized. As with all drilling, it is important to keep the drill aligned to the hole being drilled. Start with a small dimple mark and keep the pressure light. Drilling with a pin vise takes a long time and usually results in a fairly sloppy hole.

Use a small hand drill for drilling holes from about $1/16$ up to $1/4$ inch. Electric hand drills are useful for heavier drilling from $1/16$ inch and up. A motor tool (with speed control) is very handy for drilling holes up to about $1/16$ inch. Fixtures are available to adapt the motor tool to a drill press function that will allow fairly precise drilling operations. The best small-diameter drilling is done with a jeweler's drill press or equivalent, which is like the motor tool only more precise.

Drill speeds should be suited to the drill size and material. For hand-powered drills, there is no concern in going too fast. The smaller the drill, the faster the speed required. A good rule for motorized drilling would be to use 2400 rpm up to no. 30 drills, then 1200 rpm up to $1/4$ inch, and 800 rpm beyond that. Softer metals, such as some aluminum alloys, require slower speeds.

Drill lubrication is always helpful, even though it might not be necessary for brass, copper, or zinc alloys. Use cutting oil for all steel alloys. Use bee's wax or paraffin for drilling aluminum.

Tapping

Tapping is used to provide threads in metal surfaces so that machine screws can be used to attach other parts. Before using a tap, drill the hole to the proper diameter (and deeper than the threads will go) using a conventional drill bit of the *tap drill size*. This is a size that will leave just enough metal so that the tap will not bind and yet will cut clean threads with maximum holding power. Tap and clearance drill sizes are listed in the Appendix.

Keep the tap aligned in the hole and turn it very carefully. Back up slightly each half to full turn. Every one or two turns, back it all the way out so that you can clear out chips around it and the hole. A tap is very brittle, and excessive torque can easily break it. For metals, thread cutting oil is recommended to reduce tap breakage. For plastics, soap or bee's wax can be used as a lubricant.

Rivet Detail

The best rivet detail is provided by having all rivets of the same diameter and height and spacing. This is most easily done by using a purchased or homemade rivet embossing machine. Such machines use male and female dies, properly oriented to each other, and a hammer-like mechanism that provides the same force for every impression. Some machines have micrometer advancement for precise rivet spacing.

If the material is thicker than about 0.010 inch, it is better to not try to emboss the rivets. The alternative is to drill a hole where each rivet is to be, then insert a wire into the hole, soldering from behind. Then file the rivet faces to height and profile.

Soldering

Soldering is a very useful art to acquire because it lets you form strong, permanent joints in metal. The assumption made here is that brass is being soldered to brass (or copper). Soldering of other metals is more difficult and beyond this description. These soldering techniques are also *not* for soldering of electrical connections or components.

Solder performs its bonding by binding molecularly with the base metal. This cannot occur if the metal is not clean and free from oxides. Ordinary cleaning is not enough, which is why a flux must be used. The flux cleans away the oxide and slightly etches the metal, allowing the solder to get to where it has to to make the bond.

Although resin-core solder must be used for electrical connections, and both acid-core and paste fluxes are available, the only flux that should be used for metal-to-metal soldering is a liquid acid type. The solder should be solid core. Do not use acid fluxes for electrical connections!

It is helpful to have solders available that melt at different temperatures. This allows the largest pieces to be soldered with the highest-melting-point solder; with progression down to the smaller detail attached with the lowest-melting-point solder. This way, the first pieces will be less likely to fall off as subsequent items are attached.

A selection might include 4S solder, which melts at 400°F; 50:50 tin-lead solder, which melts at 325°F; and Tix solder, which melts at 275°F. If only one solder is used, the tin-lead solder is cheapest and most readily available. The flux for all three is diluted hydrochloric acid.

Soldering can be done with a soldering iron or with a miniature torch. Soldering guns are not recommended for this type of work. Use irons with the largest size in watts and with the largest tip possible for the job being done. Use replaceable tips made of copper with nickel-iron plating. All other things being equal, the iron should be light in weight and should have some sort of a heat deflector or insulator to keep the heat from the handle. Many modelers have more than one soldering iron, ranging from 50 to 150 watts.

A miniature torch, such as the one made by Microflame, can be useful, but it is a little trickier to use than the irons. It is also more expensive to operate.

Keep the tip of the soldering iron thinly coated with solder. Also keep the tip clean of accumulated oxides and flux residues. This can be done by an occasional quick wipe with a cloth. If the iron needs retinning, apply flux to the tip, followed by solder.

There are four different techniques for making the soldered joint:

Technique #1:

1. Clamp together the items to be soldered.
2. Apply flux to the joint.
3. Heat the joint with the iron (or torch).
4. Apply solder to the joint.
5. Remove the iron (or torch).

The flux is pulled into the joint by capillary action. This also pulls the solder in. The flux is pulled into the joint by capillary action. This also pulls the solder in.

Care must be taken so nothing moves while the soldering is occurring or before the solder "freezes".

Technique #2:

1. Clamp together the items to be soldered.
2. Apply flux to the joint.
3. Apply the solder to the iron tip.
4. Apply the iron to the joint.
5. The solder flows from the tip into the joint.
6. Remove the iron.

The main advantage to technique #2 is that this leaves one hand free to hold the items or adjust things. This works best for small items being soldered to bigger ones.

Technique #3:

1. Apply flux and solder to each item to be soldered.
2. Clamp the items together.
3. Heat the joint with the iron (or torch).
4. Remove the iron (or torch).

The pretinned surfaces of the two items become soldered together during the heating. This takes more time and might not result in as good a joint. Sometimes it is necessary, however, particularly if two large sheets are to be laminated together.

Technique #4:

1. Paint solder paste on both items to be soldered.
2. Clamp the items together.
3. Heat the joint with the iron (or torch).
4. Remove the iron (or torch).

Solder paste is a mixture of flux and powdered solder. When heated, the flux boils off first, then the solder melts. This technique probably does not result in as strong a joint as the others.

Besides using solders with different melting points, parts can be soldered close to previously soldered parts without the first parts falling off if a very hot iron with a large tip is used. This high heat capacity causes a rapid heat flow to the work, allowing a local heating to the solder melting point before adjacent areas can reach the same temperature. A small iron would not have this heat capacity, and the process would take longer with more chance of raising the temperature in undesired areas. A microtorch is even better in this respect because the flame can be made very small and it has a very high heat content and fast-heating capability. The use of heat sinks, wet paper toweling, etc., might still be necessary to help keep heat flow constrained.

Clean up is necessary to improve the looks of the joint. This is best done mechanically using knives and files, being careful not to mar the details. A dull blade is as effective as a sharp one for this chore. A motor tool with a short-bristled wire brush will remove the soft solder while not harming the brass detail. As your soldering facility increases, the joints will be neater and less clean up will be required. All soldered joints should be washed to remove flux residue.

Bonding

Besides soldering, ACC or epoxy can also be used to bond metal parts together, if there will be little or no stress placed on the parts.

OTHER MATERIALS

Other common building materials include glass, plaster, and foam plastics.

Glass

You can cut glass by scribing a line using a glass cutting tool drawn along a metal straightedge. Place the glass so the scribed line is along the edge of the workbench. Use a sharp downward motion on the portion sticking out to create a clean break. A thin coat of oil on the surface will help the process.

Cutting rectangular or circular holes in glass is something best left to the experts. See "Adhesives and Fasteners." chapter 7, for techniques to bond glass to other materials.

Plaster

Plaster can be cut, filed, and drilled in much the same way as wood. Do not use your best and sharpest tools because the plaster will tend to dull them. Plaster is quite fragile, and care must be taken so that it does not fracture. Usually, you can repair breaks by reattaching the piece(s) using white glue. White glue is the usual best adhesive for bonding plaster to itself or to other porous surfaces.

Foam

Do not cut foam plastics by using the hot wire technique because this produces dangerous fumes. Cut with ordinary woodworking tools or with a serrated steak knife. Smooth foam plastics with a coarse file or a surform tool. The dust sticks to everything; remove it frequently with a vacuum cleaner. Because foams dissolve in many adhesives, the safest one to use is white glue. Special white cements (such as Wilhold R/C 56) are specially formulated for use with foams. Some contact cements can be used, but test them first.

CASTING

For many of your projects, the wide range of ready-made castings that are available will be more than adequate. Commercial castings can be obtained (in general) in plastic, white metal, plaster, resin, and foam. In some cases, however, you might wish to make your own castings from one of these materials to create something that is not available or to cheaply reproduce a part in quantity.

The simplest casting jobs are done with plaster in reusable latex (or RTV) rubber molds, such as for rocks for scenery. No particular precision is needed, so deformations are unimportant. This subject is covered at length in "Rock Casting," chapter 17.

You can make accurate and detailed castings for bridge foundations, retaining walls, building foundations, and brick or stone walls using silicone rubber molds. You can also use resins for castings of these same types of modeled objects as well as for other objects such as metal bridge members, storefronts, etc., having considerable delicacy. FIGURE 8-1 shows some examples of such model castings.

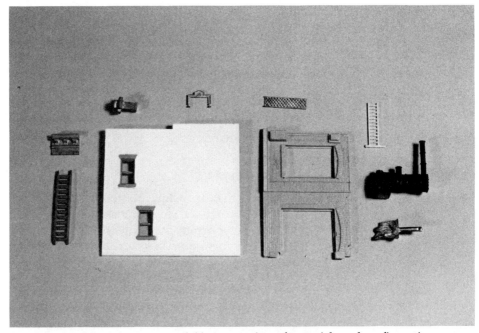

Fig. 8-1. Model castings are available in a variety of materials and configurations.

This topic will discuss model casting in general, then give some specific techniques that can be used with different size castings and with different casting materials.

A casting must be made in a mold that provides a negative image of the contours of the part to be cast. The mold must include all the detail desired in the casting, and it must not be deformed by the casting process so that the resulting casting will be true to its dimensions. How the mold is made and formed, what it is made of, and how it is supported are the keys to differences in casting.

Commercial castings are made by a variety of techniques, some of which are beyond the capabilities of the normal modeler because they involve equipment and facilities that are large and expensive. This discussion will be restricted to techniques that can be done in the home workshop at minimum cost. The casting process is quite fast for all techniques. What takes the time is the making of the molds.

Casting Material

Plaster castings should be made using molding plaster, patching plaster, or dental plaster. Metal castings can use low-melting temperature alloys, such as Cerrobend, or fluxless lead/tin alloys used for soldering. Resin materials include polyester and epoxy resins and liquid metals. Other plastic materials are probably beyond the capability of nonprofessionals.

Metal Casting

Use extreme caution when using metal for casting. The molten metal is very hot and can easily cause bad burns. It must be poured slowly into molds that are completely dry so that no splattering occurs. Molten metal poured into plaster molds that are damp can cause explosions. Be very careful when using any metal alloy containing lead. The fumes are poisonous and so is the residue left in the container used for melting the metal. Never use these containers for cooking or eating once they have been used to melt metals.

Plaster Casting

Plaster castings are best made using dental or casting plaster. Partially fill the mold with soapy water. Mix the plaster to a thick cream consistency; try not to create bubbles. You can add up to 10 percent white glue to the water (by volume) to give added strength. Add the plaster to the water, then stir. First paint the plaster mix on the inside of the mold, then slowly fill the mold while avoiding creating any bubbles. Try using the vibrations of a saber saw, held against the mold, to dissolve some of the bubbles.

For a one-part mold with a flat surface on the back of the casting, slightly overfill the mold. Slowly tilt a piece of glass or acrylic against the back of the mold to squeeze off the excess plaster and form a smooth, flat back surface.

If many castings are to be made, you can speed up the process by using seasoned water, as described in "Rock Casting," chapter 17. The casting will heat as setting occurs. The casting can be removed from the mold when the mold has returned to normal temperature. If a mold release is needed, 3M Scotchgard can be sprayed on.

Resin Casting

In spite of the bad odor, polyester is probably the best resin to use for castings. It hardens and can be removed from the mold in only 2 hours (instead of 24). This allows more castings to be made in a given time. It is also somewhat less expensive, and it is a little less wearing on the molds than epoxy resin.

Because of the smell, do resin casting outdoors at temperatures of 70°F or warmer. For additional strength and toughness for the castings, you can add milled fiberglass fibers (a powder) to the resin during the mixing. You can use a volume of fiberglass equal to the resin. Do the mixing before adding the catalyst. Add about 20 percent extra catalyst.

For a mold release for all resin casting, use petroleum jelly dissolved in methyl ethyl ketone (MEK). Paint this on the inside of the mold. The MEK will evaporate, leaving a thin coating of the petroleum jelly.

If possible, paint the resin onto the mold, then carefully pour in the remaining resin, slightly overfilling. This should help eliminate any bubbles. You can fill a polyethylene syringe with the resin and use it to fill all the voids. Pieces of wire can be embedded to add strength.

Mold Materials

Molds for metal casting should be made using room temperature vulcanizing (RTV) rubber or plaster. Molds for plaster or resins can be made from RTV or silicone rubber. Latex rubber can also be used for plaster molds, usually for the flexible ones such as for rock castings.

Mold Making

To make a mold, you must have a master. This can be either an item that is to be duplicated or a fabricated master that is exactly like what you want the eventual cast item to be. The fabricated master can be carved or built up, and it can be made of almost any solid material. If the materials are porous, then they must be sealed. The mold master must be carefully done because the castings you make can be no better than this original.

You will need to decide if the item requires a one- or a two-part mold. One-part molds can be used only for items that are flat and that have detail only on one side (and edges). Examples are building walls, wheels, etc. These molds are much easier to make, and the casting process is also easier. *Two-part molds* are necessary to cast objects "in-the-round," that is, that have detail on two or more sides. Examples are barrels, human figures, etc.

Often, one-part molds can be used to form front-and-back castings, which are later bonded together. This can avoid the use of the two-part molds. Try to make the molds so that modular or repeating patterns are made by multiple castings made from the same mold.

Two-part molds must be made with a separation plane between the two mold halves so the cast object can be removed. They need a sprue, so the casting material can be poured into the mold. The two mold halves must be indexed to each other so they will repeatedly line up. The sprue and the *flash* (along where the mold halves meet) must be cleaned off before use.

One-part molds are poured from the open side. Because it might be difficult to pour the thickness exactly right, they are usually cast a little thick and then sanded/filed to proper thickness before use.

One-Part Molds

One-part molds are made using Silastic or RTV rubber compound. Mount the master using two-sided tape or a little contact cement applied to a flat material base, such as plastic or foam board, that extends at least two inches beyond the master (FIG. 8-2).

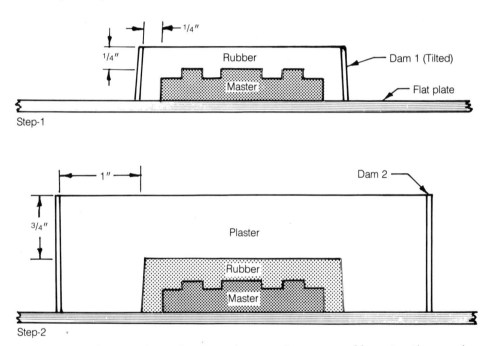

Fig. 8-2. This drawing shows the two main steps of one-part mold construction; casting the mold, and casting the plaster backing.

Build a "dam" of plastic or foam board with inside dimensions about 1/4 inch larger than the master on all sides, including the top. Tilt these side pieces slightly inward at the top. Coat the master, the base, and the dam with a compatible mold release. Silicone lubricant in a spray can is a good choice.

Next, mix the rubber, being careful not to form bubbles. First carefully paint the mix onto the master, making sure there are no bubbles and that all detail is filled. Puncture any bubbles with a pin. Slowly pour the remainder over the master, just even with the top of the dam. Allow this to thoroughly cure.

Remove and discard the dam. If the mold is small and/or distortion will not be a problem, then it can be used in this form. If this is not the case, then cast a plaster "frame" or backing around the mold. Build a new dam about 1 inch beyond the old one and 3/4 inch higher. Again, coat everything with mold release. Then fill the new dam with molding plaster and allow it to completely set.

Remove the new dam and invert the mold, consisting of a rubber inner part and a plaster backing. Carefully remove the base and master. If all went well, the rubber inner mold will be a perfect negative replica of the master. Once this is cleaned, it is ready for making castings. The rubber inner mold should be easy to remove from the plaster portion. This will facilitate releasing the castings from the mold.

Two-Part Molds

As with the one-part molds, each half of the mold will consist of a rubber inner part and a plaster outer part (backing). The mold making takes longer and the sequence is different, however. Again, start with a flat base material. Build an inner dam centered on the base, with inside dimensions 1/2 inch larger than the master and with height 1/2 inch deeper than the height of the master. Tilt the sides slightly inward towards the top (FIG. 8-3).

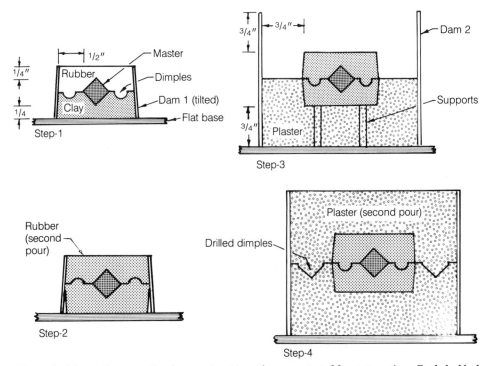

Fig. 8-3. Shown here are the four main steps of two-part mold construction. Each half of the mold and each half of the plaster backing must be separately cast.

Fill the lower half of this dam with water-base clay, pressing it down firmly all around. Smooth off the top to a plane surface. Press the master half way down into the clay in the middle of the space. Make slight "dimples" in the clay surface outside the master. Coat everything with mold release. Mix the rubber compound and paint it carefully onto the master. Pour the remainder into the dam, filling it to the top.

After the rubber has cured, remove the rubber mold (with the master still half embedded) from the dam and then clean out all the clay. Invert the mold and put it back into the dam, pressing it down to the base. Coat everything with mold release. Mix up the rubber compound and paint it carefully onto the master. Pour the remainder into the dam, filling it to the top. Let the rubber cure.

To give the mold more strength, an outer plaster backing can be used. Remove the two rubber mold halves from the dam, but leave the master inside. Build a new base and outer dam, the latter having inside dimensions $3/4$ inch larger than the outside of the rubber mold and a height that is $1^1/_2$ inch higher than the total height of the two rubber mold halves. Support the rubber mold pair so that it is approximately centered in all dimensions in the middle of the dam.

Pour the outer dam half full of molding plaster (up to the split line between the two rubber mold halves). Make sure the rubber mold does not float up and out of position. After this plaster has set, carefully drill four dimples about $1/4$ inch deep into the plaster near the four corners using a $1/2$-inch drill bit. This can be done by twisting the drill between your fingers.

Coat the exposed plaster surface with mold release. Then remove the framework used to suspend the rubber inner mold and pour the outer dam full of plaster, covering the inner mold. After the plaster has set, carefully pull the two mold halves apart at the seam line between the halves. Remove the master and clean up the mold. The dimples in one plaster mold half should be matched by protrusions in the other half that will allow consistent alignment. Cut a funnel-shaped sprue in the plaster and the rubber in both mold halves down to the cavity where the master was. This will be used for pouring in the casting material.

To make a casting, coat the two halves with mold release and clamp them together. Slowly pour the casting material into the sprue hole, taking care not to form bubbles. Shake and jar the mold a bit to help the material settle into all the spaces where it should be.

Lost-Wax Molds

In lost-wax casting, the molds are used only once, one per casting made. A wax "master" is embedded into a plaster mold with a sprue hole. The mold is inverted and heated and the wax melts and runs out (is "lost"), leaving a perfect internal cavity. The casting material (usually metal) is poured into the sprue. When it has set, the mold is broken away. The molds are easy to make, but the wax masters are not. Because it is as difficult to cast the wax masters as it would be to make plastic, resin, or metal castings by some other technique in the first place, this is not a recommended home casting technique.

ETCHING

Chemical etching (or milling) can be used to produce delicate complex parts from metal. The metal is usually brass, although copper and aluminum can be used, in thicknesses of 0.005 inch up to 0.020 inch. The process of photoetching consists of a few, simple steps:

1. Create an over-size artwork.
2. Reduce the artwork to make a photographic negative.
3. Clean the metal.
4. Coat the metal with photoresist.
5. Expose the metal and negative to light.
6. Wash off exposed photoresist.
7. Bake on the unexposed photoresist.
8. Protect the back side of the metal.
9. Etch the metal.
10. Clean up.

The negative makes a chemical mask for the photoresist. The photoresist prevents the etchant from eating away the metal in the areas so protected. The etching will tend to undercut the photoresist, limiting how small the width of remaining metal can be. That width should be from one or two times the metal thickness, on up.

Make the artwork two or more times the size of the finished item. It is crucial that the black lines be very black, as produced by India ink or equivalent. Dry transfers can be used for any lettering. The black portions will be the parts remaining in the metal after etching. Include a dimension on the drawing to aid the photographer in the reduction.

A single piece of artwork might include many items to be etched. Keep the total size consistent with the size of the negative, which will be less expensive if it is no larger than 4 × 5 inches. Connect small items together by lines, so they will not separate during etching. The lines can be cut off later.

Unless you have suitable photographic equipment, contact a professional photographer or photoengraver to make the line negative from your artwork. Shop around for the best price. The negative will be black where the metal is to be etched away.

Clean the metal thoroughly using scouring powder and water. Once clean, do not touch the surface again. The photoresist is Kodak KPR developing solution. This must be applied in a dark room with only a distant 25-watt yellow lamp. Apply a few drops along one edge of the metal, then quickly spread it smoothly using a clean, dry paper towel. It is important to completely cover the metal. Let the photoresist air dry for one hour (in darkness), then add a second coating, spreading it at right angles to the first. Let dry for another hour.

Make a sandwich of a sheet of glass, the coated metal (photoresist side up), the negative (proper side up), and a second sheet of glass (FIG. 8-4). Clamp these all firmly together and fold up the sandwich in a black cloth or towel. For exposure to light, use strong summer sunlight when the sun is high in the sky. Use an

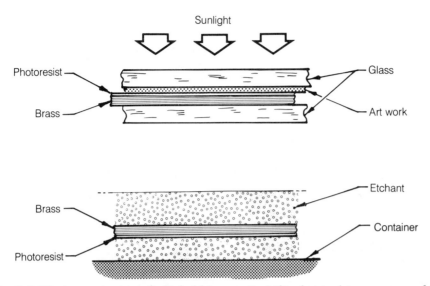

Fig. 8-4. *The two main steps of metal etching are (top) the photoresist exposure, and (bottom) the acid etching.*

exposure time of 3 minutes, lengthening this slightly for other seasons or times more than two hours from noon. Make sure the sunlight is perpendicular to the sandwich plane.

In the darkened room, disassemble the sandwich. Place the metal, photoresist side up, in Kodak KPR developing solution for three minutes at room temperature. Slightly rock the container to keep the solution agitated.

The remaining operations can be done in ordinary light. Rinse the metal in a gentle stream of running water for about 10 seconds to remove the unexposed photoresist. You should now be able to faintly see the exposed portion. Bake the metal (to set the resist) in an oven at 200°F for 20 minutes.

Protect the back side of the metal by spraying it completely with a clear lacquer such as Testor's Dullcoat or cover it with transparent clear tape. Let it dry completely. This prevents the etchant from eating away from the back. Bend up little corner tabs of the metal to keep the metal about 1/4 inch above the bottom of the container used for etching. This allows a space for the removed brass to fall into and protects the delicate top surface of the metal (which faces down) with the photoresist.

Use a glass or nonmetallic tray for a container. The etchant is 30 percent ferric chloride, which is an acid. Wear rubber gloves when handling it. You can purchase it at any radio supply shop selling supplies for printed circuit board fabrication.

The etching takes about 90 minutes for each 0.005 inch of metal (at 85°F). Do not heat the etchant above 140°F. Higher temperatures will shorten the etching time. Check the work after 30 minutes and every 10 minutes thereafter. Rock the container slightly occasionally. Place the metal in water to stop the etching action.

Remove the resist and the Dullcoat by soaking the metal in a paint stripper. Wash thoroughly and slightly sand the metal on both sides to remove any rough edges. The metal can be darkened with a chemical blackening agent, or it can be painted by conventional techniques.

Photoetching can also be used to only partially etch into the metal. Examples include making signs with raised lettering and making negative impressions in metals that are used as molds, such as for rivet heads, mortar lines, etc. The same techniques are also used for printed circuit board material where the metal is etched through but the phenolic or plastic sheet remains.

9

Finishes

Finishes, such as paint, are applied to the model to provide coloring. Except for the few materials that can be used in their natural state (representing unpainted wood or metal, for example), all modeled materials require applied finishes to give the proper color and surface appearance.

There are a large selection of model finishes available. They can be brushed, sprayed, or airbrushed on (FIG. 9-1).

FINISH OPTIONS

Finishes include paints, stains, dyes, or other chemicals applied to cover or modify the material. On full-sized objects, finishes are used for four purposes: (1) to protect from the environment, (2) to give color and improve appearance, (3) to suggest a different material, and (4) to convey information (signs). On models where there is usually no exposure to sun, wind, rain, and snow, the first purpose is of little or no importance. An exception might be to protect metals from oxidation. The third purpose is more important because you often want to finish one material to "fool" the observer into thinking it is another.

Paint Composition

Paint consists of three components. *Pigment* is the particles that give paint its color and hiding capability. *Binder* is the combination of synthetic resins and oils that surround the pigment particles. It provides paint cohesion and adhesion to the surface. *Carrier*, or *vehicle*, is the volatile thinner that evaporates away when the paint dries. For latex paints, water is the thinner; for alkyd and oil paints, it is

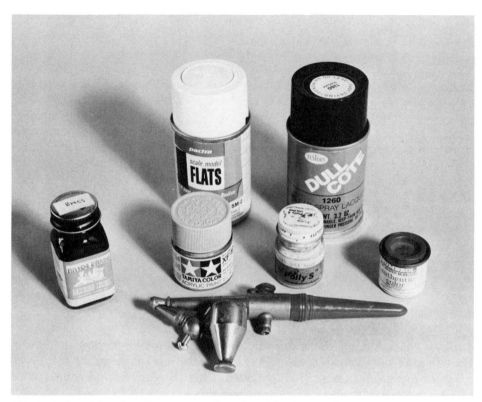

Fig. 9-1. *An airbrush and some examples of model paints and sprays.*

petroleum distillates. There are many different types of thinners, which must be chosen to be compatible with the binder resin.

Paint Types

The type of vehicle determines the designation of the type of paint, such as oil, water, acrylic, epoxy, lacquer, alcohol, etc. There are four types of paint that are of general interest to modelers: enamels, lacquers, acrylics, and oils.

Enamels dry fairly slowly and are self-leveling. They can be thinned with turpentine, mineral spirits, methyl ethel ketone (MEK), or xylene. *Lacquers* dry quickly and are not as good at self-leveling. They can be thinned with lacquer thinner, nail polish remover, or butyrate dope thinner. *Acrylics* dry rapidly, are not as good at self-leveling, and are thinned with water. *Oils* dry very slowly (usually too slowly), are self-leveling, and are thinned with the same solvents as enamels.

If a paint is self-leveling, brush marks will tend to smooth out. A paint is not completely dry until the binder has dried (oxidized) and hardened, not just when the carrier has dissipated.

Some of the brand names of paints made for models are: Enamels: Pactra 'Namel, Testors PLA, Humbrol. Lacquers: Floquil, Scalecoat, Accu-Paint. Acrylics: Polly S, Tamiya, Scalecoat II, Badger Air-Opaque, and artist's acrylics. There are no oil paints made for models, but artist's oils can be used.

Paint Coverage

Paint will always hide some detail, with the amount depending on the size of the pigment and the number of coats applied. Because the pigment size determines the thickness of the dried paint, diluting paint with thinner will not reduce the thickness. This is why the paints you use should be those made especially for model use, with finely ground pigments. Use them where thin coverage that will not obscure fine detail is desired. Otherwise, make your paint choice based on low cost and application and cleanup ease.

Spraying generally results in thinner coats than brushing. The thinness of the paint (proportion of vehicle to pigment/binder) has a relatively minor effect on the coat thickness for brushing or spraying. The thinness directly affects the coverage and hiding power, however, resulting in decreased coverage for coats made with thinner paint.

The thinness of the paint can also affect the texture of the surface, with heavy (sprayed) coats causing rougher texture. Coverage is also affected by the relationship of the finish color to the base color. Light colors do not cover dark or bright colors as well as vice versa. Sometimes "poor" coverage is desirable. The "raw" or "primed" base color can show through to varying controlled degrees to create wanted effects.

Application Choice

Either brushing or spraying can generally be used for paint application. Spray painting usually gives better coverage and hides detail less, but it involves more preparation and cleanup, as well as the possible need for masking. Brushing might be easier, but on smooth surfaces (such as plastic or metal), the coverage is not as uniform. Brush strokes should follow the grain of wood. On either plastic or metal surfaces, spray painting a primer coat of a neutral color gives a good base for brushing on finish coats, allowing much better coverage in fewer coats.

You can vary the thinness (and sprayability) of spray paints by adding the appropriate thinner. Some paints naturally dry glossy and some dull. Although you want almost all model surfaces to eventually be dull (matte) in finish, you might want to use gloss paints, either because of availability or as a preferred base for the application of decals. You can make flat paints glossy by the application of gloss finish coats. Later, you can overspray glossy surfaces with a clear flat finish to hide the gloss.

Use masking to control the extent of spray coverage or for color separation. Masking can be done with tapes or with chemical preparations, such as masking fluid (for example, Polly S Easy Lift-Off) or rubber cement. Wiping water-base paint, applied over oils, enamels, or dried acrylics, before it is dry leaves color in texture, grooves, etc.

Dyes and stains can be used to color absorbent materials or as overcoats to modify the appearance of paints on any material. When used alone, such as on wood or plaster, apply it prior to assembly (gluing) because the glue will not retain the dye/stain the same way as the bare material will. Dyes/stains are particularly effective for making "unpainted" wood look old. Very thin water-based paint can also be sprayed/brushed on prepainted surfaces as an overcoat to give interesting effects. Chemical preparations are available that can be used to blacken metal, particularly brass and copper.

Paint Removal

You can remove old paint finishes from metal or plastic models by soaking the model in a paint removal fluid. Preparations made for models include Accu-Paint Accu-strip and Scalecoat Wash Away. Some modelers have also successfully used automobile brake fluid or model glow-plug engine fuel. Remove all rubber or organic portions from the model before soaking.

The length of soak depends on many factors, so watch the model carefully to make sure the plastic does not soften. As soon as the old paint starts to loosen, remove the model and scrub off the paint using an old toothbrush. Wash the model thoroughly with warm, soapy water. Wear rubber gloves and eye protection during paint removal operations.

Lettering Removal

Sometimes you might want to just remove old lettering from a model. This can usually be done without harm to the paint underneath. Use a cotton swab and gentle rubbing. Try water, decal setting fluid, rubbing alcohol, denatured alcohol, and lighter fluid (in that order) to find the mildest solvent that will work. Caution: the last three of these solutions are flammable. Fantastik spray cleaner has also been used successfully as a solvent to remove lettering. Protect your skin and eyes from these liquids. Wash the model thoroughly after removing the lettering and before applying new lettering or finishes.

Safety while painting is very important, particularly when spraying. The volatile ingredients of paints can cause headaches, nausea, allergic reactions, and in severe cases, damage to the lungs and central nervous system.

COLOR AND PAINTS

There are three measures of what is commonly called *color*. *Hue* is the color itself, as shown on a color wheel. *Intensity* (or chroma) is the brightness, or how light or dark, ranging from white to black. *Saturation* (or *value*) is the richness, or how strong or pastel, ranging from the pure color to gray.

The color the human eye perceives is actually the light rays reflecting off of the surface pigment. Pigments react differently to light and bounce the light off differently. To understand the colors and to mix them successfully, you must have a general knowledge of colors and their relationships to each other.

The relationships of colors of pigments are shown on a color wheel (FIG. 9-2). The three primary colors are red, blue, and yellow. They are equally spaced apart on the color wheel. From these three colors, all other colors can be made. Colors halfway between primary colors are obtained by mixing the primary colors in equal portions. For example, blue and yellow make green.

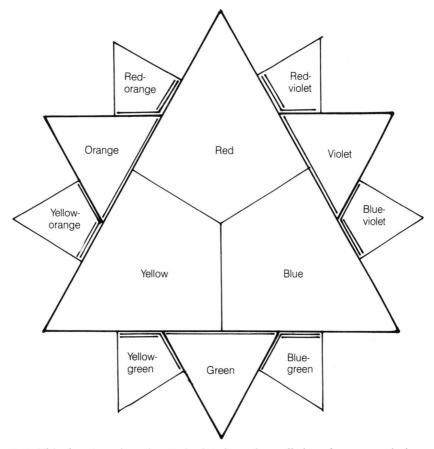

Fig. 9-2. *This drawing of a color "wheel" shows how all the colors are made from the three primaries.*

When speaking of light, black is the absence of all color and white is the presence of all colors. It is just the opposite when mixing pigments. To vary the brightness of the color, add white or black to the "pure" colors on the color wheel. In theory, a color can be darkened by adding the color opposite it on the color wheel. Practically, this usually results in a dark brown color of dubious quality. In most cases, you will make colors lighter by adding white pigment.

When using black, Mars black is warmer and redder than ivory black. Use Mars black for overall washes, and ivory black for shadows.

Floquil Paints

Floquil produces several lines of miniature paints. They include the identically formulated and intermixable Floquil Model Railroad Colors, Floquil Military Miniature Colors, and Flo-Paque Colors for Arts and Crafts. These have, respectively, RR, M, and F prefixes to their numbers. Floquil also produces stains called Flo-Stain and high-gloss, transparent lacquers called Lustre-Glaze (S and L prefixes). They also sell a water-based paint called Polly S (PS, PR, or 41 prefix). They make fluorescent and nite-glo colors, as well, but these are of less interest for models than for crafts.

The Floquil thinner is called Dio-Sol. Other thinners should not be used with Floquil paints (except for Polly S, which uses water). Also offered are a retarder, a hi-gloss finish, a crystal-cote finish, a glaze finish, and a flat finish. They also sell a barrier (used to protect polystyrene from being damaged by the regular paint solvents) and a compatible thinner.

Some of the more popular colors, the flat finish, hi-gloss finish, and barrier are available in spray cans. The liquid paints come in 1/2- or 1-fluid ounce bottles. There are a great many colors available (TABLE 9-1), including some to match specific prototype railroad equipment colors (with R or 11 prefixes).

Scalecoat Paints

Scalecoat produces two lines of model railroad paints called Scalecoat and Scalecoat II. Each requires their own thinner, and the two types are not mixable. Scalecoat II is an acrylic paint that can be sprayed directly on plastics. Shieldcoat can be sprayed over plastic to allow the regular Scalecoat paints to be used.

Scalecoat comes in a full line of colors suitable for railroad use (TABLE 9-2), including several colors blended to provide close matches to prototype paint colors. The dried finish is a semigloss. Scalecoat also makes a line of stains, called Stain Seal, that provides simultaneous staining and sealing. These colors are limited and do not include wood shades. All Scalecraft paints come in 2-ounce jars.

Badger Paints

Badger produces a line of water-based paints called Air-Opaque. These come in 1-ounce jars in a variety of railroad and weathering colors. They dry with a flat finish. They are ready for use in an airbrush, but they can also be brushed.

Accu-Paint

These paints are low odor and fast drying. They produce a semigloss finish and can be used directly on plastics. The paints come in 1-ounce jars in a variety of railroad colors and compatible thinners, primers, and over-finishes.

Table 9-1. *Most Useful Floquil Model Railroad Paint Colors*

FLOQUIL OR POLLY S

Railroad Colors	*Metallic Colors*
Engine Black	Old Silver
Reefer White	Bright Silver
Reefer Gray	Bright Gold
Caboose Red	Brass
Tuscan Red	Copper
Reefer Orange	Antique Bronze
Reefer Yellow	Gun Metal
Pullman Green	Graphite
Coach Green	
Roof Brown	
Box Car Red	

Weathering Colors	*Structure Colors*
Dust	Flesh
Grime	Earth
Rail Brown	Concrete
Grimy Black	Antique White
Weathered Black	Foundation
Oily Black	Depot Buff
Rust	
Mud	

FLO STAINS OR POLLY S

Driftwood
Rosewood
Natural Pine
Oak
Maple
Cherry
Walnut
Mahogany
Teak

Table 9-2. *Scalecoat or Scalecoat II Model Railroad Paint Colors*

Railroad Colors	*Other Colors*
Locomotive Black	Oxide Red
Smoke Box Gray	Graphite and Oil
Roof Brown	Aluminum
Coach Olive	Loco Grime

Table 9-2. Continued.

Railroad Colors	Other Colors
Tuscan Red	Black
Box Car Red	White
Caboose Red	
Reefer Yellow	
Reefer Orange	
Pullman Green	
Maint of Way Gray	

Color Selection

Except when you are trying to exactly match colors of prototype equipment, lighter colors will look best under the lighting conditions you are likely to have. For "black" steam locomotives, add a good amount of white to the black to make the engine appear more realistic. Except for new diesel locomotives, freight cars, and motor vehicles, avoid bright colors. The object is to make things look like they do in real life, not like things that just left the factory paint room.

Matching Colors

Color matching is more of an art than a science. The best way to match is with the human eye. Match the colors under the same lighting conditions that the model will normally be seen in. The color of paint will change between when it is wet and when it has dried. The color also will appear different on surfaces of different textures.

If a close match is important, use the same surface texture, lighting, and paint thickness. It is very important to measure carefully and record the exact proportions of colors that were used, so when the samples are dry, they can be duplicated; or if they still mismatch, you will have an idea of which way to go.

Measurement is best made by counting drops of paint of equal thinness from eye droppers of the same size. You should always start with a light color and slowly add the brighter and darker colors, stirring frequently. Because the colors will tend to dry slightly darker, mix them a little on the light side. Add glaze, retarder, thinner, etc., after the color is right. Once the formula is determined, keep the ratio the same and increase the quantity to mix enough paint for the whole job. As a rough approximation, 1/2-ounce is about 600 drops.

Safety

The thinners for Floquil, Scalecoat, and Accu-Paint contain mixtures of organic solvents, including toluene, acetone, xylene, and naphtha. These chemicals are poisonous to ingestion and might cause irritation to the skin and eyes. Adequate ventilation, using spray booths, and protecting your face with a respirator mask are the only safe techniques that can maximize your safety when using these materials.

FINISH PREPARATION

The preparation for painting takes far more time than the actual painting. This time is necessary, however, to achieve the best results and to avoid applications of paint that will be poor in appearance or durability.

Surface Preparation

Before painting, clean surfaces of dust and dirt. Lightly sand wood along the grain. Wash plastic and metal surfaces with a detergent, then air dry. This removes mold release agents and the natural oils from your skin. Wipe porous surfaces clean. Subsequent handling should be done without skin contact. Do not let dust settle on surfaces. The cleaning will also relieve the static electricity charge buildup from plastic surfaces.

Metal surfaces may be lightly etched to enhance the paint durability. One etchant is photographic tray cleaning solution. Put only brass or other metal parts in the solution, and only for a few seconds. The metal will be obviously "cleaner" looking when it is done. Remove the parts and wash vigorously in water.

Priming

Porous surfaces usually do not require priming. If they do, you can prime with a clear mixture of Floquil Glaze (30 percent) and Dio-Sol (70 percent), or with a spray of flat finish or Krylon. In most cases, nonporous surfaces should be etched or primed. For metal surfaces, use chemical etching or slightly etch surfaces mechanically with fine steel wool, or apply a priming coating. For castings, the latter technique is preferred. A slight roughening of plastic surfaces with household powdered cleanser might make the surface less shiny and more ready to hold the paint.

There are several priming options for plastics, depending on the type of plastic material. Polystyrene can be attacked by the solvents in Floquil or Scalecraft paints. Therefore, either use water-based paint or protect the plastic with a compatible primer. Such products include Floquil Barrier and Scalecraft Shieldcoat. If this protection is not provided, local *crazing* can occur. Usually, paints sprayed on in thin coats will not attack the plastic. In some cases, crazing can result in a desirable effect, but experiment before this is tried on a model of value to you. If in doubt of the compatibility of the plastic with the paint you want to use, test the combination on scrap or on an inside portion of the model where it will not show.

For plastic castings, it is usually desirable to apply a primer, even if the finish coat will be a water-based paint. If used, the primer should be a neutral light color, such as light gray, buff, primer, or Foundation. This provides a good color base for both lighter and darker finish colors. Drying can be hastened by heating in an oven at 200° to 250°F for about 30 minutes. Do not do this on models with wood, paper, or plastic parts, of course.

Holding

Many objects require a "handle" of some sort so that they can be held while they are being painted. Often, you can use double-sided tape to hold them to a scrap piece of wood. You might choose not to remove the casting bars (molding sprues) on cast plastic or metal parts so that you can use them as handles for painting. Sometimes with small figures, trees, etc., a small wire added to the bottom will be useful for both mounting and painting the object. When painting a locomotive or railroad car, a special holding jig might be indicated.

Masking

Masking can make any paint job easier, and it is essential for multicolor paint schemes. Masking can be done with masking tape, preferably the low-tack drafting tape or artist's frisket paper, or with masking liquids. In either case, the area where the paint is not desired is covered by the masking. Usually a base color is applied to the entire surface, and then part of this is masked off. The choice of which color is the base and which is applied second is a function of the amount of color, the shape of the model, and the colors themselves.

Do not use the raw edge of the tape to define the color separation. Instead, cut a new edge down the middle of the tape, using a sharp modeler's knife, a steel rule, and a hardened glass surface. Press the tape down firmly along the line where the color edge will be. Because it will stretch a little, it has some flexibility that will allow it to follow modest curves. Thin the paint as little as possible to reduce any chance of it running under the tape. Remove the tape as soon as possible after painting. The area beyond the tape width can be covered with newspaper that is cut to shape and taped on to the edge along the color line.

Masking liquids are probably most useful for small areas. They are "painted" on, though it is difficult to obtain smooth edges unless the edge is "cut" and the undesired part of the masking is peeled off (prior to painting). Their use remains relatively specialized, and tape is the preferred material for most masking.

Common rubber cement can also be used as a mask. The best application is to simulate paint peeling from a surface. Streak on the rubber cement to a bare or painted surface. Then apply the newer paint over all. When the rubber cement is rolled off (using an artist's pick-up-type rubber eraser), the newer paint will have streaks left that appear to be where it has peeled off. Seal the base surface with a flat finish.

Masking can also be done with chart (or graph) tape, which comes in a variety of very narrow widths. The invisible Scotch brand Magic transparent tape can also be used. Its advantage is that its thickness is minimal. Its disadvantage, relative to masking tape, is that it has no flexibility because it will not stretch. It must be cut out to the profile of any curves. Another choice is frisket paper. This comes in sheets mounted to a backing. Cut it to the proper shape, peel off the backing, and apply it. The adhesive is not as strong as either masking or transparent tape.

Tape removal can remove the base paint if that paint has not been properly applied, if it has not been allowed to dry long enough, or if the tape is removed incorrectly. Remove the tape by pulling back on the tape over that part still stuck down.

Paint Preparation

The paint must always be mixed thoroughly prior to use. This is particularly important for spray painting using an airbrush. It can be helpful to put a small, 1/4-inch diameter ball bearing in the paint jar so that shaking will be more effective. Otherwise, stirring thoroughly is usually best. Do not start painting until all the paint in the jar is of uniform consistency.

Keep the cap on the jar as much as possible because the solvent will evaporate through the top opening. A very small amount of thinner, added when you are done painting, will compensate for this loss. (If added just before using the paint, it is not as effective.)

Some people prefer to store the paint jars inverted. This can provide a better seal and prevent drying out during storage. It also can make the removal of the top easier at the time of next use. Another trick is to spread a small amount of petroleum jelly on the cap threads. Keep the plastic or coated cardboard insert as it helps in the sealing.

Another useful aid can be to apply a sticker to the cap with the paint color name and/or a color swatch. This makes finding the right color in a drawer of many jars much easier.

Sometimes, even with the best precautions, the paint will become hard or rubbery. If this happens, chemical changes have occurred and thinner cannot restore it to usefulness. Discard the paint. Save empty paint jars because they are useful for mixing or storing paint of other than standard colors.

BRUSHING

Finishing using brushes is what is normally thought of as "painting." The paint usually comes directly from the bottle and is stroked onto the surface with a brush of appropriate size and type. Depending on the type of paint and the skill of the painter, the results can look as good as a fine airbrush application, on down.

Brushes

Good-quality brushes, like all other tools, pay for themselves, if you take care of them. Proper care for brushes consists of always thoroughly cleaning them immediately after each use. They must also be stored so that the bristles will not be bent or distorted.

Buying cheap brushes is poor economy; they will not last very long, and will not permit you to do a quality job. The best choice for painting models (equipment, vehicles, people, buildings) is brushes made for water colors, with round ends (not flat) in sizes of 00, 0, 1, 2, and 3. For painting broader areas of scenery, appropriately larger brushes, designed for use with latex indoor house paints, are ideal (FIG. 9-3).

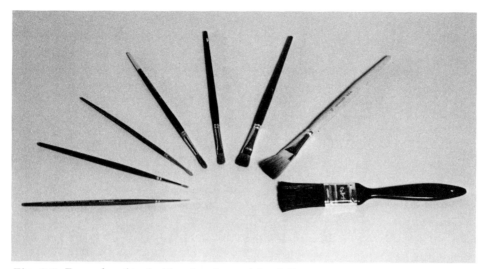

Fig. 9-3. Examples of typical brushes for model painting.

Clean the brush with the same solvent used for the paint. Make sure all the paint is out, all the way down to the base of the bristles. Wipe the brush with a cloth or paper toweling. Repeat the cleaning several times until no trace of color is left on the cloth or toweling. Before storing a small brush away, moisten the tip in water and shape the end to a point with your fingers. When you next use it, it will be as good as new. Never store or soak brushes (even temporarily) in the solvent. Save the brush cleaning solvent for use as a weathering solution after it is too dirty to do a good job cleaning the brushes.

Application

Apply paint in smooth, even strokes, overlapping each stroke slightly from side-to-side. If possible, make the stroke the full length of the object being painted. Use as large a brush as you can, consistent with the size of the object. Brush marks will be less this way. The strokes should follow the grain of wood or the natural texture of the material. Dip only the tip of the brush into the paint. Try to keep the paint away from the hairs near the metal ferrule because it is hard to clean this area. Hardened paint under and near the ferrule shortens brush life and makes the brush harder to use.

Allow adequate time before touching the painted object. The paint will dry to the touch well before it is dry enough for more painting, applying other finishes, decaling, etc. Take your time. Work on more than one project at a time. Remember that "a watched paint never dries."

Dipping

Small objects can sometimes be painted most easily by dipping them directly into the paint jar until they are fully immersed, then bringing them out, shaking them off, and mounting them to something to hold them while they are drying. Such objects should have a handling wire attached to make this possible. Some paint will likely run down or drip off, so account for this in where you place the object to dry. For dipping, the paint can be used at normal consistency, or it can be thinned up to 30 percent.

Striping

Striping is probably best done with decals or dry transfers. It can also be done by masking or with ruling pens or special striping tools. The striping tools use wheels of various widths. They are probably not useful for small models because they cannot be depended on to produce good stripes of less than 1/16 inch. Use ruling pens that are designed for ink. The pens should probably not be used for stripes over 1/16 inch.

Paint for striping may require thinning by up to 30 percent. It is best to experiment to determine what works best with the type and color of paint you are using. Note that the surface finish the striping is applied to will also affect the experiment, so duplicate the model surface.

Metallic Colors

Use separate brushes and thinner for cleaning metallic colors (gold, brass, silver, etc.) because these colors will not thoroughly clean out and will remain in the brush. Flecks of these colors can later show up in colors where they should not appear. Identify these brushes so they will only be used with metallic colors.

Dry Brushing

Use dry brushing to apply paint over other painted surfaces to simulate effects such as peeled paint, rust streaks, or wood grain. Sometimes you can use it with white or light colors to apply highlighting. Do not dilute the paint; mix the color as usual. Use a semistiff brush, drawing it first across the paint and then across a cloth or paper towel so most of the color is removed. Then lightly draw the brush across the surface, leaving just slight streaks of paint.

For highlighting, use a lighter color over the darker base color. Use white over light colors (beige, tan, yellow, flesh), earth over warm colors (red, orange, brown), and light gray over cold colors (blue, green, black).

Safety

Brushing can be safely done indoors in a room with adequate ventilation. Some paints will cause an odor that might travel to other rooms and/or be objectionable. Keep the caps on all paints and solvents, except when they are actually in use.

Some paint solvents are flammable, including those used for Accu-Paint, Floquil, and Scalecoat. These same solvents are harmful if you breathe too much of them.

Mess

Paint spills can be very messy. Never paint above a surface that would be harmed if the paint or solvent were spilled on it. If that cannot be avoided, make sure that the surface is protected with many layers of newspapers or a painter's drop cloth. A foam or cardboard holder can be made to place the paint or thinner jars in. The holder should have a cylinder to just fit the jar, which is glued to a wide base. This makes the jar hard, but not impossible, to tip over.

AIRBRUSHING

For the best quality model painting results, there is no substitute for an airbrush. This is true for locomotives, rolling stock, and buildings, particularly; but the airbrush can be useful in all aspects of miniature painting.

Airbrush Choice

There are two basic types of airbrush, single action and dual action (FIG. 9-4). The former is simpler and less expensive, the latter is harder to use and more expensive but can give the most professional results. Unless you are really going to be doing some fancy things with your airbrush, the single-action types should be entirely adequate. The mixing of the air and paint can be internal or external.

In the single-action external-mix airbrush, the only fingertip control is of the air, which is either on or off. The paint pattern is adjusted by rotating the nozzle that opens or closes the tip hole around the needle. This adjustment can be done prior to or during the painting by using the hand other than the one holding the airbrush.

In the double-action airbrush, the fingertip control can adjust both the air flow and the paint flow. This allows very precise control of spray pattern, line width, etc. It also makes the airbrush a little harder to operate for the beginner, and a lot more expensive. For either single or double action, external mixing is recommended for ease of cleaning. The paint is mixed with air outside the airbrush, right at the end of the control tip.

Airbrushes, suitable for artists or modelers, are made by such companies as Paasche, Badger, Binks, and Thayer & Chandler.

Air Supply

The best choice for an air supply is a small compressor made for artist or model spray painting. Canned (aerosol) propellant is available, but the cost is very high. The compressor will pay for itself after the equivalent of only a few dozen cans of propellant.

The compressor can be of either the piston type (preferred) or the diaphragm type. It should be an "oilless" design. It does not have to be large for model use.

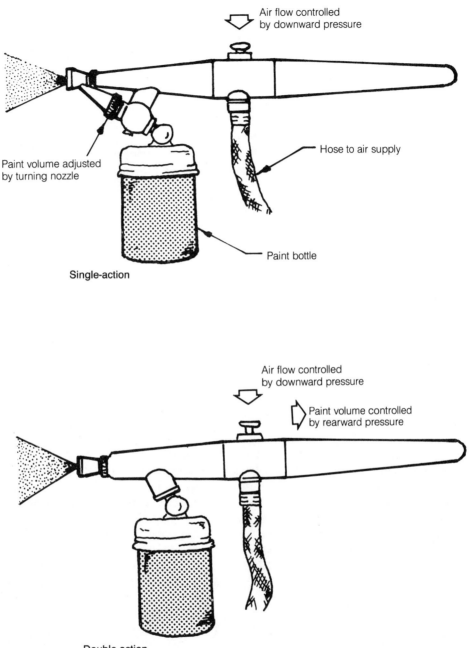

Air flow controlled
by downward pressure

Paint volume adjusted
by turning nozzle

Hose to air supply

Paint bottle

Single-action

Air flow controlled
by downward pressure

Paint volume controlled
by rearward pressure

Double-action

Fig. 9-4. *This drawing shows the single-action (top) and double-action (bottom) airbrush types.*

It is best complemented by use of a pressure regulator, a storage tank, and a moisture trap. The first two items will ensure a constant pressure, which will give better, smoother paint jobs. Choose an adjustable regulator capable of handling input pressures up to 150 pounds per square inch (psi) and with an output range of 5 to 50 psi.

The moisture trap will prevent condensed water (or oil) from entering the airbrush and being sprayed onto the model, where it will spot the surface. You can make an economical moisture trap from an automobile in-line fuel filter. Add it in series with the hose, using hose clamps.

The storage tank is not absolutely required, but it can reduce wear and tear on the compressor by letting it run less. Install the regulator just before the connection to the hose to the airbrush; install the moisture trap near the other end of the hose, as close to the airbrush as possible.

The most economical choice for an air supply is to modify a tank-type garden sprayer, of at least 4-gallon capacity, with a fitting to mate it to the airbrush hose. This requires frequent hand pumping (work), does not give a very constant pressure, and can produce a lot of moisture in the air. The latter two problems can be overcome with a pressure regulator and a moisture trap. The garden sprayer can also furnish an inexpensive source for a storage tank, when used with a compressor.

Other types of air sources, such as vacuum cleaner attachments and the electric vibro-sprayers, are not recommended for model use. They can be used for room and house painting, but are not useful for fine work.

Paint Preparation

When spraying Floquil paints, dilute the paint only with Dio-Sol thinner, beginning with about 10 percent, and using no more than necessary. Add the same percentage of Glaze as you used of thinner to compensate for the dilution of the resins. Add 2 to 5 percent Retarder to slow the drying time for best spraying.

When spraying Floquil paint on polystyrene, a protective barrier coat might not be necessary because much of the solvent evaporates before it reaches the surface. To be sure, conduct a test.

When adding an over-finish, be sure the base coats are really dry. This takes from 2 to 7 days, depending on surface, temperature, and humidity. For decal application, or if a gloss finish is desired, spray with Floquil Hi-Gloss, Testors Glosscoat, or Micro Scale gloss finish. After all decals and/or dry transfers are applied and after all aging and weathering treatments are dry, spray with several light coats of Floquil flat, Testors Dullcoat, or Micro Scale flat finish.

Water-based paints also require some thinning, but no more than is necessary to provide a good spray. Whatever paint is used, it must be completely mixed and free of any suspended particles or dried fragments. It is best to strain the paint through a fine cloth (cheesecloth or nylon stocking) just prior to use. The airbrush passages are very small and can become clogged with tiny contaminants.

For the airbrush, you can either transfer the paint into an airbrush cup, or, preferably, use siphon bottle tops that are designed for the same size jars (^{1}/2 or 1 ounce) that you are using for your paint. These siphon tops have a screw cap with an air hole in it, a sealing ring, and a siphon tube that reaches to the bottom of the jar. It is important to keep the air hole open because it is the outside air pressure that "pushes" the paint up into the airbrush. The siphon top is also a little easier to clean than the cup. The cup holds only about ^{1}/4 ounce and is open at the top so the paint is easily spilled. It is handy to have several siphon tops so that you can quickly change from color to color, saving the final complete cleanup job for later.

Spraying

Everything must be prepared before the spraying can be begin. The actual spraying takes by far the least time of the entire operation. Do not spray paint on days when it is raining or the humidity is extremely high. The water vapor in the air will affect the paint, causing it to blush.

For most simple spray painting, no particular skill is needed to use an airbrush. The main precaution is to put very thin coats on the model so that no runs develop. Spray the model from several different angles to make sure all areas are reached by the spray. If possible, keep the airbrush within about 30 degrees of horizontal at all times. Care should be taken to ensure that no paint drips from the airbrush cup or jar onto the model.

The air pressure should be no higher than will work. Start with about 10 psi, increasing this if necessary. A fine mist is what is desired. Test on newspaper before moving to the model.

Move the airbrush parallel to the surface and at a constant distance. Slightly overlap the strokes. The paint mist should just reach the surface before the droplets dry. If you are too close, the paint will tend to run. If you are too far, some of the paint will turn to dust and the surface will be rough (sometimes this is useful, if desired). There is usually a latitude of several inches in this distance. Several light coats can be applied in succession, making sure no running occurs.

Do not touch the model until the paint is dry enough so that no mark is left. Then you can can apply additional coats of the same color. Do not add coats of different colors, decaling, dry transferring, over coating, etc., until the paint is completely dry. Masking can (and should) be removed as soon as the paint is dry to the touch.

The objects must be held while they are being sprayed. It is usually best if both hands are free to use the airbrush. This requires that the objects be held in position by jigs, etc., as were discussed under "Brushing." A simple lazy susan stand can be helpful.

Cleaning

The airbrush must be cleaned after every use. Rinsing between use of different colors is usually adequate. Thorough cleaning requires disassembling the parts of the airbrush that have been exposed to the paint, immersing them in solvent, swabbing them out with pipe cleaners and/or small wires, and drying off. Failure to clean the airbrush adequately will result in paint buildup, bad operation, and poor paint jobs.

Do not store airbrush parts in the solvents in lieu of cleaning because the paint might harden anyway. This might be done for short periods of time, however, to save the time of a thorough cleaning.

Spray Cans

Painting with aerosol spray paint cans is easier than using an airbrush, but the results are in no way comparable. The spray pattern is large and uncontrollable. Generally the pressure is such that too much spray comes out too fast and most is wasted, or worse, the coat applied to the model is too thick and runs or "orange peels." The cost is also much higher, given any amount of painting. About the only advantage is that the can doesn't have to be cleaned after use and it can be thrown away when empty.

Still, with all these disadvantages, spray cans can still be useful, particularly for applying flat or gloss finishes before and after decaling, dry transferring, aging, and weathering. This is particularly true if you do not own an airbrush. Either the Floquil or Testors products appear to give the best results.

Safety

Do no spraying in an indoors room. It inevitably produces volatile liquid or solid chemicals that are harmful to health. Only do spraying outside in the open air, in a garage with the door open, or indoors using a spray booth with a fan pulling the spray to an exhaust that goes outside. Even with these precautions, wear a mask designed for protection while spraying paint. Modelers have died from the cumulative effects of paint spray!

Also be cautious because an explosive mixture is produced while spraying. This could be ignited by a stray spark, a water heater, or smoking. Water-based paints are not necessarily immune from these hazards. The dust of the pigments remains suspended for a long time, and any dust mixture can be explosive. An explosion could destroy your hobby and your life. The spray booth (with a brushless fan motor) is the safest option.

Mess

Spraying is a very messy operation. The overspray travels much farther than you might imagine. Make sure that newspapers or a painter's drop cloth are used to protect adjacent areas. Lots of newspapers are handy to have when spraying because some paint might drip or spill from the airbrush container. The cleaning operation is quite messy as well. If it is not done outdoors, protect the surface being used because the solvent will spill.

DYES AND STAINS

Dyes and stains can be applied by brush, by airbrush, or by wiping. In most cases, brushing or wiping are adequate. Ordinary paint can be used as a stain if it is thinned sufficiently and applied by brushing or wiping in the direction of the wood grain. Floquil recommends thinning with 60 percent Dio-Sol and adding 5 to 10 percent Glaze.

You also can apply these finishes in small areas and then partially wipe them off to achieve aging or weathering effect. Experiment ahead of time to obtain the exact result you want. Enough color should be retained by the wood (or other material) to give the appearance of a faded or weathered surface. For wood, two different color stains, applied in sequence, can give excellent effects.

You can apply water-based paint over any dried paint, then while it is still wet, wipe off most of the new paint, leaving the color only in the texture, grooves, etc. This is particularly effective for simulating mortar joints. In this case, use off-white or gray paint over the brick or stone color, then wipe it off from most of the surface, leaving its color to simulate the mortar.

Aged Wood

There are several ways to simulate weathered, unpainted wood. If the model material is wood, the best approach is to apply a graying stain, using diluted India ink, the "dregs" of the brush cleaning jar, a product called Weather-It, or a thin, light gray stain made from diluted paint or wood-colored stains. This can be followed by a thinned Grime stain. For any of these finishes, they are most effective if they are wiped on with a cloth and then wiped off again.

If the model material is not wood, but paper, plaster, plastic, or metal, then a different technique is needed. Paint the surface a weathered wood color, using a color such as Reefer Gray or Foundation. Then apply stains over this color using diluted India ink, the brush cleaning jar liquid, or some other "black" thin wash. This will bring out the texture and give some definition to the imitation wood.

CHALK

Powdered chalks or artist's dry pastels can be used very effectively for creating weathering effects. They have the advantage that they can be applied over any paint or lettering without risk to those materials, and with a considerable degree of control over the effect being obtained. There are dozens of brands available that are suitable. Only a few colors are necessary, including white, gray, black, and some shades of rust and brown. Unfortunately, you will probably have to buy a set with many other colors included.

Before applying any chalks, spray the model with a flat overcoat. This provides the texture necessary to hold the chalk. The chalks come in round or square sticks. They must be reduced to powder by scraping with a knife, or by rubbing the stick against sandpaper. Scrape off only as much as you need. Never apply the chalk stick directly to the model.

Cosmetics?

Left-over cosmetics can be used to apply weathering effects to models in a manner similar to the use of chalks. You might wish to experiment with these materials to determine their effectiveness and ease of use.

Candidate cosmetics include eye liner, foundation, mascara, and eye shadow. Pencil eye liner and powdered eye shadow are the easiest to work with and most predictable in results. The best colors are browns and blacks.

Dry-brush the powder onto the model using a semistiff brush $1/8$ to $1/4$ inch wide. Use the chalking brushes only for chalking and not for painting. Almost scrub the chalk onto the model, varying the amount and pressure applied to fit the result desired. Keep the direction of the brush strokes consistent with the weathering streak patterns desired. You can obtain a different effect if the chalk is applied slightly wet.

Several applications of chalk, with a light overspray of flat finish between each, might be necessary. The flat finish will slightly fade and soften the chalk colors. If you have trouble making the chalk stick, try applying it when the flat finish is fresh and slightly tacky. It is always necessary to "fix" the chalk and make it permanent with a flat overspray when you are finished.

10

Aging
and Weathering

In a prototype train, only one or two percent of the cars look clean and new. The rest are road-worn to varying degrees, with faded colors and areas worn down by the weather. They are coated with dust, grime, and stains of great variety from all parts of their travels. They might show rust, places that need repair, and places that just were repainted. Even cars from the same railroad, presumably painted with the same paint, appear to have slightly different colors.

Real buildings also only look new for a few weeks after they are built or repainted. Weather and age will gradually make their colors less bright and will coat them with soot and water stains. Automobiles are usually kept cleaner, but their colors fade with time. Trucks are often subject to the same aging and weathering tendencies as railroad cars.

If everything on your model looks new, then it does not look realistic. It looks like a toy . . . and that is probably not the effect you want to achieve. Fortunately, aging and weathering models is not very difficult. The hardest part is convincing yourself that the model you have bought or built will actually look better when it looks a little old rather than when it looks paint-shop new.

The best guide to applying realistic aging and weathering is to observe prototype equipment and buildings to see how they have aged and what and where the effects of weather have been. If possible, use photographs to capture these effects so that you can later duplicate them.

Just as an absence of aging or weathering looks unrealistic, too much can look just as bad. Make the effect subtle and vary it between different cars and buildings. If you err, err on the side of too little rather than too much. More can always be added.

DETERIORATION

The most extreme manifestation of aging is physical deterioration. Wood rots, bricks crumble, concrete cracks, paint peels, and metal rusts away. Damage, from a variety of causes, creates missing boards, dents, bent-in corners, etc. The structural relaxation of old age can cause roofs and underframes to sag and walls that are less than plumb.

Most of the representation of physical deterioration aging in the model must be done when you construct the model. It cannot be added by painting or staining. If a freight car is to sag, then the entire car must be built that way. Plastic cars can be somewhat deformed with heat and pressure to provide dents and bends. Missing stones or bricks must be cut away. Missing boards must be removed (or not put on in the first place). Aging wood that is split and rotting must be physically changed to look right.

Do all physical deterioration modeling prior to any painting or other finishing (in most cases). An exception is sanding or scraping painted surfaces to simulate peeling or abraded paint.

FADING

Fading is the natural aging process where a color becomes bleached through the action of sun and weather on the paint pigments. Simulate the effect of fading by choosing the proper model paint color, one that is lighter than it would have been if new. This means that fading effects are not added later but painted on by choosing a more pastel color. This is done by adding white to the original color, in increasing proportions, as a greater faded effect is desired.

Note that on buildings, fading does not occur equally on all surfaces. Those that are protected from the sun and weather will fade less. This includes areas under eaves and areas protected by porches or trees, etc. Also note that fading will be greater on the south and west sides of a building than on the north side.

Fading also occurs on any lettering or signs. The lettering/signs are added after the (faded) paint, and they must be faded separately. See "Lettering," chapter 11.

DEPOSITS

Deposits include wind- or water-borne dust, dirt, soot, grime, mud, etc. These deposits usually arrive first to settle on horizontal surfaces, but they are soon washed down onto vertical surfaces by rain and melting snow. Deposits might also be thrown up onto a railroad car by the wheels of the car preceding it. They might also be raised from the roadbed by the suction of the train.

Add the effect of deposits after the model is completely painted and lettered. The paint color and lettering (if any) must show through the deposits to a greater or lesser extent. This requires that the deposits be translucent, to a degree. Simulate this (with paint) by using a consistency like a stain or wash.

Simulation of deposits requires two techniques because the deposits can be relatively uniform, as left by the effects of wind or road spray, or they can be streaked, as left by the effects of rain washing them down. Uniform deposits are best applied using an airbrush. Streaked deposits are best applied using a brush to simulate the streak patterns. The brush strokes must follow the pattern that would be formed by the rain-washed dirt and grime as it runs down the roof and the sides of the modeled object. Streaking can also be effectively simulated by using chalks.

In either case, thin the paint substantially and choose colors to simulate the colors of dirt, dust, grime, etc., likely to be found on the prototype. More than one color might be appropriate on the same model because the prototype might have been exposed to several different contaminants.

Apply more road spray near the ends of the car, and with the spray direction coming from the end and below. Where it collects will be affected by the outer surface of the car, such as ribs, ladders, etc. Floquil Dust, when sprayed, effectively simulates this effect.

The soil adjacent to a building will splash up onto the lower portions of the building. This can be simulated by lightly spraying the local dirt color on these portions before the building is installed.

Another type of deposit that can be simulated is that from the load carried by the car. The load on hopper or gondola cars might blow out while en route, or it might "miss the mark" when being loaded. Tank cars might have stains running down their sides and around their domes from mistakes made while they were being filled.

The dirty solvent you used to clean brushes might serve as a useful solution to apply for a weathering stain.

CORROSION

Rust is the most common form of metal corrosion. Iron or steel surfaces eventually rust. You can simulate rust with paint, either lightly sprayed to simulate general rusting of a surface or brushed on to simulate the more-usual irregular rusty areas. The color can vary from almost a bright orange to a deep rooftop brown, although paint sold as Rust color is usually a good average color. You should mix some varieties of rust colors, based on your own observations.

Rust will, of course, stain down over wood when nails or metal bolts are used as fasteners. Simulate this using a small brush to lightly streak over the wood.

Aluminum surfaces also corrode, which usually results in a dulling or graying of the surface. Only new aluminum is bright and shiny. On the model, if the aluminum is bare metal, polish it slightly with steel wool to dull it down. Then spray it with a thin coat of light gray. If the aluminum is simulated by paint, add a little gray to the aluminum paint. In either case, use an overspray of a flat finish.

The Floquil weathering colors, particularly Dust, Grime, and Mud, are very effective when used properly. Either Grime or Mud can be brushed or sprayed. Dust should only be sprayed on. Dust is very light and has a milky appearance in the bottle. It looks hazy (dusty) on the surface after drying. Do not use too much spray. It goes on almost clear and then "blooms" and gets its true color only when dry.

Types of Aging and Weathering

Aging

☐ Fading
☐ Deterioration
  ■ Structural—sags, leans
  ■ Surface—rot, decay, cracks, splits, crumbling, paint peeling, rust, corrosion, worn-off paint
☐ Damage
  ■ Dents, bends
  ■ Crushes, scrapes
  ■ Missing pieces
  ■ Abraded paint

Weathering

☐ Stains, streaks
☐ Splash
☐ Deposits

11

Lettering

Model locomotives, freight cars, and passenger cars need lettering, but it is just as important to provide signs and lettering for the structures and roadside. Signs bring life to a scene. The signs on a building tell the kind of business that takes place inside. The name on a depot tells what town you are in. The advertisements tell about the year, where the model is located, and what other businesses might be in the locale that are not modeled.

The skill with which signs and lettering are applied can make or break the realism of a model. Fortunately, you do not have to be an artist or draftsman to produce miniature signs of quality. There are a large number of commercial decals, dry transfers, and other printed material available that you can use. They are the proper scale size and style, and are made to suit any era you are modeling.

If possible, do all lettering on car or building sides prior to their assembly. If not, provide some means to hold the model firmly so that the surface is horizontal.

Lettering styles change with the times. What was appropriate for the early part of the century might be very uncommon now. Even worse, modern lettering could not have existed at an earlier era. The style of lettering is characterized by the font used. Study photos of the buildings and rolling stock of the same time era that you are modeling to be sure that you have selected font styles that are not anachronistic.

The font style that you want to use might not be available in either decals or dry transfers. Substitutions can be made, in some cases, if the style is close enough to the one desired. Examine the shapes of both upper- and lowercase letters and of the numerals. Note the presence or absence (and shape) of serifs. Note the ratio of height to width of the letters and the relative width of the lines in the letters. Are all lines the same widths, or are some wider than others? Differences might occur particularly between vertical and horizontal lines. The same general family of fonts might have narrow, normal, and extended widths. Consider the classic fonts, such as gothic and roman, because these never go out of style.

DECALS

A decal consists of printed or screened paint on the front side of porous paper that has been coated with a thin, clear film over a water-soluble adhesive. The thin film holds the various parts of the painted lettering or design together, once the paper is soaked off. See the top half of FIG. 11-1, which shows the layers of a decal both before and after application to a model.

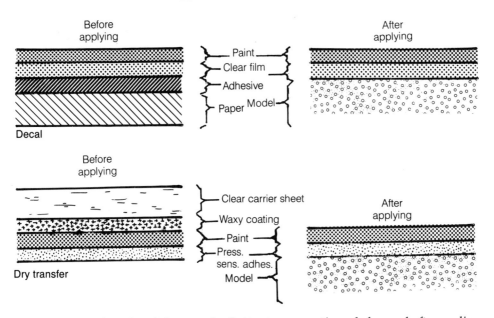

Fig. 11-1. *Decal (top) and dry transfer (bottom) cross sections, before and after application.*

The primary advantages of decals are: (1) ease of application; (2) all letters are held in place by the film; and (3) wide availability in scale sizes and subject matter. The primary disadvantages are: (1) relative difficulty in hiding the film; and (2) relative difficulty in conforming to surface irregularities.

Application

Apply decals to glossy surfaces. A surface with a flat finish has a grain that will not allow the decal to conform properly. If the surface is not glossy, spray with a gloss finish that is compatible with the paint being used (see "Airbrushing," chapter 9). Allow the finish to dry for 24 hours. The surface must be clean and free of finger oils prior to applying decals.

Carefully plan where the decal will go and make sure it will fit. Lay out all parts of the decal needed. Trim each portion of the decal you will need from the decal sheet, cutting as close as possible to contiguous groups of letters. Use scissors, knife, and/or razor blade. Do not try to trim between small letters. Before cutting out Micro Scale decals, spray the sheet with a coating of Micro Superfilm to give more body to the decals.

Arrange the surface that will receive the decals so it is horizontal. Soak the decal in water for 10–20 seconds. Use distilled water, which will eliminate any tap water mineral deposits. Remove the decal and place it on a paper towel to allow the film to loosen from the paper. Prewet the area where the decal is to go with diluted setting fluid. Do not touch the decal with your fingers. Only use tweezers, a knife tip, or a needle probe for handling the decal.

Move the decal to the area using tweezers. Hold the decal film with a knife or needle point held in one hand while pulling the paper out from underneath with the tweezers held in the other hand. Gently slide the decal on the water film to the exact area desired. Apply more water, if necessary, using a small brush. If the decal floats, remove excess water with the tip of a paper towel or facial tissue. When the decal is in exact position, lightly blot up the remaining water with the towel/tissue.

Let the decal dry for several minutes. Carefully apply undiluted setting fluid with a small brush to the edges of the decal, being careful not to disturb its position. Do not use too much fluid. Let this fluid dry completely for several more minutes. Now puncture the film over any air bubbles and slice the film to provide a good fit into grooves or along raised ridges. Repeat the application of setting fluid and the drying. This might have to be repeated several times to shrink the film around all rivets, etc.

When the decal is completed to your satisfaction, clean up around the decal using water applied with a cotton swab. Let dry completely and then overspray with a flat finish. The decal film should be completely hidden if this procedure was followed.

An alternative way to remove the decal from the backing is the float-off technique. This might work better for some types of decals. Gently lay the decal on top of the water so that surface tension will keep it floating. It will separate from the backing paper when it is ready and all the glue is dissolved. Gently lift up the decal from the water and apply it as described above. If it curls up, lay it back onto the water, let it uncurl (with some help), and pick it up again from another place.

Setting Fluid

The use of setting fluid with decals is mandatory to obtain good results. There are several brands of setting fluid you can use, including: Champ Decal-Set, Walthers Solvaset, and Micro Scale Micro Sol and Micro Set. These fluids have different strengths. Experiment to see which you prefer. All work to soften the decal film and all can be diluted and cleaned up with water. For a dilute solution, try a ratio of one part fluid to three parts distilled water.

Striping

Decal stripes can provide good-looking striping with less work than masking and painting. If the stripe covers color separations, you might wish to lightly sand the separation line to reduce the ridge. The stripe decal is cut to width and applied in the same way as for other decals. Here, it is even more important to hold one end of the decal and slide out the paper because the decal is hard to move around if it isn't close to start with.

Homemade Decals

You can make your own decals to suit special needs or to allow more control over the placement of dry transfer lettering (see next topic). Buy some sheets of plain decal paper. This is just like the paper used for regular decals but without the paint on the top surface. Use dry transfers, other decals, or paint for the letters or other material you want.

You can use the newest copy machines to reduce the size of a reproduction and print it directly onto decal paper. The fanciest machines can also print in color. Prepare oversize art work using dry transfers or other hand drawn designs. When done, overspray the top surface of the decal paper with clear flat finish to protect the printing. Apply these decals in the same way as the ready-made ones. The capability of these machines and the relatively low cost of custom decals has virtually eliminated the need for the tedious process of making your own decals using silk screening.

DRY TRANSFERS

A dry transfer consists of printed or screened paint on the back side of a clear carrier sheet that is coated with a tacky, waxlike surface that will release the transfer when the front side is rubbed. A pressure-sensitive adhesive is on the back side of the paint, which causes it to adhere to the desired surface. See the bottom half of FIG. 11-1, which shows the layers of a dry transfer both before and after application to a model.

The primary advantages of dry transfers are: (1) lack of any film that must be hidden, (2) wide availability of letter styles, and (3) relative ease of application over surface irregularities. The primary disadvantages are: (1) less availability of subject matter, (2) less availability of small lettering, and (3) care required to ensure alignment of lettering.

Preparation and Planning

Apply dry transfers to fairly smooth surfaces having a flat or, better yet, slightly glossy surface. The surface should be clean and dry and free from finger oils. The paint should have been allowed to dry for several days. The surface should be horizontal and held in such a way that it does not slip while you apply the dry transfers.

Carefully plan which parts of the dry transfer sheet will be used and exactly where they will go. The most difficult problem in using dry transfers is to provide the proper vertical and horizontal alignment of the letters. It will help a great deal to space out the lettering in advance, in pencil, on a piece of transparent (tracing) paper.

Decide on the vertical spacing between rows of lettering. Draw horizontal guidelines on the paper at this spacing and at the heights of the lettering. Mark a vertical centerline on the paper. Trace the outlines of the letters onto the tracing paper from the carrier sheet, starting with the largest row of letters. Begin with the letter (or letters) closest to the center. Use light pencil pressure.

Add letters, adjusting the horizontal spacing between them for good composition. Note that letters with straight vertical sides, such as H, M, N, B, etc., should be placed farther apart than letters with rounded or sloping sides, such as A, O, or V. Also provide more space next to thin letters (I, 1). Continue adding letters until done. Make sure the spacing looks right at this step.

Application

Tape the tracing paper along one edge (bottom or top) so that it is held in a fixed relationship to the surface to be lettered. Align the traced lettering so that it is over the right place on the surface. Slide the carrier sheet under the tracing paper and align the letter on the carrier sheet to the outline on the tracing paper. Then, without moving the carrier sheet, fold back the tracing paper, and rub on the letter. Continue this process for each letter.

The carrier sheet is translucent, but not transparent, so you can see the surface through it, but not with great clarity. Hold the sheet firmly in place, then lightly rub the portion to be transferred with a burnisher. All rubbing should be in the same direction to avoid stretching the carrier sheet. Use an old ballpoint pen tip, a rounded softwood stick, a dull soft pencil, or (preferably) an artist's burnishing tool as the burnisher.

It requires some practice to determine exactly the amount of pressure to apply to the burnishing. Too much pressure or too long a time spent in rubbing is just as bad as too little pressure and too short a time. In either case, the transfer might fail to completely re-attach itself from the carrier sheet to the receiving surface.

There will usually be a change in the "color" of the transfer, as seen through the carrier sheet, when it is free of the sheet. At that time, carefully lift the sheet away from the surface. Then place the separator sheet that comes with the dry transfer sheets over the transfer and apply further burnishing through that sheet. In some places you might need to use a pencil eraser, dabbed against the transfer, to get full conformance, such as over rivets, etc.

If a mistake is made, you can remove the faulty transfer portion with the sticky surface of Scotch brand Magic transparent tape. Another try can then be made with a new transfer without further preparation of the surface.

When all the transfers have been applied, spray on a flat finish to protect the transfers from being scratched off. This finish also covers the slightly waxy residue and keeps it from collecting dirt.

Colored Letters

Dry transfers might not be available in the lettering colors you would like to use. A lift-off technique can be used to create signs with lettering in any color as well as to create several other interesting effects. Before it is sealed with an overspray, the dry transfers are lifted off with transparent tape. This feature can be used to advantage.

Suppose you wish to have red lettering on the side of a white building. You only have white or black dry transfer lettering of the desired size available. You can make the lettering look new or with any desired degree of fading. Begin by painting the area where the sign is to go the desired color of the letters, red in this case. Let this paint dry thoroughly, then apply the dry transfers, but do not burnish them.

Now paint the entire surface the (white) color of the building. When this paint is dry, use the tape to remove all the letters. This allows the undercoat of red to show through. If you wish the letters to look faded, spray a thinned coat of the wall color over the letters until they fade into the wall to whatever degree is desired (FIG. 11-2).

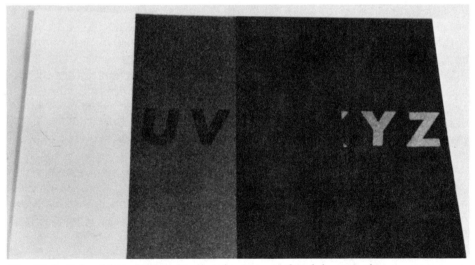

Fig. 11-2. Colored lettering can be created using uncolored dry transfers.

A second, similar technique can be used to provide faded letters. First, paint the building surface that will receive the letters white. Then spray a light mist of the red over this. Apply the transfers and spray the entire surface white. Now remove the letters. This leaves faded red letters on the white wall.

By suitable masking of areas, different parts of a sign can be created with different color letters.

CUTOUT LETTERING

Miniature signs and posters can be made from magazine advertisements or from printed material prepared and sold for this purpose. Postage stamps and the small "stamps" in advertisements for records are also good sources. Cut out these signs/posters by trimming as close as possible to the printing using a scissors and/or sharp knife.

The paper that is used is much greater than scale thickness. For optimum realism, thin the paper by sanding off the back layers of the paper. This needs to be done primarily at the edges, which are the only part that will show. This is accomplished by rubbing the paper with sandpaper or sanding sticks. Wetting the paper might help in this process.

Put the thinned sign/poster in place using white glue, contact cement, or matte medium. Posters that are coming off the wall should have loose and curled edges. You might also want to distress the front surface to make the sign or poster look old and worn. More careful sanding will accomplish this. Some of this weathering and aging can be done after the sign/poster is applied to the surface (see FIG. 11-3).

Fig. 11-3. Posters and advertisements can add color and interest to a wall, but they must be of the right era for the scene being modeled.

Freehand Lettering

Freehand lettering can be used for large letters or logos that are otherwise hard to duplicate. Plan the lettering carefully on paper, then trace it onto the surface using transfer paper (obtainable in white or black). Next, carefully paint the letters (or whatever) with a small brush and a steady hand. Transfer paper is a modern version of carbon paper and is available at craft stores.

Decal or dry transfer lettering can be partially (or wholly) colored by carefully applying paint with a small brush and a steady hand. Sometimes, you can outline or shadow the lettering by outlining below and to one side of all the letters.

Paint graffiti on freehand, using appropriate colors, or by tracing through transfer paper (if white or black). Overspray all freehand signs and lettering with a flat finish for protection and to eliminate any shine.

Signs can also be made using logos or lettering applied with stencils. This works best for the larger scales or for signs where the detail is not too small. Make the stencil by tracing the design onto a piece of stencil paper (obtained from art supply stores). Cut out the stencil using a sharp, small-tipped knife. You might need to leave small bridges between parts of the letters so they do not fall out. These areas can be painted over by hand after the stencil is used.

Apply the paint through a stencil using a brush or by spraying. If a brush is used, it should be a stiff, square-ended one, with little paint on it. Apply the paint by "pounding" the brush through the stencil, against the surface. If spraying is used, direct the airflow perpendicular to the surface so the paint does not get under the stencil.

12

Methods

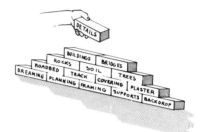

The methods used for model railroad layout, module, or diorama construction and finishing follow a usual sequence of steps. The first and most important step is "planning." The next two of these steps have traditionally been called "benchwork" and "trackwork." The remaining steps have not had any common names given to them, other than "creating scenery," or "scenicing," or "detailing," etc., none of which is sufficiently descriptive of the several steps involved.

This handbook introduces some new terminology for the entire sequence of steps in model construction. It is hoped that these clear and concise terms will be generally adopted and help to clear up a confusion in the terminology used in model railroad magazines and books.

The total sequence generally consists of eight steps. The first (planning) step is called *ideawork*. The next two steps use the names that are now common, *benchwork* and *trackwork*. The remaining five steps, which generally occur in chronological sequence, all have prefixes that explain in one word what the basic purpose of the step is. The new terms are: (1) *coverwork*, (2) *groundwork*, (3) *greenwork*, (4) *buildwork*, and (5) *detailwork*.

Model Railroad Construction Sequence

Ideawork	Dreaming and planning
Benchwork	Framework and supports
Trackwork	Roadbed and tracklaying
Coverwork	Covering and plaster
Groundwork	Rocks and soil
Greenwork	Foliage and trees
Buildwork	Buildings and bridges
Detailwork	Details and clutter

The ending "-work" is not meant to imply that these are laborious tasks, which would defeat the purpose of your hobby. The noun "work" has many meanings in the dictionary. The most appropriate ones applicable to this usage are: (1) activity in which one exerts sustained physical or mental effort to overcome obstacles and achieve an objective or result; and (2) something created by the exercise of skill, creative talent, or artistic effort. The first definition defines the activity and the second the result . . . both directly applicable to your hobby.

While these eight steps usually occur in the order given, at least in one particular area, they can all exist simultaneously in various parts of the layout (FIG. 12-1). It would be a rare situation if one step were completed over the entire layout before any portion advanced to the next step. There might also be good reasons to perform the steps out of the sequence given. It also might be necessary, during changes and reconstruction, to regress in the steps and begin at some point anew, at least in some portion of the layout.

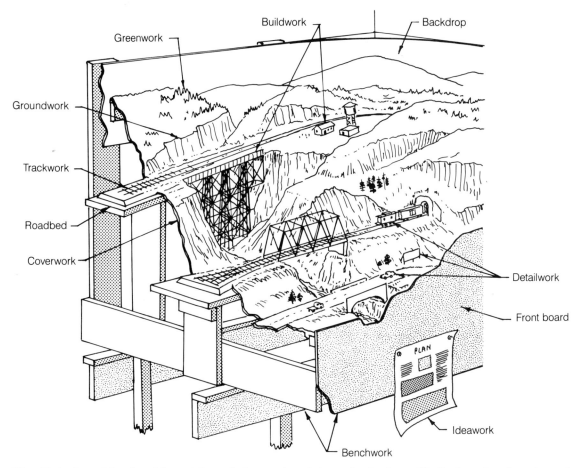

Fig. 12-1. *A model railroad layout is made in a series of steps, beginning with the bare benchwork, and finishing with the final detailwork.*

It should also be noted that the names are meant only to be a convenience. The definitions of the individual steps overlap somewhat, most particularly between coverwork and groundwork, because both involve the use of plaster coats that might, in many situations, be virtually continuous in application.

13

Ideawork

Ideawork is the name given to the dreaming and the planning necessary before any work is started on the actual modeling. It can occur over a very long time (but not too long, or you will never do anything). It can all happen in a day or two. But it must be done so that you have some sort of a mental plan, on paper if possible, of what you want to accomplish and how you are going to do it (FIG. 13-1).

In this chapter, ideawork is somewhat arbitrarily split up between two topics: model planning and scenery planning. The subjects overlap and blend, however, so that they are hard to separate. Most of the topics in chapters 1 and 2 are applicable; review them prior to and during this planning.

MODEL PLANNING

This handbook is not intended as a guide to how to design or draw plans for models, or what to select to model, or how to lay out the track plan for a layout, etc. Other books and periodicals have that as their intent and generally do a very good job of it.

There are considerations in what is modeled and how it is done that overlap with the subjects of scenery and detailing. Model planning discusses some of these considerations.

Preference

What you choose to include in your modeled scenes is determined by what you like, by what looks "right" to you, and by what it costs in time and money. Each

Fig. 13-1. Planning is essential . . . whether you build one railroad car or an empire.

separate choice is made based on some desire/appearance/cost/time trade that is made unconsciously.

Locomotives can most easily illustrate this point. You like the appearance of some locomotives better than others. You can buy them as custom-painted brass, as brass you paint yourself, as ready-to-run plastic models, as kits, or as scratchbuilt. This results in a wide range of cost, work, quality, reliability, and overall appearance. You make the choice based on what you want versus what you are willing to pay in terms of money and/or time. The choice might also be influenced because what you want is not available ready-made. Then you have to modify something else or start from scratch.

The same is also true of other rolling stock, buildings, figures, vehicles, trees, rocks, grass, and every part of the scene you are modeling. As an example, you need some human figures in a scene. You could buy them already painted, or you could buy them precast and paint them, or you could cast or carve them and

Table 13-1. *Options for Obtaining Models*

Locomotives/Cars	Mat'l	Build	Modify	Detail	Paint	Letter	Age	Cost/Time*
RTR, Custom-Painted	Brass	—	—	—	—	—	X	$$$$$$T
RTR, Painted	Brass	—	—	?	—	X	X	$$$$$TT
RTR, Unpainted	Brass	—	—	?	X	X	X	$$$$TTT
RTR, Custom-Painted	Plastic	—	—	—	—	—	X	$$$$TTT
RTR, Painted	Plastic	—	?	X	X	X	X	$$$TTTT
Locomotives, Cars & Structures								
Kit, Craftsman	—	X	X	X	X	X	X	$$$TTTT
Kit, Normal	—	X	X	X	X	X	X	$$TTTTT
Semi-Scratch	—	X	—	X	X	X	X	$$TTTTT
Scratch	—	X	—	X	X	X	X	$TTTTTT

(RTR = Ready-to-Run)
* For equivalent appearance and performance

paint them yourself. The range is from easy but expensive to cheap but time consuming. By doing the entire job yourself, you can customize what you are doing to exactly what is needed for a unique result.

Similarly, you can buy buildings as kits, you can "kitbash" them or otherwise modify them, or you can build them from scratch. If you want to model a building not available as a kit, then you must build from scratch, but you might use some precast parts, such as windows and doors.

TABLE 13-1 illustrates some of these options for selecting models from various sources. The last column shows the relative cost versus time trade values.

Accent

Everything you see is not of uniform interest, either in natural or in man-made scenes. It should be the same with the model. A good bit of blandness with occasional accented scenes, is both natural and proper and also makes for good stagecraft. (See "Stagecraft," in chapter 1).

The accented scenes should be intrinsically interesting, they should (if possible) tell a story, and they should be more detailed, more fully populated, etc. Note that the accenting is not just visual. It can include movement, sound, and smell, whatever will draw and hold attention. As on the stage, lighting can add attention, interest, and drama to a scene.

You can choose to separate the accented scenes not only with less-detailed areas, but with view blocks of one sort or another. These view blocks might be buildings, rock cuts, tree groups, or hills. They need only be large enough to prevent the viewer from easily seeing adjacent scenes. If they are done well, the view blocks will make the layout seem much larger than it really is.

Your largest and most detailed scenes should be those that set the theme for the railroad, or a part of it. This might include a mine, a sawmill, a lumber camp, a key industry, a waterfront, an ore-loading facility, etc.

Consider the viewpoint(s) of the spectator(s). This includes eye height, what can/cannot be seen from that point, the distance to the various scenes, the location of accented scenes, the general appearance of the less-detailed areas, etc. Keep the horizon at eye level. If you use mirrors, let them reflect only other parts of the model, not the viewer! There should be no shadows on the backdrop. The light should either be shadowless or appear to come from a single sun (for any scene that can be viewed at one time).

Height

Is the viewer looking at your model as if he is on a tall hill (looking down), or is the viewer at the elevation that a scale person would be in the scene? Much has been written on the proper height for a layout, both for viewing and for ease of operation, construction, and maintenance. Entirely different effects in the perception of the scene result. In the former case, the eye can see well into the scene, requiring at least moderate detailing beyond the foreground; considerably more effort must be put into detail of the tops of buildings and rolling stock. In the latter case, the perspective is more easily forced; only foreground portions of the model will require detailing.

Layout Height Considerations

The chosen height should be a compromise between comfort, convenience, good visibility, and the effect you want.

Low height:

- ☐ Difficult to work underneath.
- ☐ Access duck-unders are difficult or uncomfortable.
- ☐ Reduces layout storage space underneath.
- ☐ Requires detailing scenery further back.
- ☐ Emphasizes roof scenery.

High height:

- ☐ Difficult to lay track or maintain scenery.
- ☐ Difficult to reach derailed equipment.
- ☐ Hard to see trains being operated.
- ☐ More difficult to light.
- ☐ Requires all detailed scenes to be in the foreground.

□ Does not let children see operation.
□ Difficult to photograph.
□ Cannot suit heights of different people.

Compromise 1. Put layout just high enough to be able to duck under (probably about 40-inch clearance, which gives a minimum track elevation of about 44 inches). Use a chair of proper height to get an eye-level view. Stand up to see farther or to work on the top.

Compromise 2. Put layout at high level, chosen for normal adult eye height. Use movable platforms for viewing by children, shorter people, and for construction and maintenance.

Compromise 3. Use a two-level layout, with the upper level at eye level and the lower level spaced down enough for lighting and access (about 24 inches).

Width

Position all of the track and scenery within convenient reach from the edges of the layout (aisles or access hatches). This reach is about 24 inches if the benchwork is chest high, and up to 30 inches if you can bend above the layout from the hips. Do not exceed this reach distance at any part of the layout because it allows you to rerail equipment and construct and maintain both trackwork and scenery.

Other Limitations

Plan the scenery as a part of the initial plan of the railroad layout, module, or diorama. It is just as important as the track location. If done properly, it should make the track location look natural, as if the track was added as a minimum disturbance to the contours of the terrain—just as a real railroad would do.

Do not make tracks parallel to the edges of the layout or to the backdrop surfaces (if near). The same is also true of roads, streams, major buildings, etc. If possible, do not make separate track routes parallel to each other; give them some elevation separation. Observing these rules will make the layout seem larger and less toylike.

Making a "model of the model" can be a great aid in visualizing the eventual layout appearance. It does not have to be detailed, but it should accurately represent grade separation, track, roads, major buildings, and all topographic shapes and features. Also, build it so it can be easily changed to try out other ideas. It is not for display—it is to aid you in determining what you want and how best to achieve it.

SCENERY PLANNING

Scenery is the most obvious part of the model scene because anyone can see and recognize it and its apparent fidelity to reality. Yet scenery also needs to be unobvious or part of the background so that it does not dominate the scene. Avoid the trap of building scenery for its own sake, unless that is what you want to do. Scenery should relate to and contribute to the whole, just as stage scenery relates to the play but does not overwhelm it.

For a model railroad, the scenery has many functions. Overall, the purpose must be to support the reason for and operation of the railroad. It does this by creating both a setting and an illusion.

Scenery Functions

Create a setting:

- ☐ Indicate geographic region
- ☐ Indicate time era and past history
- ☐ Provide track routing rationale
- ☐ Show corporate identity and prosperity
- ☐ Provide operational orientation
- ☐ Provide a realistic entity

Create an illusion:

- ☐ Conceal distractions
- ☐ Suggest extended space and distance
- ☐ Suggest what isn't there
- ☐ Direct attention as needed
- ☐ Suggest longer track runs
- ☐ Separate areas and scenes

An obvious practical purpose of scenery is to keep derailed equipment from falling to the floor. The simplest bare plywood or plastic covering can accomplish this. This covering will also conceal nonscale distractions—hiding the benchwork, support legs, hidden tracks, and wiring. But covering should do much more.

Siting

The layout and configuration of the topography contours, the selection of rock type, and the presence and type of trees and ground cover all will indicate where the railroad is located geographically. Each region of the country has a characteristic appearance of its natural surroundings.

Similarly, but perhaps less obviously, the structural architecture of each region differs. This architecture, together with the signs, vehicles, and other man-made things, indicates the time era of the setting. Not to be ignored is the dating provided by the railroad locomotives and rolling stock itself.

Shaping

In full-scale reality, the topography and natural things precede the railroad and man-made things. The shape of the model topography relative to the man-made elements should provide a reason for why the man-made elements were located where they were. Bridges, cuts and fills, roads, etc., should be in logical places, just as they would be in the full-scale scene.

The model can only occupy a very small portion of the scale space taken by the real thing. Scenery can be used to suggest the extension of this fractional space to represent the near-infinity of the whole. This can be done in various ways. You need to apparently stretch the space you have and to suggest the space that isn't there. You can use backdrops to suggest distant scenery extending beyond the confines of your room. Selective compression of the scenery can give a false perspective that suggests distance and space.

Directing

Use view blocks to separate scenes that should be far apart but are actually quite close together on the model. Use the relative intensity of modeling the scenery to direct the eye from one well-detailed scene to another, across the relatively short intervals of fields or forests that separate them.

You can choose to model single-track right-of-way that makes the distances seem longer, space the line-side poles more closely together, operate shorter trains of shorter cars, etc.—all of which contribute to the illusion of longer distances of the track itself. You can interrupt the main line by using many short (rather than a few long) view blocks, such as bridges, tunnels, cuts and fills, foreground buildings, foliage, etc.—all designed to make the train's run seem longer.

Suggesting

Scenery can indicate the prosperity of the area and of the railroad. The condition of the trackwork and the line-side buildings, the time since paint was last applied, the repair of equipment and facilities, the relative newness versus shabbiness—all indicate how well the area and its railroad are doing. The age of the railroad equipment relative to the era being modeled will also indicate prosperity. Are the industries thriving or decaying? Is the signaling system modern or antique?

The naming of all towns, depots, industries, businesses, etc., can provide operational assistance, by giving the operators orientation as to where they and their trains are. These names can also be chosen to suggest a particular region of the country. Railroad-owned equipment usually has a unified color scheme. If the trackage and equipment of other railroads is present, separate color schemes can indicate this. If you are modeling actual prototypes, this must be done according to what the actual railroad did, of course.

Locale

The area modeled will be some mixture of urban versus rural scenery, with the rural varying between the sylvan wilderness of mountains or deserts to the cultivated farms of the plains, and the urban varying between the smallest towns and great cities. This ratio of landscape to "man-scape" will determine the amount and concentration of structures and of foliage, and the relative difficulty and need for detailing of the model.

The choices should not be made on what is easiest, of course, but rather on what operational effect is desired. The setting should provide a supporting role to the stage play, not the other way around. The choice of the region to model should also not be made on the basis of how easy the scenery is to create. Although it might seem that the deserts of the West would be easier to do than a wooded Eastern region, for the same effect and level of detail to be achieved, this is not necessarily true. All regions offer modeling challenges that require the study and time to note their distinguishing characteristics and to reproduce them in miniature.

A model of a large city can of necessity include only a portion of that city, and that must reflect the appropriately-large size of the structures and their density. Usually, it is an industrial or warehouse section that is modeled, not a region of office buildings (downtown) or of residences. The buildings can create the "mountains" and "canyons" analogous to the rustic areas, providing view blocks and all the other similar features.

Scenery Design

Make the design of the scenery an integral part of the design of the track layout. In real life, nature has provided the scenery—with its mountains and hills, its valleys and streams, and covered it with some blending of foliage. Into this untouched Eden, the railroad civil engineers came with the sole purpose of putting a railroad through from one point to another, at the lowest possible overall cost.

The lowest cost is not just the cost to blast the rocks, build the bridges, grade the roadbed, and lay the track, but also the operation costs thereafter. These operating costs include the maintenance costs and the cost of fuel and water and extra transit time spent. A lower average grade might soon pay for extra bridges and tunnels. A shorter mileage might be worth more cut and fill. Cut and fill will cost less to maintain than tunnels and trestles.

The railroad can be built quickly and less well, but it seldom stays that way. Economics causes changes to be made. The grades are reduced, the curves are broadened, trestles are replaced, and the weight and quality of the track are improved. How you model your railroad also indicates where your railroad exists in this process of evolution.

You must remember that the purpose of prototype railroads is to make money by moving commodities and people from one place to another. Nothing is done that does not contribute to that goal. Unless prevented from doing so by the government, the railroads will abandon any trains or services that do not provide revenue in excess of expenses.

For the model railroad, the practicalities of economics are not the same, but because you wish to model the real thing, you must understand the driving considerations that led to what it is you are trying to model, even if imaginary, so that your result will have the look and feel of realism.

Track Plans

The usual approach to planning is to draw a number of different scale track plans, trying to fit your desires into the (always) too-limited space available to you. Tracks are moved around, sidings relocated, the radii of curves changed, and efforts are made to shoehorn too much into the area you have.

If you have read and taken to heart the lessons taught in the layout and track planning articles and books, then you will eventually come up with a good track plan that avoids the "don't do's" and is not a "bowl of spaghetti" layout, but a plan of a railroad that is trying to get from one place to another just like the real one.

The plan will look entirely different than our original try, and it will be a good compromise between what you thought you wanted and what you can have because of the limitations of space. It takes several versions of plans to arrive at something that is worth building. The biggest mistake is always to try to put too much into too small a space. The next biggest mistake is to be too ambitious and try to do too much, or make the model too large, so that you risk losing interest and never having a chance to get it into operation.

Features of Good Track Plans

All good track plans will have the same positive features.

- ☐ Adequate horizontal separation between different routes
- ☐ Different routes suggested by tracks that are
  - ■ not parallel to each other
  - ■ at slightly different elevations
- ☐ Adequate space for structures and roads
- ☐ Good reasons for any hidden track
- ☐ Adequate access to all track
- ☐ A logical progression of the track through the scene
- ☐ Incorporation of integral scenery planning

Integral scenery planning is very important. If scenery is added as an afterthought, then the scene will not look realistic. There must be reasons for the hills and valleys, mountains and canyons, washes and streams, or they will look artificial rather than natural. Scenery planning must be simultaneous with the track layout planning. It is neither more nor less important, but by planning together, the entire effect can be unified and will seem right. The result should look like the natural scenery that preceded the railroad and improvements.

Topography

Topography is generally three dimensional. It has height as well as length and breadth. On the track plan, which is two dimensional, you can indicate track elevations by circled numbers along the track. On the same plan, show major scenery features along with their elevations. Sketch all roads, streets, and major structures to scale. Show all rivers, streams, and water courses together with the bridges that span them.

Show the general topography of the region, using rough contours to indicate the hills, mountains, valleys, cliffs, and other features. Indicate all cuts and fills. Locate tunnels along with portals, show necessary retaining walls. Sketch in the general layout of foliage, at least for major tree groups. Colored pencils might be an aid in visualizing different features: brown for topography, blue for water, green for foliage, etc. Make the plan as large a scale as possible, preferably an integral fractional size of the layout-to-be.

Show the backdrop. If possible, do not let the scenery abut the backdrop. It will be helpful to draw several cross sections through the layout to confirm the general contours and to check on the sight lines and the accessibility of all areas.

If you understand how to make it, the best drawing would be similar to a topographic map, with constant elevation contour lines drawn in. The best way to confirm the track and scenery layout is to build a smaller scale model of the layout (a "model of a model"), using modeling clay or other material that is easy to work with and change. This model can greatly aid in visualizing the eventual layout, avoiding painful and costly mistakes. Make this model no larger than 2 or 3 feet across.

Scenic Faults to Avoid

There are several scenic compromises or impossibilities that you can avoid by proper planning.

- ☐ Streams that have no exit or that flow uphill
- ☐ Long, high retaining walls to separate tracks that are too close together
- ☐ Excessive mainline in tunnels that do not contribute to length of run or scenic purpose
- ☐ Trick tunnels where one is left to guess where the train will emerge
- ☐ Towns or structures located on steep slopes when flatter areas are available
- ☐ Lack of natural or artificial drainage channels
- ☐ Excessive grade on streets or roads

Uniformity

Do not plan scenery that is too spectacular. You will tire of it, it will constantly require explaining, and it detracts from the overall effect. A certain amount of monotony is desirable. Scenes should blend into each other with a geological similarity and a slow change between them. A blandness in these bridging portions will make the more-detailed scenes more interesting. Complete boredom is just as bad.

Consider future photographic possibilities in the planning. What scenes will nicely compose a photo? Where can you place the camera and lighting? What will be seen in the background? Is there a place where a long train can be photographed?

Special Effects

Tunnels require special consideration. Too many of them, without justification, are bad. Use short tunnels as view blocks and to separate scenes. Use longer tunnels primarily as holding tracks, staging tracks, hidden yards, etc., because they hide what you ordinarily want to show—your operating trains. Bridges and overpasses can fulfill many of the same view blocking functions as short tunnels.

Scenery constructed all the way to the floor can be very dramatic, but it has disadvantages as well. It is damage prone and can restrict access. It also is only representative of locales where the track is situated part way up the side of deep canyons.

Scenery constructed all the way to the ceiling (or beyond) can hide building support posts, but use it only where it is appropriate to the geographic area. Tall buildings in an urban setting can be used in the same way.

Use mirrors to extend the apparent size of the area and to give the illusion of longer yards or continuing track. Plan them to reflect nothing but the model scene (never lights or the observer) and to always be at right angles to any tracks or roads or structures that they are to reflect. Keep them very clean to be effective, which requires some provision for access or (preferably) removal for cleaning.

Backdrops

Backdrops are very important to hide visual clutter, add depth to the scene, and suggest scenery or structures that are not modeled. Do not make the backdrop too spectacular; paint it in muted colors to suggest distance. Plan it so that no shadows fall on it. If possible, separate the backdrop from the three-dimensional scenery by a gap of a few inches. Use this gap to provide lighting on the backdrop from below, automatically making the lower portion lighter and eliminating any chance of shadows.

If the gap is not possible, then blend the three-dimensional scenery into the backdrop. Hide the joint by the allowed viewing aspect or by foliage, structures, bridges, etc. An examination of museum dioramas will give several ideas on how

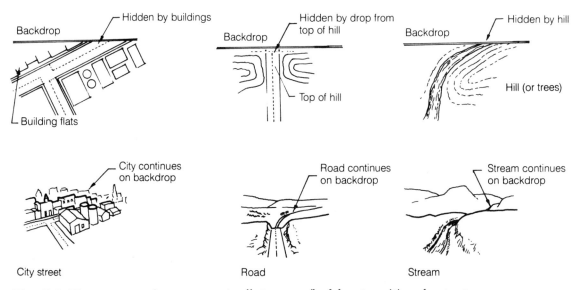

Fig. 13-2. *There are several proper ways to effect scenery/backdrop transitions for streets, roads, and streams.*

to do this. Generally, roads or streets continuing directly onto the backdrop do not work well because the perspective looks right only from one vantage point (FIG. 13-2). Curve or cove corners of the backdrop; similar coving at the ceiling/wall joints is usually not worthwhile. Plan lighting so that it will illuminate the backdrop uniformly, but not at high intensity.

Track Scenery

The track is a very important element of the scenery. In the larger sense, the degree of curves, curve easements, and super elevation can suggest the era and railroad prosperity. More closely, the size of rail, its condition; the size, spacing, and condition of ties; and the color and condition of ballast; all give indications of the class and financial condition of the railroad. You can also use the latter features to distinguish between main line and branch line, siding and yards, and between different railroads that are adjacent.

Make allowances for proper track drainage (ditches). The ballast must be the proper size, width, and depth, with appropriate contour and slope on the sides. Cut and fill slopes must be at realistic angles or with only slight exaggeration. Ditches exist even through areas of cut.

The smaller rail sizes will look better, but their choice is a compromise with the difficulty of track laying and the possible operational problems that might occur with small rail height. Rail that has been darkened on the sides will look smaller. Prefabricated, or sectional, track has adequate detail (with a little additional work) to satisfy all but the most fastidious modeler.

Hand-laid track is a luxury that should only be indulged if no other option is available, or if extremely fine track detailing is desired in the foreground. Some people have been known to go overboard on hand-laying track, even putting it through tunnels and in locations so far from the observers that binoculars would be necessary to see it.

Buildings

Choose buildings of a size and type to fit in with the era and geographic region of the railroad. They must also suit the size and prosperity of the town or city being modeled. Interconnect buildings by streets and roads, and city buildings by sidewalks as well. Buildings seldom occur in isolation. They almost always exist in groups of some sort, with the individual buildings having some relationship to each other.

In a town, the buildings should reflect the different businesses that might exist. This should include the proper mixture of shops of various types, grocery stores, cafes, professional services, etc. Not all the buildings will necessarily contribute freight traffic to your railroad.

Sometimes entire blocks of buildings were built at the same time and have common materials and architectures. In other places, the buildings date from different years, with newly built ones appearing among the older specimens. Some regions of a city might include derelict or burned-out buildings. Some buildings might be modeled as though under construction.

Modeling what "isn't there" can also be very effective. This can include vacant lots and places where buildings have been removed (FIG. 13-3).

Fig. 13-3. A demolished building still leaves its mark behind.

The depots and freight houses should reflect the size of the town. The engine servicing facilities should reflect the size of the yard and the type and size of the engines that would be serviced.

RESOURCES

Unfortunately, you probably cannot devote your full time to your hobby. Unless you are rich, you are also limited in the money you can spend. Because you are human, your wishes will always be greater than your resources.

How can you scope what you try to do to the actual time and money you have available? If you do not suit your wishes to your capabilities, then this will be a constant frustration.

Besides a lack of resources of time/money, you also probably lack the skills necessary to create the perfection you seek in your model. Skills can be learned, of course, and practice will make you better, but you might not be an artist or fine craftsman . . . at least not in all the many talents needed for model railroading. You can probably realistically never expect to really master any but a very few skills. If you are not careful, this can be another frustration.

Frustration is the last thing you need in your hobby. There is enough of that in the real world. This hobby is supposed to help you relax and bring pleasure.

My Hobby—Frustration . . . or Pleasure?

Negative approach:

- ☐ I don't have enough time.
- ☐ I can't afford the money.
- ☐ I don't know how to do things.
- ☐ I am too clumsy.
- ☐ My results aren't good enough.

Positive approach:

- ☐ My hobby is for my relaxation.
- ☐ It is my temporary refuge from the world.
- ☐ I will do the best I can with what . . .
  - ■ time I have,
  - ■ money I can afford,
  - ■ knowledge I possess, and
  - ■ skills I have acquired.
- ☐ I will share the joy of my hobby with others.

The solution is to look for the positives in what you do, in the skills you have, in what you have accomplished. Avoid the negatives of too much to do, too little money, too clumsy, too untrained, or too whatever. No one is perfect, and neither is our work, either as vocation or avocation.

You should always have an *ideal* of perfection in what is done, but be willing to accept doing things that are less than perfect. This compromise between doing only one thing and trying (but never being able) to do it perfectly, and doing everything but doing nothing well is called the art of "good enough."

"Good enough" is getting the proper balance between the results needed and the time and money taken to achieve the results. It is knowing what is important and what isn't. It is knowing where corners can be cut and where they shouldn't be. It is knowing where additional effort will result in diminishing returns of results.

What is "good enough" will vary with each of us because everyone has different goals and different things are important. You must march to your own cadence and make your own rules.

Good Enough

- Don't include details that can't be seen because of
  - hidden sides or view angle,
  - distance,
  - obscuration.
- Only include major items of detail as the first priority.
- Don't try to do more than you can do.
- Suit what you do to the trade between result versus cost of time and money.

14

Benchwork

Benchwork is defined here to include not only the framing of the layout and the construction of the roadbed, but also the construction and painting of the backdrop, the construction of the front boards, and the use of mirrors, if any.

FRAMING

The single best guide to planning and building benchwork is the book, *How to Build Model Railroad Benchwork*, by Linn Westcott. This book features a construction method using L-girder benchwork, which has proven to be low cost, strong, and amenable to later changes.

This handbook will not cover the basic construction of the framing. Take the advice given in the reference and use wood screws rather than nails for fasteners. Make sure all of these screws are accessible from underneath. Things will inevitably change, and the first such change will more than pay for the extra cost and time taken using the wood screws.

ROADBED

How to Build Model Railroad Benchwork is also a very good guide to the choices and methods for working with trackwork base materials. The base consists of a sub-base called *roadbed*, and the ballast board or strip. The added ballast on the model is a surface covering only, filling in around the ties and spilling down the slope of the ballast board (FIG. 14-1).

On a prototype railroad, the roadbed is graded much as a highway would be. It is contoured for drainage, slightly raised in the center, and has ditches at the

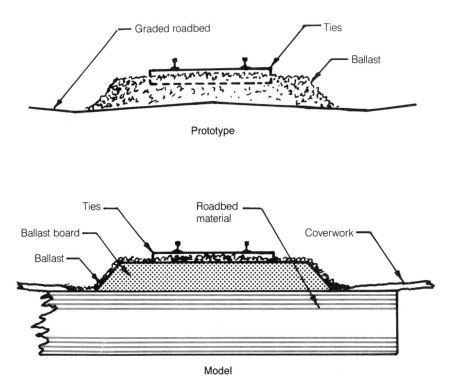

Graded roadbed — Ties

Ballast

Prototype

Ties — Roadbed material

Ballast board — Coverwork

Ballast —

Model

Fig. 14-1. The model roadbed contours are designed to simulate those of the prototype.

sides, even when it runs through cuts. On flat land, the roadbed is always raised above the surrounding terrain.

Ballast is used on top of the roadbed to hold the ties in place and, most important, to allow drainage away from the ties and rail. The ballast consists of crushed rock, gravel, or cinders of some type obtainable near or from the railroad. Prototype ballast might range from 9 to 24 inches in depth. It is usually crowned, ranging from even with the tie tops in the center of the track, to 2 inches below that at the tie ends, and sloping down from there.

On the model, the roadbed provides the proper elevation and approximate curvature and gives the necessary strength to the ballast board. The roadbed can be made of plywood, framing lumber, or (preferably) paperboard such as Homosote and Upson board. These products might be difficult to find at lumberyards, but some model railroad hobby shops now supply Homosote. Make the roadbed wider than the ballast board to keep a proper overall contour and to support the adjoining scenery.

The ties and rail (trackwork) must be supported by the ballast board, which simulates the thickness of the ballast and is attached to the top of the subbase. (This is sometimes improperly called the roadbed.) The ballast board must be firm so that it will not warp or expand or contract excessively. Unless spikes will not be used, the material should be soft enough to easily allow you to push spikes, small nails, or brads into it, and be firm enough to hold them in place. There are several possible choices.

Wood

Use the softer grades of basswood, white or sugar pine, or redwood. You can sometimes get these as precut molding at lumberyards. Alternatively, you could saw them to thickness and size yourself. Cut the thickness to about 1/4 inch for the smaller scales and possibly twice that for 0 scale and up. The width should correspond to the ballast width. Bevel the shoulders at an angle to form the ballast contour.

A company named Tru-Scale makes a milled wood product in HO and N scales of proper contour. This is available both with and without ties/tie plates milled in. It is available in straight, curved (2-inch increments of radius), turnout, and flexible configurations.

Paperboard

Paperboard is the best and most economical material to use. Either Homosote or Upson board are recommended. Homosote is now available precut from at least one supplier. Cutting is easy with power tools (skill saw or saber saw), but sawing creates a lot of fluffy "sawdust" that floats around and should not be inhaled. Use a knife blade in a saber saw. This will cut without creating sawdust, but it is slower.

Some people have experienced shrinkage with paperboard if the material had been stored in areas of high humidity. As with wood, the proper width and beveled shoulders are important. The material called Celotex is too soft to hold spikes.

Cork

Cork ballast strip consists of ground cork particles rebonded together with glue. It is made in both N and HO scales. It comes as a strip with a partially completed angled cut down the middle. To use it, cut it apart and abut the square-cut edges down the track centerline. The angle of the cut creates the shoulder bevel. Cork will not reliably hold spikes, and it should not be used except with sectional track that does not require spiking. It it flexible enough to be formed around curves.

Harder Materials

If harder materials are used as ballast board, then a method of rail attachment that does not require driving spikes or nails must be employed.

Softer Materials

A new product, named Instant Roadbed, is available. It is a soft, somewhat tacky material that comes in 2-inch widths and 30-foot rolls. It is pressed in place, and the sectional track is pressed into it. Ballast, lightly pressed on, completes the installation. It can also be used effectively to simulate roads and pavement. It has some sound-deadening qualities.

Formed Ballast Board

In some scales, formed strips of molded plastic ballast material are available. One type has a trough molded in to hold ready-made track. Another type has the ties molded in and you attach the rails. A third is like the second, but with the rails already attached. These products can save some of the work, but at a considerable increase in cost. Some added ballast and final detailing is still necessary for the best appearance.

Whatever the materials, the ballast board must offer the proper curvature for the track, and it is essential that it provide the proper vertical profile, with no dips or humps or abrupt changes in gradient. If you want superelevation, provide it by shimming between the roadbed and the ballast board or between the ballast board and the ties. The resulting track and operation will be no smoother than the roadbed and ballast board have provided.

Prior to laying any track, mark the centerline and lines marking the tie ends on the ballast board.

BACKDROP

The backdrop is the vertical surface mounted behind the three-dimensional scenery. It is used to represent the distant scenery that cannot be modeled because of the constraints of space. The backdrop represents the sky, clouds (if used), and distant hills and mountains, forests, and fields.

The backdrop also hides things that should not be seen, such as room walls, furnaces and water heaters, and other human faces. Even the simplest backdrop, painted light blue, will suffice to add realism by hiding these nonscale things.

Use backdrops behind layouts, modules, or dioramas; use them in the middle of layouts to serve as view blocks from one side to the other. They can be flat or curve around the vertical axis. Do not let seams show; gently curve them around both inside and outside corners so that no unsightly shadows can be seen. Curving the backdrop into the ceiling is not required.

If at all possible, install the layout backdrops at the beginning of construction because you need ready access to it to paint it and blend it with the three-dimensional scenery, which will come later. You can add backdrops for modules or dioramas at any time.

Material

The backdrop material can be hardboard, such as tempered Masonite, or other smooth, bendable material. The thickness should be 1/8 inch or greater. Provide support so the backdrop does not twist, bend, or deform. Some people have used linoleum floor runners, but they are not recommended because they tend to sag somewhat and form unwanted bends and dips that will catch the light and not look as good as it should.

Excellent backdrops can be made from drywall material. The 1/4-inch thickness is adequate, and it is less expensive and easier to handle and bend than thicker panels. The panels come in 4-×-8-foot sizes. Firmly nail the panels to the wall or a framework with nails every 6 to 8 inches. Cover the seams with tape and drywall joint filler.

Panels can be curved for corners. A recommended corner radius is 2 feet. Design so that there are tangent sections on each side of the curved portion. Wet both sides of the panel completely, using a sponge. Nail one tangent section, then bend the curve and nail the other tangent section to hold the bend while the panel dries.

If there is room, you can separate the backdrop and the back edge of the three-dimensional scenery a few inches. Add shadow-eliminating lights that shine upward, through the gap, onto the backdrop. Shape the back edge of the three-dimensional scenery so that no transition can be seen.

Use a damp sponge to smooth the panel surface where seams or nail holes were filled. After drying, do a final sanding. Check to see how flat the surface is by shining a light along the panel. Give the entire surface a coat of white or very light blue latex paint as a primer before starting to paint anything else on it.

Painting

A painted backdrop can be as simple or elaborate as you wish to make it, or as your artistic ability will allow. The backdrop does not have to be highly detailed and artistically exciting to be effective. You do not have to be an artist, but you do have to follow a few basics.

Entire books could be written on the subject of backdrop painting because it is, after all, landscape painting that is being done. This topic just outlines some of the principles involved and mentions the do's and don'ts that will optimize your success.

Basics

First, a few basics on perspective. Things appear smaller and lighter in color as they are farther away because of the haze in the air and the fact that you are looking through more air. Things lose definition and sharpness as they are farther away because they are smaller and "fuzzier" and because there are limits to the resolution of your eyesight. Finally, and obviously, things that are closer will hide things that are farther away and behind them.

Basics of Backdrop Painting

☐ Mute all colors on the backdrop more than the colors on the adjacent three-dimensional scenery.

- [ ] None of the backdrop has to be very detailed. Decrease the detail with the suggested distance.
- [ ] Make everything on the backdrop smaller in size than the adjacent three-dimensional scenery.
- [ ] Decrease the apparent size of objects as the suggested distance to them increases.
- [ ] Paint things farther away first, so that closer objects can be painted easily to overlap them.
- [ ] Paint the backdrop after the layout lighting is installed so that the colors will remain true.

Horizon

You will need to establish where the horizon will be. The *horizon* is the line where, in flat country, the sky and land meet. At whatever height you stand, it is always at eye level. Even though you might not be showing flat country on the backdrop, you will still need to establish the horizon line. Make it the same height as the average eye height of yourself and other spectators. Either painted or three dimensional scenery, such as hills and mountains, can and will extend above the horizon. Foreground scenery will also often be below the horizon.

You will need to plan what you are going to paint on the backdrop, then draw it on using light pencil lines. You might be able to do this from photos or from your imagination, but by far the easiest way is to obtain 35-mm slides of scenes you like, then project them directly on the wall. By moving the projector around, farther and closer, etc., and by trying a number of different slides, you can surely find some that are perfect for the locations you have.

Be sure that the scenes on the backdrop blend in with the planned three dimensional scenery. They should have the same geological and topographic character. Make sure the horizon on the slide, which you might have to guess, matches that on the wall. Generally, you will want to choose scenes that have 2/3 to 3/4 of the scene below the horizon. The most usable slides will have been taken on a level, or at a slightly downward camera angle, and usually from a hill or rise. Fortunately, most slides of scenery fill these requirements.

Also, consider the sun angle in the photos. Be sure that it is consistent with what you want and that it is the same for all photos used. The sun angle will determine the shadow patterns of the painted scenery. Note also that slides can be reversed in the projector to give what might be a better fit to your requirements.

Sky

Paint the sky color first, blending the color from light blue at the top to nearly white at the bottom. You might wish to use a roller for this. Ordinary indoor latex flat wall paint is ideal for this and offers the lowest cost. Any further painting of clouds, mountains, hills, trees, etc. should use the same kind of paint. Such details as are added can be in artist's acrylic paints. At this point you have created the minimum painted backdrop.

Clouds

Clouds painted on the backdrop can be very effective . . . or they can look totally artificial. If you are in doubt of your ability to paint the clouds, leave them out. There are always some clear, cloudless days everywhere. If you decide to add clouds, then you need to know something about them.

Clouds consist of moisture in vapor form. Clouds of the same type tend to stay at a consistent altitude on any given day. Most of us will prefer to paint the cottony cumulus clouds, which billow up on sunny days and form the most pleasing appearance. These clouds are white, with shadows that are light gray or light gray-blue. The thinnest clouds will show sky and sunlight through them. The thick ones will be quite opaque and will cast shadows on themselves and other clouds. The edges are usually sharp but ragged and not fuzzy or wispy. The bottoms of the clouds tend to be a little flatter than the tops. There can be a considerable range in the size of the clouds.

Clouds that are almost overhead will show mostly their shadowed undersides. Those a little farther away will show more of their sides and tops and less of their undersides. They will partially overlap those clouds even farther away. The clouds will become slightly more blue with distance, and their shadows will be weaker and less gray. The farthest clouds will look smaller, will seem to be more closely spaced, will overlap each other to a considerable extent. These clouds, because of the distance, will be very pale and indistinct.

Cloud Painting. Paint the farthest clouds first. Decide which direction the sun will be coming from. Keep this consistent throughout the backdrop. Decide on the location and size of the nearer clouds. They should neither dominate the scene nor be so small as to be invisible. Perhaps 2 to 3 three feet long is about right for the larger ones. It is difficult to paint clouds with a brush. Use either irregularly shaped sponges or pieces of foam rubber, or an airbrush with stencils.

If you use the sponges, twist and turn them between daubing applications so that repetitive patterns are avoided. Do the white first, then add the shadows with a different, smaller sponge. Let the nearer clouds slightly overlap the tops of the farther ones. The highest (nearest) clouds should simulate real clouds in the middle distance because you will be seeing them only 30 to 40 degrees above the horizon.

Cloud Stencils. You can use an airbrush freehand to paint clouds, if you are careful. It is probably better to make up some simple stencils that can be used to define the edges of the clouds. Stencils only have to be made for the tops of the clouds. They can then be turned over and used for the bottoms, as well. It is easiest to make the stencils the right profile if you project slides of clouds onto the tagboard or stencil paper, tracing the outline. Make four or five different stencils.

Cut out the stencils with a sharp knife. Tape the stencil to the wall and spray the top white part first. Start with the farthest clouds, then paint the bottom with a different stencil and the white paint. For the next closer clouds, use white paint for the top, but add a little gray to the white for the bottom. Continue adding clouds, overlapping the first ones and on toward the nearer ones, making the bottoms of the clouds more gray as you go.

Be careful that the paint is mixed thick enough to spray but not to run. The clouds can be made less distinct by holding the stencil an inch or so away from the wall. Be sure to add body and internal billows to the clouds by alternating stencils and white and the proper shade of gray.

With the clouds completed, you are at another point where you can stop and still have an acceptable appearing backdrop. The next steps, should you add them, are slightly more difficult but add a great deal to the effect.

Landscape

The landscape consists of the hills and mountains, fields and forests, valleys, lakes, and towns. The farthest portions of the landscape are painted first in the lightest, most pastel or grayest, shades. The landscape can be painted with brushes, sponges, or with an airbrush using stencils. Use flat, latex, or acrylic paints.

Starting with the most distant, paint the main areas, using the single most-evident color. For each area, add shadows in a darker shade of the same color. Add rock formations, forests, and snow fields (if any) in their colors. Add shadows to these features in darker shades of their colors. All the features should be indistinct.

Repeat this process for the next nearer areas, with the colors used slightly less subdued and the details slightly sharper. Give some suggestion of shape to the tree masses. The nearer area can overlap the farther one. Continue this process up to the nearest range of hills/mountains/trees, etc. For these, make the colors just a little more muted than they will be for the most-distant three-dimensiomal scenery. The nearest trees can almost be painted individually and can have some "see through" characteristics.

Add highlighting on the "sunny" side of objects, particularly for the closer areas. Use lighter shades of the same colors. Paint in any buildings or roads last. If in doubt as to your artistic ability, the less shadowing and detail added, the safer you are.

You can paint a simple (and very effective) landscape by using only silhouetted "ranges" of hills, painted in pastel colors. Make everything look as if it is viewed through a haze.

Use stencils for the main landscape areas, much the same as they are for clouds. They are most effective for mountain scenery, distant tree lines, etc. An artist can also use an airbrush freehand to do the painting, but that is beyond this description.

Forests

Keep tree shapes in distant forests very indistinct. A sponge, cut into small triangular pieces, can make good paint daubers to create the shapes of trees in distant evergreen forests. Paint nearer individual trees only if you are very sure of yourself. Make sure they are smaller than the three-dimensional trees nearest them.

Smoke

If you want to add smoke from distant factories, keep the effect subtle. Make sure that all the smoke, and any flags, all are going the same direction. Avoid painting airplanes or balloons on the sky unless you are sure you won't tire of them.

Buildings

Unless you are an artist, it is usually not a good idea to attempt to paint buildings, roads, or individual trees on the backdrop. It is difficult to capture the proper perspective, and the results can easily look worse than if these things were not included. Avoid buildings in perspective because they will only look right from one viewing point.

Haze

You can add atmospheric haze or smog by overspraying lightly with a semitransparent white flat latex or acrylic paint. Do not use too much. The object is to slightly blend and soften the backdrop colors and to help the backdrop scene to fade even more into the background.

Printed Backdrops

Photomurals can be used as backdrops, but their use is not recommended both because of the expense and because they are usually too detailed. The features depicted are also too large and out of scale.

Printed paper scenic material for backdrops is sold by several companies. These can be mounted directly to the backdrop material using wallpaper paste or rubber cement. They come in separate scenes, each several inches long, that depict city, country, and mountain vistas. They are designed so each scene flows relatively smoothly into the next one, in any order. Put them up temporarily with masking tape to be sure of the fit and confirm that you like the effect, prior to final mounting.

These paper backdrop scenes are often more effective if they are carefully cut out along the top so that you can use the sky painted on your backdrop. The height of the paper ranges from $8^1/2$ to 22 inches, so if your sky is higher than that, you will have to blend your sky into that of the scenes. An even more effective method is to cut them out, mount them to thin Masonite, and locate them slightly in front of the backdrop proper. By cutting out the scenes, you can recombine them in any order to suit your needs.

Cutouts

For urban backgrounds, you can integrate cutouts, or flats, of buildings with actually modeled buildings. The modeled buildings can reach all the way to the cutouts, which can either be placed on or slightly in front of the backdrop. There are some precautions to observe, however, to preserve the illusion.

The tops of both the modeled and cutout buildings should be above eye level. The cutout buildings should be lower than the modeled buildings, and all cutout buildings must have identical heights. The heights of the modeled buildings can vary above the minimum. Streets or alleys perpendicular to the backdrop should only "look into" another modeled or cutout building.

You can give the cutout buildings the illusion of different heights by using different window spacing and treatment, by varying floor heights, and by varying the cornices and trim. Detail the cutout buildings in relief to improve the realism. The modeled buildings should have detail such as chimneys, stacks, water tanks, small structures, etc.

Backdrop Options

In order of increasing effectiveness—and difficulty:

☐ Sky alone
☐ Sky, with clouds
☐ Sky, with silhouetted, pastel hills
☐ Sky, with hazy landscape
☐ Sky, with printed or cutout scenes
☐ Sky, with fully detailed landscape

FRONT BOARDS

Cover the edges of the layout or module with a suitable material along the front and along aisles. This enhances the appearance and can serve other purposes, such as providing mounting space for control panels, space for a shelf for ashtrays, drinks, elbows, routing cards, etc. These finished edges are called *front boards* or (*faschia*).

The front boards can be planar or curved to conform to the aisle's shape. They can be made of smooth hardboard, such as tempered Masonite, or similar materials. Firmly screw the front boards to the framing members of the layout or module. They must be strong enough to take the inevitable bumps and pressures that they will endure from the spectators.

You can profile the top edge to match the contour of the adjoining terrain. Bring the base covering (see "Coverwork," chapter 16) up to the front board and attach it using wooden blocks screwed to the inside of the front board to support the plaster. This lends strength to the scenery, which should be made extra strong in this area. The effect is that of a smooth slice taken out of the earth's surface.

Add shelves, if desired. Cut in or extend control panels from the front boards. The front boards can be added at any time, but it is probably best to add them during the basic construction, but do not trim the top profiles until the scenery contours are nearly complete. Do this final trimming with a power saber saw (FIG. 14-2).

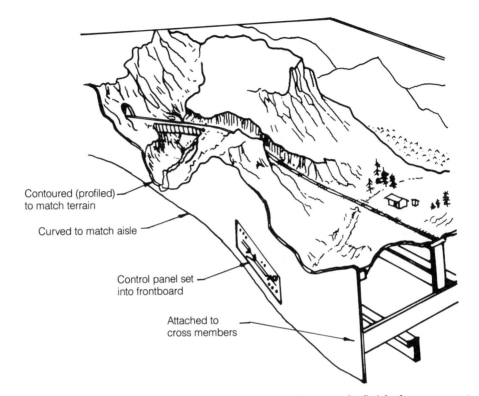

Fig. 14-2. Frontboards, contoured along the top, provide a smooth, finished appearance to the layout edges.

Paint the front boards in some dark neutral color, or in a color that complements the room. The idea is to not detract from the layout. A front board painted with the earth's strata showing is another idea, which carries the idea of the "slice through the earth" to a logical conclusion.

It should also be noted that adding skirts or curtains or cabinetry to the area underneath the layout to hide the clutter is a feature that will enhance the total appearance. Set these curtains back from the front boards by several inches to allow foot and knee room.

It is sometimes desirable to provide a plexiglass or acrylic plastic safety barrier above the front board. This might be done for modules or for layouts that will be subjected to frequent public viewing. It will keep little hands away. Such safety barriers are probably best made so that they are removable and so they fit into slots/grooves formed into a strip running near the top of the front boards. This makes them easier to clean and to remove when they are not needed. The plastic material can be ¹/₈ inch thick and 10 to 12 inches high. This, and other edge treatments, are shown in FIG. 14-3.

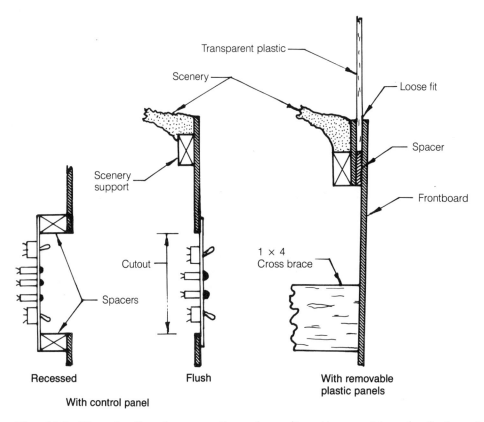

Fig. 14-3. *These frontboard cross sections show alternative provisions for flush and recessed control panels, and for protective plastic panels.*

Scenery to the floor, which is another form of edge treatment, can be highly dramatic, as John Allen and others have shown. It has several disadvantages that should be kept in mind, however. It takes more space because the slope cannot be vertical if it is to look natural. It is much more subject to damage, not just from spectators but from accidents that you might have. The lighting is more difficult because it is farther from the lights and because the shadows of spectators will sometimes get in the way. There might be nothing to stop your prized locomotive from hitting the floor if it derails. You must still provide toe space and kick boards at the bottom. In general, it is not something to be used, except on very large layouts.

MIRRORS

John Allen was the originator and master of the use of mirrors in expanding the horizons of a layout. Little new has been discovered in the over 20 years since he developed the basic principles.

If used properly, mirrors can double the apparent size of portions of the layout. They can be used so that almost no one will notice that a mirror is present.

On the other hand, if improperly used, the mirror is obvious and the illusion is lost. It all depends on how well the application rules are followed.

The mirrors must be planned into the layout from the beginning. It is almost impossible to add them later if they were not a part of the original planning. All mirrors must also be designed so they are accessible for cleaning. This can sometimes best be done by removal from below.

Never place a mirror so you can see yourself, other persons, or other full-sized nonmodel railroad objects (such as lights) in it. Do not place a mirror where the viewer will be able to see both a moving train and its reflection at the same time. An exception is for stub yards, where the tracks meet the mirror at a 90-degree angle.

A mirror reflects an image at an angle double that angle between the object and a line normal (at 90 degrees) to the plane of the mirror. Because of this, the mirrors must be absolutely vertical. The ground adjacent to the mirror should meet the mirror surface at a 90-degree angle. Tracks or roads should meet the mirror surface at only 90-degree angles. Place scenery or structures near the mirror either parallel to or at right angles to the mirror surface.

The mirrors should be of plate glass of good quality and should not be discolored. Because the mirrors are surfaced on the reverse side, the thinner the mirror, the better. Never place the mirror where strong light shines on it because this will accentuate any surface dust or dirt.

Mirrors placed below eye level usually work best. If they are extended above eye level, they might show things, such as lights, that should not be seen. Hide the sides and tops of the mirrors in some logical manner. Overlap the sides all the way to the top edge by modeled objects such as buildings or mountains. The top is most difficult to hide. This can sometimes be done by using a bridge or walkway below eye level to hide the top, or by painting clouds or smoke onto the mirror and backdrop to hide the transition between the two.

15

Trackwork

Trackwork consists of the ties, rails, and ballast, which for the model is on top of the ballast board and roadbed base. All of the electrical wiring for the track should also be completed at this step. Electrical wiring is not covered in this handbook, but a good guidebook is *How to Wire Your Model Railroad* by Linn Westcott.

TRACKLAYING

In general, there are two types of track that can be used: ready to lay and hand-spiked. Model rail is referred to by a code number that is the height of the rail in thousandths of an inch. Although there is now a fairly wide variety of sizes of both rail and ready-to-lay track available, only a few sizes exist for each scale.

The rail weight that was used by the prototype varied by the era, the prosperity of the railroad, and by the type of traffic the rails had to carry. The same railroad would use different rail weights, suiting the size to the speed and tonnage traveling over those rails. The main line would use the heaviest rail, with passing sidings, branch lines, industrial sidings, and yards using smaller rail.

On your model you can, within limitations of availability, choose the rail size to convey this same information. You can use light rail on narrow gauge lines and branches, medium on sidings and yards, and the largest for the mainline. Smaller rail will tend to look better, but larger rail will provide more reliable operation unless you are extremely careful with your wheel flange heights and profiles.

TABLE 15-1 shows the theoretical model rail scale height versus the corresponding prototype rail weight, by scale. For the generally available model rail codes, the closest equivalent model scale rail weight versus the rail code is shown

Table 15-1. *Scale Rail Height vs. Prototype Rail Weight*

Prototype		Model-Scale Height (in)					
lb/yd	Height (in)	N	TT	HO	S	1/4″	O
156	7³/₄	.049	.065	.089	.121	.162	.172
140	7⁵/₁₆	.046	.061	.084	.114	.152	.163
132	7¹/₈	.045	.059	.082	.111	.148	.158
115	6⁵/₈	.041	.055	.076	.104	.138	.148
100	6	.038	.050	.069	.094	.125	.133
90	5⁵/₈	.035	.047	.065	.088	.117	.125
80	5	.031	.042	.057	.078	.104	.111
70	4⁵/₈	.029	.039	.053	.072	.096	.103
60	4¹/₄	.027	.035	.049	.066	.089	.094
50	3⁷/₈	.024	.032	.046	.061	.081	.086
40	3¹/₂	.022	.029	.040	.055	.073	.078

in TABLE 15-2. The appearance of rail height can also be reduced by proper coloring of the rails (see "Ballasting," this chapter).

Ready-to-lay track is bought in sections with the rails already attached to the ties. The tie material is usually a plastic or fibrous material. The rail is attached to the ties by metal fasteners or by molded lugs (simulating spikes). This type of track is also sometimes called *sectional*.

Table 15-2. *Available Scale Rail*

	Closest Scale Weight (lb/yd)					
Rail Code	N	TT	HO	S	1/4″	O
172					156	156
148					132	115
125				156	100	90
100			156	115	75	70
83			132	90	55	50
70		156	100	65	35	
55	156	115	75	40		
40	115	75	40			

You can buy ready-to-lay track in most of the popular scales and gauges, with some choice in rail size. Some sectional track is only available in fixed radii, but most can be formed to suit any radius of curvature.

Hand-spiked, or *hand-laid*, track uses wooden ties that are bonded to the ballast board. The rails are then spiked to the ties. Turnouts and crossings, etc., can be bought prefabricated and ready to spike to the ties or they can be built from scratch. The range of rail sizes that can be used for hand-spiked track is fairly large.

It is quite difficult, or impossible, to hand-spike Z or N scale. Such small rail can be used by either bonding the rail to the ties using contact cement or by soldering the rail to ties made of printed circuit board material.

This handbook does not cover the design and fabrication of built-from-scratch turnouts, etc. This subject is covered in *Trackwork Handbook* by Paul Mallory, or in any of the many magazine articles that have appeared on the subject.

Use hand-spiked track where you believe the extra realism is worth the labor involved, or where the desired track scale/gauge/rail size is not available in ready-to-lay form. The two types of track can, of course, be combined on different parts of the same layout. The methods used for laying track are entirely different for ready-to-lay track than they are for hand-spiked track, but the preparation of the roadbed and the ballast board is the same.

Ready-to-Lay Track

There are at least four ways to secure ready-to-lay track to the ballast board. They are: (1) with nails/brads every few inches through the center of the ties; (2) with spikes every few inches, clinching the rails and through the ties; (3) by bonding with contact cement; and (4) by bonding with a spread bed of white glue.

Methods 1 and 2 are probably the best because when they are combined with the bonded ballast method, the track is completely bonded to the ballast board. Methods 3 and 4 can give less sound transmission because fasteners can conduct the sound to the roadbed where it can reverberate. They are most effective if the ballast board and/or the roadbed are made of a resilient material (such as cork) that will attenuate conducted sound. Use temporary nails/brads until the bonding is complete. In method 1, you can remove the nails/brads after ballasting.

Hand-Spiked Track

The first step in laying hand-spiked track is to lay the ties in place. They do not have to be prestained. They should be of a common thickness, although the length can vary slightly to enhance the appearance. Lay them on a smooth coating of white glue, one at a time, or in groups, using a tie-laying jig. After the glue is completely dry, sand the tie tops smooth and then stain the ties. Use ordinary wood stain, not varnish stain, in colors such as walnut, maple, or driftwood. Then lay the rails, spiking in place no less often than four spikes in every fourth tie.

For either type of track, the ties should not all be uniform in spacing, in condition, or in coloration. An occasional tie can be split, broken, or missing. This can be done with plastic ties or wooden ones. Color, age, and weather the rail sides. This can be done before or after ballasting. Complete all track electrical connections. Camouflage the electrical connections to the track and uncoupling ramps. Fill gaps so they will not creep shut.

BALLASTING

The natural colors of ballast can range from quite light to fairly dark. When cinders from steam locomotives are used, the color is dark red-brown. Rock and gravel ballast colors should duplicate their colors, which are usually lighter than you imagine. The ballast will also look darker under artificial light. Because ballast is continually added and renewed, there is usually a variation in colors, even over small areas. Often, blending two shades can make a better-looking result. Do not blend a dark and a light color, however, as this result in an unrealistic salt-and-pepper look.

Ballast becomes stained by rust, oil, spilled material, mold and lichen, and general weathering. This variation of coloring is best added during the track detailing following all tracklaying operations. Whatever is used to model the ballast, it should be nonmagnetic and free of chemicals that could corrode rail or rolling stock. Commercially available ballast for model railroads should meet these qualities. A grain size of a scale 2 to 3 inches is about right. You might have to buy a ballast labeled for a smaller scale to get it small enough.

The bonded ballast method will permanently bond the ties to the ballast board while providing the proper contour for the ballast bed. It provides the right shape and texture and does not alter the ballast color. Before ballasting, make all electrical connections to the rails and thoroughly test everything for proper operation.

Spread the dry loose ballast material between and around the ties to the proper shape and side slope. Keep the point area of turnouts free of ballast that could interfere with operation. Protect switch points with tape or with a petroleum jelly coating. Then spray the track with treated ("wetted") water to dampen the ballast grains.

Wetted Water and Bonding Agents

Wetted Water:

- ☐ Add 2–3 drops of liquid dishwashing detergent per pint of water.
- ☐ Alternative: use Kodak Photo-Flo in place of the detergent.

Bonding Agents

- ☐ Best choice: artist's acrylic matte medium
- ☐ Lowest cost: white glue

Diluted Bonding Agent:

- ☐ One part matte medium (or white glue) to four parts of water.

Always keep a spray bottle of wetted water handy as it will be used often. It will spread out and seep into every crack and fissure, unlike "ordinary" water, which will ball up and refuse to spread. Do not use either isopropyl (rubbing) or denatured alcohols as a solvent, thinner, or wetting agent. These alcohols have an odor, harmful fumes, a low ignition point, and they burn with a near-invisible flame.

Next, apply a diluted bonding agent using a medicine dropper. Capillary action will pull this liquid between all the grains of the ballast. When dry, the bonding agent is invisible, and the ballast (and track) are bonded tightly in place.

Diluted white glue will produce a very hard bonding with greater sound transmission. You can get a preferred and more flexible bonding (at higher cost) by using artist's acrylic matte medium, available from art supply stores and many hardware and hobby stores. Buying the least expensive brand in quart size will reduce the cost.

An alternative bonding method adds powdered dry liquid-activated glue to the dry ballast. This can be bought as dry ballast cement at the hobby shop. This mixture is then spread and shaped, and then, sprayed with the wetted water. When dry, the ballast and track is securely bonded together. This method can have an effect on the ballast color, however, so try it in advance.

You might wish to not do the ballasting until after the surrounding scenery is finished. Then the ballast can appear to partially cover the adjacent soil or grass, as it would on the real railroad roadbed. You might also add more ballast at the tails of the slope at this stage to achieve the same effect.

At some point, perhaps as a part of the detailwork, the track and ballast should receive some additional coloring. This might include a thin stain of black down the middle of mainline track, to represent grease and oil spills, and a little more black around the points of turnouts. Color the sides of the rail a light rust color, using a small brush. Some rust might also be on the ties and ballast next to the rails. Clean the tops of the rails before operating trains.

16

Coverwork

Coverwork gives contour to the model terrain, forming the hills, mountains, valleys, and stream and river beds. The best previous guide to this complete subject is the book, *Scenery for Model Railroads*, by Bill McClanahan.

This chapter concentrates only on those stages of the coverwork operations between the completion of benchwork and trackwork and the completion of a roughly contoured plaster base cover. The final stages—detail contouring and shaping, completion of rock formations, final texturing, coloring, etc.—are added, and covered in "Groundwork," chapter 17.

The object of coverwork is to "cover" the benchwork with a thin plaster base to simulate the contour of the land. Do not invest a lot of time or money, but your results must be strong and allow any degree of additional detailing (FIG. 16-1).

There are three components of the base: (1) the support skeleton, or bracing; (2) the covering material, which can be in two or more different layers; and (3) the plaster.

BRACING

The coverwork bracing forms the rough contours of the terrain and serves as a support for the covering material and plaster, at least until the plaster has set. In flat areas, the base can be plywood or Homosote, and the plaster can be applied directly without an additional skeleton. If the ground contour is not flat, however, some other method will be required to hold and roughly form the contours for the plaster, at least long enough for the plaster to harden and support itself.

There are several methods for providing the bracing. These include foam slabs and various types of wooden framework, including contour profile boards and props.

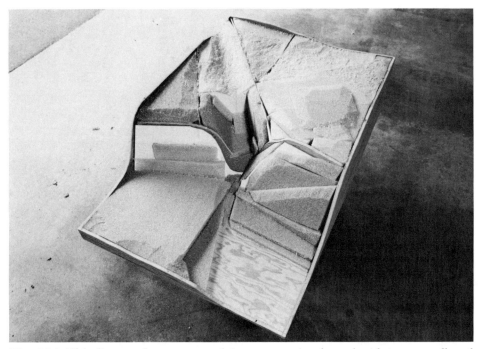

Fig. 16-1. *This diorama shows coverwork in process using foam sheet between cardboard profile sections.*

The covering material interconnects over the bracing and gives further form to the contours. It also serves as a surface to spread the plaster on and as a strengthening matrix for the plaster, once set. Many different materials can be used for covering the bracing. These include wire screen, plastic screen, cloth, cardboard, and various kinds of paper.

The plaster is spread over the covering material and forms the contours and gives strength to the entire coverwork. The plaster is usually applied in two or more coats, with the final coats being shaped to provide the detailed contours. This shaping can be done by molding the plaster while it is still wet or by carving it once it is dry. Additional plaster might be used for precast or cast-in-place rocks during the creation of the groundwork.

The choice of bracing is determined by the choice of the other two coverwork components, and vice versa. If the *hard-shell* (sometimes called *thin-shell*) method is used, then the bracing need only be rudimentary and/or temporary because the hardened plaster is so strong that it is almost completely self-supporting. If, at the other extreme, the bracing is to be foam, then the covering material is not needed because the plaster can be applied directly.

COVERING

The basic problem with any of these methods is to get the covering material to take and hold the desired shape while the plaster is being spread and is setting.

The covering must temporarily support the weight of the wet plaster and its own weight. The number of "props" necessary from the bracing are determined by the natural rigidity of the covering material.

Wire Screen

The strongest and most rigid covering materials are window screen wire (metal type), hardware cloth (1/4-inch mesh), and chicken wire screening. These materials can be cut and bent to form, wired together, and stapled to wood supports to provide almost any general contour shape. The result is strong and permanent because it is not removed after the plaster is dry. For these covering materials, occasional wood supports protruding up from the benchwork should be adequate.

Wooden profile boards that follow the contour, spaced from several inches to 2 feet apart, might be useful both for setting the contour and as supports. Note that the more open-mesh materials need a covering of paper or some other material so that the wet plaster does not just fall through the holes. Cut the screening material with metal snips and be cautious because the resulting edges are sharp. Wear gloves when handling it.

Cardboard

Cardboard strips, from corrugated boxes or posters, can be stapled between supporting posts or profile boards. These should be about 1 inch wide and at least two layers thick, with the strips forming a lattice with holes no greater than 3 inches across. Glue or staple the strips together where they cross each other. Weaving the strips is not necessary. Glue with a hot glue gun or with white glue, using clothespins to hold the joint until it dries. Bend and twist the cardboard as it is assembled to form the rough contours. This method is not as strong as screening, but it is very inexpensive.

Some additional covering material, such as paper, is necessary to prevent the plaster from falling through the holes between the cardboard strips. For this covering material, use brown paper grocery sacks or industrial-type paper towels. Tear the paper into irregular shapes of a few square inches each and soak these individually in a thin mixture of plaster. Apply them over the wire or cardboard undermaterial. Form these strips somewhat while placing them to further define the contours. Use two layers of the plaster-soaked paper, each half overlapping the adjacent layer, in one application.

An expensive, but convenient, alternative to the plaster-soaked paper is to use plaster-impregnated gauze, like the type used for casts for broken bones. Simply soak this gauze in water and spread it in place. It is very quick setting, so work fast.

Cloth

Canvas, burlap, or plastic window screening can be used as the basic covering material. These materials must be draped over a large number of wooden supports in order to form the proper contour and to have enough temporary strength. An additional coat of plaster might also be necessary. Dipping the canvas or burlap into a stiffening solution of glue or starch will help it hold the contours. Crumpled up newspapers, stuffed underneath, will give temporary support. Remove these after the plaster is set.

Tape and Newspapers

The *hard-shell* method developed by Linn Westcott is probably the easiest and lowest cost of all for forming the covering material. Erect a skeleton of a relatively small number of posts. Space these posts about 2 feet apart and make them tall enough to reach the finished scenery contour, but not the highest points of the terrain. Attach a web of 3/4-inch masking tape between the post tops. String can be used in place of or in addition to the tape.

Put wads and sheets of newspaper on top of the web to form the approximate final contours. Use additional tape to hold the newspaper in position and to hold the wads to the proper shape. A large area can be covered this way, allowing you to visualize the shape that will result. Changes are easy to make, so a few day's pause might allow you to evaluate what you are creating and make improvements.

Apply the final covering layer and the plaster together, in the form of plaster-soaked paper towels. Tear the toweling into irregular shapes of about 3 × 6 inches for rough terrain or larger for flatter areas. Place the towels directly over the newspaper, with each towel portion overlapping by 50 percent. When the final plaster coats have set, remove the tape and newspaper from underneath. The wood props will support the hard shell, which will have considerable strength between these props. Hydrocal is recommended as the plaster for hard shell.

Foam

Rigid foam slabs can also be used as the covering and as a further base for plaster. This technique is discussed later in this chapter under the topic, "All Foam."

PLASTERING

There are two general types of plaster you can use for the terrain base. They are *glue-base plasters*, which include texture paint, joint cement, papier-mâché, and most proprietary scenery mixes; and *setting plasters*, which include patching plaster, molding plaster, wood-fiber plaster, plaster of paris, gypsum plaster, and Hydrocal.

Glue-base plasters dry by evaporation, shrink somewhat, and might not take dyes, stains, or colors well. There also might be difficulty in adding more plaster at a later date because the original plaster becomes more-or-less waterproof.

Setting plasters combine chemically with water to set. They generally provide greater strength, possibility for finer detail, and better acceptance of colors. They also can be rewetted and added to easily.

Under no circumstances should asbestos plaster or plasters including asbestos fibers be used. Asbestos has a lung cancer-causing danger that you should not risk.

Plaster Types

Glue-based:

> Texture paint
> Joint cement
> Papier-mâché
> Scenery mixes

Setting:

> Patching plaster
> Dental plaster
> Wood-fiber plaster
> Plaster of paris
> Gypsum plaster
> Molding plaster (recommended)
> Hydrocal (recommended)

The two plasters recommended are Hydrocal and molding plaster. *Hydrocal*, marketed by U.S. Gypsum Co. in several different grades, is very strong, dries extremely hard, and has no shrinkage. It is best used for foundation plaster coats and for detailed (not rock) castings. You should try to get the "industrial white" or "Hydrastone," the hardest grade. It can be obtained in 100-pound bags from many suppliers of lime, cement, and plaster. Some hobby stores also carry it in smaller-size packages.

Molding plaster, also commercially known as casting plaster, is less strong but dries more slowly, takes very fine detail, and is ideal for the finish plaster coats and for rock castings. This plaster is easier to find then Hydrocal; look in hardware stores as well as building supply dealers.

Rock Formations

Rock formations can be simulated by various methods, including use of real full-sized rocks, broken cork, Celotex or tree bark, carved-in-place plaster, or precast or rubber mold-cast plaster. The use of plaster rocks is covered in "Groundwork," chapter 17. If you use real or cork/Celotex/bark rocks, then add them during the base construction, before placing the covering material or any plaster.

Real rocks are very heavy, and they are often not realistic at representing miniature scale rocks. Because of their weight, they should not be used for any type of diorama, module, or portable layout. Broken edges of cork insulation slabs or Celotex ceiling tiles can make realistic stratified rock representations in miniature. They are relatively lightweight, so their support needs are minimal. You also can use broken pieces of real tree bark in the same way. Blend in the plaster coats around them to integrate them into the scenery.

Once the plaster has been added to the layout, there is a minimum time during which it can be shaped before it has set. Some rough shaping of the rock formations can occur at this time. If molding plaster is used, the plaster can also be carved after it has set. Although time consuming, this allows you to shape the rocks exactly to your liking.

Plaster Formulations

Whichever of the two recommended plasters—Hydrocal or molding plaster—are used, mixing the plasters is essentially noncritical. Store dry plaster so that it will remain dry; for instance, in a plastic bag whose top is tightly closed. Any moisture will harden the plaster and/or affect its setting time or ultimate strength. Mixing containers for plaster should be of adequate size and made of rubber or plastic so the dried plaster can be broken away and easily removed.

Before doing any mixing, make sure that any trackwork or areas that are not supposed to be plastered at this time are completely covered. This can involve an area for several feet around where you "think" you will be working.

Mixing and applying plaster is a messy business. You will need lots of newspapers and perhaps a painter's drop cloth in both the mixing area and under the area where the plaster will be applied. Mix only enough plaster at one time that can be conveniently used before it starts to set. Because the use might involve shaping rough contours with a palette or putty knife, start with small quantities (one quart or less) to see what you can handle.

Mixing

If you want to mix 1 quart of plaster, start with 1 pint (2 cups) of cold water in the mixing container. Slowly sift in the plaster and let it soak up the water, then stir it thoroughly. A rubber kitchen spatula makes a good stirrer. Add more plaster until the consistency is like thick cream. If you are applying the plaster directly, use the spatula to transfer it to the surface. A small trowel is also useful for this operation. For very thin coats, use a cheap 1- or 2-inch paintbrush to spread the plaster.

Coverwork Plaster Formulas

For one quart of mixed plaster:

- ☐ 1 pint of cold water.
- ☐ $1^1/_2$ to $2^1/_2$ teaspoons of universal tinting color (optional, see text).
- ☐ 1 pint of Hydrocal (or molding) plaster.

To increase setting time:

☐ Add 2 teaspoons vinegar or supplied retarder, as recommended.

To decrease setting time:

☐ Add $^1/_2$ teaspoon salt or use seasoned water (see topic, "Rock Casting," chapter 17).

Paper Towels

If you are soaking paper towels, wrapping paper, or brown paper bags in the plaster, a shallow, rectangular mixing container is easier to use. Pretear the paper into pieces about the size of your hand. Make sure both sides are covered with plaster.

The paper towels should be the folded type, like the kind in dispensers. The industrial ones are light brown or blue in color. They are both stronger and less expensive than those available from grocery stores. The most important quality is good wet strength.

The mixing container should be cleaned before it is reused for another batch because the partially dried plaster will affect the setting time of the new plaster you are mixing. Do not dump this old plaster down the drain. Dump it into a separate container for use at a later time as loose rock material. Once plaster has started to set, it can't be thinned out by adding more water. It must be disposed of.

Setting Time

You will have about 15 minutes to work with Hydrocal. You can increase setting time by adding retarder, obtained where you bought the plaster. Experiment with the amount used to obtain the time you want. Optionally, 2 teaspoons of common vinegar, added to each pint of water, will serve as a retarder.

If you want to shorten the setting time of plaster, use either seasoned water (see "Rock Casting," chapter 17) or add $^1/_2$ teaspoon of salt per pint of water. Note that either shortening or lengthening the setting time of the plaster can somewhat affect its strength.

Make sure that the plaster-coated paper comes in contact with the wood props, as this will be the only permanent support. Strengthen these areas with extra layers. The hard shell will have set enough in an hour to add additional coats to thicken thin spots and for reinforcing areas needing extra strength. Full setting will take a week or more, however.

Precoloring

Finished plaster on the layout will inevitably chip and crack in some places. If only the surface has been colored, these areas will be very unsightly and will immediately reveal the truth . . . that what is being seen is not soil and rock but "only" white plaster. This does not bother some people, but to others it is an unnecessary distraction. To avoid this, precolor the plaster while it is being mixed, so when it dries, the "soil" color will go clear through and no ugly white spots will show.

If you desire to precolor, add universal tinting colors to the water prior to adding the plaster. These colors are made for tinting paints, and they can be obtained in tubes from any large paint store. The quantity and color will have to be experimentally determined based on the soil/rock colors you desire. A light tan or light brown-gray might be good choices.

Raw umber, burnt umber, and black colors should give you enough variety for what you need. A small amount of yellow or red might be appropriate for some soils or rocks. Use black in moderation. Per pint of water, $1^1/2$ to $2^1/2$ teaspoons of color are needed. Once you determine your formula, write it down so that you can duplicate the color again. Keep the colors light.

Another coloring agent that can be used is ordinary powdered clothing dye, such as Rit or Tintex. Useful colors include dark brown, cocoa brown, and tan. Use $1/2$ teaspoon of powder to a pint of warm water, dissolving the dye completely. The only disadvantage is that the plaster setting time will be cut in half because of the salts in the dye.

Note that precoloring the plaster does not omit any of the later steps of staining or dying the plaster (see "Groundwork," chapter 17). Its purpose is to prevent the white from showing in cracked or damaged plaster or in holes drilled to install trees, poles, weeds, posts, etc.

Tips on Plastering

- ☐ Always add the plaster to the water.
- ☐ Use rubber or plastic mixing containers.
- ☐ Mix only as much plaster as you can handle before it sets.
- ☐ Precolor the plaster mix.
- ☐ Cover adjacent areas to protect them.
- ☐ Do not dump plaster (mix) down the drain.
- ☐ Retain unused, hardened plaster for rock debris.
- ☐ Keep wet (and dry) plaster off your skin.

Adding On

Once the base coats of plaster have set, you can add additional coats after first wetting the lower coat completely. If this is not done, the layers will not bond together, and the upper layer will be weakened because the lower layer has robbed water from it.

The plaster can be cut away at any time for revisions or additions. Add new plaster like the old, making sure to prewet the old plaster thoroughly. Reworking the contours is so easy that there is no reason not to make needed changes that later experience indicates would be better than the original.

Note that plaster can have a very drying effect on your skin. It will deplete the natural oils of your hands and leave them rough and cracked. To prevent this, avoid contact with the dry powder or wet plaster, wear plastic gloves, or give your hands a thin coating of petroleum jelly or a skin cream before starting.

ALL FOAM

An extremely lightweight coverwork method is described by Malcolm Furlow in the book, *HO Narrow Gauge Railroad You Can Build*. This method uses carved rigid foam slabs, with added polyurethane foam rock castings. The result is strong, very light in weight, and ideal for portable modules that are moved a lot. The primary disadvantage is that fine detail (in rocks especially) will not reproduce as well.

The stronger foam is blue extruded Styrofoam, made by Dow Corning. It coems in 2 by 8 foot sheets with thicknesses of 3/4", 1", 11/2", 2" (and up). Somewhat less strong (but less expensive) is white bead board foam, such as is used for packaging. It comes in 2 by 6 foot sheets, 1" thick.

The scenery contours are built up in layers of foam. Each layer is cut to rough shape using a small handsaw or power saber saw. Do not use a hot-wire cutting tool as this produces toxic fumes. The centers of lower slab may be left hollow. The layers are glued together with white glue, latex contact cement, or foam-compatible wall panel adhesive. Finishing nails or toothpicks are handy for holding the layers together while drying.

The contours are formed with a serrated steak knife, wood rasps, or a Surform tool. The foam dust is attracted to just about everything by static electricity; vacuum it up as much as you can as you go along. The dust is also toxic. Wear a face mask when doing this work. Cover the cracks and pores with texture paint or Sculptamold (obtainable from model railroad hobby shops and art supply stores). Both are very lightweight and tough. You could also use a thin coat of plaster, but this would defeat some of the weight savings.

For lightest weight, rock castings should be made using expandable polyurethane foam. See the topic Rock Casting, in Chapter 17. All other steps, groundwork and subsequent, can be the same as those used with plaster coverwork.

17

Groundwork

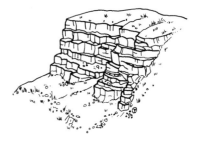

Groundwork is the step that starts with the bare base coats of mono-colored plaster coverwork; adds the rock formations, the exact ground contours, the simulated roads, highways, streets, sidewalks, and water; and provides the basic coloring. The result is something, that for the first time, starts to resemble the goal—a miniature representation of reality. It still lacks the foliage and trees of nature and the structures of man, but it finally starts to look like something that you can be proud of (FIG. 17-1). The sequence is generally to (1) add the rocks first; (2) finish the other plaster work, including the man-made roads and streets; (3) apply the coloring, starting with the rocks, then the soil, then the man-made improvements; and (4) add the water and the loose rocks and rock debris.

ROCKS

The simulation of rocks is different, depending on whether the modeled rocks represent embedded or loose rocks. Embedded rocks are those surrounded by soil, appearing as buried boulders, escarpments, or rock faces. Loose rocks include everything from large weathered round boulders, to the sharp jagged exfoliation from a cliff, to smaller talus and gravel.

You can add embedded rocks to the coverwork using a number of different methods. You can use a variety of real rocks or substitutes for real rocks, including coal, and edges of building material or cork. You can roughly shape them into the wet plaster, then carve in detail. You can simulate them with cast plaster or foam, adding the castings after they are fully set or while they are still partly wet.

The modeled rocks can be exposed in a hillside, they can constitute much of a mountain, or they can be loose at the foot of slides or as boulders in washes or streams. Add loose rocks after all the groundwork involving the rocks that are embedded is completed (FIG. 17-2).

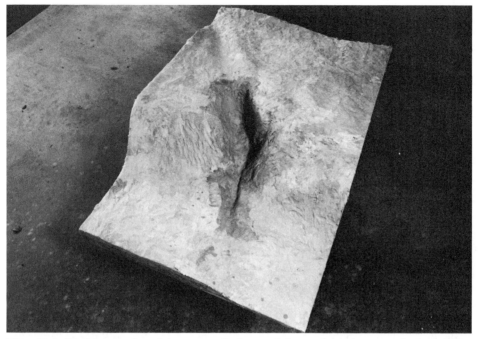

Fig. 17-1. Model groundwork in process (before applying rock castings or coloring). Plaster hard-shell covers all surfaces.

Fig. 17-2. This rock face was made up of separate castings using only two molds. Note the loose rocks below.

Added Rocks

Added rocks include both loose and embedded rocks that are simulated using either real rocks, coal, or organic building materials.

Real Rocks. Real rocks and pebbles can be used for the model if they have a texture that is appropriate, considering the scale of the rocks. For stratified rocks, this requires fine surface detailing in the real rock. Broken lumps of coal often have just the proper scale texture and are a good candidate. Another possibility, if you can find it, is petrified wood. The main disadvantage of real rocks is the weight and the need for adequate support. They will almost always need painting to simulate the colors required to match other nonreal rocks near them.

If the rocks are embedded, install them during coverwork. Fasten or glue them in place so they do not shift. If they are to simulate loose rocks, put them in place using diluted white glue or matte medium near the end of the groundwork step.

Suitable pebbles can be obtained from gravel. Sort the gravel by size and color, using only the proper color pebbles unless they are to be painted. The sizes should range from scale boulders on down to the granularity used for soil simulation.

Organic Materials. You can simulate stratified sedimentary rock formations, such as sandstone and limestone, by using layers of tree bark, cork, Celotex, ceiling tiles, or similar materials. Break the edges in a random manner to simulate the exposed rock edges. Glue the layers to each other using undiluted white glue and let them dry under weights or with clamps. You can crumble away the surface some more to further simulate the modeled rocks. Then add the entire clump with appropriate support and fastening. This is best done during coverwork.

Note that bark can be subject to insect attack and deterioration after it is installed. In fact, the insects, beetles, weevils, etc., might be in the bark when it is brought in. For this reason, bark is not a recommended rock simulation material.

The embedded material might require a light brushed coat of plaster over the surface. Even without this, it will usually require painting to provide the proper colors.

Rock Carving

If you are going to carve the rocks in place (applicable only to plaster embedded rocks), then the first coat of plaster applied in groundwork should be a thick but slow-setting mix of molding plaster. Apply this coat to the prewetted surface of the base plaster coat(s) that you put down during coverwork. Prewet or wet with wetted water (see "Ballasting," chapter 15).

Shape the plaster coat to the proper form, as far as possible, using a spatula, small trowel, small knives, brushes, etc., before it hardens. It is important to form the major cracks and fault lines and to mold the basic rock shape. A photograph of similar rocks is handy to have as a reference during this process.

As the plaster partially sets, it will accept more and better carving of details. At this stage, refine the basic profiles formed earlier by adding more detail in terms of strata, cracks, and faults. Use sharper tools, such as knives, screwdrivers, and dental picks. Even after the plaster is fully set, refinements to the detail can be added, but it is harder to do. Files might be handy for shaping at this stage.

Do not use your best tools for carving plaster because the plaster is abrasive and will quickly dull the tool. Also, be careful to keep your fingers out of the way because it is easy for the tool to slip. Take off only a little plaster at a time to avoid creating cracks or breaking off something you want to keep.

As you work on the carving, brush away the carved-away debris and dust so that you can see what the rock looks like. Save the larger pieces to break up and use as loose rocks.

Rock Casting

Precast rocks can be added to previously applied plaster surfaces. Thoroughly wet the base surface and the casting. Use additional wet plaster as the "adhesive" to fill in and blend the transitions.

Probably the best method for creating rocks is to use latex molds. The plaster is cast, then applied to the base plaster surfaces while still partially wet. This method is much faster than carving and produces more realistic results.

The latex molds can be purchased or homemade, with equally good results for the finished castings. A few different molds can suffice to populate an entire layout with rock castings, without apparent repetition of pattern. This is because each casting can be turned a different way, or it can be of slightly different size or convexity, or it can be joined to adjacent castings in different ways that disguise the common origin.

Wet Casting. Before use, thoroughly wet the inside of the mold. Fill the molds about 1/2 inch deep with a fairly sloppy mixture (so it will fill all the mold's detail) of molding plaster, mixed using *seasoned water* (see sidebar).

Seasoned Water

Seasoned water is ordinary water that has had 1 ounce (2 tablespoons) of dry plaster (per quart of water) added to it, 15 to 20 minutes in advance of use. The seasoned water rather magically shortens the plaster setting time by one-third!

Determine the amount of seasoned water required for the casting by using the mold to measure it. Slowly add the plaster to the water, stirring thoroughly, until the mixture is the consistency of a heavy cream. Pour the plaster into the mold, either while it is held in your hand or while it is supported, so the wet plaster does not run out.

Allow the plaster in the mold to partially set for 1 to 2 minutes. You can tell when it is ready by slightly flexing the mold. If small cracks and wrinkles appear, and if the plaster will not run out when the mold is tipped vertical, it is ready for application. Pick up the mold, plaster and all, and press it against the newly pre-wetted base plaster at the proper location and with the desired orientation.

Hold the plaster-filled mold in position an additional 3 to 5 minutes until it further sets and adheres to the base plaster coat(s). The plaster in the mold will feel warm. Do not leave the plaster in the mold too long or it will be harder to remove the mold. Remove the mold by gently peeling it from one corner toward the opposite corner, turning the mold inside-out (FIG. 17-3).

Fig. 17-3. The rock mold is held in place until the plaster has hardened enough to adhere.

Without the use of the seasoned water, the time for each part of the operation is three or four times as long because the plaster sets more slowly. The use of seasoned water does not seem to materially affect the strength of the plaster used for cast rocks or plaster overcoats to Hydrocal base coats.

With multiple molds and proper timing, you can set up a production line so that the casting process occurs smoothly and without excessive waiting. The following recommended sequence of operations for rock casting is for one person using two molds. This is the limit because while the molds are held in place, one hand is needed for each mold.

Rock Casting Sequence (One Person)

Get everything ready:

   *1. Measure water for molds 1 and 2.
    2. Add seasoning to water. Then, add dye to water.
    3. Wet receiving areas. Wait.
    4. Add plaster to seasoned water. Pour plaster into molds 1 and 2.
    5. Clean mixing container. Wait.
    6. Apply mold 1. Apply mold 2. Hold molds in place. Wait.
    7. Remove mold 1. Remove mold 2.
    8. Wash out molds 1 and 2.
    9. Touch up casting edges.

Repeat from * for the number of casting pairs to be made. To finish up, clean up the tools, clean up the mixing area, and clean up the casting area. Dust and store the molds.

Things can go much faster with two or more people. In a recommended sequence for rock casting with two persons and four molds, person 1 is a mixer and person 2 is a caster. Kids find the "job" of casting to be great fun.

Rock Casting Sequence for Two Persons

Person 1—mixer	*Person 2—caster*
Get everything ready.	
Measure water for molds 1 and 2.	
Add seasoning to water.	
Wait.	
*Add plaster to seasoned water.	Wet receiving areas.
Pour molds 1 and 2	
Clean mixing container.	Wait
Measure water for molds 3 and 4.	Apply mold 1.
Add seasoning to water.	Apply mold 2.
Add dye to water.	Wait. Hold molds in place.
Wait.	Remove mold 1.
	Remove mold 2.
	#Touch up casting edges.
	#Wash out molds 1 and 2.

Repeat steps from * for casting with molds 3 and 4. Alternate these steps with both pair of molds. Finish by doing the following:

Wash out all molds.	#Clean up tools.
Clean up mixing area.	#Clean up casting area.
Dust & store molds.	

Can be done by person 1 if person 2 is a child

Dust the molds with talcum powder before storing them away. Store them so they will not become deformed. Foam "popcorn" makes a good material to use for the packing.

Further steps include adding wet plaster to fully blend in the castings to the surface and to the adjacent castings. Some carving of these blended regions might be necessary, but this should be minimal because the area is small.

Dry Casting. The same method for wet casting can be used for dry casting, except allow the plaster to dry in the mold just to the point that you can remove the mold without damage. Then apply these castings to the base coat(s) using an adhesive coat of wet plaster between the prewetted casting and the prewetted base coat(s). This might be easier for some modelers, at least until they get a feeling for the timing of the wet casting method.

Foil Molds. Rock molds can be made from ordinary aluminum foil. This is useful for simulating granite and similar types of rocks or rock faces that have been blasted away. Crumple a foil piece about 4 × 6 inches tightly, then unfold and then slightly re-crumple the foil to form the mold. Use it for wet casting in exactly the same way as the latex molds. The foil is delicate, and removal will probably tear the mold, but new ones are so easy to make that this is no loss.

Mold Making. If you choose to make your own molds for rock casting, you will need the following materials and tools: liquid latex molding rubber, 1-inch wide rolls of surgical gauze, disposable 1-inch paintbrush, and scissors.

You will need some suitable rocks or pieces of coal to use as masters to form the molds. Broken coal or petrified wood can give a particularly good "rock" texture. Although these molds can be made in the field from unmovable rocks, it is recommended that rocks that can be brought to the workshop are a better solution.

Your choice of master should be a rock that looks like a scaled-down rock face or cliff. The detailing should be fine and to the proper scale. Brush the master rock thoroughly with a stiff brush to dislodge any loose material, vacuum it off, and then wash it. Wet the rock with wetted water when you apply the first latex coat. This will help in removing the mold and facilitate the liquid latex in flowing down into all the cracks and holes of the rock.

Apply the latex with a disposable 1-inch brush, working the latex down into all the fissures and surface detail. Make sure no bubbles form. If they do, puncture them. Allow this coat, and all subsequent coats, to dry completely before applying the next one. This takes about 20 minutes at room temperature. Cover only about half or less of the spherical surface of the rock for a mold. Make the molds no larger than about 4 × 6 inches and no deeper than 1 to 2 inches. After the second coat, let the mold dry overnight (if possible).

While the third coat is still wet, add a strengthening mesh of gauze, pressing it down into the latex. The gauze should be cut into pieces about 4 × 4 inches. Add a second layer of gauze with the fourth coat. In all, five to seven coats are recommended to give the mold sufficient strength to allow it to be used indefinitely without damage, and yet permit it to have enough flexibility for easy use.

After curing overnight (or longer), carefully peel away the mold from the rock. First, dust the outside with talcum powder. This will prevent the mold from sticking to itself. Some small portions of the mold will probably tear off and remain in the smaller holes and cracks of the rock, but this is normal. Dust the inside of the mold with talcum powder. Trim the edges with scissors. The mold is then ready to use. More molds can be made from the same or other surfaces of the same rock.

Several molds can be made at the same time, if several rocks are available. This takes little more time because application of the latex takes less time relative to waiting for the drying.

Loose Rocks. Save all the chunks of plaster left over from cleaning out the mixing container or that hardened before you could use them. Put these pieces in a cloth bag and hit the bag repeatedly with a hammer, breaking the chunks into smaller pieces. Spread the pieces on a newspaper, sort out the chunks that are still too big, and repeat until you have an acceptable range of sizes. After coloring and sorting (see "Debris"), you can use these bits of plaster as loose rocks and slide debris.

Foam Casting. Rocks can also be cast using expandable polyurethane foam in latex molds. The molds can be the same ones used with plaster. The polyfoam is available as a kit made by Mountains in Minutes or as industrial A-B foams. The latter are available from plastics materials stores.

These polyfoams consist of a resin part and a catalyst part, which must be combined. A chemical reaction causes an expansion (15 to 30 times) that will fill every part of the mold, and beyond if too much is used. Follow the instructions carefully and be sure to use plenty of mold release prior to making each casting. These materials will attack plastic, plastic-coated, or foam cups, so use wax-coated paper cups for mixing. When working with the material, wear gloves and avoid contact with the skin.

As with plaster castings, apply the foam castings before the foam has set or afterwards. In the former case, the fit will be better and the castings should self-adhere. In the latter case, some adhesive (foam compatible) will be necessary for attachment.

Rock Coloring

Just about any kind of paint or stain could be used to color the rocks, but there are some clear preferences in terms of cost, ease of use, material compatibility, and the results you get. Options include artist's oil colors (with turpentine thinner), and acrylic colors, polymer colors, dry-powder paints, poster colors, tempera paints, or casein paints (all thinned with water).

Every little detail adds to this attractive watering station.

This general store can add a home-town feeling to any railroad scene.

Boards can be detailed by adding nail holes and by proper coloring and weathering.

This town from the past includes an old Ford billboard that boasts a new Ford for $520.

Several 1930s-era model billboards are shown in this scene.

This freight station has everything—ladders, crates, and barrels.

This building scene includes antique cars and 1930s-era billboards.

Realism can be added to model figures by careful painting and detailing.

Is this a photo of a model or the prototype? If it is hard to tell, then the modeling has been done well.

Not only does the locomotive show detail, but the scenery as well.

Several well-modeled deciduous trees, including fallen limbs and decaying vegetation, make this scene look like an authentic landscape.

This Serranos Railroad scene cleverly displays railroad signs, Uncle Sam posters, and a telephone man.

The foam in this frothing, fast-water rapids is made from cotton tufts.

This little country shack with its older-model trucks and creek in the distance make an interesting scene.

In any case, the least expensive brand of a particular type of color or paint is quite adequate for coloring plaster. The main ingredient will be the thinner, and if that is water, it is free. Oil paints might produce slightly richer and longer-lasting tones, but the cost is higher and the smell is a lot worse, both because of the turpentine. Oils also might be slightly harder to work with. It is recommended that you use a fully water-compatible coloring method based on the use of universal dyes and/or acrylic artist's colors.

If your plaster was precolored in the mix, as was recommended in the topic, "Plastering," chapter 16, then you already have rocks that have some pale color that should approximate the lighter colors in that type of rock. If not, then the coloring you add in this step will be only on the surface. Either way, the difference will not be apparent unless the rock is cracked or damaged and the white plaster color gives away the illusion.

Do the coloring under the same light that will be used for illumination of the scenery. If this is not done, you will get some unpleasant surprises on color appearance later. The colors you will need depend on the rocks you will be simulating, but generally you will need raw umber, burnt umber, raw sienna, burnt sienna, Vandyke brown, yellow ocher, chrome yellow, white, and black acrylic artist's colors.

Staining. You will actually be staining or dying the rocks instead of painting them. Very thin washes of water consistency are allowed to run together, to run down the surfaces, and to blend themselves. The stains should add only a little color with each application. Repeated applications, often with different hues, build up the color to the darkness desired. You always can easily make the plaster darker, but it is hard to make it lighter. If you must, it is usually best to brush on a thin coat of plaster and start again. See the sidebar for a guide to color selection for rocks. Other colors in very light tints can be added to represent mineral coloration in the rocks.

Color Selection Guide for Rocks

Rock Type	*Colors to Use*
Granite, gray	Thin black wash + tint of blue
Granite, blue	Thin washes of black + blue
Granite, red	Thin washes of black + red
Limestone	Tint of black
Sandstone, brown	Thin Vandyke brown wash
Sandstone, yellow	Thin washes of Vandyke brown and light chrome yellow
Sandstone, red	Thin wash of burnt sienna
Shale	Thin washes of burnt sienna and Vandyke brown
Basalt	Washes of Payne's gray, black, and blue

Immediately after application, the colors will look somewhat wet and glossy, but they will dry flatter. Apply a bit of white acrylic paint to highlight the high spots, using the dry brush technique. Keep this subtle. By using a number of washes of watery consistency, the color will tend to collect more in the cracks and crevices, darkening these areas that would be in shadow. The portions of the rock that stick out further are naturally lighter than those that indent, just as it occurs in nature.

Clothing Dyes. Dyes can be used for coloring the rock and also for darkening or modifying other pigments, once they are in place. Use clothing dyes, such as Tintex or Rit. Useful colors are cocoa brown, black, yellow, and green. The latter two colors are used mainly to neutralize the tendency of the brown or black to look pink.

Mix the dye by adding the entire package to a pint jar, then adding warm water. This will make a saturated solution, yet leave some grains undissolved at the bottom. The concentration desired is obtained by using a medicine dropper to suck up the amount of the saturated dye desired, and adding this to a measured amount of wetted water. By measuring the number of drops of saturated dye and the amount of diluting water, you can repeat the concentration. Put leftover, diluted dye back into the saturated container. As long as there are some grains undissolved at the bottom, you can be assured that the solution is saturated.

Universal Dyes. These dyes come in tubes and are made for tinting paints. They are a better choice than clothing dyes and are easier to work with. You can buy them at the larger paint supply stores. They can be used with any vehicle, but water is the better choice for rock staining purposes. Mix them with about 12 to 16 drops of dye per 8 ounces ($1/2$ pint) of water. The tubes come in the following useful colors: burnt umber, raw umber, black, burnt sienna, yellow ochre, and ultramarine blue.

Apply the dye to the rock by spraying, dribbling, or brushing it on. Use enough dye so that it runs down into the crevices and crannies, providing more coloring in these areas. At the same time, spray with clear water, washing the color away from the high spots and down into the cracks, crevices, and lower areas. Apply the dyes to wetted plaster or to dry plaster. Dry plaster will soak it up very fast and use more of the dye, resulting in darker shades. It is best to start by applying it to wetted plaster because this is easier to control.

Follow the dyes or stains with a black relief wash, made from $1/2$ teaspoon of India ink in 1 quart of wetted water. This fills in the shadows and gives better relief to the rocks.

The most common mistake in coloring rock (or soil) is to make the colors too dark or too intense. Fortunately, when staining or dying colors, what looks about right when it is wet will dry much lighter; which will probably be the right shade in the first place.

Highlighting. Shadowing and highlighting of the rocks is necessary because the lower light intensity on the layout results in weak shadows and definition. You might wish to wait until after the completion of the greenwork to do the highlighting. The highlighting is done with a dry brush to add just a bit of white or ochre to the tops of the rocks where the brightest rays of the sun would hit.

SOIL

Add the simulated soil (or earth) after the rocks are completed. You can simulate soil with appropriately textured and colored plaster, with sawdust or ground foam, or probably the best way, with real dirt of proper size, color, and texture.

In nature, the soil is around the rocks. Your model should simulate this appearance because it will help make the rocks look like they are embedded in the soil. Place the soil everywhere, even though grass or weeds will cover much of it. Even in nature, bare spots let the earth show through (FIG. 17-4). This section will discuss methods of simulating soil on the model.

Fig. 17-4. Soil always surrounds the rocks and is under all the greenwork.

Plaster Soil

Apply a thin plaster coat over the prewetted base coat(s) in a rather liquid mix. Do this before the rocks are colored. As it is setting up, brush with an old paintbrush to smooth and form the contours and provide a light texture, if desired. Fill in this "soil" around the rocks, trying them into the scenery. Be careful to avoid forming unnatural depressions and hollows where they would not be in nature.

Coloring. As with the other plaster, color this coat in the mix to avoid future cracks and chips from showing white. Choose the colors in a lighter shade of the eventual color you want the soil to be.

Surface color the plaster that is simulating soil by using stains or dyes, as discussed in "Rock Coloring," except use appropriate colors for the type of soil being modeled. Alternatively, you can paint the plaster with a 1:1 thinned mixture of latex interior flat house paint. Choose this paint so that when dry, it matches the color of dry earth. Color all soil, even what will be eventually covered with grass or ground cover.

Color Selection Guide for Soils

Soil Colors	*Colors to Use*
Sand, tan	Wash of raw umber
Sand, grey	Washes of raw umber and black
Brown	Washes of raw umber, burnt umber, and Vandyke brown
Brown loam	Washes of burnt umber and burnt sienna
Red-brown	Washes of burnt sienna and raw sienna
Red	Washes of burnt sienna, raw sienna, and red
Ochre	Wash of yellow ochre

Zip Texturing

Zip texturing, a method devised by Linn Westcott, is named for the ease and speed with which it can be used. It is based on the use of colored dry powder pigments that are mixed with dry plaster, and sprinkled over prewetted plaster. It can be used to color soil or grass, depending on the texture of the plaster it is applied to and the colors used. The method can be combined with staining or dying; if so, the other coloring should be done first. Zip texturing does not necessarily result in the best or most realistic scenery, but it is certainly the fastest and easiest method to use. It is most effective away from the foreground, where the lack of texture is not so important.

Use molding plaster. Patching plaster can be used, but it is a less-desirable substitute. The dry pigment colors can be obtained from larger paint stores in 1 pound packages or from model railroad shops. For soil coloring, you will need raw umber, burnt umber, raw sienna, and burnt sienna. For grass coloring, you will need to add chrome yellow medium and chrome green medium.

Mix the plaster and pigment together while both are dry. This is best done in a jar or coffee can with a cover. Do not use black pigment because it will look unnatural when dry. Use burnt umber to darken the color. The proportion of pigment to plaster determines the lightness of the color. You can combine several pigments to give the desired shade of color. Mixtures having less than 25 percent plaster might not adhere well. An overspray of thinned matte medium will solve this.

Besides the mixing (and storage) containers, you will need some coarse- and medium-mesh kitchen sieves, a measuring cup, a window spray bottle, and a squeeze spray bottle modified to produce a thin stream of water.

Mix the desired colors in advance. Spray the area to be colored with wetted water. Sift the plaster/pigment mix onto the surface, as desired. It will absorb the water from the base plaster and bond to that plaster. Make the sifted coat very light to start, adding more where necessary.

Before this coat has dried, direct thin streams of water onto the scenery so that it runs down. Use a bucket on the floor to catch the stream. The water running down will follow the natural water courses, washing soil (plaster/pigment) away with it. Because this is exactly what happens in nature, the result looks realistic. The soil will be deposited in low spots and hollows along the way. You might need to add more soil near the top of the hills to replace that lost to this "erosion." Repeat these steps as needed.

Texture Materials

Either sawdust or ground foam rubber are good materials to use to provide texture to the ground. All of the groundwork that is not rock should be textured in some way. This texture is one of the primary keys to realism. If you use sawdust or foam to add texture to the earth, then dye them in earth colors. In a later topic, "Grass," in chapter 18, these same materials, colored in shades of green, will be used to simulate grass and weeds. The preparation of sawdust and ground foam will be discussed before describing how they are applied.

Sawdust. Some modelers avoid the use of sawdust for scenery believing that it always looks like sawdust. This might be because of the methods used for its preparation and application. Properly prepared and used, sawdust can provide an effective texturing material, and the price is certainly right.

You can get sawdust from your own workshop or from lumberyards. Obtain sawdust from wood that does not contain Masonite, particleboard, or building material dust or chips. These will not take the dye well. Obtain the finest possible sawdust. The finer the teeth on the saw blade, the finer the sawdust. Get at least twice what you will need because much of it will be discarded along the way. Store the sawdust in paper bags until you are ready to dye it.

Sawdust should be dyed before it is sifted and sorted. Otherwise, the finest portion, which is what you will use, would be difficult to remove from the dye solution and would dry lumpy. The larger sawdust particles help to prevent this from happening.

You should use clothing dye, with colors selected from the browns (for earth texturing) or greens (for grass/weeds). Suitable colors might include light, dark, forest, jade, olive, kelly greens, and cocoa brown. Dye several shades of sawdust from each color family at the same time. Start with the lighter hues and go to the darker in later batches. Heat 2 gallons of water to almost boiling, add one packet of dye, and stir until it dissolves completely.

Add the sawdust while stirring the mixture. Keep adding the sawdust until all the liquid is absorbed. Then set the batch aside to cool. When cool, remove the sawdust by grabbing a clump with your (gloved) hand, squeezing the liquid out and back into the container.

Spread the sawdust out in a thin layer on newspapers. There should be about 1½ gallons of dye solution remaining from the first batch. Add enough water to make 2 gallons, bring this to near boiling, add another full packet of the next darker dye, and continue to proceed in this manner until all the sawdust is dyed and all the shades have been obtained.

Keep the shades separate. After about two days, the sawdust should be completely dry. Separate the lumps and break up clumps. Now sift the sawdust through window screen to remove the larger material, which you can discard. Then sift again, using a finer mesh. You should then have two coarsenesses, medium and fine, of each shade. Store them separately in marked containers.

Ground Foam. Colored ground foam rubber can be purchased from hobby shops in a variety of colors and grinds, from several suppliers. For the quantity needed, it is relatively inexpensive. Like sawdust, it can be used to simulate dirt, sand, weeds, grass, leaves, needles, ivy, etc. You might wish to grind and dye your own foam rubber. This requires more work, but the costs will be comparable to those for dyed sawdust.

Use only genuine foam rubber. Get scraps from upholstery shops. Use a kitchen meat grinder with the finest blades. If the grind is not fine enough, run it through again. Some people have also used a kitchen blender. Experiment to see if this works better wet or dry. Another method uses a wire wheel in a bench grinder, with a cardboard box to catch the material.

Dye the foam after grinding. The dying process is identical to that for sawdust, except you will need 50 percent more dye because the rubber does not absorb the color as readily.

Some people advocate dying the foam before grinding. If this is done, dye 4-inch square blocks, then grind them. Because the dye does not color evenly through the block, this gives a natural color variation. Whether homemade or bought, store the foam rubber in marked containers, separated according to color and grind.

Application. Apply texture materials by sprinkling them onto the surface, using a salt shaker type of container. Baby food jars, with holes punched in the lid, make good applicators.

Real Dirt

Real dirt, if it is fine enough, can serve as an excellent material to use in simulating earth, gravel, and small rocks. The cheapest source of real dirt (natural earth) is free. Such dirt, obtained from your backyard or elsewhere, can simulate the soil on your model. It can, that is, if it is the right color and of small enough granularity. The finer soils are most likely to have small enough grain size. Decomposed granite is a good candidate. In some areas this can be purchased commercially from building supply dealers. Ask for the "1/4-inch × dust" size. Many model railroad hobby shops also now carry this in graded sizes.

Some of the clay-type cat box litter materials (without chlorophyll) might also be suitable. (You will have to search for the few brands that are the right color and texture.) The light earth tan clay-like dirt from baseball diamonds is also very good.

If there is any doubt, test the dirt with a magnet to make sure that it will not be attracted to the motors in your locomotives. Real dirt obtained from nature must be washed first to remove organic components, such as leaf particles, decayed vegetable matter, etc. Do not use fine clay soils because the particle size is too small and the result will turn to mud and crack.

You can wash the dirt best by adding water to a small amount of dirt in a container, shaking the mixture, pouring off the water, and repeating this several times until the water is clear. Separate the dirt from the water by pouring it out through a strainer lined with material from a nylon stocking. This can be dumped onto newspapers to complete the drying.

When dry, sort the washed dirt by size by using strainers and/or cloth of appropriate mesh size. Use the smallest granularity for soil, the next larger for gravel, etc., on up to smaller rocks. Lighten the dirt color by mixing it (dry) with Durham's Water Putty.

Several companies sell natural dirt materials for models, where all the work of cleaning and sorting has been done for you, at a price, of course. These are available in many different colors and textures.

Bonding

Groundwork simulating soil can be bare or partially, or almost wholly, covered by grass and other plants. The ground might be bare—no rocks or plant coverings—for a variety of reasons. It might be because of inadequate rainfall or excessive heat or cold that prevents plants from growing. The soil might be totally infertile or might have minerals that are poisonous to plants. It also might be freshly plowed or readied for planting. Examples of bare ground include deserts, sand dunes, beaches, salt flats, building sites, and fields under preparation for crops.

Even ground that is to later have grass/weeds and so forth should receive coloring and some texturing because the soil occasionally shows through. Use the most care in texturing of course, where the soil will be left bare or nearly bare.

The plaster should already be colored a basic earth color, as was described in the topic, "Plaster Soil." In this step, you will add texturing using a combination of sawdust, ground foam, and/or real dirt.

Application. Work in an area of about 1 foot square. Lightly spray the plaster with wetted water. Paint on diluted (1:1) earth latex paint over everything that is not rock. Be generous in this application. Apply the textures (sawdust, foam, or real dirt, as desired) by sifting them onto the wet paint. Rewet the paint with wetted water, if necessary.

For sifting, use containers such as baby food jars. Punch several holes in the screw-top lids. Use these like salt shakers. You can also use regular or crank-type sifters, tea strainers, etc. The object is to be able to put the textures where you want, but somewhat randomly.

Vary the type of texture, the color/shade, and the granularity as appropriate to achieve the effect you want. Move the material about and shape it with a soft brush, as desired. Use a teaspoon to place more dirt around big rocks, etc. It is recommended that you do not apply both earth and grass at the same time, although many modelers successfully do this.

As an alternate to the latex paint, you also can apply the textures to a brushed thin coat of acrylic matte medium (thinned 1:1), or to wet plaster, or to dry plaster. There are advocates for all these methods and they have all been successful. You might wish to experiment to see which approach you like best. In any case, the final step is the same—bond all the texture to the base.

Bonding Agents. Either of the bonding agents—matte medium or white glue—is compatible with the other and with the latex paint (all water based), so they can be used atop each other. If you apply the bonding agent by dribbling it on, you will find it most convenient to use it from and store it in a plastic squeeze bottle like the type white glue is sold in. If you spray it on, then clean the sprayer in warm water after each use. Store the bonding agent in a separate container. Small jars with screw-top lids are convenient.

Probably the best method of applying the bonding agent is to spray it on. Protect the track and any structures from the spray. Spray very gently so you do not disturb the textures. Continue to spray until the surface is saturated and milky white in color. Don't worry, the bonding agent will disappear when it is dry.

For some areas, the dribbling method might be better. Make sure that the receiving area is damp with wetted water, then drip the bonding agent on. It should spread down and around all the texture.

Repeated applications might be necessary to get full coverage and the wanted effect. Always apply the smallest sized material first, then the coarser textures, and finish with the largest rocks. Later fill in around the bigger rocks with small or intermediate size material where appropriate. The largest rocks will be found at the bottoms of hillsides and in places where erosion has exposed them.

After the bonding is dry, vacuum up any loose texture. If you place a rough cloth such as burlap over the vacuum cleaner hose end, you can save the pieces for reuse. Collect this material by turning off the cleaner while the hose end is over a newspaper. Shake out the cloth, then continue with the cleanup.

Debris

The broken-up plaster remnants that were described in the topic, "Rock Casting," need to be colored before they can be used. They can be used in addition to or in place of real rocks and stones to simulate the larger gravel, rocks, rock slides, talus, etc., found at the foot of rock formations (FIG. 17-5).

If the plaster was not precolored, then spray these rocks with wetted water: dump them into a coffee can of stain, dye, or paint, and color them to match the cast rocks on the layout. Then take them out and allow them to dry on newspapers. Some additional staining might be necessary, just as with cast rocks (see "Rock Coloring").

Spread these colored rocks onto a bed of 1:1 diluted white glue, then arrange them to suit and spray with wetted water. Dribble the preferred bonding agent

Fig. 17-5. Model rock debris can be made from a combination of real and broken plaster "rocks."

on and around them to firmly bond them in place. Put down the larger pieces first and position the smaller pieces where gravity would leave them.

If you use real rocks and stones, such as full-sized gravel, wash the material and roughly sort by size and color. Note that the colors should match other rock (which might be painted plaster) in the vicinity. To get the proper color match, it might be necessary to paint these rocks/stones.

WATER

Water is the basis of all life on Earth. It is a rare model railroad layout that would not include some modeled water in the scenery. Only perhaps in the desert is there no water to be seen. Elsewhere, there are lakes, streams, rivers, pools, bogs, and swamps. The omission of these natural features would remove a part of nature that is interesting and vital.

Theoretically, the most logical material to use for modeling water is water. But the truth is that real water does not look very "real" when used on a scale model. This is because neither the movement of water, in flowing streams, etc., nor its color scales down realistically. The color of real water comes about from reflection from the sky and is influenced by the depth of the water.

Also, unfortunately, it is not really practical to include real water, and probably everyone who has ever tried it has regretted it. It is difficult/impossible to waterproof the water courses adequately. The water evaporates, leaving mineral stains. It is very hard to keep the water purified so that strange organisms do not grow in it that smell bad and color it an unfortunate green shade. Also, real water is not very compatible with the electricity that you must use on your layout.

Fortunately, there are several ways to simulate still or moving liquid water that are quite realistic and that are not hard to do. These methods use glass or plastic sheet materials, cast-in-place clear plastic resins, artist's acrylic gloss medium, or glossy painted flat surfaces.

However it is modeled, the final test of your water will be from visitors. If they reach out to touch the "water" to see if it is wet, then you will know that you have done it well.

You also might wish to model water in its colder, solid form. If your diorama or layout includes a winter scene, then snow and ice will need to be present. Different materials are used to create snow and ice than are used to simulate "liquid" water. Some of these can be temporary (for photo purposes), but some are permanent. The test of winter realism is whether the model snow looks cold and soft, with proper drifts and banks; and whether the ice looks cold and hard and icy. The simulation of solid water (snow and ice) is covered in a separate topic.

Still Water

Still or nearly-still water, such as in lakes and ponds, is the easiest water to model because it is essentially flat and relatively smooth on its surface. This also applies to the water in large rivers, if the rivers are not fast-flowing. The ocean comes in this same category, but it needs special treatment to model the surf and any waves.

The less agitated the water, the easier it will be to model, and the more realistic it will look. The improved realism is because the modeled water does not actually move as the real water would. A wave will always stay in the same place, never moving toward the shore. By avoiding these things that our mind tells us should be moving, but our eyes tell us are not, we remove another barrier to believability. FIGURE 17-6 shows a realistic model lake made using cast plastic water.

Color. Pure water from rainfall is colorless, but as the water flows through terrain or stands in level places, it takes on color. The added color might be due to mineral discoloration, suspended silt, or microscopic plant life. A river might become quite muddy from all the topsoil that the water is carrying. Water also takes on a varying color as the depth of the body of water increases. Shallow water will be clear enough to show the color of the bed and any underwater vegetation or debris.

Depending on the sun angle, the clouds, and general brightness of the day, water will gradually look more green as it gets deeper, changing to blue-green, then blue, and for very deep water, a blue-black or deep purple. The view angle will also change the apparent water color, with low angles reflecting more sky, and thus look lighter and more toward the blues. Smooth water also takes on

Fig. 17-6. A realistic model lake made using cast plastic can show the bottom and sunken objects.

characteristics of a mirror, reflecting shoreline foliage and structures, and distant hills and mountains. Although the artist can paint these reflections onto his canvas, you will have to depend on the surface gloss of your modeled water to provide any reflections.

Choices. Any of the water modeling methods will work with still water. The choice is determined by the compromise you wish to make between realism/effect, cost, and time. The most realistic results can be obtained with liquid casting plastic resins. They are also the most expensive and have a high labor content. Sheet glass or plastic can provide very good results at intermediate cost of time and money. Painting a glossy medium on opaque flat surfaces (plywood, plaster, etc.) gives the fastest and lowest-cost solution, but at some sacrifice in realism.

Plastic Casting. The actual casting of the water is near to the last step of several necessary for this method. In this description, the word "lake" will be used, but this is only a shorthand term to describe lakes, ponds, oceans, rivers, or any other still water that is to be cast.

The first step is to prepare the lake bed. The lake does not have to be deep (in inches) to look deep because the casting plastic can be colored in its different layers to create the illusion of depth. Excessive depth will only cost more time and money and might create problems with cracking of the plastic. A maximum depth of 1 inch should be sufficient.

Because the cast plastic will need a firm and stable base, make the lake bed coverwork a bit thicker and stronger than is needed elsewhere. If you use hard shell, another layer of Hydrocal should be enough. Form the contours of the lake bed into the plaster added to the base plaster of the coverwork. The areas within $1/2$ inch of the surface are most important to model. Form and texture the shoreline and banks and the region just above the waterline at this time. The deeper portions will not be able to be seen in detail.

If rocks, debris, or tree trunks are to be in the water, press them into the wet plaster. Premodel any docks, piers, retaining walls, etc., and add them to the wet plaster, or glue them into drilled holes after the plaster is set, using white glue for bonding. Allow the plaster and glue, if any, to dry overnight.

The lake bed and the banks and all of the items in the water are then painted, stained, or dyed the color of the adjacent soil and/or rocks (see "Plaster Soil"). Just above the waterline and in very shallow areas (first $3/8$ inch), use the normal coloring that you would for the objects and surfaces. As the water gets deeper, gradually shade into deeper hues using thinned medium chrome green and ultramarine blue. Do this shading with a brush or, more effectively, with an airbrush.

Add small weeds and water plants now, using white glue for bonding. If the adjacent beach uses real sand to simulate the scale sand, then extend this into the area that will be covered with the water. Add smaller items of debris, such as old tires, etc., at this time. Make everything just the way you want it before you add the "water." Next, saturate the total lake bed with diluted matte medium. This will bond everything in place and will also prevent bubbles forming from the loose materials. Allow everything to dry thoroughly, at least two days or preferably a week.

There are two choices for the casting plastic. The best choice, because it is a little less toxic and produces less bad-smelling fumes, is two-part epoxy resins, such as Envirotex that is made for decoupage. This consists of a resin and a hardener that are normally mixed in equal parts.

A second choice is polyester casting resin, such as Castolite-SG or Clear Cast. This uses a resin and a catalyst (methyl-ethyl-ketone-peroxide), which is dangerous and highly toxic. Use only a small amount of this catalyst. This casting plastic has a very strong odor and is flammable. It also eats away most plastics, especially Styrofoam.

Handle both of these materials with caution. Keep them out of the reach of children. They should only be used in well-ventilated rooms. While working with them, you should protect yourself with goggles and protective gloves.

Follow the instructions that come with the plastics when doing the mixing. Take your time mixing and make sure the two parts are completely mixed together. Try not to form any bubbles in the mixture. You have about 15 minutes to mix and complete the pouring. Use disposable paper soup bowls for the mixing. Measure all liquids exactly using paper cups and an eye dropper (for the catalyst).

These plastics should not be used at room temperatures below 70°F because they will not set properly. Use heat lamps or ordinary light bulbs to raise the temperature in the area where the casting will be poured to between 70° and 100°F. Be careful that these lamps do not create a fire or burn hazard.

Follow the instructions on the amount of catalyst to use and measure it carefully. Too much and the plastic might crack. Too little and it will stay soft and sticky. The plastic dries to the clearness of glass. A pint of resin will cover an area of 2 × 2 feet, $3/16$ inch thick.

The plastic can be dyed with liquid dyes made for the purpose. Although the plastic can be used clear (without dye), a slight amount of dye enhances the realism of the simulated water. Add the dye to the resin/hardner or resin/catalyst mix using an eye dropper. The dyes are very strong, so err on the side of too little, rather than too much. Use either a blue-green dye or mix of half blue and half green dyes. The first coat should be very light in color.

Pour the first coat into the lake and spread it, using the paintbrush, over all the areas that will be at or below the waterline. This coat should be about $1/16$ inch thick. Guard against holes in the lake bed that would let the plastic run out and down to the floor. You might need to seal the edge of the lake toward the aisle, using a temporary dam. Puncture any bubbles that try to form. This coat will seal the entire lake bed. Let it dry overnight.

Pour subsequent coats to gradually fill the lake, starting from the deepest portion. Let these coats assume their own level. Again, puncture bubbles that form. Dye the first of these coats with the strongest hue that will be used. Each coat should be no more than $1/8$ inch thick. Subsequent coats should be lighter in hue, and the last one that "fills" the lake should be the same light color as the first coat. Make this last coat thinner and mix it with 20 percent extra hardener (for epoxy) or double catalyst (for polyester). This will make the top surface hard and nontacky when it is dry. While this coat is drying, protect it from dust.

Add floating boats, logs, etc., after intermediate coats are poured so they will appear to float in the water. Fish could even be added in this way!

Clean the container and brushes with paint and varnish remover. Do this outside where the fumes can dissipate easily. It is probably easier and safer to dispose of them instead.

The plastic will take 30 minutes or more before it starts to gel. You can test this stage by picking up a little of the plastic using a toothpick. When it starts to get a little rubbery, you can add ripples to the surface by "teasing" or otherwise disturbing or pulling the surface with a toothpick or other sharp object. Done too soon, these will all smooth out. When the plastic "remembers" them, the time is just right. You will have several minutes at this stage to do this surface texturing.

The plastic might tend to creep up the bank and on any submerged items, forming a lip or meniscus. When the plastic is dry, this will have to be painted or covered with bonded loose material to hide this unrealistic effect. This occurs more with epoxy than with polyester resins.

Swamps. Swamps or bogs are made only with a great deal of labor, but the results can be worth it (FIG. 17-7). The material used to form the water is going to be only about $1/4$ inch thick, so build up the plaster coat over the coverwork plaster accordingly, then paint it with dark brown coloring. The tedious part is adding all the weeds and vegetation, which should be put down in a bed of white glue and bonded with a spray of diluted matte medium.

The water in the swamp is normally quite dirty and can be nontransparent.

Fig. 17-7. *An effective model swamp has submerged vegetation and murky ''water.''*

The material used to model the water is diluted artist's gloss medium. Make the dilution about 3:1; the mixture will have a waterlike density and will flow like water around and among all the weeds and reeds. Gloss medium is normally not very clear and waterlike when it is diluted, but here that makes no difference. It has an advantage over casting plastic that it will not creep up on objects, so this effect does not have to be corrected later. Use two 1/8-inch coats. Alternatively, use casting plastic. "Float" dyes on the surface to simulate pond scum.

If only a wet spot, such as a puddle or spilled water, is to be simulated, the best material to use is 5-minute two-part epoxy. This will dry clear and looks realistic. Mud can be created by first painting on one of the darker wood stains, followed by the clear epoxy topping.

Sheet Materials. Sheets of smooth or rippled glass or Plexiglas or other acrylic plastic can be used to simulate still water. This method has some steps that are common to those in the casting method and some that are quite different. The material should be thin, no more than 3/16-inch thick if possible, and either clear or colored a very pale light blue. If it has a rippled texture, the scale of the ripples should be compatible with the size of waves in the water in the scale you are modeling. If the ripples really look like waves, they should face up: if not, then down is a better choice.

Add ripples to the sheet material by spraying on a thick coat of clear Krylon or brushing on a thin coat of casting plastic. While still wet, push the coat into ripples using air from an airbrush or other source of wind. Try this in advance to perfect the operation. It might take several applications of the clear plastic to get the effect you want.

An alternate, and possibly better, method is to use gloss medium on the top surface. If used full strength, this material can be built up to form waves, or the bow waves or wakes from boats. Work it up until it has gelled, to create more texture. Color the wave crests white, using acrylic paint applied with the dry-brush technique, and coat it over with a final coat of the gloss medium. A tiny amount of pearl white fingernail polish can add more life to the waves.

Cut the sheet material larger than the waterline of the lake. It must be sand-wiched between a holding framework. The upper part of this framework sup-ports the terrain above the waterline, and the lower part supports the lake bed (FIG. 17-8).

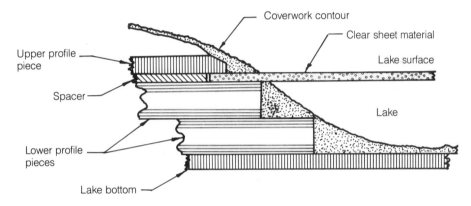

Fig. 17-8. *A cross section of a lake bed made using sandwiched sheet material construction.*

For bodies of water larger than two square feet, sandwich the clear sheet material between the two cutout pieces of 1/4-inch thick Masonite or plywood in the shape of the shoreline. Until the lake is completed, the clear sheet must be removable. This can be done in two ways: (1) make the sandwich removable from below the layout, or (2) make the sandwich removable from on top of the layout.

The first method allows you to complete the lake bed as a subassembly at the workbench, but might be harder to handle or provide the needed access. The second method prevents you from completing the coverwork very near the lake until the lake is finished, but everything is up on top where access might be bet-ter. The following method describes the second (and better) approach.

Level and attach the lower plywood cutout to the benchwork. Build the lake bed using any of the methods described in the topic, "Coverwork," in chapter 16. Because the water will be relatively clear, the simulated water depth will have to be greater, possibly up to 4 to 6 inches. Provide a finishing plaster coat and color the plaster as described previously for plaster casting, then add any sunken or immersed items. The coloring should be sandy near the shore, blending to blues and greens as the depth increases. Note that nothing can go through the clear material, so keep fitting it over the lake bed to make sure of clearances.

When everything is perfect on the lake bed, provide any desired coloring stain to the bottom surface of the clear sheet. Keep this to a minimum to just suggest the color of shallow water. Put this sheet in place and add on the top plywood cutout, attaching it to the benchwork.

Complete the coverwork around the lake, bringing it down to the water's edge, and coloring and detailing it as appropriate. Any floating boats, logs, etc., will have to be cut at their waterline and bonded to the top of the clear sheet. If you have planned ahead, you should have bonded the lower portion (less the thickness of the sheet) of these to the bottom of the sheet prior to sandwiching it in place.

If the lake is small enough, the plywood cutouts might be eliminated. The clear sheet is then supported directly from a framework brought up from the benchwork.

You can substitute a glass mirror for the sheet material. This will give a highly reflective surface, but the water will have no depth. To be most effective, this method requires the addition of slight ripples to the top surface, using gloss medium, as described previously. If you can find it, you could use a half-silvered mirror, which would allow you to see below the top of the water.

Painted Surfaces. The paint used on an opaque surface should be glossy so that it looks like real, wet, water. This finish can be shellac, high-gloss varnish, Varathane finishing plastic, urethane finish, poured casting plastic, or almost anything besides actual paint. It must dry hard and nonsticky so that the dust that collects on it can be removed, preserving its shiny surface.

The surface itself can be made of any material that can provide a flat, level base. Because it lends itself so well to creating some water surface texture, plaster is an ideal candidate. Model all of the desired details, including ripples and waves, into the plaster while it is wet. Rocks and other items that are immersed in the water are pressed into the wet plaster. The lakeshore and banks are modeled at the same time as the water surface. The water surface must be level and smooth, except for surface texture.

The key to the realism of this method is how well the "water" is painted. All of the color of the water must be painted on, including the simulation of depth and of sand/rock colors showing through near the shoreline. High-gloss paints are not required because the gloss will be added later.

Paint the entire lake first a medium light blue. Near the shore, add some light brown or tan colors. In deeper water, use more green and blue. White can be drybrushed onto wave tops.

After painting, let the surface dry for a week. Then add the clear, glossy surface finish using shellac, high-gloss clear varnish, urethane varnish, or equivalent. Make sure that this is only applied to the "wet" water, not to adjacent areas/things that are supposed to look dry. Use two or more coats of this, allowing adequate drying time between each coat. Some people put on twenty or more coats for added thickness and glossiness. Protect the area from dust during the finishing and drying.

If plywood or other sheet materials are used to provide the lake surface, add a little texture both to hide the texture of the materials and to form some ripples/ waves. First thoroughly seal these materials with shellac, paint, or waterproofing so that they do not warp. Avoid joints that fall across the lake. If this is not possible, tape and fill them using drywall materials.

Use texture paint on the surface, using the brush to form ripples and waves. When dry, paint and finish the surface as with plaster. Acrylic modeling paste can also be used. Note that this material is white and not transparent when dry.

Gloss medium makes a good material to use for resurfacing the water when it becomes scratched and old looking. Vacuum the surface first, then wash it with a detergent, then with clear water, then vacuum again. When dry, recoat with the gloss medium.

Moving Water

The material used for modeling moving water, such as in small streams, rapids, and waterfalls, can be either type of clear plastic casting resin combined with clear silicone sealant and acrylic gloss medium. The silicone sealant should be the type that dries semitransparent.

The methods used are approximately the same as those described in "Still Water," with some important additions to simulate the effect of movement and resulting bubbling and frothing of the water. The streambed first must be formed, painted, detailed, and sealed with a saturation of acrylic matte medium.

Falls. If the water descends in a free fall (FIG. 17-9) then some preliminary work will be necessary to form a transparent framework to hold the material used to simulate the water until it can set. The choices are to use strands of clear cellophane, surgical glass wool, aquarium angel hair, thin clear plastic strips, or preformed gloss medium or silicone sealant. If the glass wool or angel hair is used, it should be the shiny, straight type.

For the preforming, string the gloss medium or sealant out in strands on a glass plate. Build it up to three to six layers. Between some of these layers add white flow lines with white paint or with thin strands of white yarn. The waterfall is then scraped from the glass using a razor blade, cut to shape, and bonded in place using ACC.

Rapids. For rapids (FIG. 17-10 AND COLOR INSERT) similar methods will provide a framework for the steeper sections. Use silicone sealant to form part of the water in the rapids. Lay down a bead of the material, working it into proper shape with a knife. Work in the direction of the water flow. This will form a surface for the poured material to form around.

An alternate method is to put down beads of the silicone on a glass plate, let it dry, then peel it off and tear the strips into small chunks. These can be added to the stream bed to give body to deeper rapids, etc. Use the same method with chunks of the casting resin. Let this almost set up in a paper cup, then tear the cup away and break up the resin (using gloves).

Pouring. Apply the first coat of lightly tinted material, starting at the top and letting gravity direct it around the rocks and into pools, etc., just as real water

Fig. 17-9. A model waterfall can look wet, wild, and real.

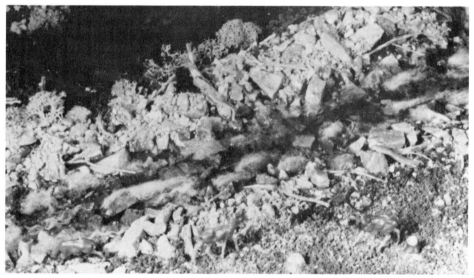

Fig. 17-10. The foam in this frothing fast water rapids is made from cotton tufts.

would flow. This water is allowed to run down the silicone material of the water-falls and rapids, adding to their thickness and blending in with the other water. Little or no dye should be used.

The larger spray in the rapids and at the bottom of a falls can be created with balled-up glass wool or shredded cellophane, temporarily held in place by pins until it is coated with some layers of gloss medium. Use a lot of white to simulate the foam.

The more vertical surfaces will only be wetted by the first coat. If using the polyester resin, use 1¹/₂ times the recommended catalyst for this coat. Guard against letting pools fill over ¹/₄ inch deep or they may crack when setting. Let this coat dry overnight.

Use a double catalyst (polyester) or 20 percent extra hardener (epoxy) for the second and subsequent coats. The tinting can be increased slightly. Some pearl dye might also be added to the mixture. Again, pour from the top, guarding against this layer becoming too thick in the pools. Let this coat dry overnight.

Now, using the dry-brush technique, add wisps and streaks of white acrylic paint to places where foam would form. Let this coat dry, then add a third coat, etc., until the more-vertical areas are built up to the right depth. Add the white foam at each step. At the proper stage in the setting-up, these latter coats can be teased by dragging an object through the plastic to build more swirls and waves into the flowing water.

Following the first two coats, using the casting plastics or silicone compound, you might wish to switch over to the use of gloss medium. This is applied unthinned by pouring and/or brushing it into place. It is easier to tease this material to simulate the swirling white water. While the last coast is still wet, string some small tufts of cotton balls downstream from the rapids to simulate the finer spray.

Finish the water by dry-brushing some final wisps of white foam onto the tops of the foaming areas, using white acrylic paint.

Snow and Ice

The modeling of winter scenes, with snow and ice, can be very effective if the correct methods and materials are used. The snow can generally cover the terrain of a diorama, or be present only at the highest mountain elevations of a layout.

Snow. Almost every white powder has been tried to simulate snow. All of them have advantages and disadvantages of various sorts. If the snow is to really be temporary, as might be used to coat a diorama and railroad equipment to take winter photographs, then the choices include baking soda, baking powder, flour, cornstarch, salt, white sugar, dolomite, and dry plaster. The material is sifted on and spread around as desired. It is removed by vacuuming. Foodstuffs should not be left as permanent snow because they attract insects and rodents.

If the snow is to be permanent and bonded in place, a good choice is common baking *soda*. Do not use baking *powder* if the snow is to be bonded because it will dissolve and make a mess. Baking soda can be corrosive, particularly if both moisture and electricity are present. Another good choice is plain, dry casting plaster or commercially available equivalents made to model snow.

If the snow cover will be thin, then the scenery that will be covered with snow should be completed just as though the snow were not going to be added. If the snow will be quite deep, then the coverwork should be prepared with a final plaster surface simulating the depth and shape of the snow, including the drifts and piles. If none of the groundwork will show through the snow, there is no need to color this plaster, either prior to or following pouring.

Any trees, weeds, ground cover, structures, etc., should be completed and in place before the snow is added. First spray the area to receive the snow with wetted water, followed by a spray of diluted matte medium. Sift on the baking soda using a tea strainer. It should stick only to horizontal surfaces, as real snow would. Then bond the baking soda with an overspray of diluted matte medium. Repeat the process as necessary to create the proper snow depth and drifts.

You also can add soda to dry surfaces, or to previously applied, but now dry, snow surfaces. Move the soda around with small brushes or miniature vehicles to simulate ruts, plowed roads or sidewalks, etc. Make the snow thinner toward the top of structure roofs or over heated areas to provide realistic effects. Clear the snow off areas where it would naturally melt away. All this shaping is followed by additional bonding.

Another method uses a mixture of equal parts of acrylic matte medium, acrylic modeling paste, and acrylic titanium white tube paint. Keep this mixture in a jar with a tight cover so it does not dry out. Brush on the "snow" mixture either thin or thick and pile it up to make snowdrifts. Because this snow is not a powder that can be sifted on, it requires somewhat more artistic skill to create realistic effects.

Either of these snow creating methods results in permanent snow that cannot later be removed from the buildings, rolling stock, trees, groundwork, etc.

Ice. Melted ice is best simulated with artist's acrylic gloss medium, thinned as appropriate, and spread on the surface. It will dry shiny. A little white coloring in it will help simulate the not-always totally clear look of ice. Ice blocks can be made by cutting small cubes of clear plastic to scale size, then coating them with the same finish, or by using paraffin.

Icicles are best made separately and then added where they should be. String unthinned gloss medium on a piece of glass with a toothpick. Use several layers to build up a thickness. When dry, remove the icicles with a razor blade, trim them, and apply them where desired using ACC. Clear nylon toothbrush bristles can also be used as a "frame" to make icicles. Coat the bristles with the gloss medium, tapering it from the point of attachment.

Make sheet ice, such as on frozen ponds or streams, using the same methods as were used for still water, but add color to make the water look frozen. What is desired is a pearly-white color, somewhat translucent, but not transparent. Experiment by adding white and pearl dyes to the top plastic resin or gloss medium.

Note that ice is usually snow-covered, except where the snow has blown away or been cleaned off. An example of the latter would be a skating rink. You might even make tiny scratches to indicate the marks left on the ice by the skates.

ROADS AND HIGHWAYS

The base plaster for roads and highways should have been put down with the plastering step described under the topic, "Coverwork," in chapter 16. This topic included the methods for completing (less the detailwork) these man-made necessities.

The width, surface material, and condition of roads and highways tells much about the area you are modeling. The choices range from the simplest one-lane dirt road up to modern super-highways. Because of space limitations, most of the modeling you will want to do will be of two-lane concrete or asphalt (black-top) highways, or smaller, more primitive equivalents (FIGS. 17-11 and 17-12).

Fig. 17-11. An example of a dirt road and a railroad grade crossing.

The narrowest, one-lane dirt road will be about 8 feet wide. Two-lane dirt or gravel roads will be 14 to 20 feet in width. Paved roads will usually measure 12 feet per lane. These dimensions do not include shoulders, if any, and ditches, which are usually necessary. You can cheat downward a little on these dimensions for the model, but not by more than 20 percent.

All but the most rudimentary roads will have some kind of ditches. Most roads have a very slight crown that raises the center a little higher than the edges so that water will run off.

Make the road surface of plaster. Sculptamold, drywall joint compound, or papier mâché. Make it as level and smooth as possible because texture, ruts, etc., will be added later. Scrape the material smooth while still wet, then sand and rasp smooth when dry. Precolor the material an earth, concrete, or dark gray color, as appropriate.

Sculptamold is a particularly good material to use because it is clean to work with, it sets in about the right time (30 minutes), it can be used in thin layers, and it is easy to sand, file, or rasp when it is dry. It can be precolored using the same methods as for plaster (see "Rock Casting").

Drywall joint compound is also a good material to use. It comes premixed and it sets slowly. It shrinks slightly when it dries. Its main advantage is that it is water soluble after drying, so it can be smoothed with a damp sponge without creating dust.

Dirt Roads

Create a dirt road by spreading fine dirt material of suitable color (see "Soil") onto the road base. A gravel road is done exactly the same, only using slighty coarser material. Spread and rut the material to simulate the kind of road being modeled. Ruts can often be done best by using a model car. When satisfied with the contour and roughness, spray the road with wetted water, then saturate it with diluted matte medium.

When completely dry, scrub the road slightly in the direction of traffic using a track cleaning abrasive pad or a coarse typewriter eraser. Some further repetition of adding, shaping, and bonding dirt can result in exactly the type of road you want. Vacuum up any loose material. A final spray of Dust can give the road the true dusty look.

Paved Roads

Paved roads are usually either concrete or blacktop (asphalt/tar/Macadam) composition. The prototype concrete roads are cast in place in sections, with expansion joints down the centerline and every 15 to 20 feet between sections. The blacktop roads are either made by mixing tar compounds with gravel on site, then spreading this out and rolling it down, or in more recent times, by using premixed asphalt laid down by machine and then rolled. In either case, there are no seams or expansion joints because the asphalt is resilient to temperature changes.

Either type of road is simulated by starting with a smooth base that has been scraped, filed, rasped, and/or sanded. Preferably, the material was precolored. For blacktop, paint or stain the surface to the proper color, which is not black but a deep slate gray. The edges of blacktop roads are often not distinct but are sort of wavy and blend into the dirt alongside the road. A concrete road might have blacktop shoulder paving.

For concrete roads (FIG. 17-12), scribe lines to simulate the joints between sections. If the concrete is old, it will have cracks, which can be scribed in using jagged lines. Note how the real thing looks to most effectively reproduce this. Then paint or stain the material a concrete color, which is a quite light grey. A thin wash of a slightly different light grey should then be brushed over the first, with the brush strokes in the direction of traffic.

Carefully brush dark gray paint into the crack and section lines to simulate the asphalt used for expansion joints and repair filler. Again, look at real examples to capture the effect properly. For an alternative method, use a wash of a somewhat diluted dark gray water-soluble paint spread over the concrete and

Fig. 17-12. An asphalt highway and a grade crossing.

into the cracks. Then wipe this off the surface before it dries, leaving color only in the joints and cracks.

The final coloring of roads and highways to simulate the brake marks, dripped oil, road markings, etc., and to add a dusty look, is discussed under "Detailwork," chapter 20.

Grade Crossings

Where a road, street, or highway crosses a railroad track, some type of material is used around and between the rails to continue the road, yet allow the track to be maintained. This is usually done with wood, although a more modern material is a hard rubber compound. Sometimes the dirt, gravel, concrete, or blacktop is continued across the track, with timbers next to the rails, or with only gaps left for the flangeways, although this is more unusual. Precast concrete slabs have also been used for these crossings.

Whatever the type, make the crossing slightly lower than the rail height so that coupler pins do not snag. Bevel the ends (as on the prototype) to lift up any dragging equipment. Simulate the wood with wood or with styrene plastic by bonding piece-by-piece to the tops of the ties. Make sure to leave adequate clearance for the flanges on the inside of the rails.

Cast blacktop or concrete crossings in place at the same time and in the same way as the adjoining road surfaces. The insides of the rails should have a stretched twine or a plastic strip abutted to the rails. This will prevent the plaster (or other road material) from forming next to the rails. Remove it after the plaster is dry and finished.

STREETS AND SIDEWALKS

The streets in towns and cities are made the same way as the roads and highways in the country, with a few exceptions. In urban areas they will usually have curbs and might have storm drains. They might also be wide enough to accommodate parking. In bygone eras, town streets were made of dirt, then of planks, and then progressed to wooden blocks, cut stones, and bricks; finally, asphalt paving and concrete became common. You must suit your streets to the time being modeled. (FIG. 17-13).

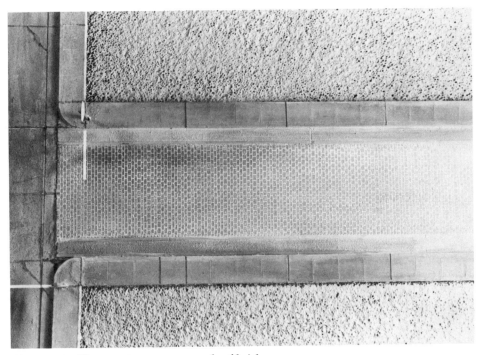

Fig. 17-13. *City streets were once made of bricks.*

Some city streets also have streetcar or railroad tracks in the street. These often use bricks around the rails to facilitate repairs. The rails for streetcars usually had a built-in flangeway. In some scales, a commercial product, called *girder rail*, is available for such streetcar rails. City streets also have manhole covers and are lined for pedestrian crosswalks and other warnings. They might use storm drains to sewers to carry away rainfall.

Sidewalks can be adjacent to the curb or separated from it by a strip of grass, which might also have trees planted in it. The sidewalk width is proportional to the foot traffic being carried. Sidewalks were, at one time, made of wood planks. Some were (and are) brick, some are asphalt, but most are now made of concrete. FIGURE 17-14 shows a photo of model city street and sidewalk detail.

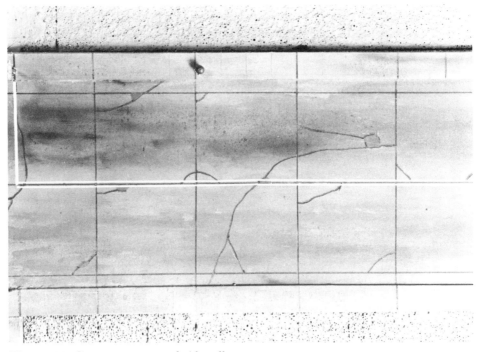

Fig. 17-14. Concrete streets and sidewalks.

Concrete sidewalks can be made of plaster, poured and sanded smooth; or they can be built up from paperboard, foamboard, or styrene, and painted to simulate concrete. The joints can be scribed or carved in. These joints occur between the sidewalk and the curb and between sidewalk sections. The joint spacing varies from 2 to 4 feet.

18

Greenwork

Greenwork is the construction sequence that duplicates nature's green things—all the items of the plant kingdom such as grass, trees, weeds, and brush. This does not restrict the subject to things that are always green, because many of these plants are other colors (tree trunks) or change color with the seasons. Greenwork also includes the dead remnants of once-green things.

GROUND COVER

Ground cover is a broad term that includes anything living, or once-living, that is not mineral or animal and that covers the ground or buildings. This includes grasses, weeds, crops, shrubs, bushes, ivy, etc., but not trees.

By the standards of most humans, Mother Nature is not a very good house-keeper. Neither is she a very neat gardener. She lets everything grow where it wants to, not separating the good plants from the weeds. She doesn't keep the grass mowed to a uniform height and neatly edged and bordered. When things die, they are just allowed to stay where they fall. That natural look is not at all what mankind has tried to create with his lawns and gardens.

Her groundskeepers are the wild grazing animals who trim things a bit here and there to suit their culinary taste. The fallen limbs and leaves are eventually converted into humus by her microbes and insects. The system works quite well. It just does not look neat and pretty by our standards.

Yet, if you want to create a realistic model, you must duplicate nature's jumbled garden, not what you wish it looked like or what it would look like if it were a rich man's estate cared for by a horde of gardeners. You must recognize that there is a good bit of randomness and clutter to natural plant growth, as well as death.

The grasses have a wide variety of heights, depending on microclimate, shade, water, animal grazing, and other factors. The types of grasses and weeds are all mixed together, but even this mixture is not uniform. There might be fair-sized areas where some type of plant is dominant, then clusters of new types appear, and one of these might then predominate for a while. There is randomness, but even the randomness gives over occasionally to some semblance of regularity.

There are no sharp demarcations between plants of different types. There are no straight lines or smooth curves. Every plant is located where its struggle with the elements and with competing plants allowed it to succeed. The result is, for that place and time, the current score in the battle of the survival of the fittest.

Every plant will live and die in one place. When it is dead, it will turn brown, wither, blow away, or stay in place. Eventually it will decay and form food for new plants. At all seasons of the year there are always some dead plants that can be seen among the living ones, ghostly remnants from the previous year. The more woody the plant, the more of these can be seen.

Plants are not all green during the same seasons. Some grow early in the spring and are brown by summer. Others grow in early summer but don't die until fall. The flowering time varies widely with plant type and climate. Almost all green plants die and turn brown in winter if the temperatures drop below freezing.

The lessons for the modeler in creating miniature ground cover are:

1. Blend several shades of color together.
2. Vary the texture of the materials used.
3. Vary the height of vegetation.
4. Model some dead plant life.
5. Keep the edges nonregular and semirandom.
6. Observe nature's examples.

It should be noted that there are some places where these rules do not apply, such as when you are modeling lawns or crop-filled fields that mankind has trimmed to suit his desires. Then, everything can be regular, repetitive, nonrandom and smooth edged . . . if that is what the real thing looks like.

It is assumed that you have prepared the ground to be covered according to the methods described in "Soil," chapter 17; that is, that all "earth" is of the proper texture and color to simulate bare ground. Ground cover should always be applied so that some of the earth shows through, particularly when viewed from above.

Grass

Grasses vary in height, color, and texture. In warm climates, grass grows and stays green year-round if it is watered regularly. If it just receives winter rains, as in much of California, it turns a golden yellow by midsummer. If freezing occurs, the grass usually deadens and turns a yellow-brown. The first rains of spring cause the brightest greens of all as the new grass sprouts up.

If grass is not mowed, depending on the variety, it can grow a few feet tall. It is usually quite tangled together when this high. The winds will often create swirls and patterns in it. The wild grasses of the North American prairies often reached several feet in height.

Materials you can use for grass include paint, zip texture, sawdust, flock, ground foam, grass paper, fake fur, and felt. Only use grass paper to simulate smooth lawns or areas where the grass is kept mowed.

The color of grass is not as bright green as your mind remembers. Most grass varies from pale yellow to deep olive green. The hues tend to be light. In wild areas, the grass is darker where the soil stays damp. Some lawn colors might be slightly blue.

Zip Texture. Zip texturing is not recommended for foreground grass because it does not provide the proper texture. It might be used in areas away from the viewer, however. Zip texturing is described in chapter 17. Use a mixture of greens, light browns, and yellow ochre.

Paint. Paint is also not recommended because of the lack of texture. Only use it for distant areas. Soft greens are recommended for colors.

Sawdust/Ground Foam. Either sawdust or ground foam are highly recommended for grass because they provide good textures and colors. "Texture Materials" in chapter 17 discusses these materials. Apply them by sifting them onto a surface that has been prewet using wetted water. Use the finer materials first. Try to avoid uniformity when applying them. Use more than one shade of the materials but with shades not too far apart, so there is no salt-and-pepper effect. Bonding is described in chapter 17.

Flock. Flock, or electrostatic grass, can make a very effective grass simulation. For short grass, obtain flock with lengths of about $1/64$ inch or less. Mix two or more colors together. Use gold flock to simulate California yellow grass.

Apply the flock using an electrostatic dispenser to a surface coated with undiluted matte medium. Rub the dispenser with a dry cloth to build up a static charge. Hold the applicator $3/4$ to $1^1/2$ inch above the surface and simultaneously shake and squeeze it. The "grass" will stand up when it hits the surface because of the charge.

Protect your face with a respirator when flocking because some of the particles will float around in the air. When dry, the flocked surface might be a little shiny. This can be dulled down by lightly misting with an airbrush and a diluted light brown acrylic paint (or Polly S). An alternate method would be to spray it lightly with wetted water and then dust on a thin coating of light brown zip texturing.

Grass Paper. Simulate grass for lawns by using grass papers. These include flocked paper and other materials bonded to paper. Contact-cement the paper to a smooth, clean surface. Hide the edges with ground cover. You might wish to spray the grass to dull it and/or change or vary it in color.

Fake Fur. Simulate tall grass with a product available at fabric stores called fake fur. This is made of a polyester pile and can be bought with fibers from $1/4$ to $1/2$ inch long. Choose the yellow-brown or other light beige or light green color. Cut the material to size and then glue it down with undiluted white glue.

Comb and trim the material with sharp-tipped scissors. You might try "mowing" it in places with the sideburn cutters on an electric razor or with electric hair clippers. Vacuum up all the loose hair. Spray the material with dark green (or other color) latex paint, thinned 4:1. When it is dry, use a brass-bristled brush to tease/fluff the fur into grass/weeds. Sift dirt over it in some places to make bare spots. Hide the edges with other ground cover.

Felt. Use felt somewhat like the fake fur. Choose an olive color. Bond it down with undiluted white glue. Spray it with the desired colors. Tease the felt with a brass-bristle suede shoe brush. Lift up for taller grass. Blend in the edges.

Flowers. Add flowers to the grass by using colored zip texture or colored sawdust or ground foam. You might also use dabs of acrylic artist's paint. Any flowers should be done sparsely to look right. Overspray with dilute matte medium to fix the flowers in place.

Weeds

The distinction between grass and weeds is somewhat arbitrary. Weeds certainly include all the broad-leafed ground cover annuals, but many narrow-bladed weeds (such as reeds, rushes, etc.) exist as well.

Weeds grow wherever there is enough moisture, where they can get sunlight, and where they have some protection from the elements. Common locations are around rocks, in swampy ground, along waterways, and around the edges of forests. They also like to grow along fences, in ditches, and almost anywhere that man does not want them to grow. They follow a random growing pattern but do tend to form in clumps.

Some of the materials that can be used for weeds include sawdust, ground foam, lichen (small), real weeds, real seeds, shavings, cotton, rope fiber, and brush fiber.

Natural Materials. There are many natural materials you can use to simulate weeds that are themselves weeds. These include cattails, foxtails, barley grass, and many others whose names are known only to botanists. The head (brown part) of the cattail can be pulled apart to reveal some miniature scale weeds. The fall of the year is the best time to find and harvest these natural weed materials.

Where to Find Natural Materials

Outside (late summer or early fall)

> Fields
> Ditches
> Weed patches
> Edges of swamps

Shops

> Florists
> Decorator's supplies

Craft stores
Floral supplies
Christmas decorations

What to look for

Lichen	Twigs
Cattails	Bark
Fine-branching weeds	Seeds
Flowers	Dry leaves
Seed clusters	

Use florist's sphagnum moss to create a tangled underbrush effect. Spray it in appropriate colors and attach it with white glue.

Artificial Materials. Use green carpet material for weed clumps. Using diagonal cutters, cut off tufts from the backing and plant them in white glue. Dry brush lighter green and/or yellow on tips.

Brush felt with a file card to obtain fuzz. Ball up some of the fuzz and paint it a dry light brown color to make effective tumbleweeds. Use light green felt fuzz to build up flat piles of kudzu or heath. Use ground foam to form the leaves of these plants.

Taller weeds and reeds can be made using macrame polypropylene twine. Choose appropriate colors or paint/stain the twine before cutting. Grasp several strands in a tweezers, then cut them off and plant them in white glue. Use the same method with other materials, such as sisal string or rope and jute twine.

Unravelled and combed-out embroidery cotton can be used to make weeds. This material comes in an assortment of colors. The bristles of natural paint brushes can also be used to make some effective weeds, but this is expensive unless you use brushes that are ready to be discarded.

Choose jute or sisal twine to make matted grass/weeds. Stain, cut it, and plant it, with some standing up and some lying down. Make small broad-leafed weed clumps from bits of lichen or the larger sizes of ground foam.

The moss/algae/lichen that grows on rocks and tree trunks can be simulated with paint splotches of Depot Olive or dark green. These tend to mostly be on the same side (North) of the objects.

Crops

Crops are whatever man has planted and tended to be harvested and used for animal or human food or as raw material for various other purposes. This includes gardens as well as the large fields of grain or rows of crops such as cotton, corn, soybeans, etc. Crops can be modeled in any of the various stages of growth, from plowed ground, small plants, mature plants, to harvested fields.

Materials for crops include many of those for grass and weeds, plus toweling. Corduroy material can be used to make some types of row crops. There are also cloth materials with separated "bumps" or tufts that can simulate the regular spacing of crops. Corrugated cardboard, with the top ply removed, makes a good plowed field.

Simulate a grain field by using fake fur or a fine-cut pile carpet in the proper color. Make corn stalks from the tips of plastic asparagus ferns. Make each stalk as if it would be about 7 feet high. Mash each leaf flat, and plant in regular rows. Hay fields can be made using the same methods used for short grass.

Twist gold and yellow polypropylene cord (twine) to make harvested hay or straw. To make bales, cut the cord $1/32$ to $1/16$ inch long. Cut the bale from 12-×-18-×-30-inch wood, filing the corners slightly. Dip in matte medium and then into the fibers. For loose hay/straw, cut the cord $1/8$ inch long. Pile the fibers onto matte medium. Make bundles or shocks by building up parallel masses of fibers to the proper size. To make a hay/straw stack, carve balsa to shape and cover it with fiber.

Short row crops can be simulated by building up clumps of ground foam, or by using bits of dyed foam of the proper size. Add flowers or cotton bolls by using bits of colored ground foam. You could create entire fields of flowers this way.

Shrubs and Brush

Shrubs and brush are intermediate in size between weeds and trees. Because of this, the materials and procedures used can be from either group, depending on the size and type of the shrub/brush to be simulated.

Scrap lichen, covered with ground foam, makes effective brush. Some of the same materials used for the fine-branch structure and foliage material for trees are also useful. See the topic, "Deciduous Trees."

Make hedges from furnace filter material by cutting it into strips and sprinkling with ground foam. Model hedge material is available commercially. A large variety of ornamental shrubs seen around houses can be modeled using these methods. Some have flowers that you can simulate with colored ground foam.

Ivy

Materials for ivy include ground foam and sawdust. Ivy is usually modeled climbing on a building wall. This is done by applying a thin line of white glue or matte medium to the wall, then sprinkling on ground foam of the proper size and color. Repeat this as necessary.

Try to form the same patterns that ivy makes in climbing up and spreading on the wall (FIG. 18-1). You might wish to paint on some of the vine branches, usually a light brown color. Ivy can also be modeled climbing up rocks or trees.

Fallen Leaves

Both deciduous and coniferous trees will have dead leaves or needles under them during some or all seasons of the year. Coniferous trees also drop cones.

Fig. 18-1.*Model ivy can be made to "grow" on a wall.*

Most leaves/needles fall within the circumference of the tree branches, although the wind can spread them elsewhere.

Materials you can use for fallen leaves from bushes or deciduous trees include ground foam, sawdust, and ground-up dead (real) leaves or bark. One material to use for fallen needles from coniferous trees is brown flock, or static grass. The tiniest paper punchings, when dyed, also make good fallen leaves. Fix the leaves/needles in place with a light spray of bonding agent (FIG. 18-2).

Most leaves turn brown before they drop off, but a few, such as aspen, are a golden color. Needles are usually a medium brown. Choose the colors to be convincing. Make cones from small cone-shaped seeds that are either naturally brown or are dyed/painted brown.

TREES

Joyce Kilmer ended his familiar poem *Trees* with:

> "Poems are made by fools like me,
> But only God can make a tree."

You are probably neither poet nor fool, and certainly not God, but you *can* make trees—miniature nonliving ones, that is. To make a model tree that looks realistic, you must look at the full-sized trees in all their variety to learn what

Fig. 18-2. Fallen leaves and needles accumulate under trees.

they look like, how they are shaped and colored, how big they are, where they grow and don't grow, and how they fit in with each other.

About Trees

The two most common mistakes that tree models display are that they are too regular and too dense. Whatever the species of a tree, it is slightly different from every other tree of that same species. It displays a certain randomness of shape within constraints common to its type. The limbs leave the trunk in different places and at different angles. The branches grow to different lengths. Often these differences are influenced by the shade from or proximity to other trees or to structures.

Trees are not as dense as you might imagine. Many an art student has heard a teacher say, "Paint your trees so they look like a bird could fly through them." Most real trees allow some sky to show through. Most show some of the upper limbs through the foliage. Trees consist of much more than half emptiness. If trees were really dense, then the sunlight and air could not get to any of the leaves except those on the outside. Each leaf must have sunlight and air or it will die.

Color. The color of the foliage is not uniform. The leaves vary slightly from each other and might be different shades on opposite sides of the leaf. Each leaf is at a different angle to the light. Some are in the shadows of others. The tree appears to be lighter colored at the top and on the sides than on the bottom or on the inside. The side towards the light looks the lightest.

The color shades will vary over a considerable range, but on one tree or type of tree, the greens will all be of the same family. Avoid bright greens. Fall colors can be modeled when appropriate. In the fall, different trees will be ahead or behind others in coloration, with a variety ranging from normal greens through all the shades of yellow, orange, red, and brown, even including leafless trees. The altitude will have a large effect on this coloring, with trees at high altitudes well ahead of those lower down.

When you model trees, you cannot, because of the small scale, model individual leaves. This is probably fortunate because that would be a tedious project. You have to create a model that gives the illusion of being a tree . . . that forms an impression of a tree. To do this, model the trunk and the major limbs. Then use some natural or artificial materials to simulate the leaf groupings of branches, but not the individual branch, twig, etc. This might also serve to represent the leaves, but you often add them on as a texture- and color-providing outer covering to the tree.

When you model dead trees, or leafless trees in winter, then you must add more of the finer branches because they are not hidden. There should always be some dead limbs, some standing dead trees, and many fallen dead trees in various stages of decay in any modeled scene where man would not have removed the dead material for firewood or for neatness' sake. Also, do not forget to model the stumps, either those left from fallen trees or those that remain when a tree is cut down.

Variety. Within a given species, some trees will be young and some will be old. Suggest this with size, shape, simulated scars, and aging of the trunk and limbs. Some trees might be modeled to show the effects of man, such as sawed-off limbs, posters, a rope swing, etc. Some might have been pruned for clearances or as in orchards. Some might show recent or long-ago storm damage. Each tree can tell a story in the same way that a structure or piece of rolling stock can.

Trees that are planted in neat rows as in orchards or windbreaks are still not identical. Naturally seeded trees appear to be spaced at random, but there are always reasons for nature's plantings. Trees are more likely to take root and survive in certain places than in others. This will depend on water supply, soil conditions, winds, and on the presence or absence of other trees. Nearby trees can give either protection to the seedling, or they can starve it of the light, water, and nutrients that it needs.

Examine nature to learn about trees. Look where trees grow. They are more likely in valleys and along streams and less likely in rocky ground. They will grow where the soil is good and relatively flat and well watered, but not where it is flooded. Look at the trees themselves. For each different species, how and where do the limbs attach to the trunk? How many are there? Are they straight or crooked? What is the shape of the foliage? What are the colors? What is the texture of the trunk? Have you ever really *looked* at trees?

Choices. As with locomotives or structures, you can buy your trees ready made or in kits, or you can build them from scratch with purchased or natural materials. The ready-made trees tend to be the most expensive, but they have a wide range of prices, depending on the appearance. Those made for architectural models are the most realistic, but the most costly. Tree kits provide medium cost and a convenient supply of materials. If you make your trees from scratch, this will be the lowest cost, and only a little more work than for those from kits. Some types of trees are not available ready-made or as kits, so then there is no choice.

Also, as with the locomotives and structures, you can improve ready-made or kit-built trees in realism by performing just a few additional steps and some detailing. Scratchbuilt trees tend to have the randomness and openness desired because of the way you build them. You might want to achieve these same desirable characteristics with ready-made and kit-built trees. This adds almost nothing to their cost but takes some additional time. That time is well spent compared to the improvements in appearance that it will provide.

For a normal layout, you are going to need a lot of trees—several hundred perhaps. If each one takes several hours to complete, that might be an expenditure of time that you would rather spend doing something less tedious. Also, if you buy each tree, the expenditure of money could be more than you care to make. The solution is not to model fewer trees, but to choose modeling methods that are economical in both time and money.

You can use some highly detailed trees in the foreground and in places where they will be seen and appreciated. You do not have to make all trees to the same high standards, however. Trees in the background can be "caricatures," with less detailing, made for a few pennies and minutes each.

Types. Most trees are either deciduous or coniferous. Deciduous trees are those with broad leaves. Many of them lose their leaves in the winter, but some in southern regions are "evergreen" and continuously lose and replace their leaves year-round.

Nonevergreen deciduous trees change their appearance a great deal during the year. In spring they display their brightest greens when the new leaves come out. They might have flowers at this time of the year, either before or after leafing out. In the fall, the leaves turn colors of yellows, oranges, and reds . . . then fall off. In winter the limbs are bare. You must suit the appearance of the trees to the season you are modeling.

Coniferous trees are all evergreens, but they have needles instead of leaves, and they produce their seeds in cones. Some of these have long needles and some short. Many trees are neither deciduous nor coniferous. Most of these other types of trees grow in hot or tropical climates, in arid regions, or in jungles. Examples include ferns, palms, cacti, etc.

Location. In different parts of the United States and Canada the trees that grow naturally are quite different. This is primarily due to the differences in climate, but certain species are only native to some regions. The location of your model determines the types of trees that should be modeled.

In the eastern forests, spruce, fir and tamarack grow. The northeastern pine forests produce jack, red, and white pines. Birch, beech, maple, and hemlock might be found in northern hardwood forests. Southern hardwood forests have oak, chestnut, yellow poplar, and hickory. Southeastern pine forests consist of loblolly, longleaf, and slash pines. Southern river bottoms will grow cypress, tupelo, and sweet gum.

In the western Sierra regions, the trees include live oak, ponderosa pine, incense cedar, sugar pine, white fir, red fir, lodgepole pine, mountain hemlock, white pine, Jeffrey pine, juniper, pinyon pine, and chaparral. Douglas fir, sequoia, and redwood are found near the coast. The hardiest broadleaf trees are aspen and white birch.

In eastern towns and cities, plantings will include American ash, willows, linden, maple, poplars, sycamores, oaks, and elms. In the southeast, magnolia and dogwood grow. The great plains and lower valleys in the west have cottonwood and birch. In the Rocky Mountain towns, boxelder, catalpa, and locust are present. In California, pepper trees and eucalyptus grow. Fruit and ornamental flowering trees in large variety are found everywhere.

Single, isolated trees are rare in nature. Trees tend to grow in clumps of three or more. These will usually be of varying sizes and might not all be of the same species. Often the tallest tree will be in the center of a group. Some of the outer trees might be seedlings of those in the middle.

Sizes. Trees of the same species can vary a great deal in height. It is best not to make your model trees too tall because they will overpower other scenery. Model your trees to 45 feet for deciduous trees and 75 feet for conifers for the tallest specimens.

Typical Heights of Mature Trees

100' and up	Sequoia, redwood, cypress, Douglas fir
70'	Black larch, maples, pin oak, beech, linden, elm, hickory, white & red pines, ash, magnolia, poplar, cherry, red and white birch
60'	Spruce, catalpa, paper birch, chestnut, hemlock, black, red and live oaks
50'	Cedar, arbor vitae, red mulberry
40'	Chinaberry, American holly
30'	Mimosa, dogwood, redbud, apple, grey birch

Shapes. Different types of trees have different shapes. Most conifers are oblong, conical, or columnar. Deciduous trees can be round, oblong, flat, vase-shaped or columnar. The shape changes as the tree gets older. A young conifer will usually be denser than an older one. Just the opposite is true of most deciduous trees. For all trees, the trunk becomes more textured as the tree ages.

Tree symmetry might change with age. This will be determined by the location relative to the wind and weather, and relative to other trees and objects. There will be less foliage on the windward side, on sides near cliffs or structures and other trees, and less lower foliage on trees in the middle of a grove.

Conifers tend to have more lower dead branches and a general thinning of foliage as the tree ages. In old trees, there can be large bare areas, and most of the needle clusters will be near the branch tips. The roots might become more exposed with time.

Sometimes fires will leave their scars on trees and forests. On the model, this can range from charred areas on the trunks of a few living trees, to whole burned-over areas with blackened trees and stumps. The latter might also be modeled at a stage of regrowth, with brush and small trees making a comeback among the derelicts.

Occasionally, trees die from disease or insect attack and retain their leaves or needles. Such trees often have a "rusty" color to the foliage. Do not overdo this effect.

Most trees are vertical, and the foliage is balanced over the base of the trunk. Exceptions are palms and trees that are dead or dying, or that were undermined or pushed aside as they were growing, such as along river banks. Almost without exception, modeled trees that are not vertical, do not look realistic.

Deciduous Trees

Generally speaking, deciduous tree models consist of an armature that represents the trunk and major limbs, some type of foliage material representing the smaller branches and twigs, and a texture material to represent the leaves.

The trunk/limbs can be cast in plastic or metal, made of metal wire, or made from natural twigs or roots. Either of the cast materials must be purchased.

The foliage material must simulate the openness of the tree while providing a support for the leaves. The choices are lichen moss, expanded fiber material, rubberized horsehair material, and steel wool. Some natural growths, when used for trees, will simulate both the trunk/limbs and the foliage material.

Make the leaves from any of the ground cover textures, particularly ground foam, sawdust, or tiny paper punchouts.

Trunks/Limbs. There are several options for making the trunks (FIG. 18-3). These include castings, twisted wire, string and natural materials.

Fig. 18-3. Some model deciduous tree trunk options.

Castings. The cast plastic or metal trunk/limb armatures are very realistic, but the most expensive. Use them in the foreground where this realism will be appreciated. For trunks, the first step is to drill a small hole in the center of the bottom of the trunk. Put a 1-inch wire into this hole and bond it in place with ACC. This will be used for all handling and painting of the tree and for the eventual mounting of the tree to the layout. A block of foam makes a good holder for a number of trees.

Next, bend the cast trunk and limbs to the shape desired. For the plastic trunks, this might require softening the plastic over a candle flame or soldering iron. Don't get them too hot or they will melt or ignite.

Twisted Wire. Trunks/limbs made from twisted wire are also very realistic. Use seven or more strands of wire of a gauge appropriate to your scale and the size of the tree. Leave one wire long at the base of the trunk for holding/mounting. Twist the other wires, using a vise and pliers. Use all of the wires for the lower trunk, but break out wires for limbs at higher elevations. Form the proper twists to the wires. The more wires that you use, the more realistic the tree will be, but the longer it will take.

For the most realistic twisted wire trunks, use two 0.060-inch tinned wires per major branch. Form the bottom of the trunk and solder the wires. Helically wrap the trunk with two or three times as many 0.032-inch tinned wires. Split these and continue forming the branches, then splitting again. Add 0.020–0.025-inch wire for the finest branches, starting where major branches leave the trunk. Solder all the strands. Use several thin coats of Durham's water putty on the trunk to fill in.

Another trunk coating is to use a resilient material, such as silicone cement or rubber (like you used for mold making). Dip the trunks in these liquids, then add another layer later by brush to fill out the valleys between the wires. Let these dry thoroughly before coloring.

String. Various types of strings can be used to make tree trunks. Possible materials include carpet thread, cotton string, jute cord, and clothesline cord. In each case, partially unravel the material down to where the first branch leaves the trunk. Below that point, harden the trunk with ACC. Then unravel more until the next branch, and repeat the process. Form the smaller branches with more unraveling and more stiffening with the ACC. Continue to do this until the finest branches are made up of only one strand.

Sewing thread can be used to wrap and hold the materials where each branch splits off. Run a thin wire up the middle of the trunk to serve as a holding and mounting means. This process is a lot of work, and consumes a lot of ACC, but it can produce extremely realistic trunks, which is particularly useful for winter scenes because of the fine branch structure possible.

Natural Trunks. Nature often duplicates herself in miniature. Many plants and parts of plants reproduce the natural branching patterns found in deciduous trees. There are a number of natural twigs and weeds that you can use for the trunks/limbs. Some of these come equipped with scale-size bark.

Examples include some types of weed roots, sagebrush or mesquite twigs, broomweed, wild rosebush tips, mountain ash (rowan), fruit clusters (without berries), smoke brush (or tree) flower clusters, and hydrangea flower clusters (with flowers pulled off). Some wild weeds such as spirea, cudweed, and yarrow are excellent. Florist's shops can provide dried floral plants, including baby's breath, caspia, yarrow, and sugar bush. Hedge cuttings from privet (use the flower portion when budding), crepe myrtle and nandina can also be used.

Caspia makes particularly effective aspen trunks, if colored white with black markings. Use yarrow or spirea without their blossoms/seed clusters in the small scales, though you can use them in 0 scale and larger.

For any of these natural materials, try to collect them in the late fall or in winter when they are dry. Dry them in an oven at 250°F for an hour before use to eliminate moisture and residual sap. Some people further preserve them in a glycerin solution, but this is not really necessary. Once they are painted, they will, although fragile, last a long time.

Some of the natural materials can not only serve as the trunks and branches but as foliage material as well. Materials that might be suitable include sugar bush and cudweed. Often, only the outer portion of these are used, bound together to form the trunk. You also might add branches of one natural material to a trunk of another to make a more convincing tree. Drill a hole and glue the "branch" in.

Make some more trunks and limbs that will be used to model either standing or fallen deadwood. Use the same materials and methods, except make the colors different to simulate the grayer colors of old and dead wood. These pieces of wood will often have part or all of the bark missing. If the material used is not natural, then the bark will have to be built up by using whatever material was used to form the trunk contour. Sagebrush roots make very effective deadwood snags.

Trunk Colors. Whatever the material, paint the trunk/limb armatures in appropriate colors. Most deciduous trees have trunks and major branches that are colored more gray than brown. Look carefully at the type of tree you are modeling to duplicate the color. The coloring is most easily done by dipping each trunk or by spraying a large number of them at once. For foreground trees, add some texture coloring. A wash of a dark color to form the shadows, followed by dry brushed highlights, will add much realism.

Foliage Material. There is no perfect foliage material that really does an ideal job of simulating the network of branches and twigs of a tree (FIG. 18-4). The best and most expensive choice is a material made by Bachman consisting of a gray-brown polyfiber matrix of fine "hairs," which is then covered with fine-grind green foam rubber. To use it, pull it apart so that it is very thin and expands out to about ten times its original area. This is necessary so that it will have a see-through look, similar to real foliage.

Woodland Scenics makes a similar, but coarser product, with the ground foam already attached. While stretching it out, some of the ground foam will fall off. Save this and use it again. Use scissors to cut the material into small, irregular clumps.

Another choice of foliage material is a type of rubberized horsehair, sometimes used for packing material. This also must be stretched out considerably

Fig. 18-4. Foliage materials and foam ''leaves,'' with bare and completed deciduous trees.

before use. Only use the brown or olive green colors of this material. Steel wool is not recommended as a foliage material. There is just too great a chance that it will cause trouble with permanent magnet motors in locomotives. Many people have used it successfully, but why take the chance when there are other low-cost choices?

Whatever the choice, glue the foliage material in small clumps to the branches of the armature, starting on the lowest limbs, to form realistic-appearing masses of foliage. The glue can be ACC or contact cement. White glue could also be used if you are willing to wait for the longer drying time.

Make the foliage clumps simulate the foliage shapes of the type of tree you are modeling. Work on several trees at once. Continue to add clumps, moving up the tree, and generally making the clumps smaller. After the glue dries, trim with scissors if necessary to finish forming the shapes. The resulting trees can make very interesting models (FIG. 18-5 AND COLOR INSERT).

Lichen. A very popular foliage material is natural lichen moss. The best grades are fine tipped and come from Norway. Lichen can be obtained precolored and pretreated from a number of companies. Choose the finest texture/density available and buy a variety of subdued colors.

Lichen also grows naturally in several areas of North America. Some of this lichen is as fine tipped as that you can purchase. If you live near a source, you might wish to collect, color, and preserve your own lichen. Collect a lot of it because the parts you will be able to use will be only a fraction of the total. Try to sort out the coarser pieces from the debris, pine needles, etc., which you can throw away.

Fig. 18-5. Several well-modeled deciduous trees, including fallen limbs and decaying vegetation, make this scene look like a real woods.

Raw lichen must be dyed and preserved. You will want to dye it several different shades of green and brown. This is most easily done by using a mass-production approach with large quantities of lichen.

For tree foliage, use only the very finest tip ends of the lichen. Save the medium-fine lichen for bushes and other scenic applications. Never use the lichen as is because it will always look artificial. Always cover it with some type of texture to simulate leaves. You can chop up and use the coarsest lichen to create brush tangles and debris.

Lichen Preservation and Dying

1. Mix one package of the lightest chosen color of powdered clothes dye, 1 gallon of industrial glycerin, and 2 gallons of water.
2. Work outside because this is a messy and smelly process.
3. Wear rubber gloves and use a wooden rod to stir the hot mixture.
4. Heat the mixture to just below boiling and then allow it to cool for 5 minutes.
5. Submerge the lichen and allow it to soak until the mixture cools to the temperature of warm water.
6. Remove the lichen, wring it out, and spread it on newspapers to dry.
7. For the second batch, replenish the glycerin by adding 1 quart. Also add a packet of the next darker dye color.

8. Reheat the mixture and repeat the process until you run out of lichen, dye, glycerin, time, or patience.

Leaves. Ground foam provides the most realistic deciduous leaves. Use the fine grind, in shades of green and yellow-green unless the tree is in fall foliage. Dyed sawdust or the tiny paper punchings (dyed) from computer cards, telex machines, check cashing machines, etc., can also be used.

Hold the tree upside-down while spraying the foliage material with a diluted matte medium solution. Sprinkle on the darkest of the green "leaves" you will be using. Work over a newspaper so the material that falls off can be retrieved and reused. Put the tree rightside-up. Spray the top and sides. Sprinkle on a little of the darker green, followed by a lighter green. Brush any "leaves" from the trunk or limbs. Let the tree dry.

Spray the top of the tree and dust on just a little light (almost yellow) green to simulate the highlights from the sun striking the leaves. When this is dry, do some final trimming and shaping. The tree is ready to plant.

The procedure is the same for fall trees, except for the color of leaves used. Flowering trees or fruit trees can be simulated by careful applications of the proper color foam or other material as a last step.

Upgrades. Even if using the cheapest, most toylike plastic tree models, take the time to color the tree the proper shades and to cover the foliage with additional leaves, as described above. This takes only a few minutes per tree, but it can transform the tree and bring it to life.

Distant Trees. Trees in the background do not have to be modeled as well (FIG. 18-6). The details will not show, and your time is better spent in doing other things. Use materials that have less fidelity to real trees. The trunks do not have

Fig. 18-6. Background deciduous trees hide the layout/backdrop transition.

to be well modeled. Here is where the best use of many natural twigs/weeds/roots, etc., for trunks can be made.

The foliage material that is most useful for distant trees is lichen. Entire forests can be formed (see "Forests") using this as the primary material, with few or no trunks being modeled. Even the distant trees will still need ground foam or other material to simulate the leaves and give the proper color and texture. Remember to make the colors slightly more subdued because of the added distance.

Fruit Trees. Fruit trees can be best modeled by including the fruit. Make the fruit of very small spheres of Fimo (see the sidebar in the topic, "People," in chapter 20) or the tiny "pills" in time-release cold capsules. Choose the color for the fruit you are simulating. Sprinkle them onto the foliage material just before the final leaf material because the fruit is usually partially covered by leaves. Make orchards of regularly spaced fruit trees. Simulate nut trees or fruit trees without fruit with properly sized tree models.

Coniferous Trees

Coniferous trees tend to have a relatively straight trunk that is much larger than any of the other limbs. The limbs of most conifers tend to droop down from where they are attached to the trunk. The height is usually about five times (or more) greater than the width. Model conifers, for foreground use, usually consist of a trunk with no limbs, foliage material that includes limbs and branches, and some texture material to simulate the needles.

Several companies provide kits for conifers that consist of wood, plastic, or metal trunks combined with suitable foliage material. Scratch-building model conifers, particularly the tall pines, firs, cedars, sequoias, etc. is quite easy.

The most effective model conifers are made using a long, tapered trunk. Branches of natural material are attached, and "needles" are added to complete the tree.

Trunks. Trunks are most easily made from wood. Start with a square piece of hard balsa wood, a hardwood dowel, or a sliver of a cedar roof shake of appropriate length. Carve or shape these to a circular cross section. Taper the trunk from the desired maximum diameter at the base to a fine point near the top. This taper should be smooth and continuous. Using a file, scratch vertical grooves in the trunk to simulate the roughness of the bark. Note that the bark texture is different for different types of trees. Drill a hole in the base and bond in a holding/mounting wire.

Trunks can also be made of wire, using a method similar to that described for deciduous trunks. Use an 18-gauge wire for the trunk. Wrap some lengths of 24-gauge florist wire around this, forming loops where branches will be. Coat the trunk with latex rubber mold compound or with liquid metal. When this is dry, cut the loops in the smaller wire to form the branches. You might need to add a second coat to the bottom of the trunk to make it thicker. These trunks work best when foliage material is added to the individual branches, rather than when natural material is used.

Paint the trunk a flat color appropriate to the type and age of tree being modeled. Add a dark wash for shadows and dry-brush on some lighter color to highlight the bark.

Branches. When the paint is dry, add the branches, starting from the bottom. The best choices for branches are either caspia, pimosa asparagus fern, or air fern. These can be obtained at hobby shops or from florists. Asparagus or air ferns are best used for short-needle trees, while caspia is a better choice for long-needle types. Use only the trimmed ends of the materials.

Using a small drill in a needle vise, drill a hole in the trunk, angled level or slanting slightly downward. Add white glue or rubber cement to the tip of the branch and push it in the hole. Use the larger branches at the bottom of the tree. Remember to add a few dead branches toward or at the bottom of the tree. If you use caspia, include the flowers and precolor it to an olive-green.

Continue drilling holes and adding the branches at somewhat random vertical and rotational spacings. Use smaller branches as you reach the top. Near the top, the trunk might be too thin to allow drilling a hole. If so, just glue the branch to the outside of the trunk. Let the glue dry thoroughly.

Needles. Added needles are not necessary with the asparagus or air fern branches, and they are optional with the caspia. For artificial branch materials, spray the branches from the top with diluted matte medium or 3M spray adhesive, then sprinkle on the needle material. Use the finest ground foam for the needles. Use the darker green first, followed by a slightly lighter green.

Another possible needle material is flock (see "Grass" for application hints). Some people have also used a fine dust, such as what is produced when cutting Homosote. This is attached first, then colored while on the tree. Whatever material you use, when finished, clean any "needles" off the trunk. When dry, the trees are ready for planting (FIG. 18-7).

You can use caspia without the flowers to simulate dead branches. Add after the foliage/needles are completed. You might also wish to add a little "moss" to the north side of the trees with olive-green paint. Make whole, dead trees from a plant found on the West Coast, called "Pride of Madera."

Background. Conifers for the background can be made in several ways. One method is to make them with tapered trunks, but with less detailing. Some people use wooden meat skewers as raw material. Paint them the proper colors.

Use either expanded Woodland Scenics foliage material or rubberized horsehair, formed into triangles and pushed onto the trunk. Rotate these clumps relative to each other and vary the size and spacing. They should decrease in size toward the top of the tree. The final step is to spray them with adhesive and sprinkle on the "needles."

Another method uses the rubberized horsehair without expanding it. Cut it into conical shapes using scissors, coat it with adhesive, sprinkle it with needles, and it is done. You might need to add a brown toothpick or dowel to simulate the bottom of the trunk.

Some smaller or more distant conifers can be simulated with natural pine cones. These must be dried thoroughly before use. Stand them up, spray them with adhesive, and sprinkle on the "needles."

Fig. 18-7. Modeled conifers, showing trunk and foliage variations.

Bottle-Brush Trees. One type of ready-to-use "pine" tree looks something like a bottle brush. It consists of fibers twisted between wires and cut to a conical shape. This type of tree can also be homemade. Cut a lot of sisal rope fibers to 2 to 3 inches in length. Stretch a wire about twice as long as your tree is to be tall along your workbench. Lay a thin strand of rubber cement along the wire and add the sisal fibers close to and parallel to each other and at right angles to the wire.

When the cement is dry, add another wire of the same length. Clamp one end of the two wires into a vise and the other end into the chuck of a hand drill. While exerting a pull on the drill, twist the wire tightly together. This will cause the fibers to "bristle" out in all directions. Trim the bristles to length and shape, spray on the proper color, and coat your tree with needle material.

Furnace Filter Material. Background conifers can be made quickly using a material made for furnace filters. The proper material should be of plant fiber (cellulose), about 1 inch thick, and fairly compact and not too open. Choose a green color. Make the trunks from dyed, tapered dowels.

Cut the material into strips of various widths, ranging from $1/4$ inch up to 1 inch. You will need at least three different sizes for each tree. Cut the strips into two or three layers and each of these into squares. Starting with the larger squares, impale them on the trunk and slide them to the right spot. Use smaller squares as you go up the trunk. Trim and shape the squares with fine-tipped scissors. When the tree is the proper shape, dip it in shellac. Let this drip off a bit, then apply the needles. Some final trimming might be necessary before planting the tree.

Bumpy Chenille. A product called bumpy chenille is available from craft shops in various sizes. The smaller size has "bumps" spaced 2 inches apart. This size can make coniferous trees about 3/4 inch high. The medium size has bumps at 3-inch spacing and can make 1- to 2-inch trees. The largest size has bumps at 5-inch spacing and can make trees 2 to 3 1/2 inches tall. You should buy the material in the green color.

Cut the material to length and trim the top of the tree to a taper. Spray paint the trees to hide the metal trunk and to give the proper color. You might also wish to add needles.

Toy Trees. Even the most unrealistic looking plastic pine trees can be made to look good enough for background use by a few minutes work. Spray them the proper color; this also hides the plastic shine. If the trunk shows, paint it a dark gray. Add needles by applying ground foam over wet paint or a sprayed contact cement (see FIG. 18-8).

Fig. 18-8. Model conifer upgrades can improve the realism with very little work.

Other Trees

Other trees include ferns, palms, cacti, and the various types of desert plants. Because they look quite different from either deciduous or coniferous trees, the modeling methods are also different.

Ferns. Ferns grow in moist areas, as undergrowth in forests, and as ornamental plants in cities. Ferns are best modeled using feathers. The feathers should not be those from the wings, but body feathers that are softer, fluffier, and have some curvature to them. Trim them to the proper profile for the frond, which usually removes much of the fluff from the base of the quill. Then dye or paint the appropriate green color and glue them together into a clump, representing the type of modeled fern. Note that some ferns have trunks. They should be modeled using the same methods described next for palm trunks.

Palms. There are some beautiful palm tree models available commercially, but they are quite expensive. It is possible to make palm trees from scratch, but there is a fair amount of work and time involved.

Palms grow in climates that are warm all year-round. They do not really grow in the desert unless they have a good source of water. Common locations are in

Southern California, in Florida, and in cities throughout the southwestern United States. There are many different types of palms, and they come in a lot of sizes and shapes (FIG. 18-9).

A young palm tree has fronds almost as large as an older one. The new fronds only grow at the top of the tree. They start out sticking almost straight up,

Coconut palm

Ornamental palm

Fig. 18-9. *Two types of palm trees are shown in this drawing.*

then relax as they get older, bending downward. When the frond dies, it turns from a light green to a dirty yellow, but it usually does not fall off the tree. With more time, the color becomes a gray-tan, and the fronds shrivel up some and hang straight down. On some trees, this skirt of dead fronds falls off, but on most it must be cut off.

The trunk of the tree keeps getting taller, always carrying a sphere of live fronds above the cylinder of frayed dead ones. The live fronds span about 10 to 15 feet, and the cylinder of dead fronds is 4 to 5 feet in diameter. The trunk stays nearly the same diameter (about 12 to 15 inches) all the way up, except for the first 6 to 8 feet, which is conical and tapers from 24 inches or more at ground level up to that diameter. The trunk has a ragged appearance from midway on up due to the frond stubs. It is usually smoother below that, with a texture like an elephant's skin.

The trunk color is medium gray-brown, except where fronds have just been cut off, where it has a light red-brown color. The trunks can be straight or they can be slightly curved. The heights range from a few feet up to over 100 feet. It is recommended that model palms be restricted to 60 feet or less so they do not overwhelm the scene.

Some palms have dates; flowers precede the dates. These grow out from among the live fronds and hang down a few feet, overlapping the dead fronds.

In creating a model palm tree, you must model the trunk and both the dead and the live fronds. There are no known natural plant materials that duplicate any part of what is needed.

Carve the trunk from wood, including the flared bottom and any curvature. The upper trunk texture can be best simulated by making short, light knife cuts, from the top on down, that raise slivers of wood. Alternatively, some modelers use Campbell's shingle material, wrapping it around the trunk. If you use this method, start from the top and spiral down the trunk, overlapping all but 1 foot or so. Compensate for this thickness when forming the trunk. The lower trunk can have some texture added by cross-sanding with coarse sandpaper. When finished, paint the trunk a suitable light brownish-gray color, followed by a thin black wash.

Simulate the dead fronds with 5 foot long pieces of brown hemp twine. Partially unravel the twine. Glue this to the trunk, starting with the lowest fronds. Overlap successive layers about 2 feet apart and continue to about 2 feet of the top. If the twine is not the correct color, spray it, after first masking off the trunk.

There are several alternatives for the live fronds. Some people make a pattern and laboriously cut fronds out of paper. Some etch them from brass. Others use the individual flower petals from plastic carnations. Perhaps the best effect is obtained with feathers, trimmed to relatively uniform shape and size. The fronds should be about 5 to 6 feet in diameter, on a 2 to 3 foot stalk. Whatever the frond material, they should be dyed or sprayed a light medium green color. You will need 30 to 40 fronds per tree!

Glue the live fronds onto the top of the trunk, starting just above the dead fronds. Curve them down over the dead ones. Continue to add the live fronds, curving them less until the top ones point almost straight up. The plane of the fronds should be parallel to the surface of the imaginary sphere of the frond cluster. A spray of a little light ochre and a thin wash of gray will add to the realism.

Cacti. Everything that grows in the desert is not a cactus. In fact, there are only a few true cacti that grow in the American deserts. These include the barrel cactus, saguaro cactus, prickly pear cactus, and chollo cactus.

The American deserts occupy much of Arizona, Nevada, and Utah, and parts of California, Oregon, Idaho, New Mexico, and Texas. The desert vegetation varies quite widely within this vast region, as determined by latitude and rainfall. It has been divided into six regions: The Sonoran desert (southern Arizona), the Colorado desert (around the lower Colorado River), the Mojave desert (eastern California and southern Nevada), the Colorado plateau (southern Utah and northern Arizona), the Chihuahuan desert (New Mexico and Texas), and the Great Basin desert (northern Utah and Nevada and northward).

The chollo cactus is found in all the more-southern deserts (Sonoran, Colorado, Mojave, Chihuahuan). The barrel cactus is found in the Sonoran and Colorado deserts. The saguaro is found only in the Sonoran desert. FIGURE 18-10 shows examples of prickly pear, barrel, and saguaro cacti.

Saguaros get to be 30 to 40 feet tall. They have a central trunk and none, one, two, or more arms, which are never as tall as the trunk. The arms have curved elbows, not L-shaped ones. The trunks usually have a slight barrel shape.

Cut the trunk and arms from balsa wood. Glue up the arms from several segments. Attach the arms to the trunk one-third to one-half the way up the trunk. Score vertical grooves in the trunk and arms with a razor saw or file. Paint brown, then dry-brush depot olive. Flowers occur in early spring at the tops of the trunk and arms. They are white with a yellow center.

Barrel cacti are made the same way, but only 3 to 8 feet tall and without arms. They usually grow in clusters. The flowers are yellow, orange, or red, depending on species.

Prickly pear cacti are low growing and have flat "beaver tail" segments. Use bristol board punchouts glued together. The color is light green. These tend to grow in dense clusters.

Cholla cacti can be made from cypress or juniper twigs, up to 25 feet long. They are light green in color, with yellow flowers at the branch tips.

Desert Plants. There are many other desert plants that are not cacti. Some are succulents and some are broad-leafed evergreens. Examples include sagebrush, mesquite, paloverde, smoke tree, creosote bush, manzanita, Joshua tree, ocotillo, yucca, and agave.

Sagebrush is found mostly in the northern deserts. It grows about 2 feet high. You can model it using the methods for any other small bush. It is "sage" green color. Creosote bush is found in the southern deserts. It is about twice as high and has a short trunk. It is olive-green color. Manzanita looks about the same as creosote bush, but the trunk and limbs are red-brown. Manzanita is found in the western deserts at higher elevations.

Smoke tree and paloverde are found in the Sonoran and Colorado deserts. They are made by tree modeling methods. Smoke trees are about 10 feet tall and have a very transparent gray-green look to them. The paloverde grows up to 25

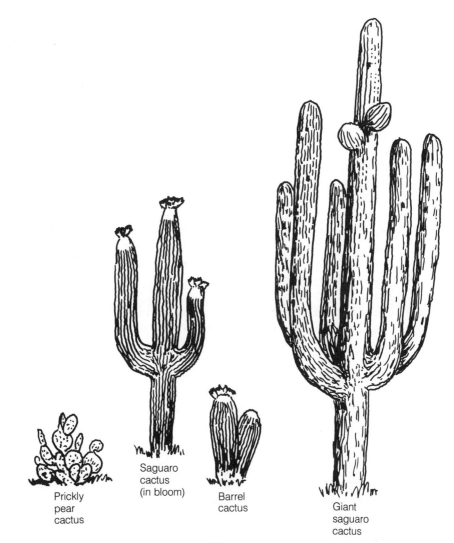

Fig. 18-10. This drawing shows some different common cactus types.

Prickly pear cactus

Saguaro cactus (in bloom)

Barrel cactus

Giant saguaro cactus

feet tall. They are a depot olive color. Mesquite grows more in New Mexico and Texas. It grows about 20 feet tall and has a "willow-like" appearance and a light gray-green color.

Joshua trees are unique to a few parts of the Mohave desert. They grow up to about 30 feet tall. They branch much like a deciduous tree, but the branches have tufts of leaf clusters for a couple of feet at each tip. These can be modeled with pipe cleaner segments in the smaller scales or with shaped chenille in the larger scales. The outer leaves are depot olive, shaded to yellow-brown for the inner (dead) third. The trunk is light gray, topped with a wash of pine stain. White flowers occur at the tips.

There are a number of different kinds of yucca, some of which are found in all American deserts. The shrub yucca grows about 2 feet high and can have a flower cluster at the end of a long stem that tops out at 8 feet high. The tree yucca has a short stem between the ground and the leaves, which cover about 4 feet, with the 3-foot blossoms (when present) just above the leaves. The foliage is best made of chenille, cut and shaped. The flower clusters can be built up with modeling putty. The colors are the same as for the Joshua trees.

The ocotillo grows about 10 feet tall, with 10 to 20 thin stalks radiating upward from the base. The ocotillo grows in the southern-most deserts. They can be modeled with a cluster of wires with slight random kinks in them. The ocotillo has red flowers near the tips in the early spring. There are only a few leaves on the stalks, which can be added with ground foam. The colors are depot olive for the top two-thirds, shaded to light gray at the base.

The agave, or century plant, grows naturally in the Chihuahuan desert and artificially in many city gardens. It has a cluster of grass-shaped leaves from 3 to 6 feet long, radiating upward and outward from the base. It blooms infrequently, shooting up a spectacular stalk 20 to 30 feet tall that subdivides into smaller branches and yellow flowers. In a group of agaves, only 10 percent or less will be in bloom at a time.

You can model the leaf cluster by finding a suitable plastic pine needle cluster of the right size. The leaves are medium green color. The stalk is best modeled from wire (see "Deciduous Trees"), unless a natural twig can be found that is suitable. Build up the flower clusters with modeling putty. The flowers go through several stages of bloom, with a considerable change in appearance. Obtain photographs of the plant to provide an accurate model. FIGURE 18-11 shows some of these other desert plants.

Forests

You might have heard of people who couldn't "see the forest for the trees." A forest is a closely grouped collection of trees. From the top, it is difficult to discern individual trees. From the edge, the only trees that can be seen are those closest to the edge. If the forest is dense, those in back are hidden by the ones nearer to the observer.

You could create a model forest by modeling every tree and then planting them close together. If the forest is thin and you want to catch a glimpse of something beyond it, you might have to do this. It is usually adequate, however, and less expensive in time and money, to not model the forest by individual trees but to model it as an entire forest, with the upper canopy of leaves and the outer few rows of trunks being the only part that is actually modeled. Your visitors will then not be able to "see the trees for the forest."

This can be done most easily for deciduous forests by using ground foam or other leaf material over lichen as the foliage material. Lay down the lichen directly onto the plaster, which you build up to the proper height in anticipation of this, or onto a screen suspended above the plaster. Vary the shading of the trees and the height and contour of the tree tops.

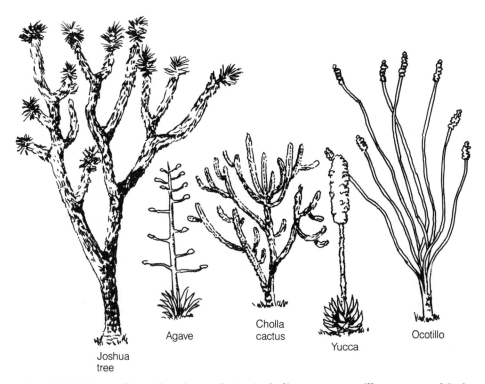

Fig. 18-11. *Some of the other desert plants, including agave, ocotillo, yucca, and Joshua tree.*

Fill in at the edge of the forest with a few fully modeled trees and enough trunks to make the forest appear dense. Fill in underneath with bushes and scrub undergrowth.

Coniferous forests can be made using any of the background tree methods described in that topic. Model only the tops of the trees, again varying the type, color, height, etc., to get some variety to the forest.

Stumps

Stumps result either when trees are cut down or they fall down from natural causes. Model stumps with the same care as the trees around them. As with the trees, the quality of the stumps should be best for those in the foreground (FIG. 18-12).

Stumps can be purchased as metal or plastic resin castings. You can also make your own stump castings. Start by carving the stump from modeling clay. Form several of these, spaced about 1 inch apart, and mounted on a base. Make a rubber mold and pour the castings using the techniques described in the topic, "Casting," in chapter 8.

You can also make stumps from twigs or round wood stock of the proper size

Fig. 18-12. *Stump castings can be used to show the remnants of trees that are no longer there.*

that you saw or break off to simulate the modeled stump. Form the roots with plaster, blending them into the twig.

Paint the bark and roots of stumps to match the trunks of nearby trees, but make it somewhat more bleached. Color the wood where the tree has been cut or broken off to match bare wood, taking into account the weathering that has taken place since the severing occurred.

Color fresh cuts with a paint of one part each of burnt sienna and yellow ochre in eight parts of white. Paint for old cuts needs to double the white and add one part black. These same formulas can be used for fallen logs and logs cut for sawmills.

19

Buildwork

Buildwork is the construction sequence that adds the structure and other non-mobile works of man to the modeled scene. The mobile things (railroad equipment, vehicles, and creatures) are covered in "Detailwork," chapter 20.

The word *crossings* describes the general category of structures that are man-made but not inhabited. These are the constructed things associated with the tracks or highways that are necessary to allow them to overcome natural obstacles of rivers and streams, hills and mountains, or to cross over each other. The inhabited structures are called *buildings*.

Structures come in ready-to-use models (usually brass), kit-built models, or partially or wholly scratchbuilt models. The kit-built models are built per the instructions, or they can be mildly or radically modified by kitbashing, cross-kitting, or by adding on scratchbuilt portions. Any of the structures modeled can use a variety of materials and techniques to simulate the prototypes (see "Construction," chapter 8).

You can enhance any model structure by painting it in flat finishes, by adding more details, and by aging and weathering. This is true, whatever the cost of the model. See FIG. 19-1 for an example using a low-cost plastic building kit.

BUILDING FROM KITS

The beginning modeler should build a few kit models before launching off on his/her own. There are some general tips to follow that are applicable to building both wood and plastic kits (of anything).

Fig. 19-1. A few additions (added painting, lettering and detailing) can make a big difference in a low-cost plastic kit structure!

Tips on Building Wood Kits

Read the directions! *Look* over the plans and drawings. *Envision* the steps of how the model goes together. *Plan* what can be major subassemblies.

Castings:

1. Separate from wood parts. If on sprues, do not remove until ready to glue in place. File off flash lines. If not on sprues, attach to a board with double-sided tape.
2. Spray or brush a primer paint coat. Paint individual colors and details.
3. When ready to use, cut off sprue with nippers and file away residual material.

Wood Parts:

1. Sort stripwood by sizes, measuring carefully to make sure dimensions of similar-sized pieces are together.
2. Remove precut door/window openings from sheet material. File and sand to exact size.
3. Lightly sand all wood to remove fuzz.
4. Add board end and nail hole detailing and physical aging, if desired.
5. Stain or prepaint all wood before assembly.
6. Always measure twice and cut once.

Assembly:

1. Use recommended adhesives in moderate amounts.
2. Add door and window castings to walls.
3. Fabricate stripwood portions.
4. Glue two walls together at a time, being careful that they are square.
5. Use jigs, clamps, and weights to hold while gluing.
6. Assemble two wall-pairs to make a box. Use plenty of interior bracing.
7. Add window material as late in sequence as possible.
8. Add interior view blocks, floors, and interior lighting (if any).
9. Add roof bracing and roof sheets.

Complete with detailing, paint touch up, and weathering.

Tips on Building Plastic Kits

Read the directions! *Look* over the plans and drawings. *Envision* the steps of how the model goes together. *Plan* what can be major subassemblies.

Castings:

1. If on sprues, do not remove until ready to glue in place. File off flash lines. If not on sprues, attach to a board with double-sided tape.
2. Spray or brush on a primer coat. Paint individual colors and details.
3. When ready to use, cut off sprue with nippers and file away residual material.

Sheet Parts:

1. File off all flash and sprue residue.
2. File all openings to accurate size.
3. True up corners with a file. Do some test fitting.
4. Spray or brush on a primer paint coat. Paint individual colors.

Assembly:

1. Use recommended adhesives in moderate amounts.
2. Add door and window castings to walls.
3. Glue two walls together at a time, being careful that they are square.
4. Use jigs, clamps, and weights to hold while gluing.
5. Assemble two wall-pairs to make a box. Use plenty of interior bracing. Reinforce corners with extra glue.
6. Add window material as late in sequence as possible.
7. Add interior view blocks, floors, and interior lighting (if any).
8. Add roof bracing and roof sheets.

Complete with detailing, paint touch-up, and weathering.

CROSSINGS

Structures for crossings include bridges of all types, trestles, tunnels, under-passes, overpasses, culverts, and retaining walls. Both rail and vehicular traffic need these structures to provide passages over, through, and across natural barriers, or across each other. The use of a variety of bridges, together with trestles, and tunnels will give a strong flavor or railroading to your layout.

One reference to the design and construction of model (and prototype) bridges, trestles, and culverts for railroads is the book, *Bridge & Trestle Handbook*, by Paul Mallery. *Model Railroader* magazine has had a series of articles on bridges that is especially detailed and informative.

Bridges

There are an enormous variety of different types of bridges. The bridge type and configuration is determined by the span required, the traffic load, and by the technology available at the time the bridge was designed. To be realistic, the model bridge must be designed with the same sound engineering practices that would have been used for its full-scale brother.

At each location that requires a bridge, you must select a bridge based on the type of bridges suitable for the time you are modeling and for the conditions of length and loading required. The bridge should also look good and be a favorite of yours. If it is inappropriate to the site and era, however, it will be anachronistic and/or technologically unsound.

Bridges can be made of timber, iron, steel, masonry, or reinforced concrete. The traffic can run over the top (*deck bridge*) or through the bridge structure (*through bridge*). The bridge can be of a truss, plate girder, arch, or suspension configuration. The bridge can be movable or fixed. (Note that a turntable is also a bridge). A bridge can have one or many spans. There are literally dozens of types of bridges within each general configuration (for example, steel truss bridges). Certainly, the potential variety of bridges is very large.

The railroads prefer to use deck-type bridges whenever possible because they are quicker and less expensive to build. Deck girders are, for this reason, probably the most common type of bridge.

As with any other structures or features on the layout, avoid the more spec-tacular bridges. Great height might be acceptable, but do not attempt large single spans because they would require suspension or steel arch bridges that would dominate everything else in the room. There should be no "Golden Gate" or "Brooklyn" bridges on the normal-sized model railroad.

Fortunately, there are many kits available for normal-span bridges that can usually be combined or shortened to fit any particular situation. There are also many plastic and wood beam materials (I and H sections, channels, etc.) you can use to fabricate bridges for custom applications.

Often, bridge kit or structural materials made for one scale, can be used in a different scale. The kit bridge width might require modification to suit the new scale requirements. For example, N scale railroad bridge kits can be easily modi-fied into HO scale highway bridges or O scale foot bridges.

As with other scenery, model your bridges in a degree of detail that is consistent with what can be seen. If the bridge will be close to the viewer, it will call for more detailing; if far away, then less detail. If it can only be seen from one side, why spend time detailing the side that cannot be seen?

The bridge floor provides the roadbed for the tracks or the road for the vehicular traffic. For railroads, this floor can be open or ballasted. If it is open, use no ballast and attach the ties to longitudinal timbers, trusses, or plates. If it is ballasted, close the deck into some sort of a trough, with the ballast contained in the trough and the ties located in the ballast in the conventional manner. In either case, track guard rails are usually used across the bridge and for a distance on either approach.

Sometimes there is a separate walkway, with or without handrails. On timber bridges there might be barrels of water to douse fires. Sometimes the bridges will carry the power/telephone/telegraph lines across the span on crossarms protruding from the side of the bridge.

Other bridge detail might include the rivets on steel bridges (before welding became common), and the nut/bolt/washer representation and truss rods of timber bridges. Brick, block, or cut-stone masonry bridges offer good opportunity for textural detailing. See the topic, "Retaining Walls."

Piers, abutments, and pedestals support the ends of bridge spans. For either bridges or trestles, they are made of concrete, masonry, or cribbing. They must be modeled so that they look like they are firmly built into the rock or earth and that they are strong enough to support the loads that they have to carry. You can build them up out of scale wood, cast sheet material, castings, etc., as appropriate to the situation. In N and HO, there are a variety of precast piers available.

Trestles

Trestles are really a series of bridge spans supported by piers, though people think of them as a continuous structure, that are usually made of wood and allow a track to cross a valley. More modern trestles are made of steel or concrete. Trestles can be one of the more interesting structures on the model railroad and the one most evocative of the feeling of railroading (FIG. 19-2).

Timber trestles are made of vertical bents, either made by driving piles into the ground (*pile trestle*) or by having the bents rest on some kind of a foundation (*framed trestle*). Pile trestles are limited in height by the lengths of timbers available. Framed trestles can be made in two or more stories to provide much greater heights. Timber trestles usually have open floors.

A bent for a single-track trestle usually consists of either four or six vertical timbers, which can be round (on old trestles) or sawn square. The outer timbers slant outward toward the base. A timber cap atop, or alongside the top, of the vertical timbers supports the longitudinal stringers. You also can use other horizontal bracing as well as diagonal bracing between each group of horizontal braces.

There is usually horizontal and diagonal bracing between the bents to give more rigidity to the entire structure. If a framed trestle is multiple stories, it is

Fig. 19-2. Timber trestles are easy to build and add an important "flavor" to the model scene.

built almost as a trestle atop a trestle, etc. The lower stories can have more vertical timbers than the upper stories.

The timbers are attached together by large bolts. Unless the trestle is in the background, or modeled in one of the smaller scales, these should be modeled. This is most easily done with nut/bolt/washer (NBW) castings. After the wood is stained, drill a hole and bond the prepainted casting in place.

Fabricate a jig to make up the bents. You can use a single jig to make all bents, even though they are of different heights. Prestain all wood before use. Support unequal height bents for pile trestles on fill blocks and fill in the earth around them. Add the longitudinal stringers and horizontal and diagonal braces on site at the trestle location. As with the bridges, don't forget to model guard rails, walkways, fire barrels, and "duck-into" refuges; as appropriate.

Piers. Piers are really trestles built over the water, with the pilings driven into the bed of the river/lake/ocean. Usually, the piles are vertical. The framework at the top and the bracing can be quite varied, depending on the application. The piles are ordinarily protected with tar, creosote, or other preservative.

If the piles are in salt water, tidal variations will leave a range of water marks. Form barnacles or clams with modeling paste and color them white or gray, as appropriate. If ships and boats dock to the pier, remember to include old tires for buffers, as well as suitable posts or cleats for tying up the lines.

Tunnels

The only parts of tunnels that need to be modeled are the portals and the lining portion immediately inside the portal (FIG. 19-3). The portals and interior walls of tunnels might be easier to complete as a part of the coverwork, rather than waiting until later. This depends on how difficult the access will be.

Fig. 19-3. Railroads in the mountains will have many tunnels, often with different types of portals.

Model the tunnel interior only as far inside the portal as someone can see. Farther than that, it is an impediment to access to derailed trains. Make the tunnel interior so you can remove it from inside, if this is needed for access. Give the tunnel interiors some kind of guard edges, raised above the trackwork, to keep derailed equipment from falling to the floor.

Portals. Portals are made of concrete, masonry (stone/brick), or timbers. In some cases there is no portal as such, and the tunnel entrance consists of natural rock. Cast portals are available for N, HO, and O scales. You can carve concrete or masonry tunnel portals from plaster, wood, or linoleum block. If a number of portals are needed, cast them from molds made from the first carving. Fabricate wooden portals from scale timbers.

Lining. Tunnel lining depends on the type of soil or rock the tunnel has been cut through. If the rock is solid, then there might be no supports, and the interior has the appearance of rock that has been blasted away, rough and angular, and exactly like the rock just outside the tunnel in type and color. Often, however, at least near the portal, the rock is crumbly or unstable, or there is soil rather than rock. Then, you must use supports and cribbing to hold up the roof and sides of the tunnel to prevent cave-ins and falling rocks.

The cribbing is usually made of wooden timbers, but sometimes it is made of concrete, mortared stone or brick. The interior usually gets very dirty from smoke and diesel exhaust, as well as staining from water and dissolved minerals. A tunnel wall might also have water seepage that can be modeled.

Snowsheds. Although snowsheds are not actually tunnels, they can become like tunnels during the winter when the snowfall and avalanches cover them. Their purpose is to eliminate the need for clearing the snow from the track in regions of particularly heavy snowfall. The design of snowsheds varies a great deal between different railroads.

In almost every case, the snowshed is built against a rock wall or mountain-side, so only one side and the roof needs to be built (FIG. 19-4). The construction is like a timber-covered through bridge, with a roof slanting to carry off as much snow (and rock) as possible and relieve the load. The snowsheds are usually not kept well painted and are, therefore, the color of weathered wood.

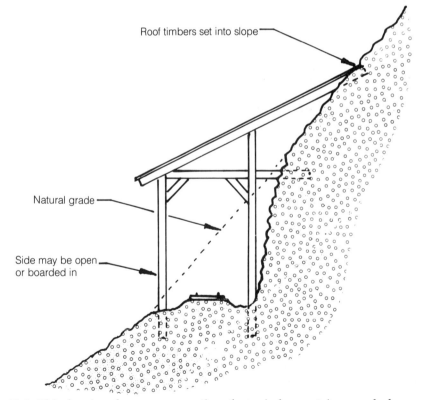

Roof timbers set into slope

Natural grade

Side may be open or boarded in

Fig. 19-4. *This drawing shows a cross section of a typical mountain snowshed.*

Underpasses/Overpasses

An *underpass* is a type of bridge that crosses over another track or road. Usually, they are of short span and moderate clearance height. Deck plate girder bridges or various types of masonry or poured concrete spans are commonly used. In most cases, abutments reduce the span. For roads crossing under tracks, the road usually makes the accommodation in elevation, dipping down to go under the track grade.

An *overpass* is just an underpass from the opposite point of view. The term is generally used for roads crossing over railroad tracks. Again, the road usually is built up by transition grades to gain the elevation to cross the tracks. In flat land, overpasses take more space on the model.

Culverts

Culverts are used to carry water under either the railroad roadbed or the highway. This water might be a continuously flowing stream, or the intermittent run-off from rainfall or melting snow. In any case, the culvert must be designed to carry the maximum flow of water that can be expected.

Culverts are made of concrete, stone, brick, metal pipe (corrugated or smooth), or clay. They can be round, oval, or box or arch shaped; single or multiple; with or without head walls and wings that are either concave or convex. Sometimes short trestles or bridges are used instead of culverts, but their cost is usually greater. Culverts can also be large enough to provide passage for stock or farm vehicles.

There are no kits for culverts, so you are on your own to scratch-fabricate them from raw materials. Plastic tubing, including that for lawn sprinkler systems, can provide a selection of round culvert shapes. Roll up corrugated aluminum material to make corrugated culverts. You can make castings for some types of culverts; others you can fabricate from wood or styrene material.

A tunnel portal in a smaller scale (N, for example) can sometimes be used as a culvert for a larger scale (HO or larger).

Retaining Walls

Retaining walls are used wherever a slope is steep and the slope consists of rock and soil that would otherwise collapse without this barrier to gravity. Retaining walls are expensive and they are not used if there is any other alternative. If possible, the slopes are graded to angles where the material will be stable. For most materials, these angles are about 30 degrees from the horizontal, but on models you can cheat a little and get away with angles up to 45 degrees.

Retaining walls are made of mortared stone, concrete blocks, bricks, unmortared stone, or cribbing made of wooden logs, ties, timbers, or precast concrete. Modern retaining walls are also sometimes made of metal. Note that the abutments used for bridges, underpasses, and overpasses are really just retaining walls that also serve the function of holding something up.

Fig. 19-5A. Modeled wood cribbing and retaining walls are used to "hold back" steep slopes.

Fig. 19-5B. A wood (or cast concrete) retaining wall.

A type of retaining wall is made from pilings, driven into dirt that is soft enough. These are often seen around streams, rivers, lakes, or the ocean. Round, wooden piles are most common, but modern steel and concrete equivalents exist.

There are some precast retaining walls available in the popular scales. You might have to shorten or combine these to fit a particular location. You also might try scales other than the one for which the wall is made. Fabricate retaining walls from scratch using cast sheet material, your own castings, or fabricated strip-wood. Prefabricate cribbing, then add to the site, filling in the rock/dirt behind it. Almost any retaining wall must blend into the groundwork and greenwork to integrate it into the scene (FIG. 19-5).

BUILDINGS

Buildings can be scratchbuilt, kit-built, or kitbashed with equally satisfying end results. They can also be made from a variety of different materials, simulating the same (for wood) or different materials of the actual modeled building. The topics that follow are organized according to the type of building construction material that is being modeled.

See the tips for building wood or plastic kits, at the beginning of this chapter. If you want to modify a plastic or plaster-cast building kit, there are certain restrictions on what can and what cannot be easily done. It is relatively easy to change the length or width of a building, to add wings, to change rooflines, or to close up or add in windows or doors. It is much more difficult to change floor height or separation or to change (all) window or door heights and widths. If the modifications are too great, it might be easier to start from scratch. FIGURE 19-6 shows an example of how the same kit can be made into two quite different-looking buildings.

When choosing buildings, try to avoid the spectacular. Suit the size and grandeur of the structure to the space you have available so it does not dominate the scene. Concentrate on providing only a few theme structures. One large industry can take up the room that several smaller ones could fit into. The latter might give more operating and scenic possibilities.

Wooden Buildings

You can model wooden buildings using wood, paper, plaster castings, styrene plastic sheet/strip, plastic castings, and high-density urethane/polyester castings. All the materials other than wood require color, pattern, and (usually) texture (grain) simulation.

You can model wood as new or relatively new, or age it with some degree of physical deterioration, including damage, rot, decay, etc. Wood can be unpainted and either new or weathered; or painted/stained, with varying degrees of aging and weathering.

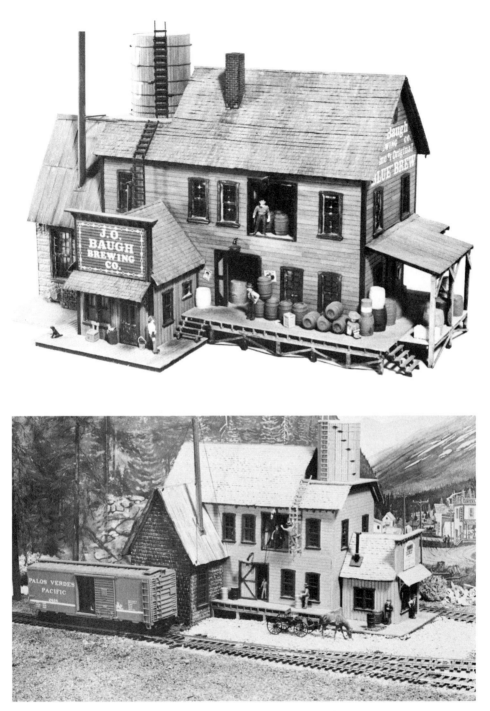

Fig. 19-6. *Two persons used the same kit, with different modifications, to create quite different buildings.*

You can fabricate wooden buildings with whole-wall castings; with sheet materials with cast/milled boards; or with a board-by-board method, building up from stripwood or plastic strip just as a full-sized building is. The windows and doors can be cast into the walls, can be separate metal or plastic castings, or can be built up from stripwood or plastic strip.

Wooden buildings will usually have masonry or poured concrete foundations, or basements, and might have fireplaces and/or chimneys of masonry construction. Sometimes, a wooden wall can have a brick facing for decorative reasons. For masonry modeling methods, see "Masonry Buildings."

Wood works best for modeling wood. Basswood is the best wood to use. It comes in blocks, sheets, stripwood, milled sheets, and milled shapes. Wood might require sanding to remove the fuzz. The techniques for wood modeling are covered in "Wood Construction," chapter 8.

Siding. Wooden siding usually runs horizontally and sometimes vertically. Types of siding include clapboard, V-groove, strake, tongue and groove, and board and batten. When using sheet siding material, scribe lines across the boards to simulate where the boards butt together. Studs are usually on 16- or 24-inch centers. Joints occur over studs but are staggered between rows. Add nailheads with a sharp, fine pin set into the end of a dowel to press them in. Use two per board at each stud location, plus two per butt end, per stud, at joints. (see FIG. 19-7 AND COLOR INSERT).

Fig. 19-7. Boards can be detailed by adding nail holes and by proper coloring and weathering.

There are three different methods to form the corners of wooden buildings when using sheet siding (FIG. 19-8). The Campbell (HO scale) corner material is milled to provide both the simulation of the exterior corner trim and the needed physical interior bracing. For any of these methods, the corners must fit well so that no externally-visible unsightly gap is left.

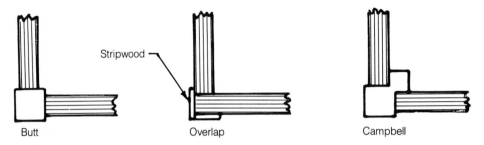

Fig. 19-8. There are three commonly used corner treatments for wooden buildings.

Stripwood. Stripwood is available in both fractional sizes of 64ths of an inch or millimeter and in scale dimensions of inches (but only for O or HO). TABLE A-8 in the Appendix provides conversions between these two systems and allows a determination of the closest size available for use in scales other then O/HO. The table is equally applicable for styrene strip materials. You also can cut stripwood at home using a full-sized or miniature table saw and a very fine-toothed blade. It is quite difficult to make the smaller stripwood this way.

Board-by-Board. Board-by-board construction is done the same way as on the full-sized building, only with glue replacing nails. Scale-size lumber is mandatory and all wood must be prefinished before starting assembly.

Do this construction over a drawn pattern covered by wax paper or plastic food wrap. Cut the stripwood very accurately and use only minute amounts of glue. Use white glue, diluted 1:1, and apply it with the tip of a toothpick. Use pins and/or small weights to hold the pieces in place while they are drying. Apply individual boards over the joists/studs/rafters. Prefabricate entire walls and then erect them into a building.

Use this method for portions of a building such as a loading platform, for an entire building, or for a building under construction. You can model a derelict shack if suitable care is taken in aging and weathering the lumber and in simulating all the ravages of time (FIG. 19-9). For a building under construction, all the wood should look new. These procedures take time, but the results cannot be matched by any other methods.

You also can build up windows and doors using stripwood. Whether these are prefabricated, using jigs if very many need to be constructed, or built in place will depend on the building. Windows made in this manner can be very satisfying, but the time required is considerable.

You also can construct stairs, ladders, railings, etc., from stripwood. If many need to be made, jigs will be worthwhile. For stairs, precut the stringers, then

Fig. 19-9. *Board-by-board methods can be used to construct either abandoned or new buildings.*

mount them into a holding jig and add the precut treads. Prefabricate this subassembly and add it to the model as late in the construction sequence as possible. These parts also are available as castings.

This same method can be used to make pallets, crates, and boxes. Fabricate pallets using a jig and precut boards. Build closed crates and boxes by gluing the cut stripwood over a wooden core. Make open crates and boxes by building the ends and then adding the side and bottom boards.

Deterioration. Old wooden buildings can sag or lean. If desired, these effects must be simulated during the construction. When lean occurs, the entire wall and all the doors/windows on it will lean together. The horizontal lines will stay horizontal, but all vertical lines will tilt at the same angle. Sag occurs because of loss of support, which allows a roof, wall, porch, etc., to curve (sag) downward between such supports as still remain. Either effect is probably easiest to obtain using board-by-board construction.

A common result of physical deterioration is missing boards or siding. When using sheetwood, carefully cut out a board or cut it partly away and curl it up. When using stripwood, leave out a board or put it in as though it is loose. Simulate rot by distressing the boards with a knife, a small, stiff brass wire brush, and/ or sandpaper.

Castings. Prefinish plastic or metal window and door (or other) castings. Mount several to a cardboard square with double-sided tape. Prime paint them, let them dry, apply base paint, apply any detail paint, and put on a relief (black) wash.

Scribing. Scribe close-grained wood to provide individual board simulation. The scribing must be along the grain. Do it using a knife against a metal straightedge in the same manner that cutting is done, but use only one or two strokes to create a groove of the proper depth. The effect achieved is that of tongue-and-groove boards, not lapped siding. You also can scribe plastic to simulate board siding. Follow the techniques described in "Plastic Construction," chapter 8.

Bracing. Wood or paper have a great tendency to warp and curl with age and humidity change. Models made of these materials need adequate bracing to prevent this. Another help is to laminate the material with alternate layers at right angles (of grain) to create a plywood-like effect. The biggest help of all in preventing warping is to seal all of the wood or paper to prevent moisture entry. This means painting or otherwise finishing the interior as well as the exterior of the model. Buildings made of plastic also need bracing to counter thermal and aging distortion.

Finishing. Apply finishing to the materials prior to assembly. For aging or stain-type finishes, this is mandatory because any glue residue will not stain the same way as the bare material. It is also desirable to obtain the subtle board-to-board variations when using stripwood. Apply the paint or stain by wiping it on with a cloth, following the grain of the wood.

Bare Wood. Coat new, unpainted wood with a colorless clear finish, such as Dullcoat. If it is to simulate aged but never painted wood, use Weather-It, a very thin wash of black or gray paint, or a thinned Driftwood stain.

To simulate the light red weathered tone of faded wood that was once painted red, red-brown, or barn red, use a brushed-on solution made from dissolving steel wool in vinegar. Use the finest steel wool and dissolve it for one week in white vinegar. Brush this on for a light red weathered tone. Repeat for darker red coloring. The wood might warp, so hold it down on a piece of glass. Use a hair dryer to hasten drying, if desired.

To simulate worn wood that has been painted, first paint the wood Reefer Gray or Driftwood. Paint over with the paint color. Use sandpaper and/or a knife to remove the color from the gray. Add a thin black stain. Another method is to first paint with color and then dry-brush on faded gray so the color shows through.

Nails will often rust, causing streaks on the wood or aged paint. Add these streaks, after the building is completed, by using some rust-colored stain or paint and a fine brush.

Paper. An excellent material for the construction of wood and other buildings is Strathmore paper or illustration board. The surface is smooth and grainless and the cost is very low. Strathmore can be obtained from art supply stores in one-ply through five-ply thicknesses. The actual and equivalent scale thicknesses are shown in TABLE 19-1.

Laminate the material for greater thicknesses. Scribe horizontal or vertical siding directly, being careful to maintain even pressure. Always use internal bracing to prevent warping.

The surface can be lightly textured, but it is better to suggest texturing by the finishing method. Finishing can be done with stains or paints of any type, followed by weathering applications. If done properly, the result will look as much like wood as wood itself.

Table 19-1. Strathmore and Illustration Board Scale Thickness

	Actual	Scale Thickness (inches)				
Plies	**Thickness**	**Z**	**N**	**HO**	**S**	**O**
1	.005″	1.1	.8	.4	.3	.2
2	.010″	2.2	1.6	.9	.6	.5
3	.015″	3.3	2.4	1.3	1.0	.7
4	.020″	4.4	3.2	1.7	1.3	1.0
5	.025″	5.5	4.0	2.2	1.6	1.2
—	1/16″	13.8	10.0	5.3	4.1	3.1

Assembly. Do as much painting and finishing as possible before assembly. Assemble into subassemblies, then combine these into larger subassemblies, etc. Add the window and door and other castings to the walls just prior to final assembly. Put the window material in as late in the assembly sequence as possible. Be careful to avoid smearing adhesive on the "glass." Add window shades, curtains, etc.

Assemble walls in pairs, gluing each corner. Use jigs, clamps, weights, etc., to ensure squareness and alignment. Glue wall pairs together to form boxes. Add other wall sets to the main set to form all the wings of the building. Provide internal bracing and separators for floors, if any. Add internal view blocks and lighting provisions.

Building Sites. The building bases need to be tied into the coverwork. You might wish to construct the building on its own base to make removal for cleaning easier. Bases also are often useful for transporting modules to reduce damage. Provide foundation planting, if appropriate. Except for the few that are modeled as leaners, make all building walls vertical. Remember to add the sidewalks or paths that would be found around the buildings.

Burned Buildings. Burned wooden buildings, or burned pieces of wood, are best made with the real thing—fire. Construct the building using the board-by-board method, but only build the part that will remain as a charred remnant. When ready, work outdoors. Use a lighted candle to selectively ignite portions of the wood, let them burn a bit, then blow them out. Avoid too large a conflagration. Keep some water handy to put out the fire, just in case.

Work slowly and try to create the burned-away ends of the boards and the charring that a fire would cause. Let some loose boards burn more completely in an ash tray. Add them and other charred ashes from your fireplace to the debris left behind by the building fire. Bond them in place with dilute matte medium. You might also wish to spray the entire area with this bonding agent or with a flat finish.

Masonry Buildings

Masonry buildings include those that are made of brick, stone, block, and cast concrete. The first three materials are laid up by masons using mortar between the joints. There are many different course patterns that can be used for modular (brick and block) materials. The stone used might be available from close by or brought in from far away. The stone can be natural, either round or stratified, or it can be cut, such as granite or marble would be. On prototype buildings, any of these materials can be their natural colors or you can paint them.

Chimneys and fireplaces and foundations for other wood or metal buildings can be made using any of these same materials. Concrete walls can be cast in place in vertical forms or cast while flat and then tilted up into place.

Materials for model masonry buildings include entire walls cast in plaster, plastic, or resin; cast embossed plastic wall material; and printed wall material. Chimneys are also available cast in metal or plastic. In addition, the walls (or portions thereof) can be cast at home.

Cast Walls. Kit walls take the least work to complete because all the detail is already cast in. Usually, the door and window framing is a part of the casting, although sometimes these are separate. Handle plaster castings carefully because they are usually quite fragile.

The first step is to clean away any flash or mold marks. Sometimes these castings do not have a uniform thickness. This can be corrected by using a large file and sandpaper. Also check the corners for fit and file and sand until the gaps are minimized. If other castings must fit into holes, check the fit and file and sand the hole or the casting until the fit is proper. Seal plaster castings with a spray coat of Krylon Crystal Clear or other flat finish.

Embossed Sheet. Embossed plastic sheet can be bought with almost any desired brick/block/stone pattern. You will have to cut the material and any openings using the techniques covered in "Plastic Construction," chapter 8. Laminate layers to make pilasters, cornices, etc. You might need to add unembossed plastic material for some details, with added scribing, carving, etc., as needed. Printed paper sheet is only suitable for quite distant buildings.

Sheet. You can scribe smooth paper or plastic sheet to create brick, block, or cut stone textures. Mark lines with a pencil for the courses and scribe all horizontal lines first. Use care in scribing the vertical lines so they do not overcut the horizontal lines. This process is very laborious, but sometimes necessary, to duplicate a material or prototype that is not otherwise obtainable.

You also can scribe cast plaster in this same manner. Some have also used linoleum blocks (such as artists use) for this purpose. These materials are easily scribed or carved.

Piece by Piece. Make stone walls the same way you make the real ones—stone by stone. Select the stones (small pebbles) that are nearly all the same size. First, glue the stones to a backing sheet. When this is dry, brush on a quite-liquid mix of plaster, filling in all the cracks and holes. When this partly sets up, wipe it off the surface of the stones with a damp paper towel. If the plaster is precolored the mortar color, no additional painting might be necessary. You can use modeling paste instead of plaster, if this is more convenient.

Sometimes, in the larger scales, there is no alternative to building a brick/block/cut stone wall piece by piece. Cut the individual pieces out of plastic or paper, or cast them in plaster for the larger scales. Glue them onto a backing sheet one at a time. Add plaster mortar if necessary. Cast bricks and tiles are available for dollhouses. These also can be useful for some of the larger scales.

Casting. If there is a repetition to the wall sections, then casting is often a good method for constructing masonry buildings. Chimneys are also good candidates for home casting (see "Casting," chapter 8). Home casting is particularly easy for simulating cast concrete walls because the mold can be made of stripwood, which directly forms the same lines in the casting as those formed in the real concrete by the wooden forms. You can simulate mold lines on "concrete" walls made from paper or sheet material. Press stripwood pieces of appropriate size into wet paint and then remove them. This technique will leave slight "form board" impressions behind.

Deterioration. Masonry buildings don't deteriorate the same way that wooden ones do. They don't sag or lean, without falling down, and they can't rot. What usually happens is that some of the bricks, stones, etc., come loose or break off. This can be simulated by knife cuts. Otherwise, the aging is almost totally that caused by changes in the color of the materials and/or the paint that was used to cover them.

Coloring. Color the walls as much as possible before assembly. You might wish to prime any plastics before painting. Unless the wall is to simulate a relatively recently painted masonry, paint (brush or spray) the base color to match the new color of the material. Brick can be a variety of colors depending on the clay used. Red brick is really often rust, red-brown, or roof-brown in color. A good base color for concrete is Concrete. Let the base color dry completely.

The mortar is usually a medium to dark gray. It is easiest to color the mortar by wiping on an overall coat of Polly S, acrylic, or latex paint, then wiping it off before it dries. It will do two things: collect in the mortar lines, giving the masonry the proper color, and age the masonry somewhat, graying the colors. FIGURE 19-10 shows the steps in coloring the precast walls of a building.

Painted Walls. If a masonry wall is relatively freshly painted, the model just needs painting and no aging needs to be applied. As the paint gets older, some of the previous paint colors or the natural colors of the materials will show through. In cases where the aging is extreme, only a hint of the last paint color might be visible. The simulation of these effects can do a lot to add character to older masonry buildings (FIG. 19-11).

The methods vary and range from minor abrading with knife or sandpaper, to scraping off a little of the most-recent paint color from a few bricks, to more drastic treatments to simulate really aged surfaces. The most-recent paint should probably be water-based, in any case. Apply the paint by lightly spraying or wiping it on, then using water and a paper towel (before it is completely dry) to remove much of this coat from the base paint. Another method is to overspray lightly with the base color instead. If lettering on the wall is involved, consider how these methods affect the lettering and its aging relative to the wall. See "Aging and Weathering," chapter 10, and "Lettering," chapter 11.

Hand paint the details of cast doors and windows, sills and headers, etc., and also any cast-in windows and doors or other trim that is painted wood or

Fig. 19-10. *Shown are four steps in the finishing of pre-cast masonry walls: Trim painting, ''brick'' color painting, wiped off mortar, and final details.*

Fig. 19-11. *Examples of model masonry walls.*

metal. Apply signs or lettering while the wall can be worked on in a horizontal position. Apply weathering at this point or after final assembly.

Assembly. Follow the same assembly procedure as given in the previous topic for wood buildings. These materials will not warp, but they must be carefully fitted together because they will not distort to accommodate lack of squareness in the fit.

Windows

Cover model windows with any suitable transparent material to simulate the glass. The best and most expensive material is microscope slide glass. This is a special, very thin glass that will never discolor or warp. It looks like the real thing because it is.

Other materials include clear plastics of various compositions, including acrylics and clear styrenes. Sheet materials, such as those used for protecting paper sheets, also are available in office supply stores. The thinner materials will not reflect light properly, and they might warp with time.

Add the material to the window after the window framing is completely painted and any aging/weathering is applied to it. Some clear sprays might fog the windows slightly. If the window is a casting, it is easier to apply the glazing to the casting before the casting is bonded into the wall, if that is possible.

A very important precaution is to use an adhesive that will permanently hold the glazing in place, yet is either very transparent or that can be applied with minimum chance of smearing onto the "glass." Only apply the adhesive around the outer periphery of the glass. Recommended choices are clear Silicone cement, ACC, and white glue. Whichever the choice, use it in moderation.

For industrial buildings, particularly in the distance, you might wish to use printed window material. This has the mullions printed on the clear material, usually either in black or white.

Details. Almost any window is enhanced by adding shades, curtains, venetian blinds, etc., to the interior. These, of course, should be appropriate to the building being modeled. Make the shades from colored paper. Paper curtains can be obtained commercially in some scales, or you can hand draw them with colored pens on paper. Venetian blind decals are available in some scales. They can also be made by careful use of a ruling pen. Some industrial windows are painted on the inside. Do not place all shades in a building at the same height or make them a uniform color or style.

For older buildings, you might want to crack or break some of the glass. You can simulate cracks with knife cuts. Make breaks by cutting all the way through and removing some of the material. Notice the pattern of cracks formed in broken glass and try to simulate that. Be sure that the cracks in the individual panes of glass in a window are independent of each other. Some panes might be left out entirely.

FIGURE 19-12 shows two scratchbuilt window construction approaches. These windows could be made of individual wood pieces. The double-hung window

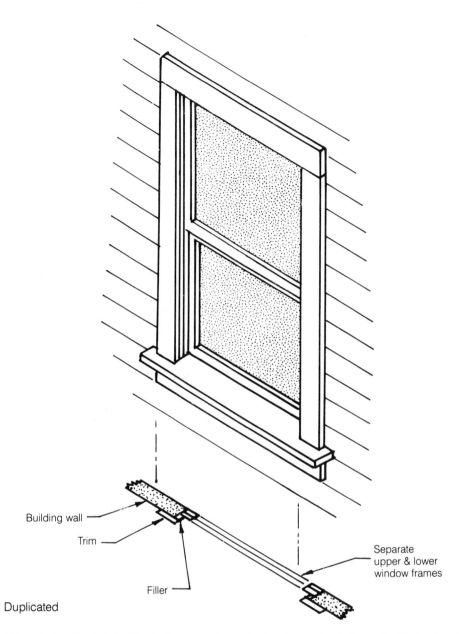

Building wall

Trim

Filler

Separate
upper & lower
window frames

Duplicated

Fig. 19-12. *Scratch-built windows can be made to either simulate or duplicate double-hung windows. A simulated double-hung window is shown on page 257.*

on the left could be built with the lower portion partially open. This figure also shows the typical trim used around windows in wood frame construction.

Not all windows are clear. Some are translucent. These can be simulated by lightly sanding the back of the plastic window material or by cutting the material from a translucent plastic. Some windows are colored. These can be dyed with

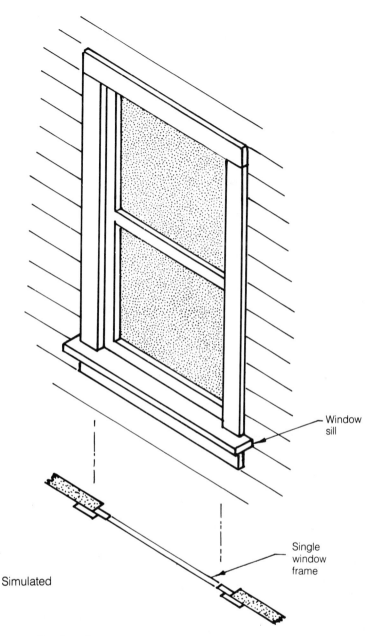

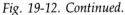

Simulated

Fig. 19-12. Continued.

special dyes made for plastics or by using colored transparent plastic material. Stores selling dollhouse supplies can give you some ideas.

Skylights are very effective. Castings are available in the more popular scales. Otherwise, fabricate the frame from suitable materials and add the glazing. Be careful to not let the edges of the glazing material show.

Screens. Window or door screens are difficult to model because there is no mesh material that is small enough, at least for the smaller scales. Some very fine weave brass screen is available, but this is expensive in any quantity. There is a type of material that can be used to suggest screens that is available at art supply stores. It is made to provide half-tone shading backgrounds for graphic art. It comes in black in varying patterns and "tones" on sheets. You peel it off and press it onto the desired surface.

Metal Buildings

Metal is usually found in buildings in the form of corrugated panels for roofing or siding. Cast ornamentation was also once used, but this is treated (for the models) just like any other cast plastic/metal part.

Model corrugated metal is available that is suitable for most scales. One type is made of embossed plastic. The more common is made of actual metal, with scale corrugations. You can also easily make your own using heavy aluminum foil. Use some of the embossed plastic siding as a form. Place the foil over the form and press (emboss) the grooves into the foil by pressing it down with a soft balsa stick, one groove at a time.

Cut the corrugated metal with a sharp knife and light cuts to avoid deforming the corrugations along the cut. Do not use scissors. Cut it into panels of the proper scale width and length. Use some steel wool on the panels to slightly roughen them.

The metal panels are much too shiny as is. They need to be aged, weathered, and/or painted, as appropriate. Some of these finishes must be applied before putting the panels on the model, and some can be done after.

One method that gives a very realistic aged, rusty appearance is to brush olive oil onto the panel, then heat it over the kitchen range. Let it smoke but not burn. It will turn color and look old, and no two panels will be just alike. Spray these panels with a flat finish.

Another, more conventional, method can be done after the panels are installed. Spray the panels with Dullcoat or other flat spray. Let the panel dry completely, and then spray or brush on light to medium gray paint. When the panel is thoroughly dry, apply rust streaks using the proper rust colors of Polly S or acrylic paints. When the paint looks right, follow up with a spray of flat finish. If the panels are to simulate those with painted finishes, then substitute the proper color paint for the gray. Do not overdo the rusting.

Still another method uses printed circuit board etchant (see "Etching," chapter 8). Using tweezers, place the panels in the etchant, being careful not to get any of the liquid on your skin. Chemical action will start to eat away the foil and turn it a rusty color. Stop the action by washing the panel in running water. You can also use this process to eat away whole sections of the panels to suggest extreme aging. FIGURE 19-13 shows an example of corrugated metal simulation and finishing.

Apply the panels to either a backing sheet (paper, wood, or plastic) or to a wooden framework, using Goo or contact cement. The panels normally overlap each other. Start at one end of the bottom of the wall/roof side. Overlap the first

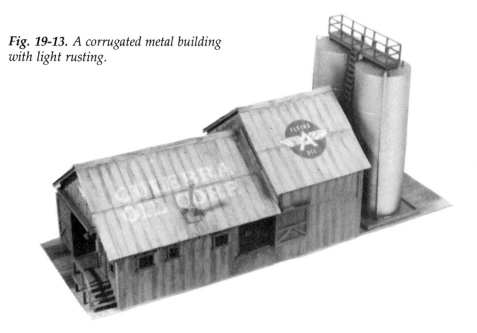

Fig. 19-13. *A corrugated metal building with light rusting.*

row from side-to-side, then add a second row, sightly overlapping the first, etc. Some panels can be bent out a bit to add aging.

Roofs

Because of their prominence in the spectator's's line of sight, roofs are one of the most important parts of a building to model well. Roofs come in a great variety of different shapes, and many different materials are used to provide the water-proofing and physical protection needed.

The most common roof shapes are gable (and variations), shed, and flat. Gable roofs are by far the most common roofs on homes. Roofs in areas having a lot of snowfall usually have steeper slopes. Flat roofs actually have some slope to allow water to run off. The roof shape of a building will depend on the type of building, the date it was built, the location, etc.

Materials. Materials for real roofs include shingles, tiles, metal, tar paper, rocks, and gravel. Thatched or board roofs are antique types that might (rarely) need to be modeled. There are usually two materials used, only one of which might be visible. The more important material, which provides the waterproof-ing, can be hidden by the outer material, which provides the physical protection. Tar paper is, more often than not, that important inner material.

Like the walls, the roof has a framework of roof joists or rafters, usually (but not always) covered with sheathing of wood or other material. Usually, this part of the roof is not visible on the model and does not need to be modeled, except possibly where the roof joists show at its edges.

Shingles or shakes can be made of wood or of composition, asphalt, cement, plastic, or metal materials. In most cases, the material is made to resemble wood, except for the composition shingle material. Shingles can be natural or colored. Tiles come in a variety of shapes, sizes, and colors, including round "Spanish" tiles and various flat tiles. Slate tiles also are in this category.

Metal roofs include corrugated metal and various seamed metal constructions, using copper or other metals. Galvanized steel is sometimes used in overlapping panels for shed roofs. Tar paper roofs might have gravel or small rocks as a coating and protection.

Wood Shingles. Wood shingles, or those materials that simulate them, can be modeled in a variety of ways. One of the most popular for HO scale is to use Campbell's paper shingle strip. This material comes in a roll. It is pregummed and has the individual shingles cut and embossed in the material. It is a natural light brown (paper sack) color.

If possible, apply these shingles to the roof panels before they are attached to the building. Use cardboard illustration board, or plastic sheet for the underpanel. Mark parallel lines on the sheet to provide guidelines for applying the shingles. If you use porous material, apply a clear finish to both sides to reduce warping.

Start applying the shingles from the bottom of the panel. Cut the strips longer than necessary. Moisten the gummed backing and put the strip in place. You might need to add white glue or clamp or weight the strips down while drying. Be careful to keep them straight, as the strips tend to curve. Let each row overlap the one beneath it. Extend the top row beyond the top of the panel.

When the panel is dry, trim the top and sides with scissors. If the panel warps, bend it back flat. After installing the panels, make ridge shingles from individual shingle clippings from brown paper or stripwood. Shingle the ridge going toward the center. Curl/lift up some shingles for an aging effect. Occasionally omit a shingle. In some places, let a few slide out of line. Make them look like they are coming loose.

Stain the shingles after the panels are installed. Wood shingles age from buff when new, to light gray, to increasingly darker gray. Use either wood stains (Driftwood is a good choice) or paints. Be sure to include the natural streaking on both the individual shingles and on areas of shingles. Study shingled roofs on buildings for good examples. Generally, the upper part of a shingle ages/weathers a darker color than the part that is more exposed. Use a darker stain first, followed by a dry-brushed lighter stain. Wood shingles also are sometimes green from moss or algae.

Embossed material is also available to make shingled roofs. This needs to be bonded to the panel with contact cement. Use printed paper for distant roofs. Make shingle roofs using individually applied shingles. This is often necessary in the scales larger than HO. The cedar wrappings from cigars have been used as a good source of material; also paper, bristol board, etc. You also can simulate the

Campbell material by first cutting paper strips, then cutting the individual shingles part way through the strip using a sharp knife or scissors.

Metal. Make corrugated metal roofs using the methods described in "Metal Buildings." Simulate metal roofs with seams from paper or plastic panels with raised stripwood or plastic strip ridges. Color the material properly to suggest the material (copper, galvanized, etc.) being modeled. Copper roofs usually age a deep, rich gray-green color.

Tile. Tile roofs are best modeled using embossed plastic sheet materials. You can obtain the realism desired only by carefully observing the color of the material and how it ages and weathers, so you can duplicate it on the model. The most common tiles are a red-brown color.

Composition. Embossed sheet material or printed paper material can represent composition roofs. In either case, bond the material to the roof panel using contact cement. One type of composition shingles can be created by cutting strips of paper using a pinking shears. Overlap the strips to form a diamond-pattern shingled roof.

Tar Paper. You can simulate tar paper by laying down strips of toilet tissue onto a wet coat of Floquil's Weathered Black or Grimey Black paint. The width of the strips should match the scale width of typical tar paper, about 3 feet. When this is dry, paint it a dark gray color (lighter with aging). Form tar seams and patches with a fine brush using glossy black paint. Another good tar paper is simulated by using 3M Medical Tape, available in various widths in drugstores.

Gravel. You can make gravel or rock roofs using sandpaper of appropriate grit size that you bond down to the roof panel with contact cement. Paint it the appropriate color and add any tar seams or patches as above. The larger rock particles might need to be added using fine ballast material bonded down with dilute matte medium.

Details. Roofs include metal flashing, faschia strips, exposed rafter ends, gutters, etc., where appropriate. Also see "Rooftops," chapter 20, for other possible details and clutter to be added.

20

Detailwork

Detailwork is the steps that provide additional detailing to the models, including the special finishes that are applied to make them look older and/or more weathered. Most of the topics here cover the man-made mobile parts of the layout, such as locomotives and rolling stock, vehicles, and people. In addition, this includes all the miscellaneous minor, but important, details called *clutter*.

RAILROAD EQUIPMENT

The railroad equipment—the trains—are usually the reason for having a model railroad. The trains are the stars of the show. They are what the people look at and "pay their money to see." If the trains look realistic and run well, then the illusion works.

Unfortunately, the effect often is not what it could be. Some modelers avoid the small amount of additional time and care they should take to give some missing details to those trains and to give them the rather dirty, weathered look of the prototype.

Steam Locomotives

Steam locomotive models can be ready-to-run, such as those made of brass or plastic, and either custom-painted or unpainted. You can build the models from kits, or from scratch, to a greater or lesser degree. All but the highest-cost, custom-finished brass models can benefit from the addition of further detail and completion with a quality paint job.

Details. The amount of detail you can include on a steam locomotive is almost without limit. You could include every valve and fitting of the steam piping. All the sand piping, all the intricacies of the brakes and rigging, all the rivets, a completely detailed backhead, the seats and windows and curtains . . . all this can be added . . . if it is important to you. None of this will make the locomotive run any better. Any of it can, if well done, make it look better. TABLE 20-1 is a checklist of possible detail to add to steam locomotives and tenders.

Table 20-1. *Checklist of Details to Include on Steam Locomotives and Tenders*

Locomotives

Steam dome	Stack
Steam valves	Whistle
Steam fittings	Whistle cord
Steam piping	Bell
Sand domes	Bell cord
Sand piping	Pilot
Brake rigging	Snowplow
Brake shoes	Flags
Brake cylinders	Number boards
Power reverse	Toolbox
Air pumps/compressors	Handrails
Air tanks	Front coupler
Water pumps	Backhead
Feedwater heater	Marker lights
Headlight	Seats
Generator	Windows
Boiler lagging	Curtains
Rivets	Armrests
Drawbar & hoses	Engineer
Drivers	Fireman
Wheels	Lettering
Siderods	Smokebox coloring
Aging	Cab roof coloring
Weathering	

Tenders

Bolster	Trucks
Brake equipment	Train lines
Hatches	Toolbox
Trucks	Coal
Handrails	Shovel
Ladder	Rerailer shoes
Rear coupler	Hose
Doghouse	Oil/water stains
Rivets	Lettering
Back-up light	Logo
Marker lights	
Aging	
Weathering	

Priorities. Again, it is your decision as to what you want. If you wish to produce a contest-quality model, then you can expect to put in many extra hours in super detailing. What you add should have a priority in terms of the contribution each addition makes to the overall appearance. Add the larger and more important details before those that are more minor. Remember that if the locomotive is viewed from more than a few inches away, much of the detail cannot be seen.

The inclusion of backhead detail is a case in point. Unless you really look closely, you cannot see any of this detail. If you cannot see it, why add it? Putting an engineer and a fireman in the cab is different, however, because they easily can be seen, and if they are absent, then the engine looks empty.

Certainly, when getting started in super detailing, it is better to not make it too "super" on the first tries. Look at photos of the prototype and compare them with the model. Add only the detail that is most obviously missing.

Those details usually consist of items that can be bought as brass or plastic castings. Examples are pumps, tanks, domes, stacks, toolboxes, pilots, etc. (FIG. 20-1). You can add them during the construction (for kits). For ready-to-run models, you must disassemble the model before the details are added. You can solder on cast details, if they and the receiving surface are both brass, or attach them with ACC. The latter can be surprisingly strong. If possible, drill a hole and use a protrusion from the casting into the hole to add strength.

Another detail often needed is additional piping. Bend the proper size of brass wire to shape and solder it on or use ACC, as for castings. A dummy, or working, front coupler can be a useful addition. Don't forget to add the crew, having prepainted them first (see "People"). Add details such as armrests, cab curtains, etc. Add a lens to the headlight. Make the headlight work, if that is desired. Add marker lights, flags, number boards, and a detailed bell.

You can enhance the appearance of the locomotive by reducing the length of the drawbar that connects to the tender. Make it as short as possible, but be careful that no binding or short circuits occur on your tightest curves.

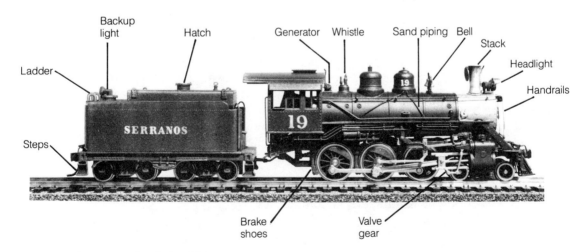

Fig. 20-1. Important detail should be present on a steam locomotive model.

Don't neglect the detailing of the tender. Add handrails or a ladder if they are missing. Add coal, if the engine is coal burning, using commercial material of the proper size. Would a backup light be appropriate? Be sure the trucks are of the proper type.

Color Choice. Even more than adding physical details, the creation of a good paint job will enhance the appearance and illusion of reality of the locomotive and tender. Running this equipment around in its gleaming lacquered brass color, or even worse, as an unpainted melange of brass and white metal, does not add much to the effect of the layout being a miniature of a real railroad. It is almost as bad to have locomotives that are painted a shiny black.

The first decision to make is what color to paint the locomotive. Black, you say? But which black? There has been a great deal of debate as to the shades of black that real locomotives were and how best to represent those blacks on the models, which are viewed under different lighting conditions.

When a real steam locomotive is new, it usually is painted a true semigloss black, with no gray in it. Because it is a major investment on the part of the railroad, for the first few years, at least, it is kept clean and is repainted regularly. Some areas are easier than others to keep wiped down, and they remain shiny. Other areas, subject to heat from the stack, smokebox, and smokebox door, gradually discolor to a flat black or graphite color. Some of the pumps and piping are subject to stains from oil and water.

Horizontal surfaces, such as the pilot and cab decks, the top of the tender, foot boards, running boards, etc., are subject to wear from foot traffic and so are worn or discolored. The domes, cab roof, and the top of the tender are blackened from soot. As the locomotive gets older, and/or as the fortunes of the railroad decline, less attention is given to appearance and all the blacks fade. This fading makes the black look more gray.

For the model, another effect enters in. The layout lighting is much less intense than sunlight. This produces less-defined shadows. If the locomotive is painted a deep black, no shadows will be seen, and all the detail of the locomotive will be lost. An exaggeration of the amount of graying can allow the shadows to be seen, providing definition to the details so that they do not remain invisible.

The conclusion is that you should paint these models black mixed with some white to make a gray. The amount of gray can then reflect the age and condition of the engine, ranging from little (new) to much (old).

Preparation. Before doing any finishing, make sure that the model runs well. Fixing bad operation is best done before this extra handling, which could result in damage to the model's finish. Similarly, install any lighting or sound systems and check them out.

Finishing Steam Locomotives

1. Assemble kit, if necessary.
2. Test run and confirm good operation.
3. Disassemble.

4. Strip off old finish, if necessary.
5. Prime paint. Paint finish coat(s). Paint other colors, if any.
6. Add lettering.
7. Add weathering.
8. Reassemble.
9. Add smallest details.

Unless it has been done already, disassembly is the first step. Paint each removable part separately. Do the disassembly systematically so that nothing is lost and so that you can get things back together again. Keep notes on the order of removal of the parts. Put screws back in the holes from which they came. Remove weights, trucks, and running gear. Remove wheel sets from trucks. Take off or mask off the couplers. Store the motor where it will not be demagnetized. Keep all parts together in a box.

Brass locomotives are often coated with a clear lacquer finish. It is optional whether you remove it prior to painting. If it is well applied, leave it on and use it as a primer for the color coats. If not, remove it so that you are starting with the bare metal.

If necessary, strip off the old paint or clear lacquer, being sure that no harm occurs to plastic parts (see "Finish Preparation," chapter 9). Etching the metal parts to improve paint adhesion is an option. Do not etch wheels. Wash the parts to be painted in warm, soapy water. Do not touch them with your bare hands after this washing. Rig up some kind of holding fixtures to hold the parts during painting and drying.

Painting. Mask all electrical contact points or places that will later need to be clean and lubricated. A thin gray primer paint coat is recommended. If at all possible, spray on this and subsequent paint coats using an airbrush (see "Airbrushing," chapter 9). Let the primer dry for 24 hours. A second primer coat, followed by another 24 hour drying period, is advisable.

The finish coat should be black, with enough white added to create the shade of gray desired. Finishes that will remain semigloss will require less graying than those that will be flat. Thin the mixture appropriately for spraying. If the locomotive is to have decals applied, or if the end result should give a semigloss appearance, then use a semigloss paint. Record the paint color and thinner proportions used so you can duplicate it later. Use only one manufacturer's paint on the model to avoid possible incompatibility problems.

Spray the hard-to-reach areas first, then the broad surfaces. Examine the model in a strong light to make sure that no areas are missed.

If you use a brush, try to keep the brush strokes in a direction so that they will be invisible or overlap each other (see "Brushing," chapter 9). You can get excellent results, approaching those obtainable with airbrushing, when care is taken with brushing.

If the locomotive is all metal, then bake on the paint in an oven (or toaster oven) set at the lowest setting for 2 to 4 hours. Make sure nothing is put in the oven that will be damaged by the heat. This baking will make the finish much more durable. After baking, let the parts dry for an additional day. For plastic models, two days drying (without baking) is recommended.

If the cab roof or the smokebox are to be different colors or shades, then mask off the remainder of the engine and spray these colors. Often, the smokebox is painted a silver-graphite color. If the locomotive has striping or multiple colors, see the next topic, "Diesel Locomotives," for these application methods.

Paint the wheels, couplers, and siderods (if not plated) using a brush. This is easier than to do all the masking necessary for airbrushing. Make sure you do not get any paint on the working surfaces of couplers. The trucks can be brushed or airbrushed. Keep paint off the wheel (tire) surfaces by masking, or be prepared to clean it off later with solvents and/or abrasives.

Lettering. Now apply the decals or dry transfers (see "Lettering," chapter 11). Most locomotives have the railroad name and/or logo on the tender side. The number is on the cab side and rear of the tender. Don't forget the numbers in the number boards. Overspray the lettering with either semigloss or flat clear finish, as appropriate.

Weathering. The amount of weathering applied will determine the apparent age and condition of the locomotive. It is better not to overdo this effect. For weathering, use water-based paints or chalks. Sprayed weathering can include grime or dust sprayed from below to simulate road dirt, and flat black soot applied from above to the cab roof and tender deck. The drivers and side rods were usually kept wiped clean.

Brushed weathering can include streaks of stains from water and oil, soot and discoloration on the stack, wear on the horizontal surfaces that receive foot traffic, etc. Paint the cab interior if it is to be other than black (see "Aging/Weathering," chapter 10).

Use chalk to provide the final weathering (see "Chalk," chapter 9). Use chalks to add stains, as an alternative or augmentation to brushing, and to generally tone down some of the areas, such as the firebox and the top surfaces of the locomotive and tender, which will fade more than the vertical surfaces. Use white chalks primarily. If some rusting is desired, do this with red-brown or orange-red chalks. Fix the chalks with semigloss or flat overspray, where appropriate.

Reassembly. Reassemble the locomotive in the reverse order of disassembly, consulting the notes you made. Make sure there is no paint where you need electrical contact or in wheel journals, etc. Provide a very small amount of lubrication for moving surfaces.

Do any final paint touch-up, then add headlight lenses, marker light jewels, bell and whistle cords, and the other, tiniest details. Add window glass, if any. Put the people in the cab. The result should be a realistic-looking locomotive that was done with comparatively little effort.

Diesel Locomotives

Diesel locomotives might not seem to have as much detail as steam locomotives, but this is not really true. It is just that most of the detail is smaller and more subtle. With their multiple colors, the painting of diesel models is even more important, however, in achieving prototypical reality.

As with their steam predecessors, diesel locomotive models come in the full range of types—from ready-to-run, to kits, to scratchbuilt. The materials are usually brass or plastic. Many fine plastic prepainted diesels are available that need only a little additional detailing to make them into first-class models.

This topic is also applicable to electric and gas-electric locomotives, and (in part) to streamlined passenger cars. TABLE 20-2 provides a checklist of details that you can add to diesel or electric locomotives.

Table 20-2. *Checklist of Details to Include*
on Diesel or Electric Locomotives

Diesel Locomotives

Handrails	Windshield wipers
Headlights	Antenna
Marker lights	Horns
Mars light	Cab interior
Number boards	Windows
Grills	Doorknobs
Draft gear	Couplers
Cooling fans	Speedometer cables
Radiator screens	Snowplow pilot
Louvers	Crew
Stacks	Lettering
Aging	Logo
Weathering	

Electric Locomotives

Same as for Diesel Locomotives, plus:
Pantographs
Brake resistors

Details. The most important detail on a diesel locomotive to have correct and of proper scale is the handrails. These should be correctly sized and located. The problem is usually to make them thin enough to be realistic and yet sturdy enough to survive handling. If possible, the handrails should be soldered brass construction.

Other details to consider adding if they are missing include number boards, windshield wipers, horns, headlights, windows, snowplows, louvers, stacks, and doorknobs. Don't forget to have a crew in the cab to operate the locomotive (see FIG. 20-2).

Color Choice. The variety of colors and color combinations that have been used for diesels is almost unlimited. The only guide in color choice has to be research to determine what colors were used on the prototype you are duplicating and where these colors were located. Determine color separation striping, warning striping, handrail colors, lettering colors, and other information necessary to duplicate the appearance of the engine.

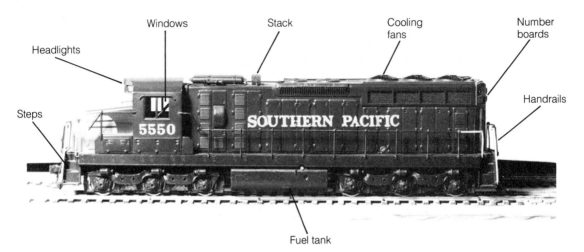

Headlights · Windows · Stack · Cooling fans · Number boards

Steps · SOUTHERN PACIFIC · 5550 · Handrails

Fuel tank

Fig. 20-2. Additional detail can be present on (or added to) a diesel locomotive model.

If you are modeling a fictitious railroad, then you should use a prototype paint scheme that you like as a model for your own, changing the colors or color locations to suit your taste. Remember that the more colors and color separations used, the more difficult the finishing job will be.

Determine how new you wish the locomotive to appear. If it is to be factory new, then the colors will not need to be lightened. An exception might be the very dark colors, where some graying can improve shadow definition. As the paint job and engine get older, the paint fades, making it lighter. Simulate this by adding more white to the paint colors.

Preparation. Make sure the model is free of mechanical problems and runs properly before doing the final finishing. Check out any lighting or sound systems. Disassemble the body from the running gear and the trucks. Remove windows and headlight lenses, if any. Usually it is not necessary to remove handrails from the body. If you do not remove the couplers, cover them with masking. If possible, remove the side frames from the trucks for separate painting. Make a holding fixture for the body so it can be held and manipulated during painting and while the paint is drying.

Finishing Diesel Locomotives

1. Assemble the kit, if necessary.
2. Test run and confirm good operation.
3. Disassemble.
4. Strip off old finish, if necessary.
5. Prime paint. Paint first finish color.
6. Mask for second color. Paint second finish color.
7. Repeat masking/painting, as necessary.

8. Add striping.
9. Add lettering.
10. Add weathering.
11. Reassemble.
12. Add smallest details.

Remove any unwanted old finish using one of the techniques in the topic, "Finish Preparation," chapter 9. Be careful of material compatibility with the paint stripping liquid. Wash the parts thoroughly, even if no paint has been removed, in warm, soapy water. Rinse in clear water and let air-dry. If the model is brass, you might want to etch the surface slightly, as described in the topic, "Finish Preparation." If the brass has a clear lacquer finish, see "Steam Locomotives."

Painting. For either metal or plastic, priming with a thin gray primer paint coat is recommended. If at all possible, spray on this and subsequent paint coats with an airbrush (see "Airbrushing," chapter 9). Let the primer dry for 24 hours. A second primer coat, followed by another 24 hour drying period, is advisable.

Determine the order of application of the colors, based on the following considerations:

1. It is better to put lighter colors on before darker/brighter colors because coverage is more difficult otherwise.
2. Apply the colors in an order that minimizes masking or makes it simpler.
3. Consider using decals for striping instead of painted stripes.

Thin the mixture appropriately for spraying. If possible, use a semigloss paint. Record the paint color and thinner proportions used so that you can duplicate them later. Use only one manufacturer's paint on the model to avoid possible paint incompatibility problems.

Spray the hard-to-reach areas first, then the broad surfaces. Examine the model in a strong light to make sure you did not miss an area. Paint the first color. If you use brushing, make the paint strokes so they overlap and become invisible (see "Brushing," chapter 9).

If the locomotive is all metal, then bake on the paint in an oven (or toaster oven) set at the lowest setting for 2 to 4 hours. Make sure nothing is put in the oven that will be damaged by the heat. This baking will make the finish much more durable. After baking, let the parts dry for an additional day. For plastic models, drying for two days without baking is recommended.

Provide the needed masking (see "Finish Preparation," chapter 9), and then paint the second color. Do not apply the masking until just before you are ready to paint. Thin the paint as little as possible so that it does not run under the masking. Let this coat air-dry the minimum time until you can remove the tape. Then repeat the baking and/or air drying. Apply additional colors following the same sequence of steps.

Paint the wheels, couplers, and handrails using a brush. This is easier than to do all the masking necessary for airbrushing. Brush or airbrush the truck side frames. Keep paint off the wheel (tire) surfaces and out of the coupler working parts.

Lettering. Now apply the decals or dry transfers (see "Lettering," chapter 11). Most diesel or electric locomotives have the railroad name and/or logo on the side. The number is on the cab side and front and rear. Don't forget the numbers in the number boards. Apply any decal striping now, too. Overspray the lettering and striping with either semigloss or flat clear finish, as appropriate.

Weathering. The amount of weathering applied will determine the apparent age and condition of the locomotive. It is best not to overdo this effect. Passenger diesels were usually washed frequently. For weathering, use water-based paints or chalks. Sprayed weathering can include grime or dust sprayed from below to simulate road dirt, and flat black exhaust soot applied from above to the top surfaces.

Brushed weathering can include streaks of stains from water and oil, soot and discoloration on the stacks, wear on the horizontal surfaces that receive foot traffic, etc. (see "Aging/Weathering," chapter 10). Paint the cab interior, armrests, windshield wipers, whistles, bell, etc.

Use chalk to provide the final weathering (see "Chalk," chapter 9). Use chalks to add stains, as an alternative or augmentation to brushing, and to generally tone down some of the areas. Use white or black chalks, as appropriate. If some rusting is desired, do this with red-brown or orange-red chalks. Fix the chalks with semigloss or flat overspray, as appropriate.

Reassembly. Do any final paint touch-up, then add headlight lenses, marker light jewels, and the other tiny details. Add window glass. Put the crew in the cab. Reassemble the locomotive in the reverse order of disassembly. Make sure there is no paint where electrical contact is needed or in wheel journals, etc. Provide a very small amount of lubrication for moving surfaces.

Passenger Cars

Passenger cars can benefit greatly from added detail and a good finish. See "Diesel Locomotives" and "Freight Cars," because many of the methods discussed there are applicable. The methods discussed here are also applicable to interurban, trolley, and street cars. Some aspects are also appropriate for some types of freight cars, such as cabooses.

Prototype passenger cars were originally build mostly from wood, but with the gradual application of steel, first to the frame, then to the sides and ends. By the mid-1920s, many cars were all metal. Streamline cars were all metal, some with smooth and some with corrugated sides. Many of them used stainless steel exterior surfaces.

The earlier cars had open platforms, clerestory roofs, truss rod bracing, and arch bar trucks. Gradually, the truss rods disappeared, the roof became round, and the platforms were closed in. The trucks became more modern, progressing from four-wheel to six-wheel types. The lengths increased from 35 to over 80 feet.

Model passenger cars are available made from prepainted and unpainted metal, plastic, and/or wood and as ready-to-run or kits, just like for locomotives.

You also can improve these cars a great deal by adding detailing, a quality finish, and a weathering job.

Details. As with other detailing, what is most important to add is what can be seen most easily and what will most obviously be missed if it is absent. For passenger cars, this includes roof and end detail and passengers. TABLE 20-3 is a checklist of possible details you can add to passenger cars and trolley cars.

Table 20-3. Checklist of Details to Include
on Passenger or Trolley Cars

Passenger Cars

Underbody

Bolsters	Trucks
Draft gear	Couplers
Center frame	Air-conditioning equipment
Truss rods	Battery boxes
Air tanks	Generators
Water tanks	Vents/drains
Brake equipment	

Interior

Windows	Tables
Shades	Dividers
Venetian blinds	Passengers
Curtains	Conductor
Seats	Porter

Exterior

Diaphragms	Roof vents
Tail gates	Stacks
Drumhead	Gutters
Safety chain	Roofing
Steps	Lettering
Handrails	Logo
Brake wheels	
Aging	
Weathering	

Trolley Cars

Same as for Passenger Cars, plus:

Trolley poles
Pantographs
Fender

Detailing the underbody has relatively little payoff in improved appearance, compared to the time spent. The underbody details cannot ordinarily be seen. If the car is a contest model, then full detailing of the underbody is essential. If not, then it is a luxury. What should be included on the underbody are the center frame or truss rods, tanks, air-conditioning equipment, battery boxes, generator, and major items of brake equipment. All the other piping and smaller details are unnecessary.

The roof is, surprisingly enough, the part of the car most easily seen, and it should be as detailed as possible. Fortunately, there is not too much detail on most passenger car roofs. You should model any stacks or vents and accurately model clerestory windows or the more modern vista-dome type windows. Include any grab irons. On the older cars, model the composition roofing with tissue paper strips (see "Rooftops,").

On the sides of the cars include all of the rivets, corrugations, window framing, etc., of the modeled prototypes. If the car was of wooden construction, then you could age and distress the boards, keeping them consistent with the suggested condition of the car. Some windows might be modeled as if they are open.

Do not ignore the ends. If possible, model the diaphragms that were used, although be sure they do not interfere or cause derailments. You can buy flexible diaphragms in most scales. Don't forget the steps, handrails, brake wheel, etc. Be sure to use the correct trucks for the car modeled (see FIG. 20-3).

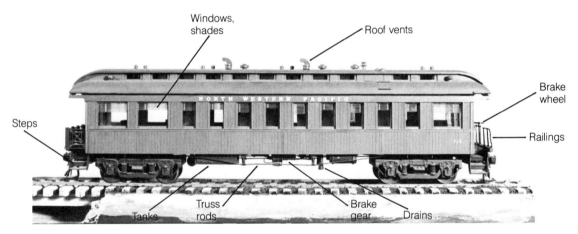

Fig. 20-3. The most important details that should be present on passenger cars are noted.

Interior. You can add a significant improvement in realism by suggesting the people that the car carries. It is not necessary to finely detail the interior because not much of this can be seen through the windows. Again, if the car is to be super detailed, then include full interior detailing, with a roof designed to be lifted off to view this detail.

Create the main areas of the car interior with cardboard or wood baffles so that you cannot see through from one side of the car to the other where that should be impossible. Only suggest the major items of furniture that can be seen through the windows by using wooden blocks shaped to size. Commercial interiors are available in many scales. Some of these are low cost and not too elaborate for this purpose.

Because the car is supposed to be carrying people between destinations, include the passengers. Most will be seated, but a few can be standing. Because they cannot be seen easily, they need only rudimentary painting and detailing.

They might have to be cut or otherwise modified to fit (see "People".) The car does not have to be full of people. Only include enough so it looks right.

The windows should have their "glass" in them. Microscope cover glass is the best, or you can use various clear plastics. Make sure to bond the window material in so that the glue does not show or smudge on the window. If some of the windows, such as in rest rooms, are to be translucent glass, simulate this by sanding the plastic on the reverse side. Sometimes the glass was tinted or colored. This can be represented by appropriately colored clear plastic. Also see the topic, "Windows," in chapter 19.

Lighting. Interior lighting can add a lot if you will be operating the trains in night conditions. Make sure this lighting is not too bright, that it is evenly distributed in the car, and that the bulbs cannot be seen from outside through the windows. Also make sure that no light escapes around removable roofs or other places provided to allow access. The light is also much more realistic if you use some means of pickup or energy storage so that the lights remain at constant brightness, independent of train speed or track dirt.

Painting. The older cars, whether made of wood or metal, were painted all over. The more modern cars, made of stainless steel, often leave some of the car unpainted. The colors can range from the older coach or pullman green to the bright colors used on streamlined "name" trains.

Paint before you add windows and complete interior detailing. Remove the trucks from the car. If you do not remove the couplers, then mask them. Devise a holding fixture for the body that will allow you to hold it during painting and drying. Remove any old, undesired finish. See the topic, "Finish Preparation," in chapter 9.

If you want paint aging effects, then lighten the paint by adding some white to it. Use the paint from only a single manufacturer to ensure compatibility. If the model is made of metal, some slight etching might be desirable. If the model is made of aluminum, which simulates finished stainless steel, then mask off the areas that are to remain clear during other painting. Dull this aluminum slightly using steel wool.

If it is necessary to color brass or plastic to simulate stainless steel, then paint this, usually as the first color. Use a gloss silver or aluminum color for the paint and add some gray. Investigate using some of the metallic paints made for finishing plastic model airplanes.

For either metal or plastic, priming with a thin gray primer paint coat is recommended. If at all possible, spray this and subsequent paint coats using an airbrush (see "Airbrushing," chapter 9). Let the primer dry for 24 hours. A second primer coat, followed by another 24 hour drying period, is advisable. Wood does not require priming.

Determine the order of application of the colors, based on the following considerations:

1. Put lighter colors on before darker/brighter colors because coverage is more difficult otherwise.
2. Put the colors on in an order that minimizes masking or makes it simpler.

3. Consider using decals for striping instead of painted stripes. See the topic, "Diesel Locomotives."

Thin the mixture appropriately for spraying. If possible, use a semigloss paint. Record the paint color and thinner proportions used so that you can duplicate them later. Paint the first color. Spray the hard-to-reach areas first and then the broad surfaces. Examine the model in a strong light to make sure that no areas are missed. If you brush, let the paint strokes overlap and become invisible (see "Brushing," chapter 9).

If the car is all metal, then bake on the paint in an oven (or toaster oven) set at the lowest setting for 2 to 4 hours. Make sure nothing is put in the oven that will be damaged by the heat. This baking will make the finish much more durable. After baking, let the parts dry for an additional day. For wood or plastic models, drying for two days without baking is recommended.

Provide the needed masking (see "Finish Preparation," chapter 9), then paint the second color, if any. Do not apply the masking until just before you are ready to paint. Thin the paint as little as possible so that it does not run under the masking. Let this coat air-dry the minimum time until you can remove the tape. Then repeat the baking and/or air drying. Apply additional colors, if any, following the same sequence of steps.

Paint the wheels, couplers, and handrails using a brush. This is easier than doing all the masking necessary for airbrushing. The truck side frames can be brushed or airbrushed. Keep paint off the wheel (tire) surfaces. Make sure no paint gets into the coupler working parts or inside the draft gear.

Lettering. Now apply the decals or dry transfers (see "Lettering," chapter 11). Most passenger cars have the railroad name and/or logo, the car number, and sometimes the car name, on the side. The number is also on the ends. Note that the lettering style used on passenger equipment is often quite different than that used on freight cars. Apply any decal striping now, too. Overspray the lettering and striping with either semigloss or flat clear finish, as appropriate.

Weathering. The amount of weathering applied will determine the apparent age and condition of the car. Do not overdo this effect. For weathering, use water-based paints or chalks. Sprayed weathering can include grime or dust sprayed from below to simulate road dirt, and flat black soot applied from above to the top surfaces.

Brushed weathering can include streaks of stains from water and oil; soot and discoloration on the roof, sides, and ends; wear on the horizontal surfaces that receive foot traffic, etc. (see "Aging/Weathering," chapter 10). Paint the car interior and furniture. Usually these should be a medium dark color so attention is not drawn to the lack of interior detail.

Use chalk to provide the final weathering (see "Chalk," chapter 9). Use chalks to add stains as an alternative or augmentation to brushing and to generally tone down some of the areas. Use white or black chalks as appropriate. If some rusting is desired, do this with red-brown or orange-red chalks. Fix the chalks with semigloss or flat overspray, where appropriate.

Reassembly. Do any final paint touch-up, then add interior details, people, and window glass. Reassemble in the reverse order of assembly. Make sure the trucks and couplers are working properly.

Freight Cars

There are an enormous variety of freight cars that can be modeled. They range from the commodity-carrying cars, such as boxcars, refrigerator cars, stock cars, tank cars, hopper cars, gondola cars, flat cars; etc., to the nonrevenue cars, such as cabooses and maintenance-of-way cars. The prototype cars include almost every combination of wood and metal, with the percentage of metal gradually increasing to 100 percent since post-World War II.

Model freight cars are available in every conceivable combination of materials—as kits, as partial kits, as ready-to-run models, etc. Many of the kits have prepainted and lettered bodies or sides. Almost all of these cars can be improved by carefully adding detail and by properly finishing, aging, and weathering. For the methods to use for cabooses or other freight cars having windows or internal accommodations for people, see "Passenger Cars" for suggestions.

Details. As with passenger cars, the least productive additional detailing to freight cars is on the underbody. Except for the contest models, such details cannot ordinarily be seen or appreciated. The only underbody detail that ordinarily should be included is the center sill (or truss rods), bolsters, draft gear, and major items of brake gear.

The most enhancing additional detailing is on the roof. Do not ignore either the sides or ends, of course. TABLE 20-4 is a checklist of possible details that you can add to freight and maintenance-of-way cars. FIGURE 20-4 shows the more important detail you should include.

In real life, you only see the roofs of freight cars from bridges or overpasses. On models, you see more of the roofs than any other part of the car. Fortunately, roof detailing is not too hard to do. Make sure you include roof walks, grab irons, or brake wheels, if any, and model them to scale. Model any roof ribs, the proper roof finish, ice hatches, etc., authentically. Be sure to include appropriate loads in open-top cars, such as flat or gondola cars. If those cars are empty, leave some debris behind.

On the sides, be sure to include all ladders and grab irons. Remove cast-on plastic detail and add more realistic and separate details, such as ladder, foot stirrups and grab irons. If the car has side doors, these and their hardware should be to scale and authentic. Model the doors open or closed as well as the interiors of boxcars. Include the animal passengers in stock cars if you like.

Include ladders and grab irons, number boards, brake wheel, and a suggestion of the coupler actuation lever on the car ends. Make sure that anything added near the couplers does not interfere with their operation.

Aging. There are two types of aging you can apply to freight cars. The first type is aging that results from damage or deterioration to the car. The second type is the aging that results in color changes. Damage can cause dents to metal or the fracture of wood. These effects must be simulated physically.

Table 20-4. *Checklist of Details to Include on Freight or Maintenance-of-Way Cars*

Freight Cars

Underbody

Center sill	Draft gear
Truss rods	Couplers
Bolsters	Brake equipment
Trucks	

Loads

Junk	Pulpwood
Scrap	Logs (with chains)
Machinery	Lading blocking
Boxes	Stock
Pipe	Piggyback trailers
Coal	Containers
Ore	Debris/residue
Cinders	
Wood chips	

Exterior

Roof ribs	Brake wheel
Roofing	Stake pockets
Roof walk	Number boards
Ice hatches	Doors
Ladders	Door hardware
Grab irons	Lettering
Platforms	Logos
Aging	Hobos
Weathering	

Maintenance-of-Way Cars

Same as for Freight Cars, plus:

Toolboxes	Drums
Tools	Gas cylinders
Cables	Chains
Rail	Snowplow
Ties	
Spare trucks	

Damage. You can create metal dents by carefully bending or pounding them into metal models. This could be a painful process if the model is an expensive brass import. Simulating the dents in plastic models is easier. Hold a hot soldering iron tip near to the area to be "bent." Make sure that it does not actually touch the plastic. Use a wooden dowel or other object to press in the dents. This process is repeated, as necessary, to simulate the damage (FIG. 20-5).

Note that dents are very common on the ends and sides of gondola cars and hopper cars, where they are loaded from above with less than tender, loving care. Most of these dents are either down along the top lip or from the inside, outward. The dents will be greater between structural members.

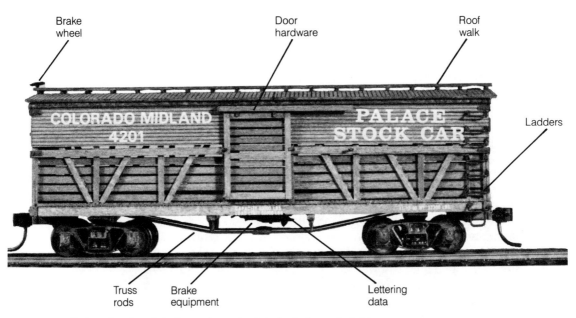

Brake
wheel

Door
hardware

Roof
walk

COLORADO MIDLAND
4201

PALACE
STOCK CAR

Ladders

Truss
rods

Brake
equipment

Lettering
data

Fig. 20-4. Only a few key details are important to include on freight cars.

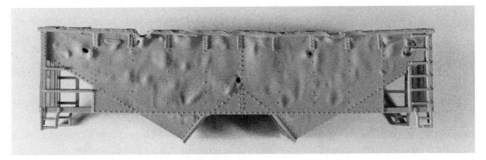

Fig. 20-5. A soldering iron can be used to form dents simulating damage to a model freight car.

Be careful about including accident damage that would cause the railroad to take a car out of operation. Most major damage that could affect operation, utility, or safety is repaired rapidly. This damage usually produces dents going inward from the outside of the car.

Wood damage can be modeled by the same methods used for wooden structures (see "Wooden Buildings," chapter 19). Again, for in-service cars, damage that is major is usually quickly repaired.

Deterioration. Deterioration of metal cars usually manifests itself in a lesser or greater degree of rusting. Rust is most likely to occur where there has been some damage, or where the paint has been removed through some damage or physical action. It also can occur almost anywhere if the car is not kept painted.

Major rust deposits cause a "bubbling up" effect that can be simulated by adding modeling paste or by teasing plastic liquid cement applied to a plastic model. Minor rusting is simulated as a part of the finishing. Note that most "wooden" cars contain at least some metal that can be subject to rusting.

Wood deterioration consists of increased surface texture, which shows the grain more, and splitting, loss of knots, and actual rotting. Model these effects using the methods discussed in "Wooden Buildings," chapter 19.

Painting. The model colors should duplicate those used on the prototype. Add some white to the paint to create the fading of aging paint. Remove trucks and couplers before painting. If the couplers are not removed, mask them off. Use a holding fixture of some sort to hold the car during the painting and drying.

Not all cars will require painting or repainting. Many kit cars have excellent prepainted and lettered sides that would take a great deal of time to duplicate. These cars might require painting of the roof, underbody, and possibly the ends. Almost all cars will need a little aging and weathering. The aging of faded paint on prepainted and lettered car sides can be simulated by a thin overspray of highly thinned white paint. The weathering is done as described below.

If you want to simulate extremely old wood, then follow the methods used for structures. Otherwise, spray or brush paint the model. Most freight cars are a single color. If not, then see "Passenger Cars" for multiple color paint finishes.

For either metal or plastic, priming with a thin gray paint coat is recommended. If at all possible, spray this and subsequent paint coats on using an airbrush (see "Airbrushing," chapter 9). Let the primer dry for 24 hours. A second primer coat, followed by another 24 hour drying period, is advisable. Wood does not require priming. If the model car is all metal, then see "Passenger Cars" for finishing methods.

Thin the mixture appropriately for spraying. If possible, use a semigloss paint. Record the paint color and thinner proportions used so you can duplicate it later.

Spray the hard-to-reach areas first, then the broad surfaces. Examine the model in a strong light to make sure that no areas are missed. Paint the first color. If brushing is used, overlap the paint strokes so they become invisible (see "Brushing," chapter 9).

For wood or plastic models, drying for two days without baking is recommended. If a second color is required, apply masking and then the second color, followed by the same drying time.

Paint the wheels and couplers using a brush. This is easier than doing all the masking necessary for airbrushing. The truck side frames can be brushed or airbrushed. Keep paint off the wheel (tire) surfaces. Make sure no paint gets into the coupler working parts or inside the draft gear.

Lettering. Apply the decals or dry transfers now (see "Lettering," chapter 11). The lettering should include the railroad name, the car number, any logo, dimensional data, and other "fine print." Make sure your cars all have different numbers. Do not forget any lettering on the car ends. Sometimes you can include graffiti. Overspray the lettering with either semigloss or flat clear finish, as appropriate.

Weathering. The amount of weathering applied will determine the apparent age and condition of the car. It is best not to overdo this effect. For weathering, use water-based paints or chalks. You can relieve the single-color effect of the base paint by brushing on a thin wash over everything using small amounts of white, yellow ochre, and raw umber in water, with a drop of detergent added. Brush along the grain of the wood and the long way on metal panels, etc. The desire is to relieve the sameness of the finish and to get a little different shade in the nooks and crannies (FIG. 20-6).

Fig. 20-6. These model freight cars (and the load) have received moderate weathering.

Sprayed weathering can include grime or dust colors sprayed from below to simulate road dirt, and flat black soot applied from above to the top surfaces. Wind-blown lading dust from coal, iron ore, grain, cement, etc., can also be added in this way.

Brushed weathering can include streaks of stains from water and oil; soot and discoloration on the roof, sides, and ends; wear on the horizontal surfaces that receive foot traffic, etc. Brushing should simulate the effects of gravity in washing dust and dirt downward (see "Aging/Weathering," chapter 10).

Use chalk to provide the final weathering (see "Chalk," chapter 9). Use chalks to add stains as an alternative or augmentation to brushing and to generally tone down some of the areas. Use white, gray, or black chalks as appropriate. If some rusting is desired, do this with red-brown or orange-red chalks. Fix the chalks with semigloss or flat overspray, as appropriate.

The order of application of the brushed, sprayed, and chalk weathering is determined by the effect desired. Did the road spray occur before or after the rains washed down the stains from above? To what extent is the rust covered by other effects? You might need to repeat some of these applications to get the result you want.

The weathering effects can vary a great deal depending on the type of freight car. The road grime spray on all cars tends to stick to the ends, in two distinct paths (wheel tracks), formed by the spray from the preceding car. This is sprayed up from below on both sides and ends. Most cars have some blackening of the areas around ladders and doors caused by dirty feet.

Rain-washed dirt and grime tend to streak the car top, sides, and ends. The color tends to accumulate at the bottom of the car side and ends, and around details such as rivets. Wind-blown dirt collects around protrusions such as external braces, doors, etc.

Trucks are originally the color of the car underbody, modified by grease stains and rust. The wheel sets are often left unpainted and age to a rich dark brown rust color. The trucks receive a lot of the road grime.

Sometimes, individual boards have been replaced on a car, and these are a newer color. This can be simulated by painting these boards with a brush in an unfaded color after the background color is painted on, or by masking off these boards, then aging the faded regions with a thinned overspray. Similarly, sometimes new lettering is applied to a portion of the car side over new paint. This effect can be simulated, before adding the lettering, by the same methods.

Rust can be sprayed on if it is general, or it can be brushed on if it occurs only in specific areas. For the former, use a very thin spray so the effect is subtle. Spray before or after lettering, depending on the desired look. The rust can vary in color from almost orange to rust to burnt sienna. Rust usually stains downward with gravity. Note that metal fittings on wood cars often stain the wood. Dry-brushing these stains is often effective (see "Brushing," chapter 9).

Car Differences. Refrigerator cars have light gray stains around the roof hatches from the water and salt brine used. Stock cars are often disinfected with a lime that leaves white stains coming out of the floor areas. These stains sometimes are other colors as well due to the lack of sanitary facilities for the animals. You can simulate this look by adding ochers and umbers. The white disinfectant gradually becomes washed away, so not all stock cars will show this to the same degree. If the ends are slatted, they need the same treatment as the sides.

Open-top cars are particularly subject to internal wear that often leaves little paint and much rust and other discoloration. The latest load will leave traces that will take quite a while to blow out or wash away. Tank cars usually are stained by the oil or other chemicals that they carry. These might occasionally be lost due to overfilling, or other such "accidents." If these spills are relatively fresh, they can be shiny. This can be simulated with enamels or with acrylic gloss medium applied over flat paints.

Cars carrying bulk commodities, such as covered hoppers, often show deposits left by spills made during loading. These recreate the colors of the bulk materials being carried.

Boxcar roofs often have very little paint left on them. The galvanized steel color shows through, which can be simulated with a mixture of reefer gray and silver. If you apply the mixture before the roof paint color, then all you need do is overspray the roof during the general painting. The ribs are then brush-painted the roof color. Use the dry-brush technique to add streaks of roof color over the silver/gray to simulate paint that still remains.

Alternatively, you can dry-brush on the silver/gray to simulate where the roof paint has peeled off. This is usually not as effective in appearance. In either case, all brush strokes should be from the center to the edge. Add rusting where desired.

You can imitate wood surfaces that are subject to a lot of wear, such as flat car or gondola decks, by following some of the methods used for buildings. See "Wooden Buildings," chapter 19.

You can make lettering look aged and faded by overspraying it with a light, thinned coat of the same color that is underneath. Do this before weathering. Sometimes the lettering on the prototype chalks off and runs down the surface as it ages. This can be simulated most safely by dry-brushing thin streaks of paint of the faded lettering color downward from the letters. A riskier alternative is to use a solvent to actually dissolve the paint in the lettering to streak it down. Chalks also can simulate this effect.

Reassembly. Reassemble the car in the reverse order of disassembly. Add any modeled loads or bulk material. Make sure the trucks and couplers are working properly.

VEHICLES

Vehicles consist of the automobiles, buses, trucks, and other motorized conveyances that do not run on tracks. Vehicles move people or freight. There are also the horse-drawn equivalents that earlier performed these same functions. Vehicles include road and farm equipment and tractors, motorcycles, bicycles, boats, and planes. Although many of these are competitors of "your" railroads, they do exist in great numbers and must, therefore, be modeled (FIG. 20-7).

Fig. 20-7. A model railroad needs a great many vehicles of many different types.

The modern vehicles offer a particular danger due to their commonality. While most people will not notice that a layout depicting 1956 has a diesel locomotive that was first produced in 1960, they will almost certainly comment on the same anachronism applied to a Chevrolet sedan. If you model your vehicles well enough so they represent particular prototypes, and you probably should, then you should pay close attention to the model years of the vehicles so you don't create impossible situations that will draw jibes from your all-too-knowledgeable spectators.

Automobiles

Automobiles constitute the predominant vehicle on the streets and highways. They are intended to transport people, but they spend much of their life parked. After their days are over, they can remain in backyards or auto junkyards in various stages of rust and decay for many more years.

Model cars are available in most scales in a fairly wide variety of prototypes and model years. Some are already built and painted, and others are kits. Some toy cars are so well modeled that they are usable. Any can be modified to improve the detail or to convert the car to a different manufacturer or model year. Cast parts for model cars are also available for semiscratch building. In this regard, the most useful parts are the wheels and tires.

Details. A supposedly moving car should have a driver and possibly passengers. If the car model that is being driven down the street or highway is unoccupied, it loses all credibility. This is the most important, and yet, most neglected detail. Add simple seats with seated people cut to fit. You might want to include the steering wheel. Convertibles might require additional interior detailing.

The second most important detail is the windshield and window glass. If there is none, this might be acceptable for cars in the distance, but for those in the foreground, it doesn't look right. At the least, include glass for the windshield and rear window. The absence of glass in the side windows can be explained by it being a warm day so that the windows are open.

In the smaller scales, some model cars are cast solid and do not have hollow interiors. Then you must suggest the "glass" by paint. No driver and passengers are needed because no one can see into the car. The suggested paint color is a dark gray, with dry-brushed highlights (reflections) of white or light blue.

Painting. Paint the car a color appropriate to the prototype. Age the color a little by adding some white, if the car is not new. Either use gloss paints or enamels, or spray the car with a gloss finish. It is probably best to paint the interior a dark color.

Paint the tires a medium gray. Make white sidewalls by carefully painting or creatively masking them. Paint the major chrome areas a chrome or aluminum color. Floquil's Old Silver is a good choice. Although most cars are kept clean, apply light weathering with Dust. Other details to include are bumpers, headlights, taillights, license plates, exhaust, spare tire, running boards, hood ornament, door handles, windshield wipers, radio antenna, and trailer hitch. Not all cars will have all of these (FIG. 20-8).

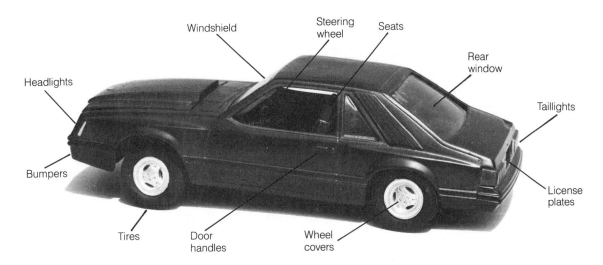

Headlights
Bumpers
Tires
Door handles
Wheel covers
Windshield
Steering wheel
Seats
Rear window
Taillights
License plates

Fig. 20-8. *This photo shows some of the more important details which might be included on model cars (and trucks).*

Unless the headlights have actual lenses (possible in the larger scales), the lenses need to be painted. They will look best if they are painted off-white, with perhaps a little touch of yellow. Use a gloss paint or coat them with a clear gloss finish. Paint the taillights a deep red, also with a gloss. Do not forget the various parking and running lights, which will be either white or amber in color.

If the car is turning a corner, turn the front wheels appropriately. These wheels might also be turned if the car is parked. You could also model a car that is jacked up, with a tire being changed. A car being towed by a tow truck, or a fender-bender accident, could also be shown.

Age junked cars by applying dents, removing parts, and liberally applying rust and weathering. Make dents by physically deforming the metal or plastic. A heated soldering iron will aid in remolding the plastic.

Trucks and Buses

Trucks and buses are the commercial motor vehicles used for transporting freight and passengers. A fairly wide selection of kits in all scales is available for trucks. Bus kits are more limited in availability. For trucks particularly, kit modifications can yield needed variations with slight additional work.

There are many different kinds of trucks, determined by the type of product being carried and the distance to be covered. TABLE 20-5 is a checklist of some types of trucks that might be modeled.

Most of the discussion on cars is also applicable to trucks and buses. Buses are like very large cars, with two additions. First, they usually contain many more passengers, who need to be modeled, if the bus is in transit. Second, they usually have some external lettering or a logo, and they might have a fancy paint job, not unlike the railroad passenger cars they are competing with.

Table 20-5. Checklist of Types of Trucks

Fire	Railway express
Ambulance	Stake
Garbage	Dump
Delivery	Tank
Ice cream	Oil delivery
Flat bed	Farm
Furniture	Armored
Glass	Horse van
Stock	Pickup
Milk	Moving van
Ice	Tow
Beer	Logging
Gasoline	Lumber
Container	Produce
Well drilling	Bread
Military	Street cleaning
Snowplow	Feed
Cement mixer	Dumpster
Semitrailer	Camper
Horse trailer	House trailer
Mail	Boat trailer

The cab (or tractor) portion of a truck is much like a car, but the load portion (or body) is different. For semi-trucks, the tractor has a fifth wheel that mounts the trailer. This is usually covered with black grease. The body might range from a flat platform mounted directly on the truck frame to various, more-elaborate tanks, boxes, etc., that perform the function or enclose the load for which the truck was built. Be sure to model these loads, in all their variety.

Trailers, such as those used for horses, stock, or boats, and house trailers or campers can be modeled using the same methods you used for trucks. Semi-trucks consist of a tractor portion and one or more detachable trailer portions. These trailers constitute an important load for your flat cars or trailer trains.

The truck often has names and advertising on the cab door and on the body. In many respects, the truck body (or trailer, for a semi-truck) has the same features as a railway freight car. Most freight cars have direct counterparts in truck bodies. In addition, there are some truck functions that are unique, such as fire trucks and ambulances.

Trucks and buses have changed in design as the years have passed. Study photos of the era you are modeling to make sure that you do not show any vehicles too modern for the time being depicted. Most people cannot recognize a particular model year, but they could detect a gross anachronism such as a 1950s truck being used in a 1930s scene.

Often the choice of truck and its location and posing can be used to tell a story. Then, too, why not use the trucks to contribute freight to the railroad, by showing them doing things in conjunction with the railroad operations, and/or with the railroad's customers?

Horse-Drawn Vehicles

Almost every modern type of car, truck, and bus had its earlier counterpart in horse-drawn vehicles. The first motorized vehicles did not appear, other than experimentally, until the turn of the century. They did not become very common until just before World War I, and they did not finally replace the horse as the principal means of urban vehicular power until the late thirties. They lasted even later in rural areas.

Horse-drawn vehicles are more difficult to model than their modern equivalents. The delicate spoked wheels, exposed springs, and the intricacies of the harness provide both a lot of detail opportunity and a great challenge. This discussion cannot even begin to list the variations in the wagons, buggies, coaches, etc., that were once prevalent.

If you wish to model these vehicles, do the necessary research to find out what they looked like and what the various parts of the vehicle and the harness were for. Model the most important parts that can be seen from the distance the vehicle will be viewed. In some scales, there are several kits or finished models of horse-drawn vehicles available. Often, the spoked wheels, which are the hardest part to model, are available separately.

Do not forget the tongues, single-trees, double-tree, etc. that allowed the horse(s) to be connected to the vehicle. Model the reins, harness straps, etc., as appropriate. Note that not all of these vehicles will always have horses hitched to them. If the vehicle is supposed to be moving, make sure it has a driver and passengers.

These vehicles, when new, were usually quite colorful. They were mostly made of wood, so the paint would fade fast and deterioration of all types, common to wood, would set in. Model both new, old, and junked vehicles, just as you would for cars.

Road and Farm Machinery

There are a lot of vehicles that are designed primarily for off-road use. These include farm tractors and machinery; road grading, earth moving, and excavation machinery and tractors; lumbering machinery; and machinery for mining, such as power shovels.

Some of this machinery have rubber tires, some caterpillar treads, some metal-surfaced wheels, and some are designed for stationary operation. Often, machinery that once had bare metal wheels, such as farm tractors and machinery, is now built with rubber tires. The sizes and styles of this machinery have also changed over the years, so make sure that recent equipment does not appear on an old-time layout.

As with other vehicles, you have the choice of using available kits or ready-to-use models. Often, toy models are available that are suitable, particularly for the grading, excavating, and power shovel equipment. If you need to scratch-build, you will need to make most of the vehicle from raw materials, with the possible exception of the wheels.

Be sure to paint the equipment the proper color because each manufacturer had "his" trademark color. Sometimes, the name of the maker is displayed and, for construction companies, the name and/or logo of the company.

This type of vehicle typically gets a lot of use, and it is seldom protected from the elements. This means that it is subject to comparatively-rapid physical deterioration and paint aging. The paint quickly wears off metal surfaces that come in contact with the earth and rock; such as treads, blades, shovels, etc,; and these surfaces have the shine and color of polished steel. This can be simulated by not painting the surface if the model is made of white metal, or by painting with colors such as Floquil's Old Silver, Bright Silver, or Gun Metal (and mixtures).

The remainder of the vehicle is often covered with the dirt that is being moved around the work site. Make sure the dirt on the vehicle matches the local earth in color and texture. Consider zip texturing (see chapter 17) as a choice when adding this dirt. Note how the dirt collects around the treads, wheels, and underbody of the vehicle.

Consider any of these vehicles as loads for the railroad's flat cars. Make sure that they are attached realistically, with wooden blocking and cables/chains so that they will not shift during shipment.

Boats and Airplanes

Among the major competitors of railroads are boats, ships, and airplanes. Unlike the trucks and buses, however, they go where the trains usually cannot go.

Boats. If your layout includes a small lake, you might wish to model a rowboat with a fisherman, or one tied up to a pier. As your bodies of water get larger, you can include larger boats. For rivers or harbors, these might include tow boats, barges, larger pleasure sail or power boats, etc. Some modelers have included railroad car ferries as an operational feature. Some have included ships as large as grain or ore boats.

It seems that most boat kits, and there are a lot of very fine ones available, are made in odd scales that do not match the model railroad scales. If you are fortunate enough to find the boat you want or need in the scale you are modeling, or close to it, then you are very lucky. Usually, you will need to build the boat from scratch. If you must compromise on the scale of the boat, it will look better if it is slightly undersized.

Railroad car ferries must be designed with rails on the deck and with an alignment system so the equipment can roll on and off the boat without derailing. Usually, the pier has some arrangement to allow for the different height of the boat deck, relative to the land, as the boat is loaded or as the water level varies.

Many books have been written on the subject of model boat construction and detailing. This material will not be repeated here. There are some principles to remember when applying model boats to model railroads, however.

Do not choose a boat to model that is so large that it will overpower the rest of the railroad. Like any other feature, keep it in balance with everything else. You will probably only have to model the boat from the waterline on up, depending on what you are using to model the "water." Make sure the boat looks like it is in, rather than on top of, the water (see "Still Water," chapter 17).

For any boats larger than the smallest ones, try to choose boats that will contribute to the freight (or passenger) traffic on your railroad. If you model a harbor, include facilities to transfer freight between trains and boats. You might wish to model the boat so it can be "moved." This would be particularly effective for a railroad car ferry, for example. The ferry can then serve as an extension of the railroad to another (unseen) place of interchange. You might also consider small boats in a boat yard or as loads on your railroad's flat cars.

Boats, like everything else, are also subject to aging and weathering. Unless the boat is supposed to be a derelict or very old, keep these effects subtle.

Airplanes. Airplanes are rarely appropriate as modeled objects for a model railroad. Usually, there is no room for an airport, or even the suggestion of one. Airplanes suspended from supposedly invisible threads look somehow toylike and contrived. Airplanes are seldom seen as freight on railroad cars, and if they were, they would be crated and protected to the point of unrecognizability.

If you wish to model airplanes, consult one of the many good books on building plastic model airplanes. The usual scales for kits are $1/72$ size (a bit smaller than S scale) and $1/48$ size (which is O scale).

Other Vehicles

Other vehicles include motorcycles with or without sidecars, bicycles, and tricycles. All of them need a rider if they are shown moving.

These vehicles usually have spoked wheels, except for the most-modern motorcycles. The spokes are too small to be easily modeled, or to be seen for that matter. There are a few kits available for motorcycles, but almost none for the smaller human-powered bikes and trikes. The latter have been made by some modelers using metal-etching techniques. They also might be made out of brass wire, bent and soldered to shape. Only the rim and tire (not the spokes) should be modeled.

Paint these vehicles like you would cars. A fine touch is necessary to paint the chrome on a bicycle, yet keep this separate from the colors of the frame, seat, pedals, tires, etc. As with cars, remember to add the head and taillights, licenses, saddlebags, etc.

CREATURES

Creatures include not only people but all the animals and birds that give living animation to the real world. Without model creatures, the layout will lack that essential life.

There are two theories on the posing of creatures. The first theory is that the people and animals are all shown as though captured frozen in time, in mid-motion, just as a still photograph would do. This allows action poses of all sorts in this suspended animation.

The second theory says that the first theory destroys the illusion of the scene because the same person will have the same limb posed in action today, tomorrow, and forever . . . something that is obvious by watching for only a few seconds. This theory suggests that you should depict creatures only in static poses—standing, sitting, leaning, resting, etc.—where the lack of movement is not so immediately obvious.

In fact, except for the trains, most of a model railroad *is* inanimate. The cars and trucks do not move on the highways and the trees do not sway in the wind. You readily accept this "suspension of disbelief" because you have no practical alternative. Extension of this inanimation to creatures can, therefore, be thought of as logical.

Which theory do you prefer (FIG. 20-9)? That is entirely up to you. Note that neither theory tries to avoid the problem by eliminating all human and animal presence. That could not be the answer because then the scene would be dead and unlived-in.

Fig. 20-9. The figures to the left are in dynamic poses, those to the right in static poses.

People

Cast figures, representing people in a variety of poses, are available from many different vendors. These figures are cast in metal or plastic. Some are available prepainted. The quality is usually proportional to the cost. Use the better figures in the foreground. Background figures do not have to be highly detailed because that detail cannot be seen.

The figures are formed to resemble people of both sexes and all ages, with dress typical of different eras. The bodies are posed in different positions, representing people sitting, standing, walking, or working at various tasks.

If there were no little people, there would be no reason for the railroad because it is for them (presumably) that it was built. Choose your figures in quality, quantity, pose, and detailing with the same care you use for all other parts of your models. The people should seem to really be doing something or going somewhere. They can tell a story as well or better than anything else you put in the miniature scenes. Plan the location and function of every figure.

Modification. You don't have to just accept the figures that you buy as-is.

Modify the figures in major or minor ways to suit your needs by carving and filing the clothing to change the era or style, or by bending or moving an arm or a leg to a different angle.

Make moderate bends by softening the plastic with solvent, then cutting out a V-shaped portion on the inside of the bend, bending, and rebonding. More extreme bends might require cutting both inside and outside the bend. Metal limbs will not bend easily, so they might have to be cut off, filed to fit, and rebonded in place at the new angle.

Sometimes it is easier to transplant parts from one figure to another. This applies particularly to hands (open versus closed, etc.). Keep a spare parts box for your figures. Use ACC (for metal) or plastic cement to reattach the limb. Make sure you do not create figures with two left or right hands, arms, or legs. Fill any gaps with plastic putty. Also use this putty to make dresses longer or to make a person fatter, etc.

If the figures are on stands, carefully remove these stands. Leave the figures on headers, if any, to make handling easier. It can be very useful to drill a hole into the foot of the figure and bond a small wire into the hole. This can be used initially for handling and later for mounting. Clean off all flash using needle files.

Seated figures will not need handling and mounting wires. For handling and painting, temporarily mount them sitting on a length of stripwood, using double-sided tape stuck to their seats. Often, to fit seated figures into a locomotive cab, railroad passenger car, or automobile, requires major surgery performed on their posterior and/or legs. If this is necessary, do not be reluctant to perform any amputations that will not show.

Some modelers have created their own figures from scratch from wood or plastic; or alternatively, by building them up and carving them to shape from wax or water putty, formed over soldered wire armatures. Others have cast their own figures from plaster or metal using molds made from purchased or hand-carved figures. Another option is to use Fimo modeling material. Any of these techniques take a lot of time.

Fimo Modeling Technique

Fimo is a clay-like modeling material, made in West Germany. It is available at most craft and dollhouse supply stores. It comes in 30 different colors, which can also be blended together to create additional colors. It costs under $2 per small packet.

You can use Fimo just like modeling clay to form almost anything. To understand just how versatile it is, visit a store selling items for dollhouses and ask to see some of the things that have been made of Fimo.

Bake the modeled item in an oven at 275°F for 30 minutes. It will then become hard and permanent. You can coat it with a clear finish for additional protection, paint it, or add more gloss.

Consider modeling figures in poses that are not the same as those available ready-made. Use your imagination so that your people do not look the same as everyone else's. An example might be someone on crutches or a handicapped person in a wheelchair. Make your children at play look like they are really having fun!

Painting. Paint several figures at a time. Wash the figures in soapy water and let them dry. If they are not on a header, attach them to a long block of wood for easier handling and painting.

Spray or brush the figures with a priming paint. Use Foundation or some other neutral shade. Paint the flesh color first, followed by the inner garments (shirt, socks), followed by the outer garments (dress, pants, jacket). If possible, paint light colors before doing dark colors. Use colors that are slightly muted by adding a little white to them. Remember to include people with skin colors other than white (black, oriental, North American Indian, Mexican, etc.) Some people also have lighter or darker complexions than others.

Make up a thin wash of dark brown or black and go over the entire figure. This will create shadows and add to the definition of the clothing and features. Wipe on black or brown antiquing stains (available at handicraft stores), then wipe off to fulfill this same function.

Then do the details, such as hair, beards, shoes, hats, belts, etc. (see FIG. 20-10 AND COLOR INSERT). Include variations in hair coloring (black, brown, blond, red). In the larger scales (O and larger), add the eyes, mouth, eyebrows, mustaches, buttons, etc. Highlight the outer folds of clothing by dry-brushing a more pastel hue on to the base colors. In the larger scales, also highlight the skin, adding a little pinkness to the cheeks and some lightening to the forehead, cheekbones, and nose.

Fig. 20-10. Much realism can be added to model figures by careful painting and detailing.

Perhaps some of your people should wear glasses? In the smaller scales, use bits of clear plastic for the lenses and paint the bows on. In O and larger, make the frames from small gauge wire.

Animals

Precast animal figures are made by the same suppliers that make human figures. The methods for preparation and painting of the figures are the same. Vary the colors of the animals, within reasonable limits, for the sake of variety. For those animals that vary in color patterns, such as some breeds of horses and cows, duplicate this variety as well.

Don't forget to model birds, chickens, pigeons, or sea gulls, if near the ocean or large lakes. Ducks or other waterfowl can float in a pond. Owls or buzzards can perch in a foreground tree or on a cactus. Pigeons are often seen on statues and rooftops. They can add much, including their droppings, to the model scene.

Domestic animals, such as cats and dogs, are appropriate to areas around buildings. Vary the breed, color, and posture (sitting, walking, lying down, etc.). Imaginative posing can add humor and interest to the scene. Dogs, trees, and fire hydrants might be shown in typical combinations.

Wild animals might be included also; for instance, deer, bears, squirrels, and rabbits. In appropriate climates, show snakes or alligators. If the circus is in town, or if a zoo is modeled, you can show a wide variety of more exotic animals.

Horses can be saddled, both with and without riders. If the horses are pulling wagons, buggies, or farm equipment, they will need harnesses, including collars for draft horses. Do not forget to paint on the bridle and use thin thread or wire for the reins.

OTHER DETAILS

There are a lot of things that man creates that are neither buildings nor vehicles, but that are essential to his convenience and are an ever-present part of the scenes you see. These *artifacts* have continuing utilitarian value.

This topic provides checklists of these artifacts and details, and discusses how to model them. Some things are the leftovers of nature or mankind that might no longer be useful, but have just not been cleaned up. These things are called *clutter*. Other things are clearly undesirable, such as trash, debris, and litter.

Artifacts

Although anything made by man is an artifact, the word is used here both more narrowly—to include only the smaller things and exclude structures, roads, etc.—and more broadly—to also include some natural details at a level below the mountains and trees. As so defined, artifacts are the frosting and decoration on the cake of life. Beyond the bareness of streets and buildings, they are the miscellaneous items that make the scenes seem "lived in."

Without artifacts, a building will look sterile and unreal. The big things might be there, but the little things will be missing. The scene won't look realistic, but you won't realize why at first. Everything will seem too neat, too clean, too uncluttered . . . to look like the real thing.

The best way to remember these many minor features and details, which you look at every day without really seeing, is to examine checklists to jog your memory. TABLES 20-6 through 20-16, which follow, are intended to serve as such memory aids. Note that not all of these artifacts would be present at each site. Use only the ones that are appropriate to the scene you are modeling.

Table 20-6. *Checklist of Artifacts*
Found Around Houses

Foundation	Fences
Basement windows	Sidewalks
Window wells	Sheds
Outside cellar stairs	Electric lead-in
Foundation planting	Electric meter
Garage	Flagpole
Trees	Birdbath
Lawns	Weathervane
Hedges	Lawn furniture
Shrubs	Porch swing
Garden	Tire swing
Flowers	Garbage cans
Gutters	Roof flashing
Downspouts	Roof faschia
TV antenna	Roof rafter ends
Doorknobs	Lawnmower
Windows	Clothes line
Curtains	Drying clothes
Shades	Bikes/trikes
Pets	Toys
Junk	Hose/sprinklers
Garden tools	House number
Mailbox	Outhouse
Chimneys	Barbecue
Incinerator	Swimming pool
Wood pile	Pump
Rose bushes	Automobile
Camper	Porches
Gazebo	Awnings
Shutters	

It is sometimes difficult to think of all the businesses you might like to have in your model towns or cities. To aid your memory, checklists of businesses, industries, and public facilities are provided in the Appendix.

Table 20-7. *Checklist of Artifacts Found Around Roads and Streets*

Crossing signs	No-parking signs
Traffic signals	Road posts/barriers
White/yellow lines	Puddles
Stop signs	Parking meters
Traffic signs	Curbs
Cracks	Gutters
Asphalt strips	Manhole covers
Lights	Poles
Dividers	Streetcar tracks
Islands	Sidewalks
Parking lines	Fire hydrants
Mailboxes	Trash containers
Vehicles	Guard rails
RR grade crossings	Power Transformers
Fire alarms	Phone booths
Drains	

Table 20-8. *Checklist of Artifacts Found Around Farms*

House (see houses)	Tractors
Barn	Machinery
Silos	Wagons
Grain bins	Junk
Corn crib	Garden
Sheds	Windmill
Outhouse	Pump
Poultry shed	Water tanks
Sty	Stock tanks
Hay piles	Horses
Straw piles	Cows
Manure piles	Sheep
Trees	Goats
Fences	Pigs
Conveyors	Poultry
Irrigation equipment	Pets
Gates	Trucks
Tools	Granary
Scrap	Orchard
Crops	Flower garden
Pastures	Vegetable garden
Pitchforks	Grain shocks
Feeding troughs	Wood pile
Pump house	Paths

Table 20-9. *Checklist of Artifacts Found Around Industries*

Chain-link fences	Poles
Corrugated fences	Distribution transformers
Block walls	Storage tanks
Junk piles	Gas cylinders
Cranes	Tools
Roof water tanks	Machinery
Scrap metal/wood	Cyclone separators
Cabling	Roof vents
Wire drums	Skylights
Fire extinguishers	Weeds
Power lead-ins	Paths
Dry spills	Flagpoles
Oil stains	Sheds
Lift trucks	Air-conditioning equipment
Lights	Loading docks
Conveyors	Cooling towers
Guard dogs	Dump
Hoists	Pallets
Dumpsters	Fire escapes

Table 20-10. *Checklist of Artifacts Found Around Mines*

Tailings	Junk
Timbers	Machinery
Cable drums	Tunnel adit
Hoist house	Retaining walls
Dynamite shed	Office
Ore bins	Conveyors

Table 20-11. *Checklist of Artifacts Found Around Railroad Passenger or Freight Depots*

Baggage carts	Benches
Luggage	Scale
LCL freight	Signs
Passengers	Porters
Baggage wagons	Conductor
Boxes	Station agent
Crates	

Table 20-12. *Checklist of Artifacts*
Found Around Railroad Right-of-Way

Signals	Cattle guards
Switch stands	Culverts
Switch machines	Derails
Relay shed	Retarders
Telephone shack	Mile posts
Fences	Train order stand
Rail racks	Mail hanger/catcher
Prefabricated switches	Junk
Yard limit signs	Ash pits
Crossing signs/signals	Water troughs
Fire barrels	Warning signs
Bumpers	Telltales
Crossing guard shack	Snowsheds
Old removed rail/ties	Poles
Abandoned track	Wheel stops
Guard rails	Grade crossings
Water/oil columns	Snow fence

Table 20-13. *Checklist of Artifacts*
Found Around Businesses

Signs	Neon signs
Awnings	Rooftop signs
Window displays	Fire escapes
Posters	Microwave relay tower
Advertisements	Power lead-in
Sign lights	Roof hatches/doors

Table 20-14. *Checklist of Artifacts*
Found Around Cities

Abandoned buildings	Newspaper stands
Construction	Shoeshine stands
Graffiti	Kiosks
Poles	Derelicts
Street lights	Billboards
Trash cans	Trees
Fire hydrants	Theater marquees
Telephone booths	Fire escapes
Mail boxes	Tenements
Statues & pigeons	Pedestrians
Benches	Clocks
Bus/streetcar stops	Fire alarm boxes

Table 20-15. *Checklist of Artifacts Found Around Old Towns*

Hitching posts	Watering troughs
Board sidewalks	Hanging tree
False fronts	Horses
Wagons	Buggies

Table 20-16. *Checklist of Natural Features Found in the Countryside*

Stumps	Weeds
Fallen trees	Rocks
Dead trees	Stones
Burned trees	Talus
Fallen branches	Rock slides
Fallen leaves/needles	Streams
Brush piles	Animal paths
Thickets	Animal bones
Swamps/bogs	Animal droppings
Erosion channels	Ponds
Wild animals	Beaver dams

Fences

There are a great many different kinds of fences. Fences keep something in, keep something out, or sometimes just hide things from view. Some fence types are chain link, woven wire, barbed wire, electric, picket, board rail, and wrought iron.

Walls can serve the same functions as fences. Wall types include block, brick, and stone. The construction of walls as fences can follow the general guidance given in the topics "Retaining Walls" and "Masonry Buildings" in chapter 19. Hedgerows and other plantings can also function as fences. This is covered in "Shrubs and Brush," chapter 18.

Note that the space along fences and walls often serves as a place where weeds can grow without much disturbance. This same space also collects more than its share of wind-blown papers and trash. Woven wire and chain-link fences often have scrap papers caught up against them.

Chain Link. This type of fence was developed in the mid-1920s. Since that time, it has become quite common because it is low in cost and easy to put up. Fence heights vary between about 3 feet to 10 feet. Metal posts, set in concrete, support the chain-link mesh. The corner posts are usually 2 to 3 inches in diameter, with intermediate posts of 2-inch size.

A $1^5/8$-inch top rail is used between all posts. The posts are set between 8 and 10 feet apart. A horizontal $1^5/8$-inch rail is used at midheight on either side of corner posts and at the top, bottom, and middle of gates. Truss rods ($3/4$-inch diameter) provide diagonal bracing at corners and on gates.

The tops of the posts stick slightly above the top rail, and they are usually closed off with caps. Sometimes an upward extension is used instead of the cap to provide for three to six strands of barbed wire. These extensions can be half-Y, Y, or inverted-A shape. The more modern fences can be topped with a coil of razor wire. Even if the fence goes up and down hills, all the posts are vertical.

For the model, make the posts and rails of suitable diameter brass rod. Make a full-sized paper pattern of the fence. Cut the posts long enough so that their bottoms can be placed in holes drilled in the coverwork. Solder the pieces together on the pattern. Form the caps from solder blobs. If top extensions are used, form them from sheet brass and solder them in place.

The choice of fence mesh material will depend on the scale. Candidate materials include tulle, nylon net, nylon mesh, Dacron mesh, crinoline and fiberglass screening. The openings in the mesh are about 2 to 3 inches. Even if the scale mesh material has openings twice that, the effect will still be realistic.

Cut the material slightly oversize and bond it to the posts and rails, with the weave of the mesh at 45 degrees to the posts, using Pliobond or a contact cement applied only to the metal. Let the adhesive dry slightly, then press down the material, stretching it to eliminate wrinkles. After the adhesive has completely set, trim the material as close as possible to the posts/rails.

The gates can be mounted on brass tubing so they open or close. In the larger scales, fabricate more realistic hinges and make gates that operate.

Before installing the fence sections, spray paint them with a fine mist of aluminum or silver paint. For older fences, a shade closer to that of concrete is more correct. Darker and less shiny colors will hide out-of-scale mesh material better. You might also wish to streak the fence with stains or rust.

Carefully drill holes for the posts and install the fence sections. You might have to do some final assembly of mesh material at the "site" in order to complete the fence. Chain-link fences are also available as commercial kits.

Woven Wire. Woven wire fences are much like chain-link fences, except that the wire mesh spacing is larger and the wires run at right angles to the posts. These fences are usually used to keep stock enclosed. The wire size and mesh spacing can vary a great deal depending on what is fenced in—small for poultry to larger for sheep, goats, and pigs.

The modeling procedures are virtually identical to those for chain-link fences, with a few exceptions. The posts are usually wood or metal, as with barbed wire fences (see next subject). Use no top or bracing rails. Apply the material used for the mesh square with the posts, instead of at a diagonal as with the chain-link fences. Sometimes the top has a single strand of barbed wire.

Barbed Wire. Barbed wire fences are almost as old as the West. These fences consist of from three to five strands of barbed wire, stapled to wooden fence posts. The fence posts vary in diameter, depending on what could be found in the area. Typical heights are 3 to 5 feet. The spacing can also vary considerably, with distances of from 10 to 20 feet being typical.

The wooden posts are best modeled using wood. If you can find them of suitable size, twigs make good posts because they have the random curves and contours of the real thing. Sometimes, the posts are split from larger logs. Drill holes in the coverwork and "plant" the posts in the holes, using white glue. The posts were almost never painted, so they should be the color of aged wood. Sometimes, some bark still remains, but usually it has all been removed or has fallen off.

The barbs on the wire are usually no more than 1 inch across and are spaced about each 12 to 18 inches. In the smaller scales the barbs would be almost invisible. They can be simulated semirealistically, however, with a fewer number of larger barbs. Make the wire from fine nylon thread with many knots tied in to create the "barbs." Attach the wire to the posts with ACC.

Another possibility is to use fiberglass window screening material. Heat-bond all the strands together so the material will not unravel when cut. Cut a single strand of the required length and trim of all the crossing strands as closely as possible to simulate the barbs. A twist to this strand will then point these barbs in random directions, and they will look surprisingly good, even though oversize.

Another alternative is to use 0.005-inch monofilament fishing line. Tie knots for the barbs using a jig. Try for 12- to 24-inch centers between the knots. Model barbed wire is also commercially available.

Use three strands of "wire" as a minimum. This was often what was used in olden times, but modern fences more typically use five strands. Modern fences also often use metal posts instead of wooden ones. The metal posts are actually a W cross section, but you can simulate this with a wood, plastic, or brass angle section. Paint the metal posts a variety of different colors, sometimes two colors on the same post. The colors age rapidly, and the posts can be rusty.

Electric. An electric fence normally consists of a single strand of unbarbed wire, strung on insulators, attached near the top of wood or metal posts. This is used to enclose the larger stock animals who soon learn the value of staying away from the "shock" of the fence.

The posts are modeled like barbed wire fences. The wire can be monofilament fishing line. The insulators can be blobs of white paint or small beads. Include a small box somewhere to supply the fence with its electricity.

Board. Board fences are usually made with wooden posts set into the ground, connected at or near the top and near the bottom by horizontal stringers. Vertical boards are then nailed to the stringers, usually butted against each other, but sometimes overlapped. These fences can be of almost any size.

Make models of board fences in much the same way as the prototypes. The construction must be, of necessity, of the board-by-board variety. It is easiest if the fence is prefabricated in sections at the workbench. Prestain or color all the wood. Work over a drawing of the fence that locates the posts and stringers. Use diluted white glue. If the fence is old, leave out some boards, or break them. If it is in the foreground, you might add the nail holes, as discussed in "Wooden Buildings," chapter 19. Board fences are sometimes painted or whitewashed. Old finishes of this type give many opportunities to try aging methods.

When the fence sections are complete, plant the posts in glue in holes drilled in the coverwork, and connect (glue) them to adjacent sections. Board fences make a wonderful place to display advertising, signs, and graffiti (FIG. 20-11).

Fig. 20-11. In the foreground is a board fence, built board-by-board, painted, aged, weathered, and with posters and grafitti.

One type of permanent snow fence, which is used to protect tracks from drifting snow, can be made in a manner similar to a board fence. Usually, the boards run horizontally, separated by 2 to 4 inches. These fences can use an A-frame arrangement of posts.

Rail. The oldest type of rail fences were built without using nails or dressed lumber. These split rail fences used an X configuration of posts, with the rails supported across the tops of the Xs and leaning against them. Rail fences can be modeled using suitably distressed wood that simulates the roughness of the unsawn posts and rails. The wood must also be grayed and blackened, to simulate its age, by using dilute Indian ink, gray stains, or other methods.

More modern rail fences are made with vertical posts and dressed lumber, either with the rails fitted into holes in the posts or nailed to the outside of the posts. Build these fences following approximately the same methods used for the board fences.

Picket. A picket fence is much like a board fence, except that the vertical boards are usually narrow and are spaced apart from each other. Sometimes, they have a sharpened top to repel water and give a better appearance. Because they are often used in the front yards of residences, they are usually kept in good repair and are repainted (often white) frequently. Their modeling is done using the same methods as were described for board fences.

Wrought Iron. These fences and gates were often made and used for their combination of sturdiness and ornamental value. They were constructed by fitting, or welding, many individual pieces of iron together. The pieces could be straight with round or square sections, and/or flat sections curved and joined to form elaborate designs. Sometimes, cast metal sections were included.

Because of its complexity, wrought iron fencing is difficult to model. There are a few metal and plastic castings available in HO scale. Beyond this, it is a matter of scratchbuilding with considerable doses of ingenuity and long hours. The options include building up from brass pieces soldered together, etching from brass (see "Etching," chapter 8), and the use of paper quillage (making items from glued strips of rolled paper).

Poles and Lines

Telephone, telegraph, and electric poles and lines are an omnipresent part of the modern scene, conveying their webs in a complex mesh above our heads and around us. Without the electricity and communications they supply, our lives would revert back to those of more primitive, but more peaceful, times.

The telegraph has been around for just about as long as the railroad. Telephones came only a few years later. From early times, the railroads used lines to carry signal commands and power. Electrification has progressed very rapidly from its beginnings, early in the century, to its almost universal availability today. For any era you are likely to model, there will be poles and lines (FIG. 20-12).

Fig. 20-12. The poles and lines can also make detailed models.

That is not to say that these poles and lines have remained the same in looks or number or function. Today, there are actually fewer telephone lines to be seen (on poles) than there were 50 years ago. There are almost no telegraph lines. Railway track signals are often radio controlled. Microwave relay and communications satellites carry much of the message data. The electric lines have grown in voltage and in power rating, and now the giant towers march across the landscape bringing enormous quantities of energy from distant dams and power plants.

As with everything else about your models, if you are to do them accurately, you must research what they look like, so that you will not make obvious mistakes. This handbook will not attempt to describe the great variety of distribution systems for electricity or telephone/telegraph service. It will only give hints at how to model the poles, lines, and other features of these services.

Decision. One of the most difficult decisions to be made is whether to model the lines themselves. The poles should be modeled, of course, but the lines give some considerable problems. They are very difficult to string up in the first place, they tend to look unrealistic when done, they are hard to keep free of dust and webs, and they are frequently damaged by accidental bumps or snags from arms or hands trying to rerail equipment or work on other parts of the layout.

Whatever is used to form the lines, the stuff just does not hang right or look like the graceful arcs, called *catenary curves*, formed by real wires. It either kinks, sags up or to the side, or is so taut that it has no sag at all. It is difficult to find a "wire" material that will not change tension with changes in temperature, humidity, or age. It is difficult to string the material with uniform tension and attach it firmly, yet invisibly, to the insulators on the poles. This is before even considering the problem of providing proper color, texture (shine and smoothness), etc., to accurately simulate the real wires.

The strong recommendation is *not* to model the lines . . . to just leave them off. While this might sound like the coward's way out, it is also the practical person's solution. The chances are that their absence will not be noticed. In the full-sized world, from the equivalent distances that your layout will be viewed, those lines cannot generally be seen. Try an experiment to convince yourself. Measure off the distance on the model that will be between the viewer and the lines. Convert this into scale feet. Then go outside and look at real lines from that distance. How well can you see them? Can you see them at all?

There are some exceptions to this drastic recommendation, of course. On an enclosed diorama, where they will be protected from dust, insects, pets, and human error, it might be appropriate to include the lines. Doing this on even a small diorama should convince you of the wisdom of avoiding all this tedious work on a larger application. In some cases on the layout, the larger lines might be modeled. Examples include high-tension lines, bundles of telephone/telegraph lines, where the size of the line is large, and where there aren't too many of them. Also, all guy wires should be modeled.

Routing. Most pole lines follow along the railroad tracks or along highways or streets. Sometimes they strike off across country or deviate from the tracks or roads to cut corners, saving distance or avoiding natural barriers. They usually do not go through a tunnel but go up or around the hill or mountain. Sometimes, water crossings use the same bridges to support the lines that are used for the tracks and highways.

Poles. Poles are normally made of wood from straight trees (generally conifers) with the branches and bark removed and with a continuous taper from bottom to top. They vary in diameter and height depending on the quantity and weight of wires they must support and the desired height above the ground. This height is determined by both safety and clearance, with the power transmission poles generally being taller than telephone poles.

The poles are placed in holes drilled in the ground, with the dirt tamped back around the pole. To protect the pole from insects and decay, at least the bottom part of the pole is often coated with tar or creosote. Sometimes the entire pole is protected, giving the new pole a black appearance. The poles might have foot irons to facilitate access to the top. This occurs particularly on poles with transformers.

A line of poles might carry both electrical power and telephone lines, but these lines are more normally on separate poles. If combined, the electric lines are at the top. If a cable of telephone, telegraph, or signal wires is present, this is usually the lowest of any of the lines.

Crossarms. If only a few wires are carried (up to 3) there might be no crossarms, but the more usual situation is a pole with one or more crossarms that are used to increase the space for mounting the insulators and separating the wires. The crossarms per pole reached quite high numbers in big cities when each telephone line required a separate wire.

Each crossarm has from 2 to 10 (or more) insulators mounted on it. The crossarms are made of surfaced wood, typically 3 × 4 inches, and they are usually notched into and bolted to the pole and supported by metal braces. Rows of crossarms are kept about 2 feet apart as a minimum. The crossarms mount to opposite sides on alternate poles.

Doubling. Sometimes crossarms are doubled, one on either side of the pole, to give more support. Sometimes the poles are doubled and they support the crossarms near their ends, which allows greater weight and more stability. This arrangement is called an H fixture or configuration. Usually, the crossarms are doubled on H fixtures.

Dimensions. It is difficult to give dimensions for the poles and crossarms because they vary so much. As with all peripheral things on the layout, it is better to downscale the sizes so they do not overpower the trains or other more-important scenery.

Typical poles that follow a railroad right-of-way might be 30 feet tall and 12 inches in base diameter. The crossarms are probably no longer than 10 feet. These poles are taller where lines have to cross over highways, tracks, or other lines. The spacing between poles is no greater than 100 feet. Shortening this distance even further, to about 80 feet, will contribute to the illusion of distance, or forced perspective.

High-power transmission towers are spaced much farther apart, of course.

The best guide is to measure the real thing, then reduce the spacing, and the size of the towers, somewhat to make them look better on the layout.

Guy Wires. Guy wires provide both longitudinal and lateral stability for the poles and the lines they carry. Guy wires along the line of the poles relieve unbalanced tension caused by the weight of the lines. Lateral guy wires on the outside of curves absorb the tension of the lines pulling toward the center of the curve.

The guy wires usually attach to the pole just below the lowest crossarm and extend at about a 30-degree angle to the pole. They might attach to another pole, a short pole, or to a loop in a metal rod attached to a concrete anchor buried in the ground. The guy wire might also come down at an angle, then drop straight down, this transition being maintained by a horizontal brace back to the pole. The bottom portion of guy wires might have a wooden or metal wrapping to provide protection from and to traffic and to provide better visibility. One pole can have more than one guy wire to provide support in different directions.

Insulators. Insulators separate the lines from the pole or crossarm. An exception is for cable bundles, which have an overall insulation. Telephone or telegraph insulators are made of glass, often light blue or green in color, mounted onto wooden or metal pegs, which connect them to the wood of the pole or crossarm. When mounted to the pole, a small wooden wedge keeps the insulator nearly vertical.

Insulators for electrical power must be larger and more elaborate as the voltage is higher. These insulators are made of ceramic and are often brown or white in color. At higher voltages, they consist of several segments, stacked atop each other. At still higher voltages, these insulators hang down from the crossarms, rather than stand up. Each segment looks a bit like an inverted soup bowl.

Lines. Electric power lines usually occur in either three's (three-phase or one-phase, three-wire) or four's (three-phase with center conductor). At higher voltages, they sometimes occur in sixes. The lines entering homes, businesses, or industries usually are three, although these lines are now sometimes combined into a single cable.

Sometimes, a single *static line* runs along the top of the power poles to provide lightning protection. It is occasionally connected to the earth through a wire running down the pole to a ground rod. Power wires are usually transposed, shifting which of the three insulator positions they are connected to, every dozen or so poles.

Most lines are made of copper and are uninsulated. They weather to a dark brown with green overtones. Some electric lines are now made of aluminum. Cables are wrapped with an insulation, which is typically black, but can be of almost any neutral color.

Sometimes, lines have weights hanging from the middle of them. These weights are intended to reduce oscillations caused by wind, particularly where the spans are great. Some high-voltage power lines use three or four conductors per line, separated by spacers every 50 feet or so.

Transformers. Transformers are mounted on poles where some power must be tapped off and reduced in voltage before further distribution to users. This often occurs in residential or light industrial areas. Other lines come out of the transformers and continue divergent routes to the individual buildings. The transformers are usually cylindrical or rectangular. They are located on the pole just below the higher voltage lines. Larger transformers can be mounted above the ground on platforms supported by two to four poles, or in larger fenced facilities located at ground level.

Transformers are usually colored black, blue-gray, or silver. Older transformers might have visible insulators. The smaller, more modern ones usually have lines feeding out from apertures and separate to go to the insulators on the transmission lines. There are also circuit breakers and switches involved, but their description is beyond the scope of this discussion.

Modern Poles. Modern power lines use concrete or metal poles that are also round and tapered. High-voltage power lines usually use towers that are fabricated from pieces of metal angle with bolted, riveted, or welded joints.

Modeling Poles. Plastic ready-made poles are offered in HO and N scales. These can be modified by trimming off crossarms and/or insulators to suit. Paint the poles a bleached wood color. Make the insulators an off-white or a very light blue or green, and the braces a rusty-gray. You might want to add black "tar" at the bottom of the poles. Use track spikes or bent wire to make climbing foot straps. Glue the poles in holes drilled in the groundwork.

Poles also can be made of wood. Scratchbuild them from appropriate diameter dowels, tapered by sanding, with stripwood for crossarms. Stain the wood before assembly. Make the insulators from the tiniest beads, such as Indian beadwork, or from tiny globs of plastic cement or epoxy.

There are few metal transmission towers available as kits. You can fabricate them from wood, plastic, or brass angle shapes to meet nearly any prototype configuration. Use large beads or cast shapes, suitably colored, for the insulators.

The poles often serve as the location for posters and advertisements. These signs might remain for a long time in varying stages of deterioration. The poles are also distressed by the points of the linemen's climbing spikes, which cause a ragged texture. These are details that might be added to foreground poles.

Stringing Lines. If you wish to string wires between poles, consider using silk thread or very thin copper magnet wire. Avoid cotton thread because it is more likely to catch dust. Nylon thread, "invisible" sewing thread or monofilament fishing line are other candidates. Select the smallest size thread that you can find to simulate all but the larger wires. Choose a color that is appropriate. A light orange color can simulate new copper. A medium green will look like copper with patina. A dark green or gray will look like older wire. Simulate aluminum wire with a light gray or silver (if you can find it) color.

Before stringing the lines, complete the detailing of the poles, including all insulators, transformers, posters, etc. Make sure the poles are rigidly installed in the coverwork because they will be under tension from the lines. Install the guy wires before stringing the lines so that they can perform their function on the model, just as they do on the prototype.

String the lower wires first, starting from the center of the pole, and attach them to the insulators with a touch of ACC. Maintain a constant tension, insofar as possible. Add wires on alternate sides of the pole and complete the lower crossarm before going to the next higher one. Proceed in this manner along the entire length of a single pole line. Don't forget to add the leads to the factories and houses.

One other point to mention, which should be obvious, is that the lines should be strung as one of the last operations in the construction of the scenery for the model, diorama, or layout. This will help, but will not prevent, accidents from happening. Stringing model lines, whether on a railroad or a three-masted ship, is something that, once done, should not be redone. If the worst happens, remember that you *were* advised to leave those lines to the imagination of the viewer!

Rooftops

Because the tops of roofs are the most readily seen portion of most model buildings, it is particularly important to provide all the detail that might be present on the real building roof. This topic supplements "Roofs" in chapter 19, which discussed the construction and aging/weathering of roofs. That topic gave you a variety of roof types, bare of any adornments or details other than the basic means of waterproofing and overhead protection that a roof provides to a building. To make roofs look realistic, there is a great deal more that can and should be added. As with any details, use discretion and moderation because most buildings will not have all of these details.

Sloping Roofs. Sloping roofs (gable or shed) are not designed to be walked on, so the details that they can have are somewhat different than for flat roofs. Some of the details that might be included are chimneys, TV antennas, lightning rods, signs, skylights, access hatches, dormers, gables, gutters, ladders, air-conditioning equipment, vents, and water tanks (FIG. 20-13). Metal or tar paper flashing waterproofs the area where roof planes meet, or where vertical walls or chimneys intersect the roof.

Model the chimneys using the methods discussed in "Masonry Buildings," chapter 19. Chimneys normally extend a few feet above the highest portion of the roof peak. They might have various kinds of metal hoods or wind deflectors. The top part of a masonry chimney might consist of sheet metal. Industrial buildings might have chimneys or smoke stacks made entirely of metal, with large metal flashing to protect the roof from the heat.

Make TV antennas from suitably sized wire. Look around your neighborhood for good examples to model. Lightning rods were once more common than they are now. They usually stuck up from the several highest points of the roof. They were connected together and to the ground by copper wire or pipe.

Mount signs on sloping roofs on vertical metal or wooden panels, braced up and out from the roof and normally locate them near the bottom of the roof slope. Paint some signs directly on the shingles of the gable roofs of barns. For more information on signs, see "Signs."

Skylights on sloping roofs are relatively infrequent. They are usually mounted at the same slope as the roof to form a window in the roof, raised slightly above the level of the roof itself by a frame. These skylights can be glazed

Fig. 20-13. *In addition to shingle weathering and aging, sloping roofs can have many other details.*

with clear, obscure, or colored glass. Access hatches on sloping roofs are usually much like the skylights, only without glazing. They provide for infrequent entry onto the roof without using a long, separate ladder.

Dormers and gables are ways to both bring more light into the attic areas under sloping roofs, while also increasing the usable volume and headroom. Model them just like the small portions of building and roof that they are. Be sure to include flashing all around them, wherever they intersect the roof panels.

Gutters are often used around the periphery of the lowest portions of sloping roofs to collect the water and direct it away from the walls of the building via downspouts. Not all buildings will have gutters. Sometimes the gutters are not in good repair. They are also a handy collection point for leaves and old newspapers. Model them using wood or plastic channel material, and paint them an aluminum color, or match them to the other trim.

Ladders are sometimes left on sloping roofs to allow quick access in case of fire or for repair. They are usually adjacent to any access hatches. They would be most likely on older wooden buildings; and in that case, the ladders would also be made of wood.

In hot climates, air-conditioning equipment has now become a necessity of life. Although the compressor and condenser unit is often at the base of the building, you also can locate them on the roof. If so, make a small platform to mount them level. The details of the air conditioner vary greatly between different size and type units. Do the model fabrication using a variety of scrap materials.

Any building has a lot of roof vents that are used to vent the plumbing drain lines, water heaters, etc. Roof vents always have flashing where they exit through the roof, and they usually stick up about 2 to 3 feet above the roof at their point of penetration. They are almost always made of metal, in a variety of diameters and cap configurations. Paint them a natural galvanized color or a color to match the roof or the building trim.

Industrial or commercial buildings will sometimes have water tanks on the roof. To model the tank, see "Tanks." On a sloping roof, mount the tank on a wooden platform to keep it level. Because the weight is considerable, build up the platform so it looks strong and so it could logically have suitable structure on the floors beneath it to carry the weight.

Flat Roofs. Flat roofs can be walked on and, therefore, are often used as extra space above a building for a variety of activities. Some of the details that might be included are chimneys, TV antennas, lightning rods, signs, skylights, access hatches, parapets, drains, ladders, fire equipment, clotheslines, sun bathers, air-conditioning equipment, fans, vents, storage sheds, and water tanks (FIG. 20-14).

Fig. 20-14. A few of the many possible details that can be included on flat roofs are shown here.

Masonry chimneys for flat roofs are usually similar to those for sloping roofs, except that they are most likely to occur at the edges of the roof or above interior walls. Sometimes, many flues are clustered together in a wide chimney. The tops of the chimneys or flue pipes normally extend 8 to 10 feet above the roof. Metal chimneys or smoke stacks, TV antennas, and lightning rods are generally similar to those for sloping roofs.

Mount signs on flat roofs on vertical metal or wooden panels, braced up from the roof, and normally locate them near the roof edge. These signs might include large billboards. Be sure to provide adequate bracing to protect the signs from being toppled by the winds.

Skylights on flat roofs are quite common. They can be flat and parallel to the roof, but raised above it by a frame, or they can be mounted at a slant, forming a gable or sawtooth configuration. Often, the frames are made of metal. These skylights can be glazed with clear, obscure, or colored glass.

Provide access to flat roofs with simple hatches or stairways with their own walls, roof, and door. Slope the stairway roof to follow the slope of the stairwell beneath it. *Parapets* are the raised portions of the exterior (or sometimes interior) walls that rise above the roof. They are of the same construction as the walls of the building. Cap them, so they appear suitably waterproofed, and add flashing and lots of tar to waterproof the junction with the roof.

Drains are needed on flat roofs to allow the water to flow off and down to the ground or sewers. Add grated drains at various placed on the roof that use internal drain pipes; or add *scuppers*, like on a ship, that are holes in the parapets that allow the water to escape to external downspouts.

Use ladders on flat roofs to provide access from one level of roof to another or for access to an external fire escape. These ladders are usually metal. Add some kind of fire equipment to the flat roof of your building, ranging from simple hand-held extinguishers to hose-on-reel configurations. Paint these details red so they will be easy to see.

Flat roofs of buildings with living accommodations often have practical purposes. They are often a place to hang a clothesline to dry clothing, a place for tending children, or a place where someone can sunbathe (with or without covering) privately. Certainly, such locations could be used for trysts and other hanky panky from time to time? A flat roof also could be used for potted trees or small gardens.

A flat roof is a convenient place to store all sorts of things, some outside and exposed to the weather, and some in a variety of different quality sheds. These sheds usually do not match the building architecture or each other. They are often of galvanized corrugated sheet metal construction, but can be of any material. They usually have flat or shed roofs with slight slope.

The things stored outside on a roof can be almost anything that you would store in a garage or in a backyard, if there was one. Use your imagination and create a point of interest.

A flat roof is a typical location for a building's air-conditioning equipment. Locate the equipment on a platform, slightly raised above the roof surface. Add various kinds of exhaust fan outlets on the roof, using a variety of metal ductwork and toppings to keep the weather out. Look at pictures of buildings, or the real thing, for examples. Castings are available in some scales.

Flat-roofed buildings have a lot of roof vents to provide for the many plumbing drain lines, water heaters, etc. Show them sealed with copious amounts of tar where they exit through the roof and model them about 4 to 6 feet above the roof at their point of penetration. In all other respects, they are similar to the vent pipes on sloping roof buildings.

The water tanks on the flat roofs of industrial or commercial buildings are similar to, but usually larger than, those on sloping roofs. They are usually mounted on a heavy framework, somewhat above the level of the roof, with a ladder for access. Also, be sure to model the pipes that connect them to their inlet and outlet.

Tanks

Many different types of tanks are used to store liquids or pressurized gases. These tanks differ considerably in size, shape, and materials used. Other tanklike structures store solids. Examples are silos, grain elevators, bins, etc.

Most tanks are made as horizontal or vertical cylinders, or some variation of these. The material used can be wood, metal, or reinforced concrete. A vertical tank has only a top end visible that forms a flat, hemispherical, or cone-shaped roof. Horizontal tanks have two ends, usually identical, that are flat, ellipsoidal, or hemispherical.

Wooden tanks are made of staves that run parallel with the axis of the tank. Hoops of metal hold the tank together and resist the internal pressure of the (usually) liquid. On a vertical wooden tank, these hoops are closer together at the bottom than at the top because the pressure is greater there. The hoops usually incorporate turnbuckles to allow tightening as the wooden staves age.

Metal tanks can be made of corrugated metal for the smaller sizes or for those containing lightweight materials such as grain. More commonly, metal tanks are made of curved steel plates, riveted or welded together. Separate hoops usually are not used. Metal tanks usually have tops or ends made of the same metal as the tank. Sometimes, old railroad tank cars are used as stationary tanks.

Concrete tanks are used for water storage, for silos, and for grain elevators. They are usually of poured construction, not concrete blocks. They are almost always vertical tanks, with a roof made of some other material.

Tanks for pressurized gases for heating might have an external metal skeleton framework made of truss sections. The tank portion rises and falls, depending on how full it is, guided by rollers bearing against tracks on the framework.

Tank Models. There are several ready-to-use or kit models of different types of tanks available in most scales. Railroad water tanks and oil storage tanks are the most common subjects. Consider using tanks made for one scale in a different scale, being careful of obvious differences such as ladder size, etc. This can be a particularly good source for water tanks for buildings.

Build wooden tanks by wrapping grooved siding around a cylindrical form or by using individual lengths of stripwood (FIG. 20-15 AND COLOR INSERT). The form can be a convenient section of a cardboard mailing tube, a section of plastic pipe, a turned wooden section, or other suitable material of the correct size. Stain or paint the wood before gluing it to the form. Styrene strip "wood" can also be used, of course.

Fig. 20-15. Examples of large wooden water storage tanks are shown.

Form the hoops from wire or thread, with cast or formed turnbuckles. Be sure to keep the hoops tight, very straight, and evenly spaced all around the cylinder.

Wooden tanks often leak and this will cause stains on the side of the tank. Add these stains, taking account of the greater probability of leaks lower on the tank than higher. The leaks might leave deposits of minerals as well.

Mount your wooden tank on a wooden platform that simulates heavy planking over timbers of appropriate size and spacing. If this is elevated, the posts and braces holding it up should look very strong because the liquid weight is considerable. Model a roof like you would for a building (see "Roofs," chapter 19).

Make metal tanks from plastic or paper formed into a cylinder. If you are lucky, you might be able to find a ready-made piece of plastic of the correct diameter. Examples might be plastic pipe sections or the plastic caps from paint spray cans. Simulate the individual plates by scribing or with overlays of paper. Emboss rivets, if they are present, into the overlay (FIG. 20-16).

Metal tanks leak sometimes too; add these stains over the aged color of the tank. The tanks might also rust, with the rust streaks being more probable at the joints between the plates.

Make concrete tanks in much the same way as metal ones, but without the plates or rivets. You might get ambitious and create a mold and cast the tank in

Fig. 20-16. Three examples of modeled metal tanks.

plaster. Paint the tanks either an aged concrete color or the color appropriate to the prototype.

Note that tanks often have signs painted on their sides. Hand paint or apply these signs as decals or dry transfers. Add any needed piping, ladders, catwalks, access hatches, etc., to the tanks. Larger tanks that contain flammable liquids are usually surrounded by earth dams to halt the spread of the liquid in case the tank ruptures.

Signs

Many different kinds of signs convey information about place names, business names and products and advertise a host of different products and services. The application of lettering to signs was discussed in "Lettering," chapter 11. This topic will discuss the location and construction of signs.

Paint signs directly on the surface of railroad equipment, trucks, bridges, or buildings; or apply them to separate sign boards that are attached to the surface.

You also can separate signs from the equipment or structure surface to improve the viewing and make the sign more visible. Signs also can be freestanding and unconnected to any vehicle or structure.

A sign can be as simple as some lettering applied to a post. The next, more complicated sign uses a painted wooden board or metal panel with lettering, mounted to one or more posts. The sign can have framing around the panel. A more elaborate version of the freestanding sign is the billboard.

Billboards. Billboards come in a variety of sizes, in wood or metal, and with painted-on or pasted-on-paper lettering and messages (FIG. 20-17 AND COLOR INSERT). Locate billboards at ground level or high atop buildings. If they are very far off the ground, they usually have some sort of a catwalk to help the workmen when the sign must be changed.

Fig. 20-17. Several thirties-era model billboards are shown in this scene.

The ground-mounted billboards will often use a lattice work to close off the area from the bottom of the sign to the ground. They can have decorative moldings used at the top and sides, and often have electric lighting for night viewing. Some billboards might have the upper part of a ladder built onto the framework. Your billboards must simulate relatively heavy framing and bracing if they are large, to withstand the wind loads.

Printed material suitable for billboards is available in several scales. Often, you can use magazine advertisements to make your own. You might even show the workmen pasting up the strips for a new billboard, or you might show the paper or paint on some old billboards peeling off.

Business Signs. Signs on businesses can range from simple to complex. Sometimes the sign stands out from the building so it can be viewed from both directions by passing foot or vehicular traffic. Sometimes the signs are illuminated by exterior floodlights and, more recently, by interior lighting shining through the plastic material.

You also can paint business signs on glass windows. These are often used for offices of attorneys or doctors that are located above the ground floor. Advertising signs, such as "For Sale," often consist of posters that you paste to the glass windows or the surface of the building.

Neon signs were very common in the thirties and are now making a comeback. Some attempts at making model neon signs have used back- or edge-lit plastic, with the neon tubes represented by scratched-away portions of the black rear coating of the plastic. You can also try making model neon signs by painting wire with various phosphorescent colors which will glow under black (ultraviolet) light.

Theaters, and some businesses, once used chase lighting for signs, consisting of many bulbs that would light sequentially, giving the illusion of light in motion. Some modelers have simulated these signs by using fiberoptics with individual fibers laid down in order. Multiple-bulb signs also use fiberoptics, without the chase feature.

Clocks, as used for jewelry-store advertisements, or clocks on public buildings are another form of signs. Often, you can salvage wristwatch faces for this use on the model. See "Graffiti" in "Trash, Debris, and Litter" for another, less desirable, type of sign.

Miscellaneous

There are a great many other small details, besides those discussed in the previous topics, that add to the model scene. This topic gives hints on how to model some of the more common of these.

Cloth. Cloth might need to be modeled to simulate tents, tarps, awnings, and flags. Real cloth has too coarse a weave to simulate a model of itself. The best material to use is tissue paper, particularly if it is to be draped and colored. Form tents, tarpaulins, or awnings over a wire frame or wooden form. Coat a reusable form with a mold release so the formed "cloth" can be removed. Use diluted white glue or matte medium to saturate the tissue. When dry, this also furnishes a surface that will accept paints without bleeding the color.

Another alternative is to use aluminum foil. This has the correct thin appearance, and when painted appropriately, looks very much like cloth. This technique is particularly effective for clothes hanging on a line.

Flags. Flags are probably better made from a slightly harder paper, such as typing paper. In some scales, preprinted flags are available. Make the flag with the proper folds in it, depending on how it is hung and how the wind is blowing. Note that the flags should correspond to the time being modeled. In the United States, the 48-star flag was adopted in 1912 and the 50-star flag in 1959. In Canada, the maple leaf flag was adopted in 1965.

Containers. Large containers are very common around a railroad or almost any industry. Examples are wooden barrels, steel barrels, steel or plastic trash cans, and gas cylinders. Wood, plastic, or metal castings are available for these in most scales. Gas cylinders can be made easily by using proper size wood or plastic dowel and turning down an area for the neck and top of the cylinder.

Any of these containers must be painted properly so that they look realistic. Let wooden barrels age naturally. Paint steel barrels and gas cylinders, the latter with different colored tops to indicate different contents. The steel barrels often have a different color for the center band than they do for the two end bands and/or the two ends. Trash cans are often left their natural color, which can be galvanized or aluminum or whatever color the plastic was molded in.

With the exception of the gas cylinders, all containers get much abuse and usually show it in terms of their physical deterioration, faded colors, and stains. These can be modeled by distressing the item before painting, by choosing an aged color, and by applying stains and streaks. Where appropriate, such as on steel barrels, add rust and rust stains.

Containers are now also used for shipment and storage of freight. These containers are used on railroad cars, on ships, or on trucks. They are made exactly like the rear portions of trucks, which they resemble in size, shape, coloring, and fittings.

Crates and Pallets. Model boxes, crates, and pallets are covered in "Wooden Buildings," chapter 19. Add lettering and labels to these, if they are necessary.

Lights. Model lights can be working or nonworking. If they work, they give out light (illumination) in night scenes. This can be very effective, but it requires some extra work on each item of railroad equipment, street vehicles, and buildings that use the lights. This includes (at a minimum) the headlights of locomotives; lights in passenger cars; headlights for cars, trucks and buses; and interior and exterior lighting for buildings and signs.

If you are ambitious, you can get even better effects by adding real lights for railroad marker lights, number boards, and cab interiors; for taillights for road vehicles; and for sign lighting for businesses, etc. As with any modeling activity that is really well done, there is almost no limit to the detail you can add with working lights.

Even if the lights are not working, they still must be modeled so they appear to be what lights look like in daylight when they are off. Lights in the interior of railroad equipment or buildings do not have to be modeled because they cannot be seen. All exterior lights must be modeled because they are a part of the detail that makes the scene and the models look realistic.

The use of small "jewels" to represent lights is to be discouraged for everything except possibly marker lights or other relatively small fixtures designed to focus the light. In most cases, a light with a lens should show the lens as a shiny surface of the proper daylight unilluminated color. This might consist of paint with a gloss finish or a plastic "lens" painted on the back side.

The most common exterior light is the ordinary light bulb in a fixture that includes a metal shade, usually shaped with a very shallow cone. These fixtures are used for lights above doors, for sign lights, for yard lights, etc. In some scales, the shades are available as metal stampings. Represent a light consisting of a bare bulb or a globe over a bare bulb by a white sphere of the proper diameter. Some map or dressmaker's pins have colored heads of the needed diameters. If the light would be yellow, use a yellow colored pin head, etc. Fluorescent bulbs are long and narrow and usually white in color. Model these with plastic sprue material, colored white.

Street lights come in a great variety of types. Some of these have globes that look like light blue in sunlight. Model the standards for the street lights using methods appropriate to the prototype selected. There are many styles of street light castings available in most scales. Make sure these styles are not too recent for the period being modeled.

Signals. Signals are used to govern the traffic of railroads or streets or to give warnings. Railroad signals include those that tell the locomotive engineer the status of the track ahead, such as semaphores and target signals; and grade crossing signals, which warn road traffic about on-coming trains. Street signals include traffic signals and flashing warning lights for various purposes.

As with the lights, the signals can be working or nonworking. Working signals for the tracks are very impressive and add a great deal to the railroad, but they take a lot of time to install, to make work right, and to keep in working order. If this effort is worth it to you, then by all means put in the signals, but only where they can be seen by operators and spectators.

Nonworking signals also must be modeled. For most of the common scales, there is a large selection of kits available to construct almost any desired type and size of railroad track signal. If the signal is nonworking, represent the lenses as you did for lights. Make sure to add the ladders, handrails, wiring conduits, cables, etc., that adds the detail to make each signal its own separate "model," worthy of all the detailing it needs proportional to its prominence and location.

Grade crossing signals are also readily available as models. These include crossing gates, the alternate flashing types, and combinations thereof. These can also be made so they work, and this can be very impressive when the gates lower, the lights flash, and perhaps a bell rings to warn of the approaching train. If they are static, the gates should probably be fixed in the "up" position.

There is somewhat less choice of model traffic signals available. Fortunately, these are quite easy to fabricate from scratch if you can't find what you want. The earliest electric traffic signals were usually suspended in the middle of the street. Later, they were put at the corners, and now they are again above the street on long standards coming out from each corner.

Street Details. There are many, many details present on the streets of a town or city. Many of the details are available as castings in the common scales. These include fire hydrants, mail deposit boxes, parking meters, fire alarm boxes, and manhole covers. Paint all of these prior to installation. The manhole covers must be inset into the street surface.

The traffic signs must represent the era being modeled. Stop signs were black on yellow until after World War II, then the white on red was adopted. The no turn/parking/stopping, etc., signs vary somewhat from city to city. Some international signs are now in use, particularly in Canada. Different cities use different colors for painting lines and curbs, although these are now becoming more standard.

Besides the centerlines, the turn lane lines, the parking lines, the pedestrian crossing lines, etc., there are also words painted on the street. Because these are meant to be read from the vehicles, and not from overhead, the letters are stretched out much longer than normal to allow for this foreshortening.

Paint curbs with different colors to indicate parking or standing restrictions. Common colors are red, white, yellow, and green. Make handicapped spaces for parking larger, color them blue, and add the special logo. Do not forget signs for hospital or school zones, fire stations, etc. Flashing lights are often used to give warnings before sharp corners or places that require slowing.

House Details. The bare structure of a house needs a few extra simple little details to make it look more real. These details include gutters, downspouts, power entrance/meter, and doorknobs. Make gutters from wood or plastic channel of the proper size. Close off the ends with tiny bits of paper. Use wood dowel or plastic sprue to make the downspouts. Note how they bend inward to the wall from the gutter, then bend away from the wall again at the bottom. Wire solder can be used for the downspouts.

Most houses have external power meters that can be bought as castings or fabricated from scrap materials. Meters are usually located near the point of entry of the power to the building. There is often an exterior conduit down from the roof to the meter or power box. Add external gas meters near the foundation. Make door knobs from the ends of common pins.

Usually the furniture in a house is not visible, and so does not have to be modeled. But if the building is super detailed, and you want to include complete interior detailing, then model all the furniture. Also, sometimes furniture is found outside, either as junk or as furniture being moved or being displayed outside at a store.

For the smaller scales, making model furniture is quite an undertaking, except that (particularly for HO) there are a great many castings available. These must be painted and detailed appropriately.

Houses offer many opportunities for interesting mini-scenes. You can show a man watering or mowing the lawn or sleeping in a hammock. Children can be depicted at play. The house might be in the process of being reroofed or repainted, with appropriate ladders and some surfaces bright and new and others old and faded. Maybe a barbecue or pool party is in progress. Use your imagination to show what real people might be doing.

Railroad Details. There are other details that are common around the railroad tracks. Examples include switch stands, switch machines, rail racks, cattle guards, hose and telltales.

Switch stands and switch machines are often available as kits or castings. Some modelers use operating switch stands that are used to change the track turnout position or that move when the turnout is remotely actuated. Even if the switch stand is nonoperating, the target, and signal indication light if any, should be accurately modeled and colored.

Rail racks hold spare rail lengths for handy access in case of need. They were once made of wood but are now made of metal; often rail sections are used. Rail racks hold several lengths of rail of the proper scale length. This rail can be new or rusty.

Cattle guards are used to discourage stock from crossing over a gap in a fence through which a railroad track or a road passes. They consist of a number of pipes or rails running at right angles to the direction of the track/road, spaced apart about 4 inches. They usually have a quite shallow "pit" underneath. Model cattle guards by using stripwood or plastic, assembled in a frame of similar pieces.

Hose is common around railroad and other facilities. One of the easiest methods to model hose is to find wire solder of the proper diameter. This bends easily to any shape and looks and lays right. Some types of string can also be used, with some stiffening provided by white glue or matte medium.

Telltales are used to warn persons atop the railroad equipment of an on-coming low clearance from a bridge or tunnel. They are actually made of many ropes hanging down from a frame, held above the track. One way to model them is to use wire screen. Remove about half of the horizontal wires. Hang this from support(s), being careful to check clearances to all equipment.

Clutter

Clutter is the term used to describe all the detail leftover artifacts that need to get added to the model scenery so that it more closely resembles the modeled scene. Neither nature nor man is a very good housekeeper when it comes to having everything always look neat and clean. If all your grass areas look freshly mowed, if all your trees are the same size and with no imperfect limbs or fallen branches, if your streets are clean and there is no litter anywhere . . . it just isn't a representation of the real thing. Clutter might not be very pretty, but it exists and should be modeled.

Clutter can be either natural or man-made. In nature, as with mankind's creations, your scene should not look perfect, as though it had been created by a landscape architect and tended by a host of gardeners. Real life is full of lots of debris and junk and other unsightly things. TABLE 20-17 is a reminder list of examples of natural and man-made clutter. All of these examples do not have to be in every model scene, of course.

Trash, Debris, and Litter

It would be great if the real world were nice and neat and clean all the time. It could be if people picked up after themselves and did not throw away bottles, cans, newspapers, trash, garbage, and heaven-only-knows what else. But the world isn't like that. Even cavemen left bones and arrowheads in their caves. Mankind has always left behind his droppings of trash, debris, litter, junk, and other discarded artifacts.

This unfortunate reality of the full-scale world must be reproduced in the miniature one if the scenes are to ring true. It might hurt to do it, but you need to trash up your streets and sidewalks, ditches and alleys to make them look realistic.

Table 20-17. Examples of Clutter

Man-Made	Natural
Tin cans	
Bottles	Stumps
Paper	Fallen trees
Fences	Fallen branches
Junk piles	Fallen leaves/needles
Dirt piles	Brush piles
Bricks/blocks	Thickets
Wood scrap	Weeds
Graffiti	Erosion channels
Old ties, rails	Rocks/stones
Old tires	Slides
Abandoned cars	Animal droppings
Abandoned buildings	Animal bones
Mine tailings	Animal paths
Scrap	
Cloth/fabric	
Short-cut paths	
Poles	
Wire	

Scrap Paper. The most obvious trash that can be seen is paper. This is usually white and ranges in size from newspaper pages down to soft drink cups and hamburger wrappings. Full-scale paper is ordinarily too thick to properly represent model paper. Only the thinnest paper should be used, such as cigarette paper or tissue paper. Either facial or toilet tissue tends to be too thick and too fragile.

The paper can be left white, or it can be grayed or yellowed with age. Use a wide distribution of sizes and shapes to represent different kinds of trash. Distribute this trash paper where the wind would blow it, such as up against fences, in corners, and where it might collect because of the wind patterns.

Sometimes you might want to model a rolled-up newspaper that has recently been tossed down by the newsboy. Create this by wrapping the paper around a wire, securing the ends with white glue, and smashing it down to the proper shape.

Bottles. Another common type of trash is bottles or glass. Some can be broken. A large variety of colors of the glass are possible. Modern bottles are often made of plastics, but at model scales there is no discernible difference in appearance, except that the colors might be different.

Metal or plastic cast bottles are available in some of the scales. Paint these the proper color and then coat with a glossy clear finish, such as acrylic gloss medium. Paint on a suggestion of any labels, such as beer bottles might have. "Break" some of the bottles by carving away a portion of the casting. Bottles can also be turned from dyed acrylic rod. Broken glass can be represented by bits of dyed cast resin.

Locate the bottles where they might end up, along the road, in the gutter, etc. Some might be standing up on a fence or a rock or anywhere you can plausibly imagine someone leaving them.

Cans. "Tin" cans are another common eyesore of litter. They can be made by cutting off lengths of metal, plastic, or wood rod/dowel and painting them appropriately. If the can is to be open or squashed, you can make it from aluminum foil wrapped around a suitably sized wire.

The color of the cans vary from that of new "tin" or aluminum to that of any degree of rustiness. Paint the outside of the can to represent the product it once contained. Locate the cans with the same criteria used for placing the discarded bottles.

Junk. There are many other discards that might be found along the highway or railroad right-of-way. Some examples are pieces of wood/lumber, coils of wire, old wooden or steel barrels, metal parts of machinery, old tires, auto parts, etc. One might also see discarded piles of coal, gravel, cinders, or dirt.

Most of these items are discussed under other topics, insofar as modeling them is concerned. Usually, the discards are old, battered, worn out, rusty, and weathered. Tires often have holes in them. Barrels are missing staves or are dented beyond any consideration of use.

These items of junk might be semi-randomly distributed, or they might be collected together into piles. They also make up the ingredients of the contents of trash barrels. In the largest sense, entire junkyards can be modeled, consisting of various types of junk. Most common is the ubiquitous automobile junkyard.

In N and HO scales, there are precast junk piles available. These need some extra painting for best realism. They also need to be cut into sections to fit exactly into the available space. The same companies also offer open gondola loads of precast junk.

Graffiti. These "writings on walls" have become at once one of the most common and most obnoxious forms of mankind's leftover junk. They have become the human equivalent to the male dog's marking of his territory . . . and just about as welcome. But the world is the way it is, and like it or not, if you are to model it, you should model parts you don't like as well as those you do.

Graffiti changes very rapidly with the times, so you must be careful to model the style, colors, and wordings appropriate to the year you are modeling. At one time, it was done by hobos with chalk, or sometimes by others with paint and brushes. Now, through the magic of technology, spray cans have made it easy for any fool to deface any wall they can reach, quickly and with little chance of being caught.

Be sure not to use a "Kilroy was here" before the mid-forties. Use "peace" symbols and political slogans in the late 50's and early 60's. Gang names and warnings have largely become common since then. Simple names, hearts, and "Bob loves Suzy" are good for any time.

Graffiti themes and styles vary greatly by city and even within a city. There are strong ethnic influences on the words and symbols used. Strict authenticity might be hard to obtain, but try to recreate the effect, if not the message. You might also show some graffiti as being painted over, as though the citizens of your model city were trying to make things look better.

The topic, "Freehand Lettering," in chapter 11 gives some hints on applying graffiti. A limited amount of period graffiti is also available in decal and dry transfer form.

FINISHING TOUCHES

When you think you are all done with a model or a scene on a layout, then that is a good time to go back and look at it as though you had never seen it before. Look at it critically to see what you have forgotten that can easily be added. See if a little more weathering won't tie everything together better. Make mental notes of what you will do different the next time. Different does not necessarily mean better. It might mean to achieve just the proper effect, which might mean more or less detail than what you did, with the right expenditure of work, which might mean more or less than you did.

Often, photographs taken of the scene can reveal unrealistic aspects that the directly-seen view cannot. Sometimes, it just takes a few weeks working on something else, followed by a new look, to reveal those last few details that are missing. It is easy to see things that are there, but it is much more difficult to see those things that are not there, but should be.

Road Weathering

Paved roads and streets become discolored from the rubber worn off tires and from the oil droppings from the traffic. This can be simulated by spraying a raw umber/lampblack mix in the traffic lanes. Look at the real thing to properly vary the coloring and its location in the lanes.

A light dulling coat of dust often covers everything in country areas, where it has been stirred up by the wind or by passing vehicles. This can be simulated by a 10:1 diluted earth latex paint spray used as a wash over dirt roads and adjacent foliage, ballast, trees, structures, etc. Keep this effect very subtle. This can also make concrete highway look more travel worn.

Highlights

Look back over the entire layout, particularly the foreground scenes. Consider adding more dry-brushed highlighting to rocks, tree trunks, structures, people, etc. Again, try for subtlety. Try to bring out the highlights by considering the location of the "sun" in the scene.

Tips to Remember

- ☐ Measure and record formulas for paint colors, plaster mixes, etc., so you can repeat your results, duplicate your successes, and avoid the failures.
- ☐ Don't throw much away. Keep all:
  - ■ Leftover kit parts
  - ■ Figures and figure parts

- Truck and coupler parts
- Cutoff ends of stripwood or plastic
- Nice-sized plastic sprue pieces
☐ Be a collector of junk. Examples are:
  - Jewelry items
  - Caps from cans, tubes, etc.
  - Small plastic parts of all kinds
☐ Use resources for ideas. This includes:
  - This handbook
  - NMRA membership—Bulletin and Handbook
  - One or more model railroad magazines
  - How-to-do-it model railroad books
  - Library periodicals and books
☐ Organize what you have. This saves time.
  - Label and sort paint
  - Sort stripwood by size
  - Sort parts by type
  - Sort references by date and subject
  - Put tools in a toolbox
☐ Try not to start too many new projects without finishing some old ones first.
☐ Keep reminding yourself of what is "good enough" for each thing you do.
☐ Do what gives you pleasure, and don't worry about what others think, because the hobby is for YOU!

Appendix

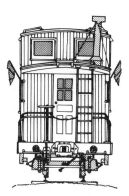

CONVERSIONS

Conversions are often necessary between different systems of units. One type of conversion is between full-sized modeled objects and the scale models, and vice versa. These conversions are covered in the figures in the topic, Reality and Scale, Chapter 1. The second type of conversion is between different units in the same system of measurements; for example, between feet and inches in the English system, or between centimeters and meters in the metric system. The third type of conversion is between units in different systems of measurements; for example, between inches in the English system and centimeters in the metric system.

The following tables cover the second and third type of conversions. TABLE A-1 gives the conversion factors to multiply by to convert units of length, liquid volume, mass/weight, or pressure between the English and metric systems, or vice versa. At the bottom of the same table are the conversion formulas between temperatures in the Celsius and Fahrenheit systems.

Liquid conversions are given in TABLE A-2. In the metric system, liquid measures are in liters and milliliters (1/1000 liter). One liter of liquid weighs one kilogram, and one milliliter weighs one milligram.

In the English system, dimensions are often given in fractions. TABLE A-3 allows a ready conversion of fractions of an inch into decimal inches or millimeters.

DRILL AND WIRE SIZES

TABLES A-4 and A-5 provide the decimal inch and millimeter equivalents of numbered drill sizes. TABLE A-6 gives the tap drill and clearance drill sizes (in numbered drills) for the most common model tap sizes. TABLE A-7 provides the dimensions for wire and metal gage sizes common to modeling.

Table A-1. English/Metric Conversions

Property	English Units		Metric Units		
Length	ft.	in.	m	cm	mm
	3.28	39.37	1	100	1000
	1	12	.305	30.48	304.8
	.083	1	.025	2.54	25.4
	.033	.394	.01	1	10
	.003	.039	.001	.1	1
Liquid	qt.	pt.	l	cl	mg
Volume	1.057	2.113	1	100	1000
	1	2	.946	94.6	946
	.5	1	.473	47.3	473
	.011	.021	.01	1	10
Mass/	lb.	oz.	kg	g	
Weight	2.205	35.28	1	1000	
	1	16	.454	454	
	.063	1	.028	28.3	
	.0022	.035	.001	1	
Pressure	psi		kPa*		
	1		6.89		
	.145		1		

* kPa = kilo Pascals

To convert temperatures:

°F to °C: °C = (°F + 40)/1.8 − 40
°C to °F: °F = (°C + 40)1.8 − 40

(Add 40 to the temperature. If converting from °F to °C (which will give a lower number), divide by 1.8 (which is 9/5). If converting from °C to °F, multiply by 1.8. Then subtract 40 to get the result.)

Table A-2. Liquid Conversions

(All weights are in fluid ounces or pounds)

1 teaspoon			=	1/6 ounce		
1 tablespoon	=	3 teaspoons	=	1/2 ounce		
1 cup	=	16 tablespoons	=	8 ounces	=	1/2 pound
1 pint	=	2 cups	=	16 ounces	=	1 pound
1 quart	=	2 pints	=	32 ounces	=	2 pounds
1 gallon	=	4 quarts	=	128 ounces	=	8 pounds

1/4	1/8	1/16	1/32	1/64	in	mm
				1	.0156	.3962
			1	2	.0312	.7925
				3	.0469	1.1913
		1	2	4	.0625	1.5875
				5	.0781	1.9837
			3	6	.0938	2.3825
				7	.1094	2.7788
	1	2	4	8	.1250	3.1750
				9	.1406	3.5712
			5	10	.1563	3.9700
				11	.1719	4.3663
		3	6	12	.1875	4.7625
				13	.2031	5.1587
			7	14	.2188	5.5575
				15	.2344	5.9538
1	2	4	8	16	.2500	6.3500
				17	.2656	6.7462
			9	18	.2813	7.1450
				19	.2969	7.5413
		5	10	20	.3125	7.9375
				21	.3281	8.3337
			11	22	.3438	8.7325
				23	.3594	9.1288
	3	6	12	24	.3750	9.5250
				25	.3906	9.9212
			13	26	.4063	10.3200
				27	.4219	10.7163
		7	14	28	.4375	11.1125
				29	.4531	11.5087
			15	30	.4688	11.9075
				31	.4844	12.3038
2	4	8	16	32	.5000	12.7000
				33	.5156	13.0962
			17	34	.5313	13.4950
				35	.5469	13.8913
		9	18	23	.5625	14.2875
				37	.5781	14.6837
			19	38	.5938	15.0825
				39	.6094	15.4788
	5	10	20	40	.6250	15.8750
				41	.6406	16.2712
			21	42	.6563	16.6700
				43	.6719	17.0663
		11	22	44	.6875	17.4625
				45	.7031	17.8587
			23	46	.7188	18.2575
				47	.7344	18.6538
3	6	12	24	48	.7500	19.0500
				49	.7656	19.4462
			25	50	.7813	19.8450
				51	.7969	20.2413

1/4	1/8	1/16	1/32	1/64	in	mm
		13	26	52	.8125	20.6375
				53	.8281	21.0337
			27	54	.8438	21.4325
				55	.8594	21.8288
	7	14	28	56	.8750	22.2250
				57	.8906	22.6212
			29	58	.9063	23.0200
				59	.9219	23.4163
		15	30	60	.9375	23.8125
				61	.9531	24.2087
			31	62	.9688	24.6075
				63	.9844	25.0038
4	8	16	32	64	1.0000	25.4000

One inch = 25.4 mm = 2.54 cm
One mm = 0.03937 inch

Table A-4. Drill Equivalents—Small
Numbered Drills (Diameters)

Drill	in.	mm	Drill	in.	mm
80	.0135	.3429	65	.0350	.8890
79	.0145	.3683	64	.0360	.9144
78	.0160	.4064	63	.0370	.9398
77	.0180	.4572	62	.0380	.9652
76	.0200	.5080	61	.0390	.9906
75	.0210	.5334	60	.0400	1.0160
74	.0225	.5715	59	.0410	1.0414
73	.0240	.6096	58	.0420	1.0668
72	.0250	.6350	57	.0430	1.0922
71	.0260	.6604	56	.0465	1.1811
70	.0280	.7112	55	.0520	1.3208
69	.0292	.7416	54	.0550	1.3970
68	.0310	.7874	53	.0595	1.5113
67	.0320	.8128	52	.0635	1.6129
66	.0330	.8382	51	.0670	1.7018

Table A-5. Drill Equivalents—Large Numbered Drills (Diameters)

Drill	in.	mm	Drill	in.	mm
50	.0700	1.7780	25	.1495	3.3797
49	.0730	1.8542	24	.1520	3.8608
48	.0760	1.9043	23	.1540	3.9116
47	.0785	1.9939	22	.1570	3.9878
46	.0810	2.0574	21	.1590	4.0386
45	.0820	2.0828	20	.1610	4.0894
44	.0860	2.1844	19	.1660	4.2164
43	.0890	2.2606	18	.1695	4.3053

Drill	in.	mm	Drill	in.	mm
42	.0935	2.3749	17	.1730	4.3942
41	.0960	2.4384	16	.1770	4.4958
40	.0980	2.4892	15	.1800	4.5720
39	.0995	2.5273	14	.1820	4.6228
38	.1015	2.5781	13	.1850	4.6990
37	.1040	2.6416	12	.1890	4.8006
36	.1065	2.7051	11	.1910	4.8514
35	.1100	2.7940	10	.1935	4.9149
34	.1110	2.8194	9	.1960	4.9784
33	.1130	2.8702	8	.1990	5.0546
32	.1160	2.9464	7	.2010	5.1054
31	.1200	3.0480	6	.2040	5.1816
30	.1285	3.2639	5	.2055	5.2197
29	.1360	3.4544	4	.2090	5.3086
28	.1405	3.5687	3	.2130	5.4102
27	.1440	3.6576	2	.2210	5.6134
26	.1470	3.7338	1	.2280	5.8115

Table A-6. Tap and Clearance Drill Sizes

Tap Size	Tap Drill	Clearance Drill
00 – 90	60	55
0 – 80	56	53
1 – 72	53	49
2 – 56	50	44
4 – 40	43	33
6 – 32	36	28
1-mm	65	59
1.4-mm	55	52
1.7-mm	53	48
2-mm	50	45
2.6-mm	42	36
3-mm	36	29

LUMBER CONVERSIONS

Stripwood, cut to simulate model lumber, is available in fractional sizes and in sizes for HO and O scales. TABLE A-8 allows the determination of the scale size of this stripwood in the more popular scales. The underlined sizes are the scale sizes available in HO and O.

STANDARDS

The definitive guide to standards for scale model railroads is the NMRA Handbook. This may be obtained as one of the benefits in joining the National Model Railroad Association.

Table A-7. *Wire and Metal Gauge Sizes*
American Wire Gage (AWG) and Brown and Sharpe (B&S)
Used for most nonferrous metals

Gauge	in.	mm	Gauge	in.	mm
26	.0159	.4039	12	.0808	2.0523
25	.0179	.4547	11	.0907	2.3028
24	.0201	.5105	10	.1019	2.5883
23	.0226	.5740	9	.1144	2.9058
22	.0253	.6426	8	.1285	3.2639
21	.0285	.7239	7	.1443	3.6652
20	.0320	.8128	6	.1620	4.1148
19	.0359	.9119	5	.1819	4.6203
18	.0403	1.0236	4	.2043	5.1892
17	.0453	1.1506	3	.2294	5.8268
16	.0508	1.2903	2	.2656	6.7462
15	.0571	1.4503	1	.2893	7.3482
14	.0641	1.6281	0	.3249	8.2525
13	.0720	1.7780	00	.3648	9.2659

Table A-8. *Fractional and Scale Lumber Conversions*

Dim (in.)	Fract. Size	Scale Size (in.)*					
		O	S	OO	HO	N	Z
.0156	1/64"	1/2	3/4	7/8	1	1 7/8	2 1/2
.0197	.5-mm	7/8	1 1/4	1 1/2	1 5/8	3 1/8	4 1/4
.0208		1	1 3/8	1 5/8	1 3/4	3 3/8	4 5/8
.0230		1 1/8	1 1/2	1 3/4	2	3 5/8	5
.0313	1/32"	1 1/2	2	2 3/8	2 3/4	5	6 7/8
.0344		1 5/8	2 1/4	2 5/8	3	5 1/2	7 1/2
.0394	1-mm	1 7/8	2 1/2	3	3 3/8	6 1/4	8 5/8
.0417		2	2 5/8	3 1/8	3 5/8	6 5/8	9 1/8
.0459		2 1/4	3	3 1/2	4	7 3/8	10 1/8
.0469	3/64"	2 1/4	3	3 1/2	4	7 1/2	10 1/4
.0625	1/16"	3	4	4 3/4	5 1/2	10	13 3/4
.0689		3 1/4	4 3/8	5 1/4	6	11	15 1/8
.0781	5/64"	3 3/4	5	6	6 3/4	12 1/2	17 1/4
.0788	2-mm	3 3/4	5	6	6 3/4	12 1/2	17 1/4
.0833		4	5 3/8	6 3/8	7 1/4	13 3/8	18 3/8
.0916		4 3/8	5 7/8	7	8	14 3/4	20 1/4
.0938	3/32"	4 1/2	6	7 1/8	8 1/8	15	20 5/8
.1148		5 1/2	7 3/8	8 3/4	10	18 3/8	25 1/4
.1181	3-mm	5 5/8	7 1/2	9	10 1/8	18 3/4	
.1250	1/8"	6	8	9 1/2	10 7/8	20	
.1378		6 5/8	8 7/8	10 1/2	12	22	
.1563	5/32"	7 1/2	10	11 7/8	13 5/8	25	
.1576	4-mm	7 1/2	10	12	13 5/8	25 1/4	
.1608		7 3/4	10 1/4	12 1/4	14	25 3/4	
.1667		8	10 5/8	12 3/4	14 1/2		
.1837		8 7/8	11 3/4	14	16		
.1875	3/16"	9	12	14 1/2	16 3/8		

Dim (in.)	Fract. Size	Scale Size (in.)*					
		O	S	OO	HO	N	Z
.1970	5-mm	9³/₈	12¹/₂	15	16⁷/₈		
.2067		9⁷/₈	13¹/₄	15³/₄	<u>18</u>		
.2083		<u>10</u>	13³/₈	15⁷/₈	18¹/₈		
.2188	7/₃₂″	10¹/₂	14	16⁵/₈	19¹/₈		
.2296		11	14³/₄	17¹/₂	<u>20</u>		
.2364	6-mm	11¹/₄	15	18	20¹/₄		
.2500	1/₄″	<u>12</u>	16	19	21³/₄		
.2756		13¹/₄	17¹/₈	21	<u>24</u>		

* - To nearest 1/8 in.

When planning the model railroad layout, adequate clearance must be left around the track so that the rolling stock will clear scenery and structures. Suggested standards are shown in TABLE A-9.

*Table A-9. Minimum Clearances
for Track Side Structures
(Based on NMRA recommendations)*

Scale	Center to Side*	Height
Z	¹/₂″	1¹/₄″
N	⁵/₈″	1⁵/₈″
TT	³/₄″	2¹/₈″
HOn	⁷/₈″	2¹/₄″
HO	1 ″	3 ″
OO	1¹/₈″	3¹/₂″
S	1³/₈″	4¹/₈″
On	1¹/₂″	4¹/₄″
O	2 ″	5¹/₂″

* For straight track
For critical clearance conditions, see NMRA standards.

CHECKLISTS

The following three tables (TABLES A-10 through A-12) provide check lists of the various types of businesses, industries, and public facilities that might be found in small towns or large cities. These lists can serve as a memory aid when you are trying to think of things to model, particularly those that might serve to create traffic for your railroad.

Table A-10. Checklist of Businesses to Model

Accountant	Antique Store
Appliance Store	Architect
Art Gallery	Art Studio
Attorney	Bakery
Bank	Bar

Barber	Beauty Shop
Bicycle Shop	Blacksmith
Book Store	Bottled Gas
Bowling Alley	Brake Shop
Broker	Builders
Cafe	Candy Store
Car Wash	Carpet & Rug Store
Cat House	Chandler
Children's Clothing	Chiropractor
Cigar Store	Confectionery
Convenience Market	Cooper
Dairy	Decorator
Dentist	Department Store
Diner	Doctor
Donut Shop	Dressmaker
Drug Store	Dry Cleaners
Dry Goods Store	Fast Food Shop
Five and Ten Cent Store	Floor Coverings
Flower Shop	Food Lockers
Fortune Tellers	Fraternal Organizations
Fruit Stand	Furniture Store
Garage	Garden Supplies
Gas Station	Gift Store
Glass Shop	Goldsmith
Grocery Store	Gunsmith
Haberdashery	Hardware Store
Hobby Shop	Hotel
Ice Cream Store	Ice Rink
Inn	Jewelers
Kennel	Laundry
Livery Stable	Lumber Yard
Meat Market	Men's Clothing
Milliner	Mortuary
Motel	Movies
Music Store	Newspaper Office
Nursery	Pharmacy
Photographer	Plumber
Radio/TV Store	Real Estate Agency
Realtor	Restaurant
Roller Rink	Saddlery
Saloon	Savings & Loan
Self-Service Laundry	Service Station
Shoe Repair	Sports Shop
Stationers	Supermarket
Taxidermist	Telephone Office
Toy Store	Travel Agent
Undertakers	Used Furniture
Variety Store	Vegetable Stand
Veterinarian	Video Store
War Surplus Store	Wells Fargo
Western Union	Wheelwright
Women's Clothing	

Table A-11. *Checklist of Industries to Model*

Auto Wrecking	Boat Yard
Book Bindery	Brazing Shop
Brick Yard	Building Supplies
Cabinet Maker	Cannery
Chemical Plant	Cold Storage
Corrugated Metals	Cotton Gin
Creamery	Die Casting
Die Making	Distillery
Drayers	Drilling Equipment
Dyers	Earth Moving Equipment
Electric Light & Power Co.	Equipment Rental
Express Service	Farmer's Market
Feed Mill	Foundry
Furniture Mfg.	Gasoline Storage
Grain Elevator	Greenhouse
Grinding	Hatchery
Hauling	Ice House
Ice Mfg.	Kilns
Laboratories	Landscaping
Machine Shop	Meat Packing
Metal Fabrication	Metal Plating
Milling	Movers
Moving and Storage	Oil Storage
Ore Crushing	Paint Mfg.
Pipe Mfg.	Plastics Mfg.
Printers	Public Scales
Refinery	Rock Products
Roofer	Sawmill
Scrap Metal	Slaughter House
Stamping	Storage Yards
Warehouse	Welding Shop
Well Drilling	Wholesale Grocers
Wholesale Produce	Winery

Table A-12. *Checklist of Public Facilities to Model*

Bandstand	Bus Depot
Cemetery	Churches
City Hall	Court House
Fire Station	Foot Bridges
Golf Course	Hospital
Jail	Library
Museum	Parks
Police Station	Post Office
Public Utility	Rest Home
School House	School Yard
Sheriff	Synagogue

Glossary

adhesives—Liquids used to cause materials to adhere or bond together.

aging—The process of creating the look of age through surface deterioration and paint-fading effects.

anachronisms—Things that are impossible because they do not exist for the time depicted.

approach—How one goes about accomplishing something.

architecture—The appearance and characteristics of buildings that distinguish them from each other.

artifact—A product of human activity; anything made by man.

artificial materials—Materials that are made by chemical or manufacturing processes.

backdrop—A two-dimensional representation of scenery lying off the layout itself.

ballast—The crushed rock or cinders that holds the track in place on the roadbed and allows drainage.

ballasting—The process of simulating the ballast for model trackwork.

barrier—A finish, applied to plastics that prevents other finishes from reacting with the plastic.

believability—The effect created by making models that are not real seem like miniatures of real things.

benchwork—The steps in framing the layout and constructing and painting the roadbed, backdrop, and front board.

binder—The portion of paint providing surface adhesion.

board-by-board—A construction method using individual pieces of stripwood/plastic.

bonding—Using adhesives or other liquids to attach materials to each other. Often applied to loose materials.

botany—The study of plant life. Here used relative to where and how trees and other vegetation form and grow.

bracing—The physical supports for the covering material; a part of coverwork.

buildwork—The steps that add the basic structures to the model.

carrier—The portion of paint that makes it liquid and that evaporates away when the paint dries. Also, see *vehicle*.

carving—Forming shapes by removal of material.

casting—Forming shapes by solidifying liquids and pouring into molds or forms.

catalyst—A chemical that enables a reaction between other chemicals or materials.

cement—A type of liquid adhesive.

checklists—Memory aids for what might have been forgotten.

clutter—That part of details involving miscellaneous leftover things.

color—The perception of hue or the chromatic variation of the light or light reflected from surfaces.

coloring—The process of providing color to a surface.

compression, selective—The artificial reduction in the dimensions of modeled things so they will fit better.

construction—The building of things by shaping, cutting, forming, and joining of materials.

contour—The shape of the land. The points of equal elevation in a landscape.

covering—The surface material(s) used to hold the plaster; a portion of coverwork.

coverwork—The steps in forming the contours and topography of the model.

creatures—All living things, including people and animals.

cross-kitting—Using parts from more than one kit to create a model of something.

crossings—The general category for bridges, trestles, overpasses, tunnels, etc.

debris—Broken rock fragments.

detailing—The process of applying smaller elements of design and finish to models.

details—The small elements that make the larger item look real.

detailwork—The steps that provide model railroad equipment, vehicles, creatures, and other details.

deterioration—Aging resulting from physical damage, rotting, corrosion, etc., applied to surfaces.

dioramas—Static models of scenes or situations that usually do not allow operation.

dry brushing—The use of a brush with most paint removed to provide subtle highlighting to a surface.

English system—The system of measurements primarily used in the United States.

era—The time period that is being represented in the model.

fasteners—Mechanical devices, such as screws, bolts, etc., used for joining materials.

features—Another word for details.

fidelity—The faithfulness and accuracy of the model, relative to the modeled object, in all details.

finishes—The paints, stains, etc., that give color and protection to the model.

finishing—The steps in modeling, beyond the construction, that make the model look real.

foliage—A general term that includes all plant life but applies especially to the leaves and needles on trees and bushes.

formulas—The recorded ratios of the mixtures of combinations of colors, solids/liquids, etc.

framework—The wooden structure portion of the benchwork beneath the model railroad.

front boards—The finished aisle edges of the model railroad layout.

gauge—The distance between the rails of a railroad track. Also the thickness of metal sheet or the diameter of wires.

geology—The study of how the earth is formed, particularly rock and land formations.

glue—A type of adhesive; usually used to describe white or yellow glues.

goals—What you want to accomplish, both as a process and as an end result.

greenwork—The steps in applying simulated grass, weeds, shrubs, and trees to the groundwork.

ground cover—Organic vegetation, but not trees, that covers the ground, such as grass, weeds, leaves, etc.

groundwork—The steps in applying color and final shaping to coverwork; providing rocks, roads, etc.

hard shell—A thin coverwork method involving the use of Hydrocal and paper towels.

highlighting—Using artificial lightening on surfaces to simulate sunlight reflections.

hue—The actual color of something.

ideas—The dreams, the thoughts, the creativity of what and how to do the modeling.

ideawork—The steps of dreaming and planning the model.

illumination—Lighting the model scenes to represent natural sunlight.

illusion—The magic of making something seem to be something other than it really is.

jigs—Devices used to allow cutting or assembly of multiple copies of something.

kit-built—A model built from a kit.

kitbashing—A model built primarily from a kit, but with some degree of changes.

kits—Collections of materials and instructions for making a particular model.

layout—A fixed model railroad, representing a real railroad, that allows operation of trains.

lighting—The lights used, inside or outside the models, to represent artificial lights. See *illumination*.

locale—The particular place being represented.

man-made—Things made by chemical or manufacturing processes, as distinguished from things that are natural.

materials—The raw ingredients, such as wood, brass, etc., from which the models are made.

matte—A finish or surface that is flat and nonreflective of light.

methods—The specific steps and procedures for creating modeled scenic and detailing effects.

metric system—The universal system of measurements used in most of the world, except for the United States.

modeled objects—Real, full-sized things that are used as prototypes of models.

modeling—The process of making models and miniatures to scale.

models—The miniatures of full-sized, modeled objects made to scale.

modules—Transportable portions of an operable model railroad.

molds—Reusable forms used for repeatable castings.

natural materials—Materials found directly from nature, such as rocks, twigs, and plant life.

overspray—A sprayed transparent or semitransparent finish to alter the appearance or gloss of another finish.

perspective—A viewpoint. Also, the property of things appearing smaller and less distinct with distance.

perspective, forced—The creation of the effects of perspective through artificial means.

piece-by-piece—A method of construction using individual pieces of materials to build up a wall or surface.

pigment—The portion of paint that gives color and has hiding capabilities.

planning—Determining in advance what will be done and how it will be accomplished.

plaster—A powdered material that, when combined with water, forms a castable hard substance.

plastering—The process of applying plaster, usually to coverwork.

plastic—Any of several hydrocarbon chemical compositions that can be produced as cast or formed solid shapes.

plausibility—How believable the model or modeled scene is relative to real, full-sized things or scenes.

preparation—The steps necessary to get ready to do something, prior to actually doing it.

prototype—The full-sized modeled object. The real building, railroad car, etc.

ready-to-lay track—Prefabricated model track with the rails attached to the ties.

ready-to-run—Equipment bought ready for operation.

ready-to-use—Models bought ready to operate without additional work, assembly, or finishing.

real—Anything that can be seen or touched, but used here to mean things from the non-miniature world.

reality—The world of nonminiature, full-sized things. Not the models or miniatures.

reference sources—The sources of information that allow learning about prototypes, history, geology, etc.

resources—The time and money that can be expended.

roadbed—The support for the railroad trackwork and ballast.

scale—The proportion in size that a model bears to a full-sized, modeled object.

scenery—The broad category of foreground, background, detailing, etc., that duplicates nature in a model setting.

scenes—The individual portions of the whole that can each be seen at one time.

scratchbuilt—A model built from individual parts or materials rather than from a kit.

simulate—The process of making something appear to look like something else.

siting—The planning of the locations of things.

size ratio—The ratio of model size to modeled object size, using the same units.

skills—The technical capabilities learned that enable one to do things well.

spectacular—Things that appear to be far more important than those around them.

stagecraft—The art of creating a theatrical illusion. Here, applied to creating that illusion on the modeled scene.

standards—Requirements on dimensions, etc., that need to be observed to allow clearances and equipment compatibility.

structures—Buildings, bridges, and other nonmobile things made by man.

techniques—General knowledge of how to use tools and materials to create models. See *skills*.

texture—The smoothness/roughness of a surface that affects its light reflection and appearance.

texturing—The process of providing artificial textures to surfaces.

tools—The various instruments used for cutting, shaping, holding, etc., the materials being worked on.

topography—The relief surface and contours of the land and its depiction on maps and plans.

tracklaying—The process of providing the model railroad trackwork on top of the roadbed.

trackwork—The steps in adding the model ties, rails, etc., for the track, to the benchwork.

uniformity—The creation of oneness by avoiding excesses.

vegetation—A general term that includes all trees, grasses, and other plant life.

vehicle—The volatile portion of paint that evaporates when the paint dries. See *carrier*.

vehicles—The man-made cars, trucks, buses, etc., that are used to convey passengers and freight (other than railroads).

weathering—The application of finishes to duplicate the effects of weather staining, etc., on surfaces.

Bibliography

Magazines

Monthly, all scales

Model Railroader, Kalmbach Publishing Co.
Railroad Model Craftsman, Carstens Publications.
Model Railroading, Rocky Mountain Publishing.
NMRA Bulletin, National Model Railroad Association.
Narrow Gauge and Short Line Gazette, Benchmark Publications.
Mainline Modeler, Hundman Publishing.
Prototype Modeler, Interurban Press.

Other magazines also exist that cover only a single scale or more limited ranges of interest.

Books

Scenery Tips and Techniques. Staff, Kalmbach Publishing Co., 1989.
HO Narrow Gauge Railroad You Can Build. Malcolm Furlow, Kalmbach Publishing Co., 1984.
Modeling Narrow-Gauge Railroads. Brick Price, Chilton Book Co., 1984.
Model Railroad Structures from A to Z. Wayne and Mary Cay Wesolowski, Carstens Publications, 1984.
The V&O Story. W. Allen McClelland, Carstens Publications, 1984.
Building an HO Model Railroad with Personality. John Olson, Kalmbach Publishing Co., 1983.
Scenery & Dioramas. Robert Schleicher, Chilton Book Co., 1983.
Realistic Model Railroad Scenery. Dave Frary, Kalmbach Publishing Co., 1982.

Model Railroading with John Allen. Linn H. Westcott, Kalmbach Publishing Co., 1981.

Modular Railroading. Ron Tarjany, Tarjany Publications, 1980.

Building Plastic Railroad Models. Robert Schleicher, Kalmbach Publishing Co., 1979.

Design Handbook of Model Railroads. Paul Mallery, Carstens Publications, 1979.

How to Build Model Railroad Benchwork. Linn H. Westcott, Kalmbach Publishing Co., 1979.

Track Planning for Realistic Operation. John Armstrong, Kalmbach Publishing Co., 1963.

ABC's of Model Railroading. Staff, Kalmbach Publishing Co., 1978.

Creative Layout Design. John Armstrong, Kalmbach Publishing Co., 1978.

How to Operate Your Model Railroad. Bruce A. Chubb, Kalmbach Publishing Co., 1977.

Trackwork Handbook. Paul Mallery, Boynton & Assoc., 1977.

Bridge & Trestle Handbook. Paul Mallery, Boynton & Assoc., 1976.

N Scale Primer. Russ Larson, Kalmbach Publishing Co., 1974.

Scenery for Model Railroaders. Bill McClanahan, Kalmbach Publishing Co., 1967.

How to Wire Your Model Railroad. Linn H. Westcott, Kalmbach Publishing Co., 1959.

Magazine Articles

The following are some of the better magazine articles that have appeared in the recent past. They cover the subjects of scenery and detailing.

GAZ = Narrow Gauge and Short Line Gazette
MM = Mainline Modeler
MR = Model Railroader
RMC = Railroad Model Craftsman

1990

"Weathering with and without an Airbrush," David Bontrager, RMC, Jan 1990, p. 77.

"Wild Water and Furious Fjords," Carla Black, RMC, Feb 1990, p. 84.

"Paint as a Detail," Bill Geracci, RMC, Feb 1990, p. 92.

"Fat-Fat Fibers," Jory Tetzlaff, MR, Sep 1990, p. 74.

"Airbrushing Made Easy," Leigh Hareton-Arnold, RMC, Oct 1990, p. 78.

"Bring a Scene to Life," Charles D. Carter, RMC, Dec 1990, p. 96.

1989

"Improved Lichen Bushes," Jim Wild and Dwayne Easterling, RMC, May 1989, p. 69.

"Modeling Trees with Mother Nature," Robert & Nancy Turner, RMC, Jun 1989, p. 58.

"Modeling Western Foliage," Carl Caiati, MR, Jun 1989, p. 76.

"Modeling Junk," Carl Caiati, MR, Jul 1989, p. 76.

"Making Waves," Phil Chiavetta & Frank diBonis, RMC, Aug 1989, p. 48.

"Simulating Peeled Paint with Pastels," Dwayne Easterling, RMC, Sep 1989, p. 68.

"Marker Magic," Bill Alspach, RMC, Oct 1989, p. 93.

"Weathering with Water-Base Media," Carl Caiati, MR, Nov 1989, p. 88.

1988

"Pine Tree Art," Carl Caiati, MR, Feb 1988, p. 108.

"Making Big City Signs," Robert Smaus, RMC, Feb 1988, p. 82.

"Modeling a Marsh," Jim Wild and Dwayne Easterling, RNC, Jul 1988, p. 78.

"Building Demolition," Earl Smallshaw, MR, Aug 1988, p. 100.

"Creating Realistic Conifers," Laszlo Dora, MR, Oct 1988, p. 84.

"Tracks in the Street," Robert Smaus, RMC, Oct 1988, p. 72.

"Three-Dimensional Backdrops," Harry Brunk, RMC, Nov 1988, p. 64.

"Modeling a Winter Wonderland," Bruce Nall, RMC, Dec 1988, p. 76.

"The Basics of Wood Weathering," David Spence, RMC, Dec 1988, p. 81.

1987

"Building Timber Retaining Walls," Jim Wild and Dwayne Easterling, RMC, Mar 1987, p. 61.

"Easyshell Scenery," Brad Short, MR, Apr 1987, p. 72.

"How to Apply Decals," Andy Sperandeo, MR, May 1987, p. 62.

"Trees," Nat Howard, RMC, May 1987, p. 55.

"ABC's of Scenery," Jim Kelly, MR, Jun 1987, p. 100.

"The Charisma of Trivia," Carl Caiati, MR, Oct 1987, p. 98.

1986

"Weathering Figures," Richard and Bill Gardner, MR, Jan 1986, p. 108.

"Sweet n' Sour Weathering," Dwayne Easterling and Jim Wild, RMC, Jan 1986, p. 88.

"Making Signs for the Layout," Earl Smallshaw, MR, Feb 1986, p. 94.

"Deciduous Anyone?" Bill Haynes, MR, Feb 1986, p. 116.

"Better Backdrops," John Lowrance, RMC, Mar 1986, p. 63.

"String Trees," Art Curren, MR, Jun 1986, p. 83.

"New Horizons," Miles Hale and John Lowrance, RMC, Jun 1986, p. 70.

"Making Mud," Jim Wild and Dwayne Easterling, RMC, Jul 1986, p. 55.

"Modeling California's Golden Grass," Jack Burgess, RMC, Aug 1986, p. 69.

"Modeling Cuts and Fills," Gordon Odegard, MR, Sep 1986, p. 96.

"Scenery Without Plaster," Dick Walker, RMC, Sep 1986, p. 52.

"Painting Faded Signs," Bob Kress, MR, Sep 1986, p. 100.

"Building Plaster Structure Kits," Bob Hayden, MR, Nov 1986, p. 96.

1985

"Weathering with Dry Colors," Gary Schmarch, RMC, Apr 1985, p. 72.

"Modeling Barbed Wire," Jack Burgess, RMC, May 1985, p. 95.

"Creating Your Own Backdrop," Robert Hamm, MR, Jul 1985, p. 71.

"Falling Water," Jim Wild and Dwayne Easterling, RMC, Jul 1985, p. 67.

"Rapid Water," Jim Wild and Dwayne Easterling, RMC, Aug 1985, p. 48.

"Water and How to Model It," John Nehrich, MR, Oct 1985, p. 78.

"Rushing Water," Gary Hoover, MR, Dec 1985, p. 112.

1984

"Modeling Water with Acrylic Gloss Medium," Dave Frary, MR, Jan 1984, p. 152.

"Blended Backdrops," Joe Kreiss, RMC, Jan 1984, p. 75.

"Quick Weathering with Chalks," Don Mitchell, MR, Feb 1984, p. 64.

"Signs & Philosophy," C. J. Riley, RMC, Feb 1984, p. 93.

"Lightweight Module Construction," Roger Malinowski, RMC, Mar 1984, p. 71.

"Modeling Tall Grass," Bill Kennedy, RMC, Mar 1984, p. 86.

"Soils for Scenery," Jack Burgess, RMC, Apr 1984, p. 56.

"Building Rock and Timber Retaining Walls," Lee Brown, RMC, May 1984, p. 93.

"Weathering with Pastel Pencils," Pete Moffatt, GAZ, Sep/Oct 1984, p. 34.

"Spray Weathering with an Airbrush," John Schick, MR, Oct 1984, p. 98.

"Painting People," Steve Shoe and Dwayne Easterling, RMC, Nov 1984, p. 70.

1983

"Coloring Track for Maximum Effect," Gordon Odegard, MR, Feb 1983, p. 104.

"Layered Backdrops," Jeff English, RMC, Apr 1983, p. 74.

"Backdrops and Clouds," John Nehrich and Brad Toole, RMC, Jun 1983, p. 72.

"Floral Shop Trees," Jim Grupe, MR, Aug 1983, p. 70.

"Jute Trees," Irvin Riffel, MR, Oct 1983, p. 124.

"Modeling the Great American Desert," Mark Junge, MR, Dec 1983, p. 111.

1982

"Felt Grass and Weeds," Art Curren, MR, Jan 1982, p. 118.

"Painting Signs," Terry Metcalfe, RMC, Jan 1982, p. 58.

"Weathering Corrugated Roofs," Gary Nash, GAZ, Jan/Feb 1982, p. 32.

"Step-by-Step Backdrop Painting," Art Curren, MR, Feb 1982, p. 93.

"Modeling Water," Jim Kelly, MR, Mar 1982, p. 98.

"Modeling Track," George Sellios, RMC, Mar 1982, p. 72.

"Tunnel Portals," Jim Findley, RMC, Apr 1982, p. 51.

"Weathering with Pastels—Five Projects," Robert Zenk, MM, May 1982, p. 54.

"The Fleet and the Airbrush," Robert Zenk, MM, May 1982, p. 54.

"Eight-Step Sure-Fire Weeds," Gary Edlen, RMC, Jul 1982, p. 54.

"Painting and Weathering Styrene Freight Cars," Keith Brown, John Parker, and John Busby, GAZ, Jul/Aug 1982, p. 67.

"Locomotive Painting," Jack Burgess, RMC, Aug 1982, p. 71.

"Building Scenic Forms," Jim Kelly, MR, Sep 1982, p. 70.

1981

"Weathering Wood With Dirt and Diosol," Gary Nash, GAZ, Jan/Feb 1981, p. 48.

"Making Tall Grass and Bushes from Synthetic Yarn," Terry Metcalfe, RMC, Feb 1981, p. 64.

"Modeling Furlow's Slough," Malcolm Furlow, MR, Mar 1981, p. 94.

"Signs," Frank Pearsall, MM, Mar/Apr 1981, p. 81.

"Ceiling Tile Rocks," Jim Kelly, MR, Apr 1981, p. 66.

"'Growing' Tall Grass and Weeds," Peter Watson, RMC, Apr 1981, p. 56.

"Aging Corrugated Material by Etchant," Ken Hamilton, GAZ, Jul/Aug 1981, p. 70.

"Painting Scale Figures," George Konrad, MR, Sep 1981, p. 69.

"Lichen," Jim Kelly, MR, Nov 1981, p. 112.

"The Art of Using Mirrors," John Allen, MR, Dec 1981, p. 109.

1980

"Making Your Own Dry Transfers," Ron Ford, MR, Feb 1980, p. 70.

"Furnace Filter Forests," Gail Holland, MR, Apr, 1980, p. 96.

"Modeling the Ground," Jim Kelly, MR, Jun 1980, p. 70.

"Roads and Grade Crossings," Jim Kelly, MR, Sep 1980, p. 70.

"Modeling Chain-Link Fences," G. Warren Reed, MR, Sep 1980, p. 72.

"Weathering Signs," Gary Nash, GAZ, Sep/Oct 1980, p. 48.

"A Quick and Easy Way of Mass-Producing Coniferous Trees," Bob Tyson, RMC, Dec 1980, p. 87.

Index

glass construction, 80
gloss, 93
gloss finishes, 93, 116
glue, 63-67
glue-base plasters, 166-167
goals, 39
good enough, 141
grade crossing, 201, 203
graffiti, 321-322
grass, 208-210
grass paper, 209
gravel roads, 202
gravel roofing, 261
greenwork (*see* vegetation),
   123-125, 207-234
ground covers, 207-213
ground foam, 186
groundwork (*see also* geology),
   123-125, 173-205
   roads and highways, 200-203
   rocks, 173-183
   snow and ice, 199-200
   soil, 183-189
   streets and sidewalks, 204-205
   water effects, 189-200
gutters and downspouts, 308
guy wires, 305

H

hand-laid trackwork, 138,
   158-159
hard shell coverwork, 164, 166
hay, 212
haze, backdrops, 151
hedges, 212
height of layout, 130-131
highlighting, 182, 322
highways, 202
history and era, 21-24
holding, painting, 100
holding tools, 52-54
hole filling, 71, 74
horizon, 148
horse-drawn vehicles, 287
horses, 293
hose, 319
houses, 294, 318
hue, color, 94
humidity, 32-33
Hydrocal plaster, 167

I

ice, icicles, 200
ideas, 39
ideawork, 123-125, 127-141
illumination, 28
illusion, 10-11, 132
industries, 296, 333
insulators, electric poles, 305
intensity of lighting, 29
intensity, color, 94
ivy, 212

J

jigs and fixtures, 54
joining tools, 55-56
junk, 321

K

kitbashing, 69
kits, 69, 72
knives, 49-50

L

lacquer paints, 92
ladders, 308
lakes, 190-197
lamps, 316-317
landscape on backdrops, 150
lanes, 318
layout, 10, 37
leaves, 223
lettering (*see also* decals;
   striping), 94, 115-122, 268,
   272, 276, 280, 321-322
lichen, trees from, 221-223
lighting, 27-32, 58
   baffles for, 30
   fluorescent vs. incandescent,
   29
   illumination functions, 28
   intensity, 29
   modeled, 32, 316-317
   passenger cars, 275
   photographic, 31-32
   placement, 29-31
   planning for, 28
   safety, 28
   shadows and spotlighting, 30
   wattage, 28-29

limbs, tree, 218-219, 225
lines, 302-307
lining, tunnel, 241
liquid measurements,
   conversions, 326
liquid metals, 66
litter, 319
locale, scenery and, 134
location of layout, 27
locomotives (*see* diesel
   locomotives; steam
   locomotives)
loose rock, 180
lost-wax molds, 86
Lucite, 44
lumber, size-to-scale conversion,
   329-331

M

macadam, 202
machinery, 287-288
magnifiers, 58
manholes, 317
man-made vs. natural, 10
markers, measuring tools, 49
masking for paints, 93, 100-101
masonite, 146, 152
masonry buildings, 251-255
materials, 41-44
   backdrops, 146-147
   casting and molds, 82
   commonly used, 43-44
   costs, 43
   full-sized vs. modeling
   material options, 42-43
   grass, 209
   metals, 44
   mold-making, 83
   paper, 44
   plastics, 44
   roadbed, 145
   trees, 224-227
   wood, 44
matte, 93
measuring tools, 45-49
metal buildings, 258-259
metal construction, 76-80
   casting, 82
   cutting, 76
   drilling, 76-77

About the Author

Al Sorensen has been an active model railroader for over 40 years. Like many others, he became interested in the hobby at a young age by playing with his and his friend's Lionel and American Flyer equipment. During these many years, he has explored every aspect of model railroading: building HO, N, and O scale equipment, dioramas, modules, and layouts. His current lifetime project is an early thirties' era imaginary trans-Sierra railroad in HO, the Serranos (short for El Camino de los Serranos).

Al studied both architecture and electrical engineering (MSEE). He served in military intelligence in the United States Army during the Korean War. Al is an engineering manager for a major aerospace firm in Los Angeles, responsible for the design and systems engineering of spacecraft and their subsystems.

He has a multitude of hobbies to provide relaxation from those real-life challenges. Besides railroads, he has modeled about everything else, including airplanes and sailplanes for display and flying, boats, military equipment, dollhouses, and automobiles. He is also an active stamp collector, works with leather, paints, draws, and writes articles and books on a wide range of subjects. Other hobbies include electronics and a very active application of computers, both at work and at home.

Al and his understanding wife of 30 years, Evelyn, live in Palos Verdes, California. They have five grown children, but none have adopted any of Al's hobbies. The family is quite active in their church. In another "few" years, when he retires, Al intends to spend full time on his many hobbies, probably write a novel, and continue semiannual trips to visit foreign countries.